# NEIGHBORHOOD POVERTY

· · ·

## Volume I

### Context and Consequences
### for Children

· · ·

Jeanne Brooks-Gunn
Greg J. Duncan
J. Lawrence Aber

EDITORS

Russell Sage Foundation · New York

**Library of Congress Cataloging-in-Publication Data**

Neighborhood poverty : context and consequences for children / edited
  by J. Brooks-Gunn, G. J. Duncan, and J. L. Aber.
     p.    cm.
  Includes bibliographical references and index.
  Contents: v.   1. Context and consequences for
children
  ISBN 0-87154-145-9
  1. Poor children—United States—Case studies.   2. Urban poor—
United States—Case studies.   3. Family—United States—Case
studies.   4. Neighborhood—United States—Case studies.   5. Urban
policy—United States—Case studies.   6. United States—Social
policy—Case studies.   I. Brooks-Gunn, Jeanne.   II. Duncan, Greg J.
III. Aber, J. L.
HV741.N383   1997                                              97-7864
362.5'0973—dc21                                                CIP

Text design by Suzanne Nichols.

RUSSELL SAGE FOUNDATION
112 East 64th Street, New York, New York 10021
10 9 8 7 6 5 4 3 2 1

We dedicate this volume to William Julius Wilson and to Urie Bronfenbrenner, who have inspired the serious examination of the neighborhoods and communities in which children live.

JEANNE BROOKS-GUNN
GREG J. DUNCAN
J. LAWRENCE ABER

# Contents

# Contributors

**JEANNE BROOKS-GUNN** is Virginia and Leonard Marx Professor of Child Development at Teachers College, Columbia University. She is also director of the Center for Children and Families and founder of the Adolescent Study Program at Teachers College.

**GREG J. DUNCAN** is professor of education and social policy and a faculty associate in the Institute for Policy Research at Northwestern University. He is also faculty affiliate of the Northwestern University/University of Chicago Joint Center for Poverty Research.

**J. LAWRENCE ABER** is director of the National Center for Children in Poverty at the Columbia School of Public Health, Columbia University.

**LARUE ALLEN** is professor and chair in the Department of Applied Psychology of New York University's School of Education. She is also Director of Education and Training for the National Consortium on Violence Research.

**P. LINDSAY CHASE-LANSDALE** is associate professor in the Irving B. Harris Graduate School of Public Policy Studies, University of Chicago. She is adjunct faculty member in the Department of Psychology and faculty associate of the Population Research Center at the University of Chicago. She is also faculty affiliate of the Northwestern University/University of Chicago Joint Center for Poverty Research.

**ELIZABETH CLIFFORD** is visiting lecturer in the Department of Sociology, Northwestern University.

**STEVEN P. COLE** is director of research at Research Design Associates, Inc., Decatur, Georgia.

**JAMES P. CONNELL** is director of the Institute for Research and Reform in Education.

**WARREN E. CRICHLOW** is assistant professor of education in the Faculty of Education, York University, Toronto, Canada.

**MARTHA A. GEPHART** is adjunct associate professor in the Department of Organization and Leadership at Teachers College, Columbia University. She is also senior research associate at the International Center for Cooperation and Conflict Resolution at Teachers College.

**RACHEL A. GORDON** is research scientist in the Department of Psychiatry, University of Chicago.

**BONNIE L. HALPERN-FELSHER** is assistant professor in the Department of Pediatrics, Division of Adolescent Medicine, University of California at San Francisco.

**STEPHANIE M. JONES** is research associate at the National Center for Children in Poverty, Columbia School of Public Health, Columbia University.

**PAMELA K. KLEBANOV** is research scientist at Teachers College, Columbia University and affiliate of the Bendheim-Thoman Center for Research.

**JEFFREY S. LEHMAN** is dean and professor of law and public policy at the University of Michigan Law School. He is also professor of law and public policy in the School of Public Policy, University of Michigan at Ann Arbor.

**TAMA LEVENTHAL** is doctoral candidate in developmental psychology at Teachers College, Columbia University. She is also graduate fellow at the Center for Children and Families, Teachers College, Columbia University.

**EDWARD SEIDMAN** is professor of psychology in the Department of Community Psychology at New York University. He is also the coordinator of Community Psychology Program.

**TIMOTHY M. SMEEDING** is director of the Center for Policy Research, Maxwell School of Citizenship and Public Affairs, Syracuse University.

**MARGARET BEALE SPENCER** is Board of Overseers Professor, Developmental Psychologist in the Psychology in Education Division of the Graduate School of Education at the University of Pennsylvania. She is also director of the Center for Health, Achievement, Neighborhood, Growth and Ethnic Studies (CHANGES), University of Pennsylvania.

**DENA PHILLIPS SWANSON** is postdoctoral fellow in the Graduate School of Education at the University of Pennsylvania. She received her Ph.D. from Emory University in education and developmental psychology.

**PETER A. USINGER** holds an M.S. in social psychology and in communication engineering. He is also president of Biz IQ, Inc., an organizational research and business consulting firm in Rochester, New York.

# Introduction

*Martha A. Gephart and Jeanne Brooks-Gunn*

The resurgence of interest in the influences of neighborhood and community contexts on the development of children, youth, and families who reside and interact in them is a welcome addition to social science. Through a new generation of studies, researchers are attempting to assess the combined effects of individual, family, and neighborhood/community characteristics on the development of children and adolescents. An interdisciplinary group of scholars working under the auspices of the Social Science Research Council planned and undertook a research program on the influences of community and neighborhood contexts, in interaction with family processes, on the development of poor children and adolescents. The group's collaboration resulted in the two-volume *Neighborhood Poverty*. The first volume, *Context and Consequences for Children*, presents findings on the consequences of neighborhood residence on children and adolescents, drawing upon six developmental data sets. The second volume, *Policy Implications in Studying Neighborhoods,* highlights our group's approach toward, as well as other scholars' perspectives on, investigating links between child and family outcomes, on the one hand, and neighborhood residence, on the other. In this chapter we discuss the impetus for the Social Science Research Council working group collaboration, as well as the organization of volumes 1 and 2.

## INTELLECTUAL AND ORGANIZATIONAL IMPETUS FOR THE RESEARCH

Several developments in social and scholarly life provided the impetus for the collaborative research described in this volume. During the late 1980s, after nearly two decades of relative neglect, issues concerning the causes and consequences of poverty reemerged on the U.S. political and intellectual agendas. Renewed public interest in the problems of urban poverty was sparked by the visibility of homeless people in American cities during the early 1980s and by journalistic accounts of social pathologies in inner-city neighborhoods.

The problems highlighted in such accounts included violent crime, drug use, out-of-wedlock births, school dropout, rising and chronic unemployment, and welfare dependence. Inner-city poverty and the social disorganization thought to be associated with it were often said to be "exploding."

The perception that social problems in poor urban communities were becoming more intense and interrelated led to a concern, reflected in Ken Auletta's (1982) book *The Underclass* and in Nicholas Lehmann's series of *Atlantic Monthly* articles, that an "urban underclass" was forming in inner-city neighborhoods. Academic interest in these issues was stimulated by arguments put forward by the sociologist William Julius Wilson in a series of papers that were eventually published as *The Truly Disadvantaged* (1987). Wilson argued that severe social dislocations were occurring in some neighborhoods as a result of the increasing concentration of joblessness and poverty. Isolation from informal job networks, lack of exposure to norms and behavior patterns of the steadily employed, lack of access to effective schools, and women's lack of opportunity to marry men with stable jobs were among the "effects" that Wilson hypothesized of concentrated joblessness and poverty in the inner city (see also Wilson 1991a, 1996).

As used in the media and among scholars, the concept "urban underclass" has typically included one or more of the following characteristics: (1) persistence and/or intergenerational transmission of poverty; (2) geographic concentration; (3) social isolation from mainstream society; (4) unemployment and underemployment; (5) low skills and education; (6) membership in a minority group. In the early and mid-1980s, little was known about the overlap or interaction among these characteristics. Researchers and policy makers asked whether concentrated poverty in central cities causes or reinforces unemployment, welfare dependence, school dropout, out-of-wedlock births, and involvement in crime and drugs; and whether such behaviors, in turn, lead to the persistence of poverty and its intergenerational transmission through their effects on children.

Toward the end of the 1980s, the Committee on National Urban Policy of the National Research Committee reported that poverty appeared to be worse in many large cities than it had been ten or twenty years earlier and that poverty seemingly was becoming more spatially concentrated in inner-city neighborhoods. The committee identified the phenomenon of increasing poverty concentration in inner-city neighborhoods as the national urban policy issue most meriting further attention. Meanwhile, private foundations concerned with the plight of disadvantaged families were independently becoming convinced of the need for comprehensive community-based interventions to address the problems of urban disadvantaged children and families.

In response to these developments, and with encouragement and support from the Rockefeller and Russell Sage Foundations, the Social Science Research Council (SSRC) established a research program in 1988 to improve understanding of the causes and consequences of persistent and concentrated urban poverty and to build the knowledge base needed to design and implement better policies and programs for the persistently poor in urban areas. The program sought to establish a framework for the analysis not only of structures and processes that generate or maintain persistent concentrated urban poverty but also of those that help people overcome such poverty. It also sought to recruit and nurture a pool of talented, well-trained young scholars who would advance research on the topic. Under the direction of the SSRC's Committee for Research on the Urban Underclass, several working groups of scholars were established to clarify the causes, effects, and relationships among the set of social conditions that had come to be associated with the term *urban underclass*.

A significant challenge for the program was to link larger socioeconomic and political forces, the changing context of poverty at the community level, and the outcomes and experience of families and individuals. In 1989, the SSRC's committee appointed the Working Group on Communities and Neighborhoods, Family Processes, and Individual Development to improve our understanding of the ways in which neighborhoods and communities influence the development of families and the children who reside in them. The group comprised social scientists with diverse disciplinary backgrounds, as well as theoretical and methodological orientations, to facilitate the conceptualization and investigation of links that require multilevel and cross-disciplinary analysis. The members included J. Lawrence Aber (Columbia University), Jeanne Brooks-Gunn (Columbia University) Linda M. Burton (The Pennsylvania State University), P. Lindsay Chase-Lansdale (University of Chicago), James P. Connell (Institute for Research and Reform in Education), Thomas D. Cook (Northwestern University), Warren E. Crichlow (York University), Greg J. Duncan (Northwestern University), Ronald F. Ferguson (Harvard University), Frank F. Furstenberg, Jr. (University of Pennsylvania), Martha A. Gephart (Columbia University), Robin L. Jarrett (Loyola University), Vilma Ortiz (University of California, Los Angeles), Tim Smeeding (Syracuse University), Margaret Beale Spencer (University of Pennsylvania), and Mercer L. Sullivan (Rutgers University).

## CONCEPTUAL FRAMEWORK AND RESEARCH STRATEGIES

Our working group took as its mandate the following questions: Does concentrated residential poverty, along with the associated economic and social neighborhood disadvantage, place children at risk? Are diverse neighborhood characteristics mediated by family structures and processes, or do they exert a separate and powerful influence on children's lives, over and above family influences?

We began by reviewing the existing theory and research. A review of existing quantitative research (Jencks and Mayer 1990) revealed weak and inconsistent effects of neighborhood composition on individual outcomes, but many of the studies were flawed. In the early phase of our own work and of other scholars investigating the nature and effects of the changing context of urban poverty at the community level, research undertaken by scholars working in the traditions of social ecology and social disorganization theory was largely ignored. The insights from such work have subsequently been incorporated in the thinking of our group and of others studying urban poverty (see chapter 1; Sampson and Morenoff vol. 2).

For some time, ethnographic researchers had argued for the importance of neighborhoods and communities in understanding poverty. A number of studies (for example, Anderson 1990; Sullivan 1989; Williams and Kornblum 1985) highlighted the salience of local community factors for understanding the poor's life chances and experiences. But ethnographic research had not produced systematic analyses of the effects of neighborhoods and communities on families and the individuals in them (see Furstenberg and Hughes vol. 2; Jarrett vol. 2; Merriwether–de Vries, Burton, and Eggeletion 1996).

Theory and research on family structures and processes and on individual development increasingly recognized the importance of the contexts within which individuals are situated. Most existing research, however, focused on the more proximal contents of families, peers, and social networks (see chapter 2). The growing literatures in these areas did not directly address the effects of neighborhood and community contexts or of concentrated and persistent poverty upon individual development.

After commissioning a review of existing research on differences among ethnic groups in the functioning of poor families and households (Jarrett 1990), we developed a conceptual framework to guide our research (figure A). This framework considers as exogenous the macro structures and processes that produce neighborhoods of concentrated disadvantage, including housing discrimination, racism, migration and contingent preferences, and institutional practices and policies. At the neighborhood and community levels, our framework specifies structural and sociodemographic characteristics, including formal opportunities and constraints, dangers, ethnicity, and persistent poverty, as the attributes of neighborhoods that may vary with the concentration of poverty and resource deprivation and that may affect developmental outcomes (see chapter 1; Sampson and Morenoff vol. 2). The community-level social and cultural processes are illustrated in our framework by informal networks. Such processes are assumed to mediate the effects of structural and sociodemographic characteristics on outcomes. Family structures and processes, including household demography, family theories of childrearing, and family networking to opportunities and dangers, in turn, are assumed to mediate the effects of community-level processes on individual outcomes. Individual developmental processes, such as efficacy, competence, and identity processes, mediate individual outcomes that are domain specific and appropriate for particular developmental stages. Because developmentalists expect both ontogenetic and social-structural causes for later outcomes (such as teenage

FIGURE A   Conceptual Model

## COMMUNITIES AND NEIGHBORHOODS, FAMILY PROCESSES, AND INDIVIDUAL DEVELOPMENT

**EXOGENOUS FORCES**

Macro structures and processes that produce neighborhoods of concentrated disadvantage

* housing discrimination
* racism
* migration and contingent preferences
* institutional practices and policies (for example, public housing)
* labor-market conditions

Attributes of neighborhoods that may vary with poverty concentration and affect developmental outcomes

Formal opportunities and constraints

Dangers

Informal networks

Ethnicity

Persistent poverty

Family responses to neighborhood conditions

Family processes

Family "theories" of childrearing

Family networking to opportunities and danger

Household "demography"

Individual developmental outcomes

(likely to be domain specific) For example:

* health and mental health
* achievement
* interpersonal relations
* depression, self-esteem, efficacy
* crime
* fertility
* "negotiating multiple worlds"

pregnancy and school dropout), our framework posits that neighborhoods will affect later outcomes by influencing relevant childhood outcomes. In this volume, we evaluate neighborhood and community influences in early and middle childhood and adolescence.

Our review of existing work revealed little theory or research about the characteristics of neighborhoods and communities that affect children, youth, and families; about the nature of those effects; or about the mechanisms and mediating processes at the community, family, and individual levels through which the effects operate. Multiple theoretical perspectives, fragmented by discipline and often by method, provide partial, potentially complementary (but sometimes conflicting) guidance about the characteristics of neighborhoods that may affect the development of children, youth, and families, and about the mechanisms through which such characteristics affect families and individuals. It seemed clear that new multidisciplinary and multilevel research was needed, yet existing theory and research seemed inadequate as a basis for designing a major new data collection effort. Meanwhile, policy and program solutions were making assumptions about links across levels, but existing knowledge was inadequate to assess the links hypothesized.

Given the state of existing theory and research, we took as our major challenge the development of new theory, concepts, methods, and empirical findings that would guide future research. To address this challenge, we decided to undertake several types of collaborative research that would build on and analyze existing quantitative and qualitative data. These collaborative research activities have been undertaken with support from the Russell Sage Foundation, the Smith Richardson Foundation, the W. T. Grant Foundation, and the Rockefeller Foundation. We deeply appreciate their support.

Using a common conceptual and analytical framework, the group decided to design and undertake coordinated analyses of the separate and combined effects of families and neighborhoods on children and youth. These analyses have been undertaken using six developmental data sets that vary in the developmental outcomes and the family- and individual-level mediating processes assessed, as well as in the ages and ethnicities of the children and adolescents sampled. Most of the chapters in this book are devoted to the results of these analyses.

To investigate in greater depth some of the processes through which neighborhoods and communities of concentrated social and economic disadvantage are thought to affect families and individuals, the group also established four multidisciplinary research teams. These teams focused on (1) multi-generational families, (2) household economies, (3) school/community/family links, and (4) ethnic, gender, and other identity processes. Building on ongoing research and on existing data, these teams are exploring ways of integrating quantitative and qualitative analyses to investigate the processes of mediation between the characteristics of neighborhoods and communities and the developmental trajectories of the resident families and children. These approaches are reflected in the chapters in volume 2.

The group's quantitative analyses have addressed three major questions: (1) Is there a meaningful underlying organization to the variation in neighborhood socioeconomic composition? (2) What are the direct effects of variation in neighborhood socioeconomic and sociodemographic composition on the development of children and youth, net of family socioeconomic factors? (3) Are neighborhood effects mediated by particular family and individual psychological variables?

One of the core activities of our working group was the collaborative examination of neighborhood effects in six different data sets, as detailed in this volume. The group decided to use geocoded data as the unit of analysis (see chapter 4). Six data sets were selected that focused on children or youth, had address data available, and had longitudinal data collected. Three were local site studies, and two were national studies. One was an eight-site study. The Panel Study of Income Dynamics (PSID), a national twenty-five-year study, was analyzed by Duncan and his colleagues. The Children of the National Longitudinal Study of Youth (NLSY), a national study of youth started in 1979 and now including the offspring of the females in the 1979 cohort, was analyzed by Chase-Lansdale and her colleagues. The Infant Health and Development Program (IHDP), an early intervention trial for low-birth-weight premature infants and their families, was used by Brooks-Gunn and her colleagues. The upstate New York study includes African American and white children and youth from an upstate New York school district; this data set was used by Connell and his colleagues. The Atlanta study, directed by Spencer, focused on African American youth in a number of Atlanta schools. The study by Aber and his colleagues also focused on youth, but in three different cities— New York City, Washington, D.C., and Baltimore. African American, white, and Latino youth were included, and the sample was drawn from poor schools.

The investigators all agreed to analyze their data in exactly the same way— something of an anomaly in social science research. After much discussion, the group decided how to conceptualize neighborhoods and the family-level variables to include in the analyses. Results are presented in the same format to facilitate comparisons across studies in this volume. Of importance vis-à-vis the reported neighborhood effects is the fact that three samples were "local" samples, with less variability in census tracts, while three were national (or, in the case of the IHDP, an eight-site one), which resulted in more census tracts being represented. This design detail is discussed fully in chapter 11.

## OVERVIEW OF THE CHAPTERS IN THIS VOLUME

This volume includes chapters on conceptual and framing issues and empirical findings. In this introduction and the three conceptual chapters that follow it we review the existing theory and research upon which we have drawn our analyses. Chapter 1 describes what is known about neighborhoods and communities as contexts for development, and reviews contemporary theory and research on neighborhoods and communities as contexts for development. The author describes the changing context of poverty at the community level, summarizes several theoretical perspectives that have guided our thinking about neighborhood and community influences, and discusses issues that arise in conceptualizing and measuring neighborhoods and communities. She then reviews the results of recent community and contextual analyses that are relevant for understanding neighborhood and community influences on development.

Chapter 2 builds on the framework outlined by Gephart in chapter 1. The authors include family and individual contextual factors, as those, together with neighborhood contextual effects, might influence child and youth outcomes. The developmental-contextual framework, within which this volume's analyses are embedded, is then outlined. The authors introduce a number of key concepts used in the study of development, review Bronfenbrenner's (1979b) developmental-contextual framework, and discuss how neighborhoods could influence development at each major developmental stage.

Chapter 3 provides an overview of how *neighborhood* was defined for the complementary analyses and the measures used to characterize neighborhoods. The authors describe the common conceptual framework and measurement strategy that the group developed to describe the variation in neighborhood structure and composition sometimes associated with variation in developmental outcomes. They describe the procedures and results of efforts to distill a factor structure of neighborhood conditions that was used in all subsequent analyses across all data sets. They also use data on neighborhood characteristics to place the six developmental data sets analyzed in this volume, which involved samples of children and youth from vastly different neighborhood conditions, into a national comparative context. Finally, they describe the neighborhood conditions under which children and adolescents live and describe how neighborhood poverty covaries with family poverty for black and white children and youth.

The results of our empirical analyses are presented in the next five chapters. The analyses are organized by developmental stage: early childhood (ages three to seven), late childhood and early adolescence (ages eleven to fifteen), and late adolescence (ages sixteen to nineteen). In most cases, each chapter presents results from two or more of the six data sets. Chapters 4 and 5 contain analyses from the IHDP and the children of the NLSY. Chapter 6 summarizes results of neighborhood analyses on children and young adolescents from the upstate New York, Atlanta, and Northeast Corridor studies. Chapter 7 contains results from the upstate New York data set, and chapter 8 involves findings from the PSID and the upstate New York study.

The chapters include discussions of behavioral and school achievement outcomes. The outcomes vary across chapters, since different aspects of behavior and achievement are tapped at different ages. However, comparable measures were available in the data sets that focused on each age group. For example, the early childhood data sets both included measures of verbal ability and behavior-problem checklists. Consequently, some general comparisons may be made about the specificity of findings by development epoch and data set (Chase-Lansdale and Brooks-Gunn 1995).

Analyses reported were designed so that we could look at direct neighborhood effects (chapters 4, 6, and 8). A series of analyses were conducted in order to look at the effect of the five neighborhood variables in predicting the agreed-upon child and adolescent outcomes. Then, regressions with family-level variables added were run, to see whether neighborhood effects were independent of these family-level variables. These analyses were conducted for boys and girls separately, as well as for black and white children separately (interaction terms were also entered into the original equations to examine gender and race interactions). In studies where sample size allowed, four groups were assembled—white girls, white boys, black girls, and black boys. In some cases, analyses were conducted using different "cut" points for poor neighborhoods, since black children are much less likely to live in affluent neighborhoods and white children in poor neighborhoods, so that neighborhood effects might be relative to the distribution of each group (Brooks-Gunn, Duncan et al. 1993; Duncan, Brooks-Gunn, and Klebanov 1994).

An additional set of analyses was run in order to look at possible mediated, or indirect, effects of neighborhoods on child and adolescent outcomes, as reported in chapters 5 and 7. In chapter 5, the authors use the IHDP and the Children of the NLSY data sets. Both of these have measures of the home environment, including provision of learning experiences and maternal warmth (Klebanov, Brooks-Gunn, and Duncan 1994; Sugland et al. 1995). Mediated models were built in order to see whether any of the observed neighborhood effects operated through the home environment, and evidence for such effects was found in both data sets. Additionally, the authors of chapter 5 divided their samples into those living in resource-rich and resource-poor neighborhoods to see whether the factors influencing young-child outcomes differ for these two broad neighborhood types. Chapter 7 presents an illustration of a mediated model from the upstate New York study. The authors take as their starting point different aspects of the self-system and motivational processes as possible mediators of neighborhood effects on school outcomes.

Given that neighborhood analyses are beset by a number of issues, chapter 9 describes and assesses possible sources of bias that jeopardize the drawing of causal inferences from analyses of neighborhood effects. Many of these "sources of bias" reflect the inadequacies of the conceptual model that underlies our analyses, namely, that developmental outcomes are additive functions of family conditions and neighborhood factors. The authors consider the possibility of omitted interactions between family and neighborhood conditions and between them and other moderators of their effects. They discuss the possibility that important unmeasured characteristics of families lead them to reside in certain kinds of neighborhoods and to have children with different developmental trajectories (selection effects). They consider transactional models of development that emphasize the reciprocal relationships between individuals and families shaping and creating their environments (for example, by deciding where to live), and the characteristics of those contexts influencing individual and family characteristics (such as income, family structure, and decision making). The possibility that neighborhood influences are underestimated due to suppression effects from other unmeasured variables and that neighborhood effects may not be linear across the range of neighborhood conditions are also considered.

Chapter 10 provides a lively and sometimes provocative account of the implications of this volume's findings for federal policy. The authors situate the findings presented here within a very broad context, discuss policy initiatives relevant to the findings, and outline the policy community's data needs. In effect, they suggest future directions for theoretically relevant, contextually rich, and policy-relevant research.

In chapter 11, the authors summarize the results, integrating across study, developmental epoch, and outcome domains and, whenever possible, across qualitative and quantitative data. They discuss the need for work on mediating processes, as well as for the combination of macroapproaches and microapproaches (as done by Korbin and Coulton in volume 2).

## CONCLUSION

We hope that these two volumes will encourage research and evaluation studies on the neighborhoods in which children reside. Our goal also is to stimulate more contextualized research that includes innovative ways of assessing neighborhood contexts. Finally, given that extrafamilial resources, and in some cases intrafamilial ones, are distributed via neighborhoods or other more local geographic areas (such as school districts, health districts, and counties), we hope that those who evaluate changes in federal and state allocations to children and families will take seriously variations by place or neighborhoods. Indeed, place has become even more important, given the passage of the Personal Responsibility and Work Opportunity Reconciliation Bill of 1996. States now are able to fashion their welfare programs in a variety of ways, with much less federal oversight than before. The first implementation of state requirements makes clear the fact that variations are occurring at the county and state levels. Obviously, we must be prepared to examine the new welfare bill's effects community by community.

# 1

# Neighborhoods and Communities as Contexts for Development

*Martha A. Gephart*

In *The Truly Disadvantaged*, William Julius Wilson (1987) argued that the deindustrialization of the U.S. economy, the shift of jobs from cities to suburbs, and the flight of minority middle-class families from the inner cities had led to severe social dislocations in some urban neighborhoods. Left behind, he suggested, were communities lacking the institutions, resources, and role models necessary for success in a postindustrial society. Wilson argued that people living in neighborhoods of concentrated poverty had become isolated from job networks, mainstream institutions, and role models, and that a variety of social dislocations resulted from this isolation, including school dropout and the proliferation of single-parent families (see also Wilson 1991a, 1991b, 1996).

Spurred by Wilson's (1987) conceptualization of the nature and effects of changes in inner-city neighborhoods and by evidence of the growth of concentrated poverty (Bane and Jargowsky 1988; Massey and Eggers 1990) and its increased clustering with other indicators of disadvantage (Ricketts and Mincy 1989; Ricketts and Sawhill 1988), subsequent research has tried to assess the nature and degree of changes in neighborhoods, the causes of such changes, and the influences of neighborhood and community social and economic disadvantage on adult and child outcomes. In this chapter the changing context of community-level urban poverty is described, and theory and research on neighborhoods and communities as contexts for the development of children and adolescents are reviewed.

## THE CHANGING CONTEXT OF URBAN POVERTY AT THE COMMUNITY LEVEL

During the past several decades, poverty in the United States has become more urban, spatially concentrated, and clustered with other indicators of disadvantage. The residents of neighborhoods of concentrated poverty, who experience these multiple forms of social and economic disadvantage, are disproportionately members of minority groups.

## INCREASED SPATIAL CONCENTRATION OF POVERTY

During the past several decades, poverty in the United States has become more urban. From 1959 to 1985, the proportion of poor people residing in central cities increased from 27 percent to 41 percent (Jargowsky and Bane 1990). Between 1970 and 1990, poverty also became more spatially concentrated within many metropolitan areas and cities, especially among poor blacks (Jargowsky 1994, 1997; Jargowsky and Bane 1990; Kahn and Kamerman, 1996).

During the 1970s, the overall proportion of poor people living in neighborhoods in which 40 percent or more of the residents were poor increased only modestly among blacks and decreased among Hispanics. The aggregate numbers concealed substantial regional differences, however. The spatial concentration of poverty dramatically increased in large northern cities and strikingly decreased in small- and medium-sized southern cities (Jargowsky and Bane 1990, 51). In the Northeast, for example, the proportion of poor blacks living in neighborhoods in which 40 percent of the residents were poor more than doubled during the 1970s, increasing from 15 percent to 34 percent (Jargowsky and Bane 1990).

Between 1980 and 1990, concentrated poverty among blacks grew, in terms of both the absolute number of blacks and the percentage of the black population living in neighborhoods of concentrated poverty. Between 1980 and 1990, the percentage of the metropolitan black population living in areas in which 40 percent or more of the population was poor increased from 20.2 percent to 23.7 percent (Jargowsky 1994, 1997). The percentage of the metropolitan black poor who were living in such areas increased from 37.2 percent to 45.4 percent.

The trend toward increasing spatial concentration of poverty among blacks during the 1980s was not uniform, however. Unlike during the 1970s, when increases in the number of black persons living in neighborhoods of concentrated poverty were dominated by a few large cities such as New York and Chicago, during the 1980s, smaller metropolitan areas had the largest increases. In terms of regional variations, there were decreases from 1980 to 1990 in the levels of concentrated poverty among blacks in cities along the eastern seaboard, and there were sharp increases in the western mid-Atlantic states, in the Midwest, and in the oil states.

## INCREASED GEOGRAPHICAL SPREAD OF CONCENTRATED POVERTY

In cities in which the inner-city poverty levels increased during the 1970s, many new census tracts became areas of concentrated poverty (Jargowsky and Bane 1990). This geographical spread of concentrated inner-city poverty exploded during the 1980s (Jargowsky 1994, 1997). The number of census tracts in which 40 percent or more of the residents were poor increased in the vast majority of metropolitan areas during the 1980s. Even many of the metropolitan areas with declining levels of concentrated poverty experienced increases in the number of concentrated poverty tracts.

INCREASED CLUSTERING OF POVERTY WITH OTHER FORMS OF DISADVANTAGE

Consistent with Wilson's (1987) conceptualization of concentration effects, recent research has suggested that poverty has become more clustered with other indicators of disadvantage. Taylor and Covington (1988), for example, reported links between the increasing concentrations of poor and minorities in Baltimore city neighborhoods from 1970 to 1980 and increases in violence. Chow and Coulton (1992) reviewed changes in Cleveland neighborhoods between 1980 and 1989, and they presented evidence of a structural change in the distribution and interrelationship of adverse conditions in Cleveland during that decade (see Korbin and Coulton vol. 2). Comparing factor structures for a wide range of indicators of social and economic disadvantage in 1980 and 1989, they found three evenly distributed factors in 1980 (Unruliness, Family disruption, and Dangerousness), and only a single factor in 1989, which they called Impoverishment. Land, McCall, and Cohen (1990), in an analysis of the structural covariates in twenty-one macrolevel studies of homicide, found that cities, standard metropolitan statistical areas (SMSAs), and states that had large poor populations and high percentages of blacks and single-parent families with children in 1960, 1970, or 1980 all had disproportionately high homicide rates. Their results suggest that the clustering of economic and social disadvantage precedes the period from 1970 to 1980 and applies not only to neighborhoods of large cities but also to cities, metropolitan areas, and states.

The vast majority of the residents of neighborhoods in which 40 percent or more of the residents are poor are members of minority groups (Jargowsky and Bane 1991, Massey and Eggers 1990). In 1990, there were 11.2 million persons living in such neighborhoods (Jargowsky 1994). More than 50 percent were non-Hispanic blacks, nearly 33 percent were Hispanic, and only 11.8 percent were non-Hispanic whites, despite the fact that the latter group comprises 75 percent of the U.S. population. Thus, minorities disproportionately experience the effects of concentrated poverty and its clustering with other forms of disadvantage. As a result, many minority children and adolescents face daily challenges, dangers, and obstacles that their white counterparts rarely experience.

## ANTECEDENTS AND CAUSES OF URBAN POVERTY'S CHANGING CONTEXT

Existing research suggests that the interaction of several forces in American cities over the past fifty years has led to the increased spatial concentration of poverty, the geographical spread of areas of concentrated poverty, and the increased clustering of poverty with other forms of social and economic disadvantage. These forces have altered the context of urban poverty at the community level and created the neighborhoods and communities of concentrated poverty that have been associated with the term *urban underclass*.

## INCREASES IN LEVELS OF INNER-CITY POVERTY AND JOBLESSNESS

A dramatic change in the wage structure over the past two decades has had especially negative consequences for non-college-educated minorities living in inner cities (Moss and Tilly 1991). Declining real wages overall, rising inequality in wage and income distribution, and growing numbers of low-wage jobs have placed minority city residents at a particular disadvantage in the labor market (Wilson 1996). Deterioration of labor market conditions for those in the labor force has been accompanied by a considerable increase in joblessness, especially among black minority youth in cities. The average jobless rate for black high school dropouts climbed from 6 percent in the mid-1960s to 36 percent in the mid-1980s. For high school graduates, the rate rose from zero to 14 percent. In seeking to explain these labor market trends, researchers have pointed to the impact of structural transformations in the economy, including deindustrialization, globalization, and technological change; expansion of the labor force; spatial and skill "mismatches" between inner-city minorities and job opportunities (Kasarda 1988, 1990a, 1990b; Rosenbaum 1991; Rosenbaum and Popkin 1991); decline in the number of low-wage jobs in central cities (Freeman 1991a; Kasarda 1990a, 1990b); decline in job ladders in internal labor markets; and statistical discrimination (Kirshenman and Neckerman 1991).

## PERSISTENT HIGH LEVELS OF RESIDENTIAL SEGREGATION BY RACE

Racial prejudice (Farley 1997), racial discrimination in housing markets (Galster 1986, 1990a, 1990b, 1990c; Massey and Denton 1993); and a variety of federal and local governmental policies (Bradbury, Case, and Dunham 1989; Logan and Molotch 1987; Skogan 1986) have contributed to the persistence of or, in some cases, increases in levels of urban residential segregation by race since the 1940s, forming a pattern that led to conditions of "hyper-segregation" for blacks in twenty major metropolitan areas in the 1980s and 1990s (Massey and Denton 1989). Some researchers (Massey 1990; Massey and Eggers 1990) have presented evidence that residential segregation is a major cause of concentrated poverty because segregation has confined metropolitan-level increases in black poverty to a few spatially distinct neighborhoods. In addition, Massey and Denton (1993) have argued that residential segregation, by restricting economic opportunities for blacks, produces interracial economic disparities that elicit further discrimination and reinforce segregation.

OUT-MIGRATION OF NONPOOR FAMILIES

Evidence also exists that the movement of nonpoor families out of the inner cities has contributed to the increased spatial concentration of urban poverty (Gramlich, Laren, and Sealand 1992). On the basis of detailed studies of ghetto poverty in Cleveland, Memphis, Milwaukee, and Philadelphia, Jargowsky and Bane (1990) concluded that the process by which geographical areas stayed, became, or stopped being ghettos (areas in which 40 percent or more of the residents are poor) between 1970 and 1980 was complicated. In none of the four cities was the geographical spread of concentrated poverty a simple result of migration or of increases in the poverty rate. Jargowsky and Bane described a general pattern of dispersion interacting with changes in the poverty rate and continuing high levels of racial segregation. During the 1980s, central cities continued to experience population loss, and economic segregation increased (Jargowsky 1994, 1997).

FEDERAL AND LOCAL GOVERNMENT POLICIES

Historical research shows that federal and local urban and economic policies, by contributing to the concentration of poverty and by failing to stem business disinvestment in cities, the withdrawal of services, and other conditions that promote disorganization and crime, have also played an important role in shaping labor market conditions in inner cities and in contributing to inner-city decline (Bursik 1988; Logan and Molotch 1987; Massey and Kahaiaupuni 1993; Wallace and Wallace 1990). Federal subsidization of interstates and free-ways, urban renewal and public housing policies, and the fragmentation of metropolitan areas into competing jurisdictions have all contributed to the marginalization of cities and the decline of inner-city neighborhoods over several decades.

## NEIGHBORHOOD AND COMMUNITY INFLUENCES: THEORETICAL PERSPECTIVES

Several theoretical perspectives guide our thinking about the ways in which neighborhoods and communities may influence the development of children, youth, and families. Work by Wilson (1987, 1991a, 1991b) and others (Jencks and Peterson 1991) on urban poverty and the underclass has provided the immediate impetus for much of the recent work on the effects of neighborhoods and communities on poor children and families. Wilson argued that the concentrations of male joblessness, poverty, and female-headed households, which have resulted from job losses and the middle class's flight from inner-city neighborhoods, may have led to social isolation and to a shift in neighborhoods' social and cultural norms. He posited that both the macrostructural

constraints and the behavior of other jobless families in a neighborhood influence the children and families who reside there. Wilson accorded priority to
the role of joblessness in shaping inner-city changes, arguing that the importance of work extends beyond the provision of income. "Work," Wilson
(1991b, 10) argued, "constitutes a framework for daily behavior and patterns
of interaction because of the disciplines and regularities it imposes. Thus, in
the absence of regular employment, what is lacking is not only a place in
which to work and the receipt of regular income, but also a coherent organization of the present, that is, a system of concrete expectations and goals."
Wilson's ideas have thus stimulated consideration not only of the neighborhood characteristics that might influence individual developmental outcomes,
but also of the family and individual characteristics and processes that may
mediate those influences.

The mechanisms Wilson proposed are among those identified by Jencks
and Mayer (1990) through which the effects of neighborhood socioeconomic
composition might operate. *Collective socialization* models, which are emphasized in Wilson's formulation, focus on how adults in a neighborhood
influence youth who are not their children. According to collective socialization theories, middle-class and professional neighbors serve as role models
and exercise social control, helping young people to internalize social norms
and to learn the boundaries of acceptable behavior. *Institutional* models also
focus on the influences of adults on children, but the adults are those from outside the community who work in various neighborhood and community institutions, such as schools, welfare agencies, and the police force. Institutional
models also point to the behavioral regularities that are produced through
structured and semistructured interactions with organizations and actors,
incluling employers, schools, enforcement agencies, and other social institutions. *Epidemic* models focus on how peers influence one another's behavior.
Such contagion processes result from imitating behavior and peer pressure
and are conditioned by differential susceptibility of individuals to conform.
Collective socialization, institutional, and epidemic models all assume that
growing up with relatively affluent neighbors encourages children to learn in
school, get good jobs, and avoid trouble.

A second set of models identified by Jencks and Mayer (1990) suggests
that relatively affluent neighbors can be a disadvantage. *Social comparison*
models emphasize relative deprivation and status-organizing processes. Relative deprivation theories assume that young people judge their success or
failure by comparing themselves with others around them and that an unfa-
vorable comparison can lead them to try harder or to drop out of the competition. If young people respond to failure and blocked opportunities in
school or in the job market by reducing their effort and motivation, having
relatively affluent neighbors may increase the chances of their quitting
school, becoming teenage parents, or becoming involved in the illicit economy. Disadvantaged youth who do not believe that opportunities for mobil-

ity will be available to them, and who therefore do not work in school, may be following the logic of relative deprivation theory (Leventhal, Graber, and Brooks-Gunn 1996).

Models of *cultural conflict* and *competition for scarce resources* also suggest that relatively affluent neighbors may be a disadvantage. The formation of subcultures of resistance can be a collective reaction to perceptions of blocked opportunities and lack of success (Ogbu 1991; Willis 1977). The presence of advantaged neighbors or classmates, viewed as evidence of structural inequality, may increase the likelihood of such responses. Finally, competition for scarce resources can make relatively affluent neighbors a disadvantage, as, for example, when youth compete for a limited number of jobs or for grades in school.

Theories of economic choice (Duncan and Hoffman 1991; Haveman and Wolfe 1994) consider the impact of resources and incentives in the family and neighborhood on various decisions that affect investments in the human capital of children and adolescents. According to this perspective, decisions about whether to complete high school, to have a child out of wedlock, or to engage in illegal economic activity will be influenced by incentives provided by local employment conditions, marital opportunities in the local environment, welfare opportunities, and the state of the unreported and illicit economies. In relating the outcomes of interest to opportunities and incentives in the local environment, an economic choice perspective typically assumes that decision makers are reasonably well informed about their actions' economic consequences.

Some economists have sought to formalize Wilson's role model hypothesis by assuming that the role model process is one in which young people use family, friends, and neighbors as information sources when making economic decisions. Lillard (1993), for example, argued that human capital investment may vary across neighborhoods because neighborhood characteristics affect productivity, costs of investment, and expected returns. His model assumes that returns to human capital vary with ability and that individuals imperfectly perceive the relationship between earnings and education or ability. Youth may systematically underestimate returns to education if they live in neighborhoods in which local earnings distributions are truncated.

Social disorganization theorists have identified a set of general ecological features that characterize neighborhoods with high, persistent rates of problem behavior (Shaw and McKay 1942; Kornhauser 1978). Community-level structural factors that are thought to impede systemic social organization include residential mobility and population turnover, family disruption, population heterogeneity, housing/population density, and poverty/resource deprivation (see Sampson and Morenoff vol. 2). These are linked to community-level social and cultural processes that have been conceptualized in terms of the prevalence and interdependence of a community's social networks—both informal (for example, the density of acquaintanceship or intergenerational kinship ties) and formal (organizational participation)—the span of collective supervision that the community directs toward local problems, and the shared norms that support the community's quest for common values (Sampson 1988, 1991). These community-level processes, in turn, directly affect families and individuals. The central idea in social disorganization theory is that the impact of communities is found primarily in the factors that facilitate or inhibit networks of social support and value consensus.

The concepts of functional communities (Coleman and Hoffer 1987) and social capital (Coleman 1988, 1990) overlap with social disorganization theory in their emphasis on the nature of social ties and community values. Functional communities are those in which social norms and sanctions arise out of the social structure and both reinforce and perpetuate that structure. Social capital, which is derived from the density and quality of social ties, exists within families, as well as neighborhoods and communities. According to Coleman (1990), one of the most important community characteristics that facilitates the availability of social capital is the "intergenerational closure" of networks among families and children in a community. Such closure exists when a child is related to two or more adults whose relationships transcend the household. Such adults, who may be friends or acquaintances, can observe the child's behavior in different settings, share their observations and views, and set norms. This type of relationship, for example, "where parents' friends are the parents of their children's friends" (Sampson 1992, 79) encourages monitoring and supervision of youth by community members other than their parents and guardians.

Sampson (1992; Sampson and Morenoff vol. 2) has proposed a community-level theory of social disorganization that emphasizes families and child development and reflects a convergence among several of the theoretical orientations just reviewed. The central argument of Sampson's theory is that community structure is important mainly for its role in facilitating or inhibiting the creation of social capital among families and children. His theory integrates social disorganization theory with research on child development and family management.

Noting the empirical connection that has long been recognized between the health-related problems of children and rates of crime and delinquency, Sampson (1992) linked social disorganization theory with child development theory by positing that *community-level structural features* ("residential mobility and population turnover, family disruption, housing/population density, poverty/resource deprivation, inadequate health care resources, and the ecological concentration of the urban underclass") are mediated by *community-level processes* ("institutional-family connectedness; the observ-ability, monitoring, and supervision of youth; intergenerational closure among adult–child networks; control of street-corner peer groups; local organizational participation; mutual social support and extensiveness of social networks; perceived normative consensus on parenting, social trust") "that directly and indirectly influence the care of children, and ultimately rates of delinquency and crime" (85–86). Sampson argued that in socially organized communities, the social capital that is generated enhances the health-related aspects of child development and the viability and effectiveness of family management practices, regardless of the personal characteristics of children and families. Sampson's theory promises to integrate several strands in socio-logical theory—including Wilson's (1987, 1991a, 1991b) theory of concen-tration effects, Shaw and McKay's (1942) social disorganization theory, and Coleman's (1988, 1990) theory of social capital and functional communities—and to link those strands with theory and research on child development and family management. In doing so, it bridges some of the disciplinary differ-ences that have characterized analyses and interpretations of neighborhood and community influences (see Sampson and Morenoff vol. 2).

The developmental-ecological perspective of Bronfenbrenner (1979b, 1989) views individuals as developing within a set of embedded contexts—microsystems, with which the person is in direct contact; mesosystems, which influence the person indirectly via their effects on microsystems; and exo-systems, or the institutional and social/cultural normative contexts in which microsystems and mesosystems are embedded. Neighborhoods and com-munities can influence individual development at any and all of these levels: as a direct or indirect influence; and/or, as a moderating context that condi-tions the relations among causal influences. As articulated by Bronfenbren-ner, the developmental-ecological perspective is a framework more than a theory (Moen, Elder, and Lusher 1995); thus, it can incorporate the substan-tive content of various theoretical perspectives (see chapter 2). Brooks-Gunn (1995), for example, has added neighborhood resources to Bronfenbrenner's framework. The studies reported in this volume draw on this framework's key concepts to form questions and interpret results. As Aber and colleagues indicate in chapter 2, the framework emphasizes variations across and inter-actions among person, process, context, and time in human development. It highlights the importance of nonadditive, synergistic effects of multiple dimensions of neighborhood social and economic disadvantage and the differential effects of neighborhood characteristics on individuals and fami-lies, depending on their characteristics and interaction processes.

## CONCEPTUALIZING AND MEASURING NEIGHBORHOODS AND COMMUNITIES

Conceptually, neighborhoods and communities are the immediate social con-text in which individuals and families interact and engage with the institutions and societal agents that regulate and control access to community opportunity structures and resources. Neighborhoods are spatial units, associational net-works, and perceived environments. A key issue in research on neighborhoods

understanding are contextual analyses that have investigated individual-level variations in the behavior of children and adolescents as a function of individual- and community-level factors. This review of existing research focuses primarily on such studies.

The current generation of contextual analyses has a number of serious limitations, however. Neighborhoods and communities are usually defined as the administrative units for which data have been collected. Most existing contextual analyses use cross-sectional data, making it impossible to study the transactions between individuals and communities as they both change. The fact that neighborhood- and community-level factors tend to be highly correlated makes it difficult to assess their relative importance. Moreover, most existing analyses use data that do not include measures of intervening processes at the community, school, family, and individual levels, which are needed to test competing theories. Finally, most existing studies are unable to distinguish nonrandom selection processes from genuine contextual effects. Because of these limitations, the results of recent community-level analyses are reviewed and used to help interpret the findings of the contextual analyses and to clarify some of the mechanisms of influence through which neighborhoods' structural and compositional characteristics may affect outcomes for children and adolescents. Although qualitative and ethnographic studies can also help researchers interpret the results of contextual analyses, such studies are not reviewed in this chapter.

Community-level analyses have begun to clarify relationships between the structural and compositional characteristics of communities and the differences among communities in rates and levels of behavior. To the extent that the social structural and compositional characteristics of neighborhoods and communities predict differences among communities in rates and levels of behavior, our confidence in interpreting their contextual effects on individual behavior increases.

Community-level analyses have also begun to clarify the links between the structural and sociodemographic characteristics of neighborhoods and communities and the community-level social and cultural processes thought to mediate the effects of structural conditions on individual outcomes (Brooks-Gunn, Brown et al. 1995). Such studies (for example, Darling and Steinberg vol. 2; Sampson and Groves 1989; Simcha-Fagan and Schwartz 1986) illuminate some of the community-level mediating processes through which neighborhood compositional effects may operate. Their results underscore the need for caution in interpreting the direct effects of neighborhood sociodemographic characteristics without examining the relations between them and community-level processes.

## THE GAUTREAUX ASSISTED HOUSING PROGRAM

Because of its quasi-experimental nature, one type of program has not been subject to some of the sources of bias that jeopardize the causal interpretation of most neighborhood effects identified in correlational analyses. The Gautreaux Assisted Housing Program was established by the courts in 1976 in an effort to redress racial discrimination in the Chicago Housing Authority's public housing program. Housing counselors offer participants housing on the basis of availability, not locational preference, and most accept their first offer, since they are not guaranteed another. Potential participants must meet three eligibility requirements: families must have four or fewer children; they must pay their rent and have a steady source of income (usually Aid to Families with Dependent Children, or AFDC); and they must not be bad housekeepers on the day of the counselor's visit. These three criteria together eliminate less than 30 percent of the public housing population, making the study results applicable to most public housing residents. Since its inception, the program has placed about four thousand low-income black families in private-sector apartments, and over half of these have been in the suburbs.

In 1982, Rosenbaum, Kulieke, and Rubinowitz (1988) compared the experiences of Gautreaux children whose families moved to the suburbs with those of children whose families moved to neighborhoods within the city. The effects of the move were generally positive, although the suburban children experienced some overt racism and were more likely to be placed in special education programs. In a recent follow-up study (Kaufman and Rosenbaum 1992; Rosenbaum 1991), the mothers and children were reinterviewed. At the time of reinterview, the children had been in the program from 7.5 to 13 years; most of them were about twenty years old. The sample of 107 children included 65 in the suburbs and 42 in the city. Although only 59 percent of the youths in the original study could be located for this follow-up study, the group was not significantly different from the entire population (Rosenbaum 1991, 1194–96).

Regarding education, the suburban youth were much less likely than the city youth to drop out of school (5 percent versus 20 percent). They had similar grades despite higher expectations. They were more likely to be in or to have completed the college education track (40 percent versus 24 percent), and they were more likely to be enrolled in college (54 percent versus 21 percent). Among college students, suburban movers were also much more likely to be in a four-year college (50 percent versus 20 percent).

In terms of employment, suburban movers were much more likely to be employed (75 percent versus 41 percent), to work in better-paying jobs, and to receive at least one job benefit (55 percent versus 23 percent). City youth were less likely to be employed or in school (10 percent versus 26 percent). Mothers of suburban children spoke of the move's benefits for their children, particularly the better schools and safer environment.

Two other studies of the experiences of public housing residents who move are currently underway. One is a study of public housing residents who moved to cluster-based housing in middle-class neighborhoods in Yonkers. The other is a demonstration project—the Moving to Opportunity (MTO) demonstration project—that is being sponsored by the U.S. Department of Housing and Urban Development. In MTO, two thousand families who are public housing residents in five of the nation's largest cities are being randomly assigned to one of three conditions: (1) conventional Section 8 housing vouchers for relocation within the city; (2) vouchers and assistance to move to low-poverty areas; and (3) remaining in public housing. The results from these studies should build upon the findings from the Gautreaux research and address some of the methodological limitations in that earlier work.

## COMMUNITY AND CONTEXTUAL ANALYSES

Verifying and interpreting the effects of concentrated poverty and neighborhood disadvantage on individual behavior has proved more difficult than confirming Wilson's predicted increases in the concentration of poverty or the increased clustering of poverty with other forms of social and economic disadvantage. In this section, community and contextual analyses that help to clarify whether and how neighborhoods and communities influence child and adolescent development are reviewed.

In an earlier review of research on the effects that the socioeconomic and racial mix of schools and neighborhoods had on a range of outcomes for adults and children, Jencks and Mayer (1990) found few studies that linked neighborhood conditions to individual outcomes, while controlling for family-level economic status. They argued that strong conclusions about the existence and strength of neighborhood effects could not be drawn from the existing body of empirical work. However, a growing body of research completed since their review has linked the geographic concentration of socioeconomic disadvantage and features of neighborhood social disorganization to outcomes for individuals and families. Table 1.1 contains a summary of studies published since Jencks and Mayer's review that have investigated the effects of neighborhood characteristics on child, adolescent, and young adult outcomes, plus a summary of the results of studies published between 1980 and 1990 that Jencks and Mayer reviewed.

Both table 1.1 and the review of studies following it are organized by developmental period. For ease of reference, the studies in the table are listed alphabetically by lead author within developmental period. In the text, I review the community-level analyses for each developmental period before the relevant contextual analyses. Unless otherwise indicated, contextual analyses include controls for family- and or individual-level characteristics. A glance at the table reveals that most of the studies published since 1980 have focused on outcomes for adolescents and young adults. Only a few studies have investigated the effects of neighborhood characteristics on outcomes for children.

*(Text continues on page 26.)*

TABLE 1.1 Community and Contextual Analyses Reviewed by Developmental Period

Early Childhood

| Study | Data Set(s) & Sample Characteristics | Neighborhood/ Community Level(s) Characteristics | Outcomes Level(s) Domain | Results |
|---|---|---|---|---|
| Brooks-Gunn, Duncan, Klebanov, and Sealand (1993) | Infant Health and Development Program (IHDP) 489 black, 304 non-Hispanic white, and 101 Hispanic, low-birth-weight infants, at age 3 1980 census | *Census tract* Affluent neighbors Low-income neighbors Professional/ managerial workers Female-headed families Male joblessness Welfare receipt | *Individual* Cognitive functioning Behavior problems | *Effects of tract-level sociodemographic characteristics on individual outcomes* Affluent neighbors $\longrightarrow$ (+) IQ at age 3 (Effects mediated by home learning environment) |
| Coulton, Korbin, Su, and Chow (1995) | City and county agency data 177 census tracts in Cleveland 1990 census | *Census tract* Community impoverishment Community child-care burden (family & age structure) Residential instability Contiguity to high-poverty areas | *Census tract* Child maltreatment rates | *Effects of tract-level sociodemographic characteristics on tract-level outcomes* Impoverishment Child-care burden Residential instability Contiguity to high-poverty areas $\left.\begin{array}{c} \\ \\ \\ \\ \end{array}\right\} \longrightarrow$ (+) Rates of child maltreatment |

(Table continues on p. 16.)

TABLE 1.1 *Continued*

Early Childhood

| Study | Data Set(s) & Sample Characteristics | Neighborhood/Community Level(s) Characteristics | Outcomes Level(s) Domain | Results |
|---|---|---|---|---|
| Coulton and Pandey (1992) | City and county agency data<br>187 census tracts in Cleveland | Census tract<br>Type of poverty area<br>Demographic factors<br>Social conditions<br>Poverty rates | Census tract<br>Low-birth-weight-rates<br>Infant death rates | *Effects of tract-level sociodemographic characteristics on tract-level outcomes*<br><br>Poverty<br>Races ⎫<br>Population decline ⎬ → (+) Low-birth-weight rate<br><br>Crime<br>Substandard public housing ⎫<br>Unmarried childbearing ⎭ → (+) Infant death rates<br>(Significant indirect effects of crime, poverty, race, and population decline) |
| Duncan, Brooks-Gunn, and Klebanov (1994) | IHDP<br>489 black, 304 non-Hispanic white, and 101 Hispanic low-birth-weight infants at age 5<br>1980 census | Census tract<br>Neighborhood poverty<br>Affluent neighbors<br>Low-income neighbors | Individual<br>Cognitive functioning<br>Behavior problems | *Effects of tract-level sociodemographic characteristics on individual outcomes*<br><br>Affluent neighbors → (+) IQ at age 5<br>Low-income neighbors → (+) Externalizing problem behavior at age 5 |

16

## Middle Childhood

| Study | Sample | Census tract | Individual | Effects of tract-level sociodemographic characteristics on individual outcomes |
|---|---|---|---|---|
| Kupersmidt, Griesler, de Rosier, Patterson, and Davis (1995) | Children from 6 elementary schools in small southern public school system 762 white and 509 black 2nd–5th-grade children; 656 females, 615 males 1980 census | Neighborhood SES (low/middle) | Behavioral adjustment Social adjustment | Middle-SES neighborhood → (−) Aggressive behavior of black children from low-income, single-parent homes<br>Low-SES neighborhood → (+) Teacher prediction of delinquency<br>Middle-SES neighborhood → (+) Peer rejection of low-income white children in single-parent homes<br>Middle-SES neighborhood → (+) Number of home playmates for middle-income white children |

## Late Childhood/Early Adolescence

| Study | Sample | Neighborhoods | Individual | Effects of neighborhood sociodemographic characteristics on individual outcomes |
|---|---|---|---|---|
| Peeples and Loeber (1994) | Pittsburgh Youth Study 219 white 290 black Pittsburgh public middle school students ages 12–16 1980 census | (1–7 census tracts) (underclass/ not underclass) | Delinquent behavior | Underclass neighborhood → (+) { Frequency of delinquent behavior / Seriousness of delinquent behavior } |

(Table continues on page 18.)

TABLE 1.1    *Continued*

| | | Late Adolescence/Early Adulthood | | |
|---|---|---|---|---|
| Study | Data Set(s) & Sample<br><br>Characteristics | Neighborhood/ Community Level(s)<br>Characteristics | Outcomes Level(s)<br>Domain | Results |
| Brooks-Gunn, Duncan, Klebanov, and Sealand (1993) | Panel Study of Income Dynamics (PSID) 1,132 black and 1,214 white women, ages 14–19 1970 and 1980 census | *Census tract Zip code*<br><br>Affluent neighbors Low-income neighbors Professional/managerial workers Female-headed families Welfare receipt Male joblessness | *Individual*<br><br>School dropout Teen out-of-wedlock births | *Effects of tract- and zip-code-level sociodemographic characteristics on individual outcomes*<br><br>Affluent neighbors $\longrightarrow$ (–) { School dropout { For whites only / Teenage births }<br><br>Professional/ managerial workers $\longrightarrow$ (–) { School dropout / Teenage births }<br><br>Female-headed families $\longrightarrow$ (+) School dropout<br><br>(Zip-code data produced more significant effects on school dropout) |
| Case and Katz (1991) | 1989 NBER Boston Youth Survey 585 black (299 males) 455 white (288 males) in 3 high-poverty areas of Boston's central city | *Block group*<br><br>Neighborhood peer influence (mean of neighbors' behaviors) | *Individual*<br><br>Adolescent behaviors | *Effects of block-group-level peer characteristics on individual outcomes*<br><br>Neighborhood $\longrightarrow$ (+) peer influence { Regular alcohol use / Illegal drug use / Criminal activity / Idleness / Friendship with gang members / Church attendance } |

| Study | Sample / data | Aggregation level | Individual / outcome | Effects of sociodemographic characteristics |
|---|---|---|---|---|
| Clark (1992) | 1980 census 5% sample 22,534 males, aged 15–18, from 10 largest SMSAs in 1980 | *Census tract*<br>Professional/managerial workers<br>Affluent neighbors<br>College graduates<br>Male joblessness<br>High school dropouts<br>Neighborhood poverty<br>Female-headed families<br>Welfare receipt | *Individual*<br>School dropout | *Effects of tract-level sociodemographic characteristics on individual outcomes*<br>Professional/managerial workers → (−)<br>Affluent neighbors → (−) } School dropout<br>Neighborhood poverty → (+) |
| Corcoran, Gordon, Laren, and Solon (1992) | PSID 841 males, aged 10–17 in 1968 1970 census | *Zip code*<br>Median family income<br>Female-headed families<br>Male joblessness<br>Welfare receipt | *Individual*<br>Economic status | *Effects of zip-code-level sociodemographic characteristics on individual outcomes*<br>Welfare receipt → (−) { Men's earnings, Hourly wage rate, Family income, Family income-to-needs ratio<br>Male joblessness → (−) Hours of work |
| Coulton, Korbin, Su, and Chow (1995) | City and county agency data 177 census tracts in Cleveland 1990 census | *Census tract*<br>Community impoverishment<br>Community child-care burden (family and age structure)<br>Residential instability<br>Contiguity to high-poverty areas | *Census tract*<br>Incidence of:<br>Social problems<br>Health problems | *Effects of tract-level sociodemographic characteristics on tract-level outcomes*<br>Impoverishment, Child-care burden } → (+) { Teen pregnancy, Drug arrests, Juvenile delinquency, Violent crime<br>Residential instability → (+) Violent crime |

(Table continues on page 20.)

TABLE 1.1  *Continued*

|  |  | Late Adolescence/Early Adulthood | | |
|---|---|---|---|---|
| Study | Data Set(s) & Sample Characteristics | Neighborhood/Community Level(s) Characteristics | Outcomes Level(s) Domain | Results |
| Coulton and Pandey (1992) | City and county agency data 187 census tracts in Cleveland | *Census tract* Type of poverty area Demographic factors Social conditions Poverty rate | *Census tract* Teen birthrate Juvenile delinquency rate High school dropout rate | *Effects of tract-level sociodemographic characteristics on tract-level outcomes* Poverty / Race / Population decline → (+) { Teen birthrate / Juvenile delinquency } Unmarried childbearing / Crime / Substandard housing → (+) { Teen birthrate / Juvenile delinquency } (Significant indirect effects of crime, poverty, race, and population decline) |
| Crane (1991b) | 1970 15 percent PUMS Neighborhood Characteristics File 113,997 males and females, aged 16–19 44,466 for teen childbearing 92,512 for school dropout | *Census neighborhoods* Professional/managerial workers | *Individual* School dropout Teen childbearing | *Effects of census neighborhood-level sociodemographic characteristics on individual outcomes* Professional/ managerial workers → (−) { School dropout / Teen childbearing } (Nonlinear effects) |

| Study | Sample | Community level & measure | Individual outcomes | Effects of community-level sociodemographic characteristics on individual outcomes |
|---|---|---|---|---|
| Datcher (1982) | PSID, 196 black and 356 white urban young men, aged 13–22, living with their parents in 1968, 1970 census | *Zip code*<br>Family income | *Individual*<br>Years of schooling | *Effects of zip-code-level sociodemographic characteristics on individual outcomes*<br>Family income → (+) Years of schooling |
| Dornbusch, Ritter, and Steinberg (1991) | Northern California high school students, 382 black and 3,467 white | *Census tract*<br>Community SES | *Individual*<br>Self-reported grades | *Effects of tract-level sociodemographic characteristics on individual outcomes*<br>Community SES → (+) Student reports of grades |
| Duncan (1994) | PSID, 783 white males, 818 white females, 884 black males, & 954 black females, aged 16–22, 1970 census, 1980 census | *Census tract*<br>Low-income neighbors<br>Affluent neighbors<br>Female-headed families<br>Female employment<br>Race<br>Region | *Individual*<br>Years of schooling<br>Failure to complete high school<br>College attendance | *Effects of tract-level sociodemographic characteristics on individual outcomes*<br>Low-income neighbors → (−) Years of schooling (white girls)<br>Affluent neighbors → (+) Years of schooling (except black males)<br>Racial integration → (+) Years of schooling (black males)<br>Female-headed families, Female employment → (−) Years of schooling (black females)<br>Female employment, Low-income neighbors, Black neighbors → (+) Years of schooling (white males)<br>→ (−) College attendance (black males) |

(Table continues on p. 22.)

TABLE 1.1  *Continued*

| Study | Data Set(s) & Sample Characteristics | Neighborhood/Community Level(s) Characteristics | Outcomes Level(s) Domain | Results |
|---|---|---|---|---|
| | | | | Late Adolescence/Early Adulthood |
| | | | | Female employment ⟶ (−) College attendance (white and black females) |
| | | | | Female-headed families ⟶ (+) Dropout (black females) |
| Ensminger, Lamkin, and Jacobson (1996) | Woodlawn Longitudinal Study 950 black male and female youth 1970 census 1980 census Chicago Board of Education Records | *Census tract* Neighborhood SES (poverty/middle SES tracts) Neighborhood poverty White-collar workers | *Individual* School dropout Years of schooling | *Effects of tract-level sociodemographic characteristics on individual outcomes* Middle SES neighborhood ⟶ { (−) School dropout (+) Years of schooling } |
| Esbensen and Huizinga (1990) | Denver Youth Survey 1,530 youth, aged 7–15 in high-risk neighborhoods in a midwestern city 1980 census | *Census block groups* 3 types of socially disorganized neighborhoods | *Census block groups* Prevalence and frequency of drug use  *Individual* Settings of drug use Reasons for drug use | *Effects of 3 clusters of block groups on individual outcomes* Type of neighborhood ⟶ { Settings of drug use Reasons for drug use } |

| Study | Sample | Unit / Measure | Outcome | Findings |
|---|---|---|---|---|
| Garner and Raudenbush (1991) | 2,500 students in one Scottish education authority who left school between 1984 and 1986; 1981 census of population | *Educational authority*: Neighborhood deprivation index | *Individual*: Educational attainment score | *Effects of authority-level sociodemographic characteristics on individual outcomes*<br><br>Neighborhood deprivation → (−) Educational attainment score |
| Hogan and Kitagawa (1985) | 1979 Young Chicagoans Survey; 1070 unmarried black Chicago women, aged 13–19 in 1979; 1970 census | *Census tract*: Neighborhood SES (high, medium, low) based on index of neighborhood quality | *Census tract*: Teenage pregnancy rates | *Effects of tract-level sociodemographic characteristics on tract-level outcomes*<br><br>Low neighborhood SES, Living on the West Side → (+) Teenage pregnancy rate |
| Massey, Gross, and Eggers (1991) | 1980 Summary Tape File 4A | *SMSA*: Segregation; Poverty rate | *Census tract*: Poverty rate | *Effects of SMSA sociodemographic characteristics on tract-level outcomes*<br><br>SMSA segregation × poverty → Poverty rate |
| (1991) | 1980 5 percent PUMS Whites, blacks, and Hispanics in 50 largest SMSAs who have lived in the same house for 5 years | *Public housing (by group)*; *Census tract*: Poverty | *Individual*: Male joblessness, Teen childbearing, Female-headed families | *Effects of tract-level sociodemographic characteristics on individual outcomes*<br><br>Neighborhood poverty → (+) Male joblessness (16–19-yr.-olds), Male joblessness (20–35-yr.-olds), Teen childbearing (15–18-yr.-olds), Female-headed families |

(Table continues on p. 24.)

TABLE 1.1  *Continued*

| | | Late Adolescence/Early Adulthood | | |
|---|---|---|---|---|
| Study | Data Set(s) & Sample | Neighborhood/ Community Level(s) Characteristics | Outcomes Level(s) Domain | Results |
| | Characteristics | *Locality* | *Locality* | *Effects of sociodemographic characteristics on locality processes* |
| Sampson and Groves (1989) | 1982 British Crime Survey 1984 British Crime Survey | Community structural characteristics Community social organization | Rates of crime and delinquency | Residential stability → (+) ⎫ Local friendship<br>Urbanization → (−) ⎭ networks<br><br>Community SES → (−) ⎫<br>Ethnic heterogeneity → (+) ⎪<br>Family disruption → (+) ⎬ Unsupervised peer groups<br>Urbanization → (+) ⎪<br>Community SES → (+) → Organizational participation<br><br>*Effects of community processes on locality outcomes*<br><br>Unsupervised peer groups → (+) ⎫<br>Local friendship networks → (−) ⎬ Victimization<br>Family disruption → (+) ⎪<br>Organizational participation → (−) ⎭<br><br>Unsupervised peer groups → (+) ⎫<br>Family disruption → (+) ⎬ Offending rates<br>Local friendship networks → (−) ⎭ |

Simcha-Fagan
and
Schwartz
(1986)

1980 census
294 black, 238 white,
and 21 other males,
aged 11–18, and
their mothers from
12 N.Y. City
neighborhoods

*Census tract*

3 Neighborhood
Factors:
Community disorder-
criminal structure
Community informal
structure
Community
organizational
participation

*Census tract*
*Individual*

Self-reported
delinquency
Officially
recorded
delinquency
Severe self-
reported
delinquency

*Effects of sociodemographic*
*characteristics on community processes*

Community poverty
Children in single-         →(+)   Community disorder-
family households                  criminal subculture
Maternal education          →(+)   Organizational
level                              participation

*Effects of community processes on tract-level*
*outcomes*

Organizational          →(−)
participation                      Self-reported
Disorder-criminal       →(+)       delinquency
subculture

Disorder-criminal       →(+)       Officially recorded
subculture                         delinquency

*Effects of community processes on individual*
*outcomes*

Residential                 →(+)
stability
Organizational                     Self-reported
participation                      delinquency
Community               →(−)
disorder-criminal
subculture
Community               →(+)       Officially recorded
disorder-criminal                  delinquency
subculture
Community               →(+)       Severe self-reported
disorder-criminal                  delinquency
subculture

25

EARLY CHILDHOOD: COMMUNITY ANALYSES

Communities characterized by high levels of social and economic disadvantage also have high rates of child abuse, infant mortality, and low birth weight. In a study of subareas and census tracts within a city, Garbarino and Crouter (1978) found that poverty, residential mobility, and single-parent households accounted for over 50 percent of the variation in child abuse rates. In a subsequent study, Garbarino and Sherman (1980) selected a pair of neighborhoods, matched for socioeconomic level, on the basis of correlates of neighborhood differences in the rates of child abuse and neglect. Interviews conducted with samples of families from both neighborhoods indicated that families in the high-risk neighborhood (though similar in socioeconomic status) reported a less positive evaluation of the neighborhood as a context for child and family development. Garbarino and Sherman's research suggested that high-risk neighborhoods are socially impoverished relative to low-risk neighborhoods. Mothers in high-risk areas were less likely to assume full responsibility for their children, to engage in neighborhood exchanges, or to use the resources available. The picture that emerged from the high-risk areas was one of very "needy" families competing for scarce social resources. These findings provide support for a concept of neighborhood risk for abuse that is independent of socioeconomic status and other compositional factors.

More recent support for the link between neighborhood disadvantage and risk to children has come from studies undertaken by Coulton and her colleagues in Cleveland, who have shown that children living in neighborhoods characterized by concentrated poverty, population turnover, and the concentration of female-headed families are at the highest risk of abuse (see Korbin and Coulton vol. 2). After examining the geographic distribution of poverty in Cleveland (Coulton, Pandey, and Chow 1990) and changes in the distribution during the 1980s (Chow and Coulton 1992), Coulton and her colleagues concluded that there had been a dramatic shift in the degree to which low-income tracts had become economically homogeneous. The poor in Cleveland were more than twice as likely to live in conditions of concentrated poverty in 1980 than in 1970. To take into account some of the historical and spatial differences among poverty areas, they identified three categories of poverty areas: traditional poverty areas that were already high in poverty at the time of the 1970 census; new poverty areas that became high in poverty between 1970 and 1980; and emerging poverty areas that became poor between 1980 and 1988, reflecting the dislocation of many blue-collar workers on Cleveland's outskirts. They then examined the mean rates of indicators of child well-being in these types of poverty areas. Children in all high-poverty areas were at greater risk than children in low-poverty areas. For low birth weight and infant death, low-poverty areas were not significantly different from emerging poverty areas. Rates of low birth weight were significantly higher in traditional and new poverty areas than in emerging or low-poverty areas.

Using a database developed for the city of Cleveland (which contains information on social, economic, demographic, and physical characteristics of each census tract, as well as on the incidence of selected social problems, health conditions, and educational outcomes), Coulton and Pandey (1992) identified geographic areas that pose high risk for children and adolescents. The majority of high-poverty areas in Cleveland did not seem to pose these extreme levels of risk for children and adolescents, suggesting that aspects of the social and physical environment other than poverty are important. Communities characterized by high rates of low birth weight and infant death were also characterized by substantial numbers of single-parent families with children and female-headed households, by high crime rates, and by the concentration of public housing and substandard market housing. Employed males were in short supply. After the researchers controlled for indicators of these social conditions, poverty had no effect on low birth weight, but it did have a direct effect on infant death. Demographic factors added little to the explained variance. Public housing was an important factor in infant death, and the crime rate was an important predictor of low birth weight in a neighborhood. The strongest predictor of child and adolescent risk was births to unmarried mothers, which was highly correlated with the predominance of female-headed households as a family form. These results suggest that neighborhoods' sociodemographic characteristics may affect risk to children directly, but perhaps more important are their indirect effects on child risk through their influence on social conditions and economic deprivation.

In a subsequent study, Coulton, Korbin, Su, and Chow (1995) found that three dimensions of community social structure—community impoverishment, community child-care burden (family and age structure), and residential instability—together with a measure of the geographical contiguity of a community to high-poverty areas—explained a substantial part of the variance in child maltreatment rates across areas. The impoverishment factor had the greatest effect on maltreatment rates. Areas with the highest maltreatment rates were those in which the conditions of poverty, unemployment, female-headed households, racial segregation, abandoned housing, and population loss were intertwined. The child-care-burden factor had a significant but somewhat weaker effect than Impoverishment. Impoverished areas in which there were many children per adult, few elderly residents, and a low proportion of adult males were at highest risk of child maltreatment. Residential instability had a relatively weak effect, and its effect diminished as impoverishment rose. While low residential mobility had a preventive impact on maltreatment in more affluent areas, it did little to offset the negative impact of extreme impoverishment. The geographic location of the tract relative to areas of concentrated poverty also seemed to affect maltreatment rates. Areas that were contiguous to other high-poverty areas had higher maltreatment rates, independent of their values on the structural factors associated with community social organization. The macrostructural factors that explained child maltreatment rates were less adequate as explanations of child health indicators such as low birth weight.

## EARLY CHILDHOOD: CONTEXTUAL ANALYSES

Through collaborative studies, Brooks-Gunn, Duncan, and their colleagues have investigated the effects of neighborhood compositional characteristics on preschool children. These studies have used samples of infants and children from the Infant Health and Development Project (IHDP), a longitudinal data set created to evaluate a program of support and educational services for low-birth-weight children (IHDP 1990; Brooks-Gunn, Klebanov et al. 1993; Brooks-Gunn, McCarton et al. 1994). The preschool children in these samples were low-birth-weight infants born in hospitals in eight cities in 1985. In one study, Brooks-Gunn, Duncan, and colleagues (1993) investigated the effects of neighborhood characteristics on the cognitive and behavioral outcomes of children at age three. When no family characteristics were included in the model, strong neighborhood effects were found for both IQ and behavior problems. After adjusting for differences in the socioeconomic characteristics of families, the authors found strong and significant effects of affluent neighbors (percentage of families with incomes over thirty thousand dollars) on child IQ. An important feature of this and the subsequent study is the authors' distinction between the effects of the presence of low-income families and the absence of relatively affluent families. The results provided substantial evidence for the influence of the latter, but not the former. Additional analyses indicated that part of the effect of neighborhood on preschool children's IQ at age three was mediated by the provision of learning experiences in the home, and that the addition of the home variables to the model increased the variance explained (Brooks-Gunn, Duncan et al. 1993, 385).

In a second study (Duncan, Brooks-Gunn, and Klebanov 1994), the authors investigated the effects of family- and neighborhood-level variables on the IQs and behavior problems of five-year-olds. Again using IHDP data, they found that the presence of affluent neighbors was associated with higher IQs, while the presence of low-income neighbors was associated with a greater incidence of behavior problems.

In another study, Klebanov, Brooks-Gunn, and Duncan (1994) examined the effects of neighborhood and family poverty on maternal psychological and behavioral characteristics and on the quality of the home environment. They found that residing in a poor neighborhood was associated with a worse physical environment in the home and with less maternal warmth toward the children. These results provide further evidence that the effects of neighborhoods on preschool children are likely to be mediated in part by parental behavior.

## MIDDLE CHILDHOOD: CONTEXTUAL ANALYSES

Kupersmidt and her colleagues (1995) investigated family and neighborhood influences on children's social and behavioral adjustment. Their sample included 1,271 second- through fifth-grade white and black children enrolled in one of six elementary schools in a small southern public school system. Measures of behavioral adjustment included a peer report of aggressive behavior and teacher ratings of risk for delinquency. Measures of social adjustment included peer rejections and home and neighborhood play companions. The researchers sought to evaluate the relative influence of parallel measures of family and neighborhood characteristics on the child, and to assess the impact of neighborhood characteristics, given the level of the child's risk from family characteristics.

Twenty-nine neighborhood units were selected on the basis of 1980 census neighborhood areas. A cluster analysis performed on the twenty-nine neighborhoods using twenty census neighborhood characteristics revealed two distinct types of neighborhoods, which were classified as middle-SES and low-SES neighborhoods. Each child was classified into one of eight types of families based on race (black or white), family income (high or middle income), and family structure (one parent or two parents). A series of hierarchical 8 (family type) × 2 (neighborhood type) × 2 (sex) analyses of variance (ANOVAs) was conducted for each of the dependent variables, except peer rejection, which was evaluated in a categorical modeling analysis procedure. Family type was entered into the model first, followed by neighborhood type, family-by-neighborhood interaction, and sex.

The findings provided support for several different models of neighborhood and family influence, emphasizing the complex relationships between environmental context and children's adjustment. The results suggested a protective effect of middle-SES neighborhoods on the aggressive behavior of black children from low-income, single-parent homes. Neighborhood and family factors operated as independent risk factors for teachers' predictions of delinquency. Low-income, white children from single-parent homes were at greater risk for peer rejection if they lived in middle-SES neighborhoods than if they lived in low-SES neighborhoods, consistent with an interactional model of person–environment fit. Middle-income white children had more home playmates if they lived in middle-SES neighborhoods than if they lived in low-SES neighborhoods. Although the unequal cell sizes in this study limit the generalizability of its findings, the findings do suggest that the effects of neighborhoods on children's social and behavioral development are not uniform. The same neighborhood may be "protective" with regard to one aspect of adjustment or for one type of family but may function as a "risk" factor or neutral influence for others.

## LATE CHILDHOOD AND EARLY ADOLESCENCE: CONTEXTUAL ANALYSES

Peeples and Loeber (1994) investigated the effects of neighborhood context on the delinquent behavior of black and white boys in Pittsburgh. The researchers sought to assess whether residence in an underclass neighborhood contributes to the explanation of juvenile delinquency after accounting for individual and family factors. The study also attempted to assess whether the effects of neighborhood context are similar for black and white youth.

The sample, drawn from the oldest cohort of the Pittsburgh Youth Study, included 504 black and white boys, aged twelve to sixteen, who were enrolled in public middle schools in Pittsburgh. Boys were randomly selected for an initial screening in the spring of 1987 and 1988; 83.5 percent of the seventh-grade boys (n = 850) and their parents agreed to participate. In the screening assessments, the boy, his primary caretaker, and his teacher were asked to report on the boy's prosocial and antisocial behavior. A risk score, calculated on the basis of the boy's commission of potentially indictable offenses according to the three respondents, was used as a criterion in selecting the final sample. That sample consisted of the 30 percent with the highest risk scores and roughly an equal number of randomly selected boys from the remainder. Equal proportions of blacks and whites were classified as high risk.

Measures of the frequency and seriousness of delinquent behavior were based on the boy's, caretaker's, and teacher's reports at the initial screening, when the boys were in the seventh grade, and six months later at the first wave of follow-up interviews, when the boys were in the beginning of their eighth-grade year. Neighborhoods were classified as underclass or not underclass on the basis of an index constructed with six variables from 1980 census data: family poverty, public assistance, female-headed families, families with no one employed, nonmarital births, and male joblessness. Summed, standardized factor scores based on the six variables were assigned to Pittsburgh's eighty-eight officially recognized neighborhoods, each of which is composed of one to seven census tracts. Fifteen of those neighborhoods were classified as underclass and seventy three as not underclass. Each boy was assigned the factor score and classification (underclass or not underclass) of the neighborhood in which he resided at the time of the screening.

After controlling for individual hyperactivity and parental supervision, residence in an underclass neighborhood was associated with delinquency, while ethnicity was not. When black and white youths were compared without regard to neighborhood context, black youths were more frequently and more seriously delinquent than white youths. However, when black youths did not live in underclass neighborhoods, their delinquent behavior was similar to that of white youths. Because Pittsburgh's neighborhoods are highly segregated, there were not sufficient numbers of white youths residing in underclass neighborhoods to compare their delinquent behavior with that of black youths in similar neighborhoods.

## LATE ADOLESCENCE AND EARLY ADULTHOOD: COMMUNITY ANALYSES

A substantial body of research exists on the neighborhood and community influences on adolescents' and young adults' development. Studies of community influences on delinquency and crime have a long tradition. Much of the recent empirical work on the effects of neighborhoods on other aspects of adolescent behavior has been stimulated by Wilson's (1987, 1991a, 1991b) conceptualization of concentration effects. Before reviewing studies that examined the contextual effects neighborhood characteristics on individual outcomes, I review studies that investigated the effects of structural and sociodemographic characteristics of neighborhoods on aggregate rates of behavior and community-level processes.

Massey and his colleagues (1991) used 1980 data for the fifty largest SMSAs to test the hypothesis that segregation and poverty interact at the metropolitan level to distribute economic deprivation unequally among neighborhoods inhabited by whites, blacks, and Hispanics. They found that the total poverty rate in a census tract was predicted from the poverty rate of whites, blacks, or Hispanics; the degree of a nonwhite group's residential dissimilarity from whites; the interaction of group poverty rates with their degree of residential dissimilarity; and the number of units of low-income family housing inhabited by members of each group. Their results showed that blacks were much more likely to live in poor neighborhoods than either Hispanics or whites. These intergroup differences were heightened when the focus was on the poor of each group. Poor blacks, and to a lesser extent poor Hispanics, experienced neighborhood environments characterized by much higher levels of poverty than did poor whites.

As expected, the rate of poverty that a group experienced in the metropolitan area as a whole had a strong effect on the degree of poverty concentration its members experienced at the neighborhood level. The effect of metropolitan poverty was significantly exacerbated by segregation. A high rate of total poverty led to a far greater concentration of neighborhood poverty when a group was highly segregated. The geographic concentration of poverty was further heightened by having a large number of group members living in low-income housing. Taken together, these metropolitan-level variables explained about 30 percent of the variance in neighborhood poverty rates.

Coulton and Pandey (1992), using the city and county agency data previously described for census tracts in Cleveland, found that rates of teen births and delinquency filings were significantly higher in all high-poverty areas than in low-poverty areas. Teen birthrates were significantly higher in new poverty areas than in emerging poverty areas. Three of the 204 census tracts in Cleveland were areas of extreme high risk for both infant and adolescent outcomes. These tracts were located in a traditional poverty area in the only part of the city that has experienced concentrated poverty since the 1940s, and in which the majority of Cleveland's publicly operated housing projects are located. Seven tracts in new poverty areas, which became concentrated poverty areas during the 1970s, were areas of extreme risk for teen mothers (and poor infant outcomes). Eleven tracts were high on adolescent risk (delinquency and teen childbearing); some of these were long-term poverty areas, but a few were new poverty areas. Areas that were high on delinquency, but not on any of the other adverse outcomes, had not yet reached the concentrated poverty threshold of 40 percent.

Additional analyses revealed that the effects of poverty, race, and population decline on rates of teen births and delinquency filings were largely indirect, through the rates of unmarried childbearing, crime, and substandard housing in an area. Poverty continued to have a direct effect on delinquency. Demographic factors added little to the explained variance. The impact of poverty concentration seemed to differ, depending on how long an area had been extremely poor and its proximity to the city's center.

In a subsequent study, Coulton, Korbin, Su, and Chow (1995) found that the three dimensions of community structure that predicted child maltreatment rates—community impoverishment, community child-care burden (family and age structure), and residential instability—also predicted types of adolescent and young adult deviant behavior such as violent crime, drug trafficking, juvenile delinquency, and teen pregnancy. These same dimensions of community structure were poor predictors of health outcomes, suggesting that child maltreatment and adolescent problem behavior are embedded within similar communities—namely, those with low levels of social organization, including community resources, social control, and solidarity.

Sampson and Groves (1989), using data from the 1982 and the 1984 British Crime Surveys, tested Shaw and McKay's theory of community social disorganization—namely, that low economic status, ethnic heterogeneity, residential mobility, and family disruption lead to community social disorganization, which, in turn, increases crime and delinquency rates. A community's level of social organization was measured by local friendship networks, control of street-corner teenage peer groups, and the prevalence of organizational participation. The authors found that communities characterized by sparse friendship networks, unsupervised teenage peer groups, and low organizational participation had disproportionately high rates of crime and delinquency. They showed, moreover, that variations in these processes of community social organization mediated the effects of community sociodemographic and structural characteristics, including low SES, residential mobility, ethnic heterogeneity, and family disruption.

Sampson and Groves's (1989) results demonstrate that misleading inferences could be drawn by interpreting only the direct effects of social stratification factors, such as SES. They found, for example, that 80 percent of SES's total effect on mugging and street robbery was mediated by the indicator of unsupervised teenage youth. Similarly, 34 percent and 68 percent of the total effects of community SES on stranger violence and total victimization were mediated by the level of unsupervised peer groups. In addition, their results provide support for the idea that particular dimensions of community social structure differentially predict particular aspects of community-level social organization and rates of specific behavior.

Using data from twelve neighborhoods in New York City, Simcha-Fagan and Schwartz (1986) identified two dimensions of community social organization—a community's ability to sustain organizational participation and the extent of a criminal subculture in a neighborhood—that mediated the relationship between sociodemographic characteristics of neighborhoods and neighborhood levels of delinquency. Organizational Participation was negatively related and community residential stability positively related to the level of self-reported delinquency. Criminal Subculture was positively related to the level of officially recorded delinquency.

Esbensen and Huizinga (1990), using data from the Denver Youth Survey, a sample of 1,530 youth aged seven to fifteen in high-risk neighborhoods in a midwestern city, used cluster analyses to determine whether the underlying dimensions of social disorganization—poverty, residential instability, and housing density—were differentially distributed among neighborhoods. *High-risk neighborhoods* were defined as areas characterized by both "social disorganization" and a high official crime rate. Employing the techniques of social area analysis, the authors identified two neighborhood factors—a high-SES and a low-SES factor. A cluster analysis was used to combine and identify similar block groups. Seven clusters emerged, three of which were identified as "socially disorganized." In subsequent analyses, the authors found no differences among the three types of socially disorganized neighborhoods in either the prevalence or frequency of drug use.


LATE ADOLESCENCE AND EARLY ADULTHOOD: CONTEXTUAL ANALYSES

A substantial and growing body of studies has been conducted to assess neighborhood and community influences on the individual outcomes of adolescents and young adults. The studies reviewed and summarized here assess neighborhood and community influences on four domains of individual outcomes: educational outcomes, economic outcomes, problem behavior, and teen childbearing.


EDUCATIONAL OUTCOMES     Educational outcomes have been the most frequently assessed in the existing literature. Studies have examined neighborhood and community influences on educational attainment and academic achievement.

*Educational Attainment*    Studies have assessed the effects of neighborhood sociodemographic composition on three measures of educational attainment: years of schooling, college attendance, and school dropout.

Two studies used data from the Panel Study of Income Dynamics (PSID) to examine the effects of neighborhood composition on years of schooling. A study by Datcher (1982), which was reviewed by Jencks and Mayer (1990), investigated the effects of zip-code-level sociodemographic characteristics on years of schooling. Using a sample of black and white urban young men, aged thirteen to twenty-two, who were living with their parents in 1968, Datcher (1982) examined the effect of average family income on years of schooling. She found that an increase of a thousand dollars (10 percent) in zip-code-area income raised the men's educational attainment by approximately one-tenth of a school year for both blacks and whites.

Duncan (1994) investigated the effects of tract-level neighborhood characteristics on years of schooling for a sample of white and black males and females from the PSID (see also Brooks-Gunn, Duncan et al. 1993). Taking advantage of sample sizes large enough to perform separate analyses for white males, black males, white females, and black females, and to search within each of the four groups for interactions between neighborhood factors and the family's economic status, Duncan sought to analyze more systematically than in previous studies which adolescents were most vulnerable to neighborhood influences.

He found that the presence or absence of relatively affluent neighbors was a highly significant predictor of completed schooling for all groups other than black males. The addition of an interaction between the percentage of families with incomes above thirty thousand dollars and the fraction of individuals in the neighborhood who were black to the completed schooling regression produced a significant positive coefficient on the interaction for black males only, which is consistent with the hypothesis that relatively affluent neighbors appeared to benefit black males only if those affluent neighbors were themselves black.

Duncan found that the neighborhood's racial integration appeared to benefit blacks without having a corresponding detrimental effect on whites. Both black males and black females did worse in neighborhoods with a greater concentration of blacks, while the completed schooling of white males and white females was not significantly affected. These effects persisted even after adjusting for differences in the economic and demographic structure of black and white neighborhoods. The neighborhood's racial composition was the single most important neighborhood characteristic for black males.

The proportion of female-headed families in the neighborhood was included as a measure of the neighborhood's ability to monitor the behavior of its adolescents, and the proportion of female neighbors employed was included as an indicator of a possibly beneficial role-model influence on female adolescents in the sample. Only for black females did monitoring seem to matter; female employment and female-headed families were both detrimental to black females' completion of schooling. However, more employed female neighbors were associated with increased schooling for white males. Detrimental effects of low-income neighbors on completed schooling were found only for white females.

Interactions between neighborhood- and family-level conditions suggest that affluent neighbors benefit only the more advantaged females, that the racial composition of the neighborhood has a much greater effect on black male children from more economically advantaged families than those from less advantaged families, and that the detrimental effects of working women in the neighborhood are greater for black females from more economically advantaged families. Duncan concluded from these results that no evidence existed that neighborhood effects are especially powerful for children from economically disadvantaged families.

Duncan (1994) also examined the effects of neighborhood and family influences on college attendance. Whereas only the racial composition of the neighborhood affected completed schooling for black males, more low-income neighbors and more black neighbors both appeared to reduce their chances of attending college. Contrary to the expectation that more employed female neighbors might be positive role models, female employment in the neighborhood was associated with lower college attendance rates for both white and black women. Moreover, the expected effects of affluent neighbors were not found for the outcome of attending college.

*School Dropout*   Brooks-Gunn, Duncan, and colleagues (1993), Clark (1992), Crane (1991b), Duncan (1994), and Ensminger, Lamkin, and Jacobson (1996) have examined the effects of neighborhood composition on high school dropout. Crane (1991b) tested an epidemic model of school dropout using data from a special linked family-tract cross-sectional file from the 1970 census-based Public Use Microdata Sample (PUMS). Neighborhoods were approximated using sets of census-block groups that were not necessarily homogeneous or contiguous. Consistent with an epidemic model, Crane found highly nonlinear effects of neighborhood quality on school dropout. In neighborhoods with very few professional or managerial workers (5 percent or fewer), both blacks and whites were very likely to drop out of high school. Blacks and whites who lived in the worst neighborhoods were over fifty times more likely to drop out of school than were their counterparts in less-bad neighborhoods. Apart from neighborhoods in this extreme category, however, there was little evidence that neighborhood characteristics mattered. Non-linear effects were significant for blacks and whites as groups, for young black men, for young white men, and for young white women in the largest cities. Crane's estimates of sex-specific effects showed that black male teenagers from inner-city neighborhoods were at considerably higher risk of dropping out than were black female teenagers.

Clark (1992) attempted to replicate Crane's findings on the effects of neighborhood quality on the school dropout of males by using census SMSA data from states containing the ten largest SMSAs in 1980. She linked individual boys' records to tract-level data from the Urban Institute's Underclass Data Base. Although Clark found that several measures of neighborhood resources predicted the high school dropout status of males, she failed to find evidence of nonlinear effects. She found that the probability of dropping out rose as the proportion of affluent neighbors declined for whites, but not for blacks. The relationship was weaker for boys who were poor. She also found that the probability of dropping out rose for both whites and blacks as the proportion of low-income neighbors increased.

Brooks-Gunn, Duncan, and colleagues (1993) analyzed the effects of neighborhood characteristics on dropping out of school for a sample of teenage girls in the PSID. They found that the fraction of neighborhood families who were relatively affluent was negatively related to dropping out for nonblacks, but not for blacks. Unlike Clark (1992), however, they did not find detrimental effects of the proportion of low-income neighbors on school dropout. Substituting other neighborhood characteristics in their model, Brooks-Gunn and her colleagues found that, controlling for family-level factors, the fraction of professional/managerial workers in the neighborhood was negatively related to dropping out and that the fraction of female-headed families in the neighborhood was positively related to dropping out. The authors also found that zip-code-level data on neighborhood characteristics produced more significant effects on school dropout that census-tract-level data, suggesting that their results might reflect a school district or labor market, rather than a neighborhood, effect. In a subsequent analysis, Duncan (1994) failed to find the expected effects of affluent neighbors on students' dropping out of high school.

Ensminger, Lamkin, and Jacobson (1996) investigated the effects of living in a poor or middle-class neighborhood on the likelihood of graduating from high school for a cohort of African American children followed from 1966 to 1993. Using data from the Woodlawn (Chicago) longitudinal study, which combined information gained from children, their teachers, and their families with census tract characteristics of neighborhoods and school board records of high school graduation, the authors examined hypotheses about the direct, indirect, and interactive effects of neighborhoods on leaving school before graduation (school dropout).

All first grade children ($N = 1,242$) in Woodlawn's nine public and three parochial schools were assessed by their teachers and by psychologists in 1966–1967. Their mothers were also interviewed. Ten years later, in 1975–1976, the children and their mothers ($N = 939$; 75 percent) were reassessed. In 1982, school graduation records were obtained from the Chicago Board of Education. In 1992–1993, young adults (aged thirty-two to thirty three) were interviewed again ($N = 954$, 77 percent). At the time of the 1975-1976 follow-up, two-thirds of the children had moved to other neighborhoods. Extensive information about the children gathered before and after the moves enabled the authors to examine whether and how neighborhood differences matter for adolescent outcomes.

During the time of this study, Woodlawn was a community with low median income and high unemployment. According to the 1970 census data, 97 percent of Woodlawn's residents were African American. Although poor, Woodlawn was and has remained economically diverse. The neighborhood variables used for the adolescent follow-up in 1975–1976 were averages and trends computed by combining 1970 and 1980 census data. To differentiate between poor and nonpoor neighborhoods, the authors dichotomized neighborhoods based on percent white-collar workers and percent below poverty. Poor census tracts were those with more than 20 percent below the poverty line. Middle-class census tracts were those with more than 40 percent of residents employed in white-collar positions. Analyses of neighborhood effects included controls for family background, early school performance, adolescent family supervision, and adolescent marijuana use. School leaving was measured by Chicago Board of Education data supplemented by data obtained from young adult interviews on the receipt of GED degrees.

Analyses were conducted for males and females separately. For males, the results indicated an advantage of living in a neighborhood characterized by a high percentage of residents who work in white-collar occupations. Black male adolescents who lived in a middle-class neighborhood were three and one-half times as likely to graduate from high school, with family background, early school performance, adolescent family supervision and adolescent marijuana use controlled. Living in a poverty census tract did not seem to influence the likelihood of high school graduation or leaving over and above the impact of family and individual characteristics. There were no neighborhood effects for females. Nor was there much evidence that poor performance or problem behavior heightened the impact of poor neighborhoods. Analyses conducted with years of schooling as the outcome yielded results similar to those for school dropout.

*Academic Achievement*   Two studies have investigated the effects of neighborhood sociodemographic characteristics on adolescents' academic achievement. Dornbusch, Ritter, and Steinberg (1991) examined the effects of census-based neighborhood characteristics on self-reported grades using a sample of black and white students from high schools in northern California. They used a composite index of neighborhood socioeconomic status that included per capita income, household income, the percentage of families above poverty, the percentage of adults employed as professionals or executives, and the mean level of completed education for adults over age twenty-five. They found that neighborhood SES was a highly significant predictor of self-reported grades, even after controlling for family structure and parental schooling. In contrast to most of the studies cited earlier, they found somewhat stronger effects of neighborhood SES for blacks than for whites.

They did not report sex-specific results. Dornbusch and his colleagues found that neighborhood SES and racial composition conditioned the relationship between family status and adolescent grades. For black adolescents, only the community variable, and not family status, predicted self-reported grades.

Garner and Raudenbush (1991) assessed the effects of community characteristics on academic achievement for a sample of students in one education authority in Scotland in the mid-1980s. Neighborhood risk was measured with a previously developed index of twelve economic, demographic, and housing measures from the 1981 Census of Population data. Using hierarchical linear modeling to estimate their model, they found a negative and highly significant effect of the neighborhood deprivation score on a general achievement test score at the completion of secondary school.

ECONOMIC OUTCOMES    Various researchers have investigated the effects of neighborhood and community influences on late adolescents' and young adults' economic outcomes. Corcoran and associates (1992) used PSID data, with zip-code-level census data on four community characteristics appended to individual records, to analyze family and community influences on young (aged twenty-five to thirty-two) adult men's earnings, wage rates, work hours, and family income. After controlling for many personal and family background variables, they found that the percentage of community families on welfare was negatively associated with most outcomes, but the other community characteristics had negligible effects on all outcomes. The only exception was the level of male joblessness in the zip-code area, which was related to the young men's hours of work.

Using 1980 neighborhood PUMS data from the 1980 census for a sample of whites, blacks, and Hispanics in the fifty largest SMSAs who had lived in the same house for five years, Massey, Gross, and Eggers (1991) found that tract-level poverty was positively associated with male joblessness for sixteen- to nineteen-year-olds, and even more strongly associated with male joblessness for twenty- to thirty-five-year-olds. Case and Katz (1991), using data from the 1989 National Bureau of Economic Research (NBER) Boston Youth Survey for a sample of young black and white men and women from the three high-poverty neighborhoods in Boston's central city, examined peer influences on idleness, which they defined as an individual being neither in school nor in work. They measured peer influence by assigning each individual the mean level of idleness of other youths who resided in the same or adjacent block groups. They found that adolescents who resided in a neighborhood in which many other youths were out of work and out of school were themselves more likely to be idle.

PROBLEM BEHAVIOR    Several studies have identified neighborhood and community influences on problem behavior (delinquency and substance use) in adolescence. Simcha-Fagan and Schwartz (1986), using the sample of adolescents from twelve neighborhoods in New York City described previously, found that two of the tract-level community processes—organizational participation and criminal subculture—that accounted for substantial variance in tract-level rates of delinquency, were also significant predictors of individual delinquency, after controlling for individual-level compositional characteristics. The pattern of effects of these community-level processes on individual delinquent behavior was similar to their effects on aggregate levels of behavior, although the proportion of variation in individual behavior that they accounted for was much smaller. Organizational participation was negatively related to self-reported delinquency and criminal subculture was positively related to officially recorded delinquency.

The authors also estimated a bilevel causal model of community effects on delinquency. They concluded that structural constraints characteristic of a community were associated with the nature of the community's organizational base, which, in turn, affected delinquency directly and indirectly via social bonds to key socializing institutions. Their results suggest that the organizational base's effects on delinquency are primarily indirect and operate by strengthening individual adolescents' bonds to school, the primary institutional relationship of this age group. The effects of community characteristics on associations with delinquent peers were also indirect and mediated by weak attachment to school.

Case and Katz (1991), using the sample of adolescents from the NBER Boston Youth Survey described earlier, found that related peer behaviors had significant direct effects on regular alcohol use, illegal drug use, criminal activity, friendship with gang members, and church attendance. The magnitude of effects was particularly large for illegal drug use and church attendance. Their results suggest that an adolescent who lives in a neighborhood in which many other youths are involved in crime, use illegal drugs, or attend church is more likely to engage in those activities.

Esbensen and Huizinga (1990), using the sample of adolescents from the Denver Youth Survey previously described, found that although the types of disorganized neighborhoods did not affect neighborhood-level prevalence or frequency of drug use, they did affect the settings and reasons for drug use. Their findings suggest that different mediating factors might help to explain drug-using behavior in different neighborhoods.

TEEN CHILDBEARING   An early study by Hogan and Kitagawa (1985), which was reviewed by Jencks and Mayer (1990), investigated the effects of neighborhood quality on teenage pregnancy rates by using a 1979 sample of 1,070 unmarried black women aged thirteen to nineteen in Chicago. The authors used a composite index of neighborhood quality to divide neighborhoods into high-, middle-, and low-SES categories. They found no significant difference between high-SES and middle-SES neighborhoods in teenagers' likelihood of becoming pregnant, but the chances of becoming pregnant in a given month were a third higher in the low-SES neighborhoods. Living in a particularly disadvantaged neighborhood on Chicago's West Side increased the pregnancy risk by almost two-fifths. In a subsequent study, Hogan, Astone, and Kitagawa (1985) used the same data set and found that females in the low-SES neighborhoods were about half as likely as those in the better neighborhoods to use contraception when they first had sex. These results suggest that contraception use accounted for a good part of the differences in pregnancy rates.

Crane (1991b) used the 1970 Census Neighborhood Characteristics File previously described to investigate whether the social composition of tract-like neighborhoods affected the likelihood that sixteen- to nineteen-year-old girls who were living with their parents had a child. Crane found evidence of non-linear effects of a neighborhood's proportion of professional and managerial workers on the probability of teen childbearing. The increases in childbearing probabilities were significant only for black and white females living in the largest cities. For black females living in the largest cities, the sharpest increase occurred earlier in the distribution than it did for white females in the largest cities, although the overall interpretation is similar—namely, that the childbearing probability was highest by far in the neighborhoods with the lowest percentages of high-status workers. For white females in the largest cities, the neighborhood effects were huge, with the likelihood of teen childbearing almost a hundred times greater when the proportion of high-status workers was 3.5 percent than when it was 7.5 percent.

Massey, Gross, and Eggers (1991), using neighborhood PUMS data from the 1980 census, found that tract-level poverty was associated with increased teen childbearing among fifteen to eighteen-year-old females. Brooks-Gunn, Duncan, and colleagues (1993) also investigated the effects of neighborhood social composition on teen childbearing. Using PSID data, they found that the presence of relatively affluent neighbors reduced teenage births after controlling for families' socioeconomic characteristics. A series of interactions suggest that the benefits of affluent neighbors on teen childbearing were restricted to whites. Consistent with the results reported by Crane (1991b), they also found that living in a neighborhood with few professional or managerial workers was associated with higher rates of teenage out-of-wedlock childbearing. Finally, out-of-wedlock childbearing was the one outcome for which Case and Katz (1991), using data from the 1989 NBER Boston Youth Survey, did not find evidence of the direct effects of peer behaviors.

## NEIGHBORHOOD AND COMMUNITY INFLUENCES: SUMMARY AND CONCLUSIONS

Existing research has used overly narrow concepts; inadequate methods to measure key concepts; and research designs that fail to capture the complex, dynamic, and contextualized nature of the phenomena under study.

Census-tract or zip-code-level data do not provide appropriate indicators of either residential neighborhoods or functional communities. Hence, the results of most existing studies should be viewed as exploratory analyses to see whether even weak indicators of neighborhood and community characteristics can help to clarify whether they influence child and adolescent outcomes. Because most existing data sets do not include measures of community-, school-, and family-level processes that are likely to mediate the effects of neighborhood structural and demographic characteristics, it is impossible to clarify the nature of direct and indirect effects with existing data. Even in data sets that contain measures of community-level processes, our limited knowledge of the relationships among neighborhood demographics and community-level processes, and the tendency of measures of neighborhood characteristics to be highly correlated, make it difficult to clarify the relative importance of neighborhood characteristics.

Community-level analyses suggest that forms of disadvantage other than poverty, such as the concentration of single-parent families, female-headed households, crime, and substandard housing, may constitute the most potent sources of risk for children and adolescents. There seem to be commonalities and differences in the community contexts of risk for young children and adolescents. Community contexts that are low in social organization are associated with high levels of child maltreatment, crime, and delinquency, but not with health or academic outcomes.

Community analyses also suggest that the structural and demographic features of neighborhoods and communities are likely to affect child and adolescent outcomes indirectly, through a set of community-level social and cultural processes such as community monitoring, the number and quality of social ties, organizational participation, and value consensus. The few studies that have examined peer processes have found them powerful in predicting adolescent outcomes and have suggested that such processes may mediate the effects of community-level social organization.

Few studies have examined the contextual effects of neighborhoods and communities on children and young adolescents. In the existing studies, the characteristic of neighborhoods most often found to influence children's intellectual and behavioral outcomes is the presence of affluent or middle-class neighbors. The nature of the effects, and the group of children who seem to be most affected by residing in middle-class neighborhoods, are not consistent across data sets and developmental periods, however. While researchers have recently documented the short- and long-term effects of familial poverty on child development (Brooks-Gunn and Duncan forthcoming; Chase-Lansdale and Brooks-Gunn 1995; Duncan and Brooks-Gunn 1997), few researchers have examined the effects of neighborhood poverty and disadvantage on the development of children. The studies reported in later chapters in this volume thus represent a major contribution to our understanding in this area.

# 2

# Development in Context: Implications for Studying Neighborhood Effects

*J. Lawrence Aber, Martha A. Gephart, Jeanne Brooks-Gunn,*
*and James P. Connell*

This chapter introduces the conceptual framework within which the Social Science Research Council (SSRC) studies of neighborhoods' effects on children, youth, and families reported in this volume are being conducted and interpreted. Our framework combines a model of neighborhood and community influences with an integrative model of development in context for understanding the ways in which neighborhoods could influence development. The framework as a whole is first presented. Then each component is considered in more detail. Finally, and most importantly, we discuss the ways in which neighborhoods could influence development using some of the concepts described early in this chapter.

An overview of our conceptual framework is presented in figure 2.1. The framework draws most heavily on social disorganization theory and research (Sampson 1993; Sampson and Morenoff vol. 2; Shaw and McKay 1942), related work on social capital and functional communities (Bronfenbrenner 1992; Coleman 1988, 1990), and Bronfenbrenner's (1979b) developmental-ecological framework for the study of human development in context.

In its most simple form, our framework considers the effects of three types of processes on individual outcomes. These three are labeled in figure 2.1 as neighborhood and community processes, social and interpersonal processes, and individual processes. All three of these processes may be influenced by exogenous forces, as indicated in the figure. What is of particular interest to us is the inclusion of neighborhood and community processes in this model. Typically, developmentalists have considered social and interpersonal processes and individual processes as they are linked to children's adaptation and growth. When community processes have been studied, the school usually has been the focus, rather than other institutions in the community (parental workplace, health and hospital services, and so on). Also, community influences that are not directly centered in institutions have been omitted from many developmentally oriented frameworks. The past decade has

FIGURE 2.1   Conceptual Framework

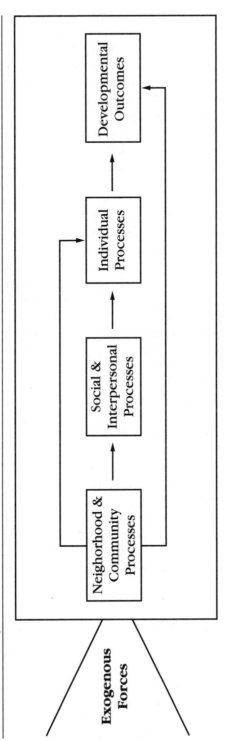

seen an increased interest in neighborhood and community influences, over and above the school. This volume is directed to a set of these influences, which have been labeled neighborhood characteristics.

Perhaps what is most important is that we have ordered the processes from those that are presumably more distal to the child (neighborhood) to those that are more proximal (individual processes). The least proximal processes, those defined by neighborhood of residence (or influence), may influence child and youth outcomes directly or indirectly. That is, neighborhoods may influence the child's social and interpersonal life, through peer networks and parental behavior, and thereby affect outcomes. Likewise, neighborhoods could exert their influence via individual characteristics such as self-regulation, which in turn would influence outcomes such as school achievement. The outcomes of individuals also may affect the character of the neighborhood, so that any framework needs at the very least to acknowledge the possibility of bi-directional effects (a point not pursued in this chapter). We hasten to add that most of the literature to date has not addressed such effects vis-à-vis neighbor-hoods but typically has treated them as a case of selection bias. (See chapter 10 for a discussion of selection bias.) Transactional models have been put forth by theorists such as Bronfenbrenner (1986), Garmezy and Rutter (1983), and Sameroff and Seifer (1983), and have been considered in long-term longitu-dinal studies (Elder 1974; Furstenberg, Brooks-Gunn, and Morgan 1987; Kellam et al. 1980; Werner 1994; Werner and Smith 1992). These models may have special relevance to researchers studying neighborhoods.

Given that this volume is devoted not only to including neighborhood influences in its schematic framework but also to testing the strength of such influences, an attempt is made to consider what is meant by *neighborhood* and by *neighborhood effects*. In this chapter, we briefly look at the neighborhood construct. More detailed and nuanced treatments of this topic are found in Sampson and Morenoff (vol. 2), Furstenberg and Hughes (vol. 2), Burton and associates (vol. 2), and Jarrett (vol. 2). A brief commentary is also provided as to the interpersonal and individual processes that are critical to an under-standing of children's growth at several different life phases: preschool years, elementary school years, middle school years, and late high school years. In a final section, possible links between neighborhood and other more proximal processes are considered.

## DEVELOPMENT IN CONTEXT

Before we consider neighborhoods, social relationships, and individual characteristics as processes that interact with one another to influence development, a brief discussion of development in context follows. Typically, *context* refers to the contexts in which an individual resides. We use Bron-fenbrenner's concept of systems in considering these varied contexts. Con-text in development may also be construed much more broadly to include different developmental outcomes, different age- or school-graded epochs of development, or individual and group differences in development. Each of these topics is mentioned here, as they inform the different analytic strategies that have been used to study neighborhood influences.

## LEVELS OF EMBEDDED CONTEXT

Following Bronfenbrenner (1979b), we conceptualize human development as a process that occurs within a set of embedded contexts. Our framework focuses on neighborhood and community contexts of development, as well as more proximal social and interpersonal contexts, such as families and peers. Both may influence development directly, as well as mediate the influences of neighborhood and community contexts on individual developmental processes and outcomes.

Bronfenbrenner (1979b) defined four "levels" of embedded contexts. Microsystems are contexts with which the child comes in direct contact, such as family, friends, teachers, and classrooms. Mesosystems are contexts that indirectly affect children's development via their influences on microsystems, such as parents' and teachers' colleagues. Exosystems are larger institutions and organizations that influence children, such as the quality of child care or community institutions or the number and nature of formal and informal community organizations. Finally, macrosystems are the broader sociocultural practices, beliefs, and values of a nation, region, or community that influence child and family life, such as racist beliefs or belief in the value of corporal punishment or violence as means of discipline or dispute resolution.

Neighborhoods could have an effect on family processes and individual development at any or all of these four embedded levels. To the extent that children and youth come into direct contact with neighborhoods (unmediated by family or institutions), neighborhoods are a microsystem, and their direct effects should be estimated. To the extent that neighborhoods influence the type of employment available to children's parents or affect the quality of children's friendships through effects on their friends' parents, neighborhoods are mesosystems, and their indirect effects should be estimated. As clusters of linked organizations (exosystems) and macrosystems (networks of beliefs and values), neighborhoods have moderating effects that should be estimated.

## LEVELS OF EMBEDDED OUTCOMES

*Development* can be defined as the acquisition and growth of the physical, cognitive, social, and emotional competencies required to engage fully in family and society. In this volume, we focus primarily on the cognitive, academic, social, and emotional domains of child and adolescent development (Brooks-Gunn 1990). Often these domains of well-being are divided into two broad areas—cognitive-academic and social-emotional. Examples of cognitive-academic development include growth in language, math, and reading abilities. Examples of social-emotional development include growth in self-regulatory and social competencies. The physical-health domain is not considered in this volume because the collection of studies we are drawing on includes few measures in the health domain. Historically, scholars pursued quite separate lines of theory and research on cognitive-academic development (for example, Piaget 1973) and social-emotional development (Erickson 1950). More recently, some scholars have attempted to forge a more integrated "organizational" perspective on the associations between domains or development (Cicchetti and Rizley 1981; Sroufe 1979, 1983). Even though domains influence one another, it makes great sense both empirically and conceptually to conceive of them also as unique and distinct but interrelated.

We retain the distinction between these two very broad domains in our collaborative work for several reasons. First, from a scientific point of view, it is valuable to attempt to discern paths of influence from neighborhood risk that are unique to each set of outcomes and that are common to both sets of outcomes (Aber, Allen et al. 1996). Second, from program and policy points of view, different audiences are concerned with the effects of neighborhoods on school and work outcomes and on social functioning and mental health outcomes. Thus, extrafamilial contexts are likely to influence developmental outcomes in these broad domains somewhat differently, just as familial contexts do (Brooks-Gunn, Duncan et al. 1993; Brooks-Gunn, Klebanov, and Liaw 1995a; Duncan, Brooks-Gunn, and Klebanov 1994).

## EPOCHS OF CHILDHOOD AND TRANSITIONS AMONG THEM

A common and potentially useful way of conceiving of development is as a series of different epochs or phases that children and youth pass through sequentially. Classic examples of stage theories of development include Freud's notion of psychosocial stages (trust versus mistrust in infancy, autonomy versus shame and doubt in toddlerhood, identity versus identity confusion in adolescence, and so on) and Piaget's theory of cognitive structural stages of development (sensory-motor, preoperations, concrete operations, formal operations). Without belaboring the point, the fundamental notions behind each of these stage theories are that children think about and relate to themselves and others in qualitatively distinct ways at different points in their lives and that early stages are the building blocks for later advances. Certain features of these classic stage theories have been discredited or reversed (Cicchetti 1989; Fischer 1977; Keating 1990; Sroufe 1979, 1983), because clear-cut differences, whether qualitative or quantitative, do not always exist between stages.

Many developmentalists do not focus on stages per se to classify or divide development into epochs. Often the childhood epochs are divided by transitions. These transitions may be in school, cognition, biology, or social events. The concentration of events may be an epoch's defining feature. Often epochs are defined by challenges to be mastered (Brooks-Gunn, Denner, and Klebanov 1995; Brooks-Gunn, Guo, and Furstenberg 1993; Haveman and Wolfe 1994). In this volume, four general developmental epochs are considered: (1) preschool childhood (three to seven years of age), (2) school-age childhood (eight to ten years of age), (3) younger adolescents (eleven to sixteen years of age), and (4) older adolescents (seventeen to twenty years of age).

The variation across epochs in the developmental *tasks* may result in different effects of neighborhoods on development. Take, for example, the transition to adolescence. A major task at that stage of development is the construction of a qualitatively different form of personal identity (Brooks-Gunn and Paikoff 1992). This task both influences and is influenced by trans-formations in adolescents' way of thinking as they begin to reason in an increasingly logical way about abstract concepts like friendship and justice (Smetana 1988) and in the nature of their social relationships as they become increasingly interested in romantic relationships (Brooks-Gunn and Paikoff 1993). Such intra- and interpersonal developmental changes are often accompanied by changes in adolescents' environments, for instance, with moves into bigger, impersonal schools; new, extralocal neighborhoods; and different peer groups (Brown 1990; Eccles et al. 1993; Feldman and Elliot 1990). Each of these challenges creates the possibility that neighborhoods may affect development differently in adolescence than in childhood.

## GROUP AND INDIVIDUAL DIFFERENCES IN CONTEXTS AND OUTCOMES

In addition to studying epoch differences like those just described, the science of human development also focuses on understanding individual differences. What predicts or helps explain why some children develop optimally, some adequately, and some poorly?

The emergence of individual differences over time is described in terms of continuity or discontinuity in adaption over time and identification of risk and protective factors (Garmezy and Rutter 1983; Werner 1994). In the former case, quality of adaptation (or maladaptation) to earlier tasks of development is studied as it predicts the quality of adaptation to later tasks. When conti-nuities are found, the sources are investigated (Brim and Kagan 1980). When discontinuities are prevalent, the mechanisms underlying change are sought.

The second approach focuses on identifying risk factors known to increase the probability of negative outcomes in development (Garmezy and Rutter 1983). Protective factors moderate the effects of risk factors on development by buffering children from the most deleterious effects of risk (Rutter 1987). Risk and protective factors could be located in the neighborhood, inter-personal, or individual processes (figure 2.1). Risk or protective factors may act as moderating influences, buffering the child from the neighborhood's influences on development (see chapters 5 and 8). The analyses presented in this volume focus on explaining individual and within-group differences in the development of children and youth. We employ a risk-protective model as a way to understand (1) the effects of neighborhood risk on cognitive-academic and social-emotional development, and (2) the buffering influence of race, family socioeconomic status, and other factors in moderating the influence of neighborhood risk on development.

In addition to epoch and individual differences, group variations need to be understood as development in context. For example, developmentalists study group variations in (1) the organization, meaning, and development of both competencies and problem syndromes; (2) the quality of adaptation and maladaptation to stage-salient tasks; and (3) the contexts within which development unfolds. If group differences in the organization, adaptational nature, and contexts of development are not fully appreciated, then theory and research on the fundamental dynamics of development can be profoundly distorted for some subgroups (Aber 1994; Gilligan 1993; Spencer 1990).

Several illustrations follow. While important latent constructs can be measured reliably and validly for black, white, and Latino youth or parents, the exact operationalizations of these constructs may take race or ethnic (or gender-specific) forms (Allen et al. 1995, under review; Berlin et al. 1995; Bradley, Whiteside et al. 1994; Sugland et al. 1995). For example, performing delinquent acts with peers appears to be a more important defining feature of the larger phenomenon of antisocial behavior for white youth than for black youth. If this group difference in organization of antisocial behavior is not recognized and accounted for, the relationship between antisocial behavior and other important constructs, such as social problem-solving skills can be obscured (Aber et al. 1995). Similarly, while it is considered a normative feature of adolescence to engage the tasks of identity formation and intimacy, the exact ages and ways that low-income and middle-income youth face these tasks may vary so much as to change their underlying meaning (Doucette-Gates, Brooks-Gunn, and Chase-Lansdale forthcoming; Spencer and Dornbusch 1990).

Most salient to this volume is group variation in the neighborhood and family context. Enormous race/ethnic variation exists in both the family and neighborhood contexts in which children and youth develop in America. As estimated by several national samples (for example, the Panel Study on Income Dynamics), the average concentration of poor, single-parent families in the neighborhood is nearly two standard deviations higher for black children and youth as for white children and youth (chapter 3; Brooks-Gunn, Duncan et al. 1993). In some studies that oversample poor, inner-city children or youth, the racial/ethnic differences in neighborhood context may be less extreme, but still striking, as seen in some of the studies reported in this volume. Even more striking are the racial/ethnic differences in the joint probabilities of living in both family and extreme neighborhood poverty or escaping any family or neighborhood poverty (chapter 3; Duncan and Brooks-Gunn 1997).

Such systematic group variation in the organization of development, in the salience of certain developmental tasks, and in the contexts of development has stimulated new theoretical orientations and modes of analysis (Brooks-Gunn et al. forthcoming; McLoyd and Steinberg forthcoming; Fitzgerald, Lester, and Zuckerman 1995). While we are not able to take full advantage of recent advances in theory and research on gender and cultural group variation in development, we have taken steps such as ensuring the psychometric adequacy of measures across ethnic groups and running analyses on the effects of family and neighborhood risk within race/ethnic groups. Through our collaborative efforts, it is clear that group variation in context is related to group variation in the organization of development and the quality of adaptations to stage-specific tasks. One principle is clearer to us after working on this volume than it was at the beginning of this collaborative work: at every phase of developmental theorizing we must consider the critical issues of diversity in developmental pathways, contexts, processes, and outcomes.

## CONTEXTUAL THEORIES AS REFLECTING A PARADIGM SHIFT

Our working group's interest in neighborhoods' effects on family processes and child development partly reflects a larger paradigm shift within developmental psychology over the past two decades. Development is no longer viewed as primarily universal at its core but also as highly variable and contextualized (Baltes, Featherman, and Lerner 1990). Many sources have influenced this paradigm shift. Demographically, the United States has become increasingly diverse. America's demographic diversity has driven interest in understanding the diversity of developmental experiences, pathways, and contexts. Politically, interest has grown in understanding the effect of contexts on development in the hope of gaining insights about how changes in contexts (for example, schools or communities) can lead to positive changes in developmental outcomes. Scientifically, developmental psychology has been strongly influenced by other natural and behavioral sciences that examine individual–context transactions such as population biology and behavioral ethology.

# EFFECTS OF NEIGHBORHOODS ON DEVELOPMENT OVER TIME

Our conceptualization of neighborhood and community influences has drawn heavily from the work of Coleman (1988), Jencks and Mayer (1990), Sampson (1993; Sampson and Morenoff vol. 2), and Wilson (1987, 1991a, 1991b). Three distinct but interrelated dimensions of neighborhood and community contexts are included: their structure and composition, their social organization, and their cultural and symbolic processes (figure 2.2).

As Sampson and Morenoff (vol. 2) point out, earlier traditions of urban sociological theory and research, especially traditional ecological models and social area analysis, have stressed the social composition of urban communities and the distribution in time and space of urban poverty, residential change, and racial/ethnic composition. Drawing on these earlier traditions of theory and research, our model of neighborhood and community influences employs a structural-ecological approach to understanding the neighborhood context of poverty. It emphasizes the role of macrolevel forces in leading to the clustering of social and economic factors in urban areas. Thus, globalization, economic restructuring, migration, and various public policies at the federal and local levels have led to neighborhood-specific increases in the geographical concentration of poverty. Such increases, superimposed on a racially segregated environment, have been associated with the clustering of adverse social conditions.

Consistent with the existing theory and research, our framework suggests that neighborhood-level concentrations of social and economic disadvantage, together with ethnic heterogeneity, residential instability, household density, and age structure, may adversely affect the development of youth and families. As indicated in chapter 1, researchers have disagreed about which features of neighborhood socioeconomic composition are the most important influences on the behavior of children and youth, and their families. Some scholars have emphasized male joblessness, in terms of both the macrostructural constraints and the behavior of other jobless families in the neighborhood, as an influence on children and families (Wilson 1991b). Other researchers have focused on the presence or absence of middle-class or

FIGURE 2.2   Neighborhood and Community Dimensions

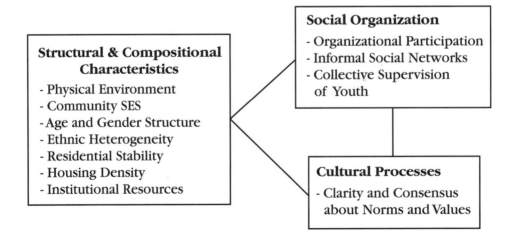

high-status professionals (Brooks-Gunn, Duncan et al. 1993; Crane 1991). The concentration of poor, minority, female-headed families is yet another neighborhood characteristic thought to be important (Hogan and Kitigawa 1985).

Researchers working in the tradition of social disorganization theory have suggested other structural and compositional characteristics of neighborhoods and communities that are likely to influence child and adolescent development. Following Shaw and McKay (1942), Sampson (1992) and others (Simcha-Fagan and Schwartz 1986) have argued that high ethnic heterogeneity and high residential instability lead to a weakening of adult friendship networks and value consensus in the neighborhood. Coulton and colleagues (1995) have argued that age and gender segregation and population density in poor neighborhoods create extreme child-care burdens (see also Korbin and Coulton vol. 2).

Previous research in the tradition of social disorganization theory provides a framework for understanding the community-level processes that intervene between concentrated neighborhood disadvantage and the experience of children and families. Social disorganization theory has specified a set of community-level social and cultural processes that, it posits, are differentially affected by particular structural and compositional characteristics. Recent research providing support for this specification has influenced our model of community and neighborhood influences (Korbin and Coulton vol. 2; Sampson and Morenoff vol. 2). Communities with high concentrations of poor, single-parent families and jobless males, and low concentrations of well-educated professional and managerial workers, are unlikely to have or attract the resources necessary to develop and sustain high-quality institutions and organizations. Moreover, the greater needs of residents in such disadvantaged neighborhoods are likely to overtax existing institutions and organizations.

A weak community organizational base impedes participation in local organization and development of informal social networks, such as friendship ties among community adults. These, in turn, reduce the collective supervision of youth in the community and diminish the resources available for child care. High levels of family disruption in a community are also likely to decrease community networks of social control.

In contrast, living in socially organized or "functional" communities should increase parents' contact with their children's friends and with the families of their children's friends (see Darling and Steinberg vol. 2). A by-product of living in such a neighborhood or community should be increased vigilance and monitoring by parents and other adults, regardless of the child's or adolescent's own household composition. As children grow older and spend less time without direct supervision, such indirect monitoring may become increasingly important. Membership in a functional, socially organized community should therefore enhance parental monitoring and benefit families with more limited economic and personal resources. When residents form local social ties, their capacity for community and social control is increased because they are better able to recognize strangers and are more likely to engage in guardianship behavior against victimization. In addition, a greater density and multiplicity of interpersonal networks in a community should increase the clarity and consensus about norms and values and lead to greater constraints on deviant behavior. The greater articulation and support for common values should, in turn, reinforce existing social ties and organizational participation (see Burton et al. vol. 2; Furstenberg and Hughes vol. 2; Jarrett vol. 2).

In summary, our model of neighborhood and community influences posits that a set of exogenous forces (figure 2.2)—including globalization, economic restructuring, migration, contingent preferences, and a variety of public policies at the federal and local levels—shapes the structural and compositional characteristics of neighborhoods and communities. Such characteristics, which include the physical environment, the demographic makeup of the community's residents, and the community's institutional resources, influence community social organization and cultural processes in ways that facilitate or inhibit healthy development of children and families.

## INTERPERSONAL AND FAMILY PROCESSES

This review is not intended to be exhaustive but rather is intended to help generate a set of hypotheses about phase-specific effects of neighborhoods and communities on development. In particular, we draw on ideas of (1) risk and resilience, (2) continuity versus discontinuity, and (3) embedded contexts to describe our general notion that how neighborhoods affect development varies with stage. We suggest that in early childhood, the neighborhood influences children's development primarily by its effects on parents. A secondary effect could be formed through the quality of care provided by other major caregivers (who are typically members of the community). In middle childhood and adolescence, the effects of neighborhoods on development may be mediated by a new set of factors, primarily schools and peers. Finally, in early and late adolescence, still other factors are hypothesized to mediate neighborhoods' effects on development. Possibilities include direct contact with certain "neighborhood processes" like adult monitoring of youth, as well as broader institutional and cultural processes like the operations of the labor market, the justice system, and the beliefs and values that guide family formation.

If neighborhood effects are mediated by different contextual factors over the life course, several questions need to be raised. Does children's sensitivity to neighborhood effects vary with age or developmental epoch? How do neighborhoods interact with other salient ecologies over time—notably, family, peers, child-care providers, schools, and other service institutions? Do different features of neighborhood composition or structure have differential impact on cognitive-academic and social-emotional processes and outcomes? These questions cannot be answered fully by the studies presented in this volume; however, they have guided our conceptualizations and analyses (and, we argue, should guide the design of future studies of neighborhood effects).

## PRESCHOOL YEARS

The epoch occurring from about three to seven years of age is one of rapid growth in cognitive and socioemotional competencies, as well as of dramatic change in the daily contexts of children's lives (Brooks-Gunn, Denner, and Klebanov 1995). Major tasks of this period of life in contemporary U.S. culture include the following: to successfully make the transitions from home to school (Entwisle and Alexander 1993); to develop the cognitive, affective, and behavioral self-regulation necessary to succeed in the transition to school (Mischel, Shoda, and Peake 1988; Mischel, Shoda, and Rodriguez 1989); to build on earlier cognitive and motivational competencies and learn the earliest, most fundamental tasks of reading and mathematics (Baroody et al. 1984; Snow 1983); and to build on the interpersonal trust and social problem-solving skills developed in the family to begin to establish competent relations with peers (Sroufe 1979, 1983). If children successfully meet these tasks, important outcomes include age-appropriate advances in cognitive development (both generally and particularly in the development of early math and reading abilities) and adequate self-regulation, as indexed by a lack of significant behavioral and emotional problems.

The specific processes that lead to positive outcomes in early childhood are many, varied, and beyond the scope of this chapter. (For more information, see Sroufe et al. 1992). In general, they involve primarily transactions in the home that directly affect children: experiences of parents' sensitivity and warmth that foster the growth of interpersonal trust (Ainsworth et al. 1978; Sroufe 1979); experiences of cognitive stimulation and exposure to stimulating materials that foster curiosity and mathematical and linguistic reasoning ability (Sparling et al. 1991); and experiences of structure, predictability, and contingent responsiveness that foster the growth of self-regulations (Emde 1980; Kopp 1982). Certainly, other processes outside the home, most importantly the quality of nonparental child care and early education (Brooks-Gunn et al. 1991; Hayes, Palmer, and Zaslow 1990; Phillips and Hofferth 1991), are central to development in early childhood. But the transactions in the home, especially between parents or other primary caretakers and the child, are thought to be key.

## ELEMENTARY SCHOOL YEARS

The ages of seven to eleven years are marked by fewer transitions than the preschool and middle school years. Children are not usually entering profoundly new school contexts and are not coping with drastically new adult expectations (such as learning to read) or new bodily experiences (such as puberty). But nonetheless, middle childhood is a period of extremely important advances in both cognitive and socioemotional development (Collins 1984; Collins and Gunnar 1990; Hartup 1989). The world of school and peers, introduced in early childhood, becomes increasingly important in the day-to-day lives of seven- to eleven-year-olds (Hartup 1989). Perhaps most important, how children think of themselves, as students and as social partners, becomes increasingly articulated and stable (Jones et al. 1996; Harter 1983). The growing differentiation and stability of concepts of the self are part of a larger transition in making meaning in their lives, which involves comparing their actual selves to others and to their own ideal selves, as well as interpreting the meaning of experience, events, and contexts through their effect on the self.

While the specific developmental challenges in elementary school shift to consolidating functioning in school and with peers and to making meaning, some of the outcomes of successful development remain similar—age-appropriate advances in cognitive development in general and in math and reading abilities in particular, plus social adaptation as indexed by lack of behavior problems. But the processes expected to affect these outcomes shift significantly. As children spend less time at home and more time at school and with peers, the quality of interactions with teachers and fellow students becomes a major contributor to the course of development during middle childhood (Stipek et al. 1995). In addition, the parental factors that influence development grow to include not only cognitive stimulation, sensitivity, warmth, predictability, and structure but also the quality of interpersonal problem solving and the indirect structuring of learning and peer experiences even when the parent is not there (Collins and Russell 1991; Dodge and Coie 1987; Smetana 1988; Steinberg, Dornbusch, and Brown 1992).

## MIDDLE SCHOOL YEARS

The epoch from about ten to sixteen years of age encompasses the transition from childhood to adolescence. Early adolescence involves dramatic changes in biological development with the onset of puberty (Brooks-Gunn and Reiter 1990); in cognitive development, with the acquisition of the ability to think logically about abstract concepts like friendship and fairness (Keating 1990); in social development, with dramatic changes in the nature and quality of peer relationships (Brooks-Gunn and Paikoff 1993; Brown 1990); and in emotional development, with higher rates of psychological symptoms and behavior problems (Petersen et al. 1993). These changes in development are usually accompanied by changes in context—notably, the transition to larger, more impersonal junior and senior high schools and increased autonomy to meet friends and travel to places with less adult supervision (Eccles and Midgley 1990; Seidman et al. 1994). Another major task of early adolescence is the consolidation of a sense of personal identity from the many strands of the meaning-making processes, which began earlier in development (Erikson 1950; Allen, Bat-Chava, and Seidman 1995).

Because sound mental health and smooth adaptation to school are such widely valued and highly prognostic indicators of successful adaptations, key indices of successful outcomes in early adolescence remain school achievement and lack of behavior problems. In addition to parents, peers, and school, early adolescents become directly involved in a host of contexts, from formal youth-serving organizations to informal neighborhood groups to features of popular culture directed toward youth (O'Brien, Pittman and Cahill 1992).

## HIGH SCHOOL YEARS AND BEYOND

The epoch from sixteen to twenty-one years of age represents the transition from adolescence to young adulthood. At sixteen, youth can leave school with parental permission and begin to drive; by twenty-one, they are permitted to vote and drink alcohol and are expected to be well on their way to the psychological and economic self-sufficiency characteristic of modern American adulthood. The major task of this developmental phase is preparation for work and for independent family life (Graber, Brooks-Gunn, and Peterson forthcoming; Graber and Dubas 1997; Sherrod, Haggerty, and Feathermen 1993). Successful adaptation to these tasks is clearly influenced by earlier developmental histories, in particular the individual's adaptation to earlier tasks in school and in social relationships (Brooks-Gunn, Guo, and Furstenberg 1993; Haveman, Wolfe, and Spaulding 1991; Masten, Neeman, and Andenas 1994), as well as by the nature of the contexts during late adolescence, for example, the nature of the labor market and the practices, values, and beliefs of peers regarding family formation (Chase-Lansdale and Brooks-Gunn 1995; Newman 1996). Indices of successful outcomes at this developmental stage can no longer be restricted to academic achievement and mental health measures, but must include real-world adaptational measures like school dropout (higher education) and teen out-of-wedlock parenthood (delayed parenthood).

In addition to the types of contexts and processes affecting development at earlier stages, new contexts and processes, ones that may have affected them at earlier stages only indirectly or not at all, begin to affect late adolescents directly. Examples include the labor and marriage markets, and employer–youth and romantic partner–youth interactions.

## NEIGHBORHOOD INFLUENCES AS A FUNCTION OF EPOCH

If tasks, contexts, processes, and outcomes do vary with epochs of development, we may ask whether or not epoch-specific effects of neighborhoods on development exist. On the basis of the theory and research summarized thus far, we hypothesize that the effects of neighborhoods on development during early childhood will be primarily indirect, through the effects of neighborhoods on the quality of the home environment and out-of-home care. The indirect effects of neighborhood composition or structure on early childhood development mediated by the quality of the home environment are examined in chapters 4 and 5.

Further, we hypothesize that by middle childhood and early adolescence, (1) children will come into increasingly direct contact with neighborhoods, so that neighborhood effects should increase in magnitude, and (2) new processes will mediate the effects of neighborhoods on development, in particular, children's perceptions of their home, peer, and school environments, as well as their self-perceptions. These "perceptions" of context and self are the psychological "meaning-making" function we described as so salient in middle childhood and early adolescence. The indirect effects of neighborhood composition or structure on cognitive and emotional development in middle childhood and early adolescence, mediated by perceptions of context and self, are discussed in chapters 6 and 7.

We hypothesize that, by later adolescence, youth are in even greater contact with the neighborhood and broader community ecologies and institutions, both because of the increased autonomy that comes with age and because the epoch-specific changes of preparation for work and independent family life propel late adolescents into new contexts deeply embedded in community ecologies and institutions (for example, networks of employment opportunities or networks of opportunities for persistent antisocial behavior). During the adolescent years, less emphasis is placed on the mediating roles of home, school, peers, and subjective perceptions of self and contexts than at earlier developmental epochs. Nonetheless, the processes by which neighborhoods affect outcomes in late adolescence are expected to be complex. The indirect effects of neighborhood composition or structure on school dropout and teen parenting in late adolescence are explored in chapter 8.

By comparing the effects of the same dimensions of neighborhood composition or structure on cognitive and emotional outcomes at distinct epochs of development and by using several data sets at each stage, we describe a developmental sequence of whether and how neighborhoods affect development. As becomes strikingly clear in chapter 3, it is not enough to pose these questions for all children. Within-group analyses must be conducted in order to test the effects separately for black and white children and youth, as well as for males and females. The joint probabilities of growing up in persistently poor families and neighborhoods are so drastically different for black and white children in the United States that separate analyses must be conducted (chapter 3). Indeed, black and white children and youth occupy almost nonoverlapping places on the continuum of neighborhood and family poverty. Similarly, both quantitative and ethnographic research findings suggest that different features of high-risk environments may prove differently important for girls' and boys' development. For these reasons, all analyses of the direct and indirect effects of neighborhoods on child and adolescent development have been conducted separately by race or ethnicity (black or white) and gender (male or female).

## DEVELOPMENT ACROSS PERSON, PROCESS, CONTEXT, AND TIME

Bronfenbrenner (1979, 1989) has argued persuasively that studies of human development must examine variations across four dimensions: person, process, context, and time. The most proximal influences in the course of development are transactions between a child and his or her immediate social and object worlds. Engagement in the increasingly complex manipulation of symbols (via language and play) and the experience of being contingently responded to by an important other (what some call sensitivity) are two examples of such transactions. Bronfenbrenner referred to these transactions as the *proximal processes* that drive development. Such processes are influenced by *person characteristics*. Some characteristics are "status" variables like age or cohort, gender, and race/ethnicity. Others describe a person's preexisting capacities, limits, and dispositions—for example, inquisitiveness, physical disability, and shyness or sociability. Proximal processes and person characteristics take on particular meanings in particular *contexts*. Again, contexts can be enduring macrosettings of development such as family structure and composition or neighborhood structure and composition. Contexts can also entail microsettings of development, as with the contrast in opportunities for cognitive development presented by the free-play and structured-play situations with adults.

The key to understanding the dynamics of development is to examine why processes vary by person characteristics and context *over time*. Once again, time can be represented to varying degrees. Longitudinal studies might follow children for months or years, ideally over major stage transitions (for example, from late childhood to early adolescence) and perhaps even over major portions of the life span (for example, from childhood to adulthood). But it is also possible to follow children over briefer periods (for instance, during adaptation to a new classroom or to an unfamiliar peer) to understand how certain basic processes are affected by person characteristics and contexts over time.

This Person × Process × Context × Time model can be employed to describe some of the strengths and weaknesses of the data sets that form the backbone of this volume. The person variables of particular interest in this volume include age or epoch, race or ethnicity, and gender. These status variables are available in all data sets. Measures of preexisting capacities, limits, and dispositions are more idiosyncratic to each study and so offer very few opportunities for joint analyses. However, some members of the working group are conducting analyses of neighborhood effects that include person characteristics far beyond the major status variables (Brooks-Gunn, Duncan et al. 1993; Klebanov, Brooks-Gunn, and Duncan 1994). Some of the data sets, like the Panel Study of Income Dynamics (PSID) and the Children of the National Longitudinal Study of Youth (NLSY), contain very little information about truly transactional *processes* between children and contexts. Other data sets, like the Infant Health and Development Program (IHDP) and Atlanta data sets, are very rich in process data. All of these studies are longitudinal, although the time frame varies from three decades in the PSID to two decades in the Children of the NLSY to almost one decade in the IHDP to only one major developmental transition in the Adolescent Pathways Project and the Atlanta study. All of these studies chart not only changes in individual and family processes over time but also individual outcomes over their course. However, limited data have been collected on neighborhood change over time. It is important to know whether neighborhoods are rapidly declining, rebounding, or remaining relatively stable (see Korbin and Coulton vol. 2). Despite the value of viewing individuals and neighborhoods as changing over time, in this volume we report analyses using neighborhood conditions in 1980 and at individual developmental processes and outcomes at one or two points of time in the 1980s. Future studies by members of this working group will be of a more ambitious longitudinal type.

The unique contribution of this collaborative research effort to the study of human development is its conceptualization and measurement of the impact of a major *context*, the neighborhood. Our collaboration has made necessary compromises in how we operationalize *neighborhood*. As described earlier in this chapter and by various authors in volume 2, a much richer conceptualization of neighborhoods exists than is currently available uniformly across the six data sets. Future multisite, multi–data set studies of neighborhood effects could be designed to take advantage of the conceptual and measurement work under way by other networks of scholars (for example, the MacArthur Foundation's Networks on Successful Adolescent Development and on Criminal Behavior and Human Development), as well as by members of our own working group. For now, we conceptualize neighborhood factors as primarily structural-compositional in nature, thereby leaving out critically important institutional and organizational factors (such as the quality of schools or the availability of primary services) and process factors (such as density of friendship networks or nonparental adult monitoring of children and youth) at the community level, all of which no doubt influence development. Further, we operationalize these factors with census data aggregated at the tract level (see chapter 3).

We believe that at this stage in the history of studies of neighborhood effects, the limits created by these compromises are offset by the opportunity to examine neighborhood effects across multiple data sets and several stages of development. And other chapters in this volume provide a window into additional pathbreaking neighborhood conceptions.

---

Work on this chapter was supported in part by grants from the National Institute of Mental Health (MH43084) and the Carnegie Corporation (B4850) awarded to Edward Seidman, J. Lawrence Aber, LaRue Allen, and Christina Mitchell. We express our appreciation to the adolescents and schools whose cooperation made this study possible.

# 3

# Neighborhood Models and Measures

*Greg J. Duncan and J. Lawrence Aber*

The decision to estimate neighborhood effects on child and youth development using multiple and varied data sets required the development of a common analytical approach to the estimation of neighborhood effects, as well as a common conceptual framework and measurement strategy for describing the variation in neighborhood structure and composition that may be associated with developmental outcomes. Some of our data sets, such as the National Longitudinal Surveys of Youth (NLSY) and the Panel Study of Income Dynamics (PSID), are drawn from national probability samples. These two studies provide large numbers of observations and national representation of both children and neighborhoods (although the Children of the NLSY is not a national representation of all children, but of children born to relatively young mothers [Chase-Lansdale et al. 1991]).[1] We also use multicity data sets (Adolescent Pathways Project, Infant Health and Development Program [IHDP]) and city-specific data sets (Atlanta, upstate New York) because they contain large samples of children and youth in poor neighborhoods and more detailed information on developmental process and outcomes.

In terms of analytic models, our strategy is to estimate neighborhood effects from data sets that combine census-based information on the socio-demographic composition of neighborhoods with developmental-process and outcome data on children and their families. Common to our analytic approach is a set of (1) simple regression models describing the nature of the associations between neighborhood composition and developmental outcomes, with and without adjustments for differences in family-level socio-economic status (SES); (2) mediated models that attempt to account for the neighborhood-outcome associations found in the first step; and (3) moderated models that test for differences in neighborhood effects between resource-rich and resource-poor neighborhoods. A first purpose of this chapter is to outline the analytic approach used in the next section of the book.

With regard to measurement strategies, our desire to synthesize findings across data sets required us to develop and use the same concepts and measures of neighborhood structure and composition and also to describe how each sample varied on these measures. Since each decennial census provides literally hundreds of measures of the demographic composition of neighborhoods, we faced the task of producing a manageable number of neighborhood factors that made sense both theoretically and empirically. A second purpose of this chapter is to describe the procedures and results of our efforts to distill a factor structure of neighborhood conditions that could be used in all subsequent analyses across all data sets.

We also use data on neighborhood characteristics to place the six developmental data sets into a national and comparative context. The six data sets employed to estimate neighborhood effects in this volume sample children and youth from vastly different neighborhood conditions. If these sample differences in neighborhood conditions are not well understood from the beginning, it will prove impossible to compare and contrast findings on neighborhood effects across data sets. Therefore, a third purpose of this chapter is to describe the six data sets in the context of nationally standardized norms developed from the nationally representative PSID sample.

Finally, many readers will be unfamiliar with the national dimensions of neighborhood characteristics, just as we were when we started our joint project. A fourth and final task of this chapter is to provide some perspective on the neighborhood conditions under which children and adolescents live and how neighborhood conditions of poverty covary with family conditions of poverty. Because these conditions are so vastly different for black and white children and youth and because most of our analyses are conducted separately for black and white youth, we described neighborhood and family conditions separately by race.

## ANALYTIC FRAMEWORK

None of the six data sets was designed explicitly to model the effects of neighborhood conditions on children's development. However, all share three core elements. First, all recorded respondents' residential addresses, which provide a linkage to census-based measures of the demographic composition of the neighborhood environment. Second, all provided at least crude measures of the SES of the child's or adolescent's family. And third, all six data sets provided interesting and reasonably reliable measures of cognitive, behavioral, or mental health outcomes of children or adolescents. The first set of items constitute neighborhood composition measures; the second set constitute family-level SES measures; and the third set constitute developmental outcomes.

Beyond these core elements, the different data sets bring very different strengths and weaknesses to the task of understanding how neighborhoods affect child and adolescent outcomes. The national and multisite samples provide the greatest dispersion in neighborhood conditions and therefore the most statistically reliable estimation of population-wide neighborhood effects. The local samples provide relatively greater coverage of resource-poor neighborhoods and of racial and ethnic minorities. The local studies also tend to provide higher-quality measures of developmental outcomes and more complete measures of family process.

A first task in modeling of neighborhood effects is to assess the simple association between neighborhood conditions and developmental outcomes. This is accomplished with two regressions run on each available outcome measure:

$$(3.1) \text{ Developmental outcome} = f_1 \text{ (neighborhood characteristics)}$$
$$(3.2) \text{ Developmental outcome} = f_2 \text{ (neighborhood characteristics,}$$
$$\text{family SES)}$$

The purpose of these regressions is to assess the descriptive associations between neighborhood characteristics and the outcomes, with and without controls for family-level SES. Although suppression effects are possible, equation 3.1 will almost certainly lead to an overestimation of the causal role of neighborhood conditions, since it fails to adjust for the family-level conditions that affect development and are correlated with neighborhood conditions. Thus, equation 3.1 is probably most valuable in pointing out *un*important neighborhood-level predictors of children and adolescent outcomes.

The addition of family-level measures of SES (such as family income or single-parent status) in equation 3.2 adjusts the estimates of neighborhood effects for differences in family-level SES. This is desirable to the extent that the values of such family-level measures are not themselves determined by neighborhood conditions. The implications from transaction models (Bronfenbrenner 1989; Sameroff et al. 1993) of the possible reciprocal causation between neighborhood characteristics and family-level SES are explored further in volume 2. In the absence of such reciprocal effects, equation 3.2 provides better estimates than equation 3.1 of the possible causal influence of neighborhood composition on child and adolescent outcomes.

Some of our data sets provide interesting and reliable measures of the family- and individual-level processes that might account for the apparent neighborhood effects showing up in equation 3.2. Our exploration of mediated models amounts to the estimation of:

$$(3.3) \text{ Developmental outcome} = f_3 \text{ (neighborhood characteristics, family}$$
$$\text{SES, family mediators)}$$
$$(3.4) \text{ Family mediators} = f_4 \text{ (neighborhood characteristics, family SES)}$$

Equations 3.3 and 3.4 constitute a simple recursive system in which equation 3.3 provides estimates of the direct effects of neighborhood characteristics that operate independently of family SES and family mediators, while the mediated neighborhood effect is the product of (1) the effect of neighborhood characteristics on family mediators in equation 3.4 and (2) the effect of family mediators on developmental outcomes in equation 3.3. The direct and mediated effects of a neighborhood characteristic sum to the total effect estimated in equation 3.2. Thus, the results from the estimation of equation 3.2 will serve as a guide to what mediated effects might be most important.

A final step in our common analytic framework is to estimate, whenever possible, moderated models of neighborhood effects. Here we divide each sample into groups representing individuals in resource-rich and resource-poor environments and then run models such as equations 3.2 and 3.3 separately for the two neighborhood-based subgroups. This will help indicate whether other aspects of the developmental process appear to be operating in different ways, depending on the type of neighborhood.

All of these analytic models suffer from a host of potential threats to their validity. A number of these issues are explored in chapter 9 of this volume and in various chapters in volume 2. Among these issues are the following concerns:

1. The decennial census does not provide measures of neighborhood characteristics that match the theoretical concepts.

2. Decennial census definitions of neighborhoods are either larger or smaller than "true" neighborhood boundaries.

3. Important interactions are omitted between family and neighborhood conditions and between these variables and other moderators of their effects at the individual and more macro levels.

4. Omitted-variable bias is introduced by the fact that families have some degree of choice regarding the neighborhoods in which they live.

5. Insights from transaction models of development, which emphasize not only that individuals shape and create their own environments but also that individual and family characteristics are *shaped by* social and physical contexts such as their neighborhoods, are ignored.

6. Neighborhood influences are underestimated because of suppression effects from other, unmeasured variables.

7. The fact that neighborhood effects may not be linear across the entire range of neighborhood conditions is ignored.

8. Insights into the estimation of multilevel data such as ours that come from hierarchical linear models and related multilevel modeling techniques are not taken into account in these analyses.

The extent to which these various concerns are addressed in the later chapters of the book varies with topic. For all of them, however, the nature of the problem is presented, and, at a minimum, an illustrative empirical analysis is presented to gauge the magnitude of the possible bias.

## OUR APPROACH TO MEASURING NEIGHBORHOOD CONDITIONS

Our data on neighborhood characteristics come from the 1980 Census Summary Tape File (STF) 3, which provides data on neighborhood-like areas that take the form of tracts, block-numbering areas (BNAs), or enumeration districts (EDs). Nearly all of the land in U.S. metropolitan areas is tracted, and a few states also were fully tracted in nonmetropolitan areas in 1980. Tract boundaries are delineated with the advice of local committees working under Census Bureau guidelines. Boundaries typically reflect important physical features that define neighborhoods, such as major streets or railroads, as well as important ethnic and social divisions.

In most states, some nontracted areas (mainly cities in nonmetropolitan areas) were blocked; aggregations of blocks, or BNAs, provide a reasonable analogue to tracts. When, in rare cases, our sample children lived in untracted and unblocked areas, we used the EDs to approximate neighborhoods. EDs are the basic work units of individual census enumerators, and since they are drawn primarily for the convenience of the enumerators, EDs are probably less well matched to true neighborhoods than tracts or BNAs.

The data provided by the decennial census about these neighborhood areas come from the census forms the population is asked to fill out on April 1 of the first year of every decade. Abundant information about the economic and demographic characteristics of the population is provided by the completed census forms. This enables us to characterize neighborhoods according to a number of key dimensions such as the extent of neighborhood poverty, female-family headship, public assistance receipt, and male joblessness. Regrettably absent from the census forms and from all other national databases on local-area conditions are measures of crime, drugs, gang activity, churches, community centers, employment opportunities, and school quality. Thus, we are forced to use a rich, but less-than-optimal, set of indicators of neighborhood conditions. The attempts of some of the members of our working group to develop alternative measures of neighborhood conditions are described in volume 2.

Until recently, empirical research on the effects of neighborhood socioeconomic conditions on children, youth, and families has relied on just a few indices of neighborhood conditions that were derived primarily from census-tract data. In the last few years, however, researchers have expressed greater interest in multiple indices.

One approach is to aggregate multiple indices into a common neighborhood risk factor: neighborhoods that scored above certain cutoffs on multiple factors are defined as especially high risk. Ricketts and Sawhill (1988) exemplify this approach by defining *underclass* neighborhoods as consisting of tracts that are at least one standard deviation above the national mean on four behavioral indicators (high school dropouts, male joblessness, public assistance use, and female headship).

Another approach is to look for critical thresholds on particular variables and to compare the relative power of several related single-index measures to predict outcomes. Crane (1991) found evidence of threshold effects with the 1970 PUMS data using a tract-level measure of whether the fraction of employed men working in professional and managerial occupations was less than 5 percent. (See Brooks-Gunn et al. [1993] for a variant of the Crane procedure.) Because of the intercorrelations among various indices on neighborhood disadvantage, very high threshold scores may also identify neighborhoods with very high scores on other indices of neighborhood disadvantage (Korbin and Coulton vol. 2; Sampson and Morenoff vol. 2).

In the collective research reported in this volume, we have adopted an alternative to these multiple-indices approaches. Specifically, the organization of community risk factors is examined, both empirically (through factor analysis) and theoretically (by ensuring that the empirical dimensions identified via factor analyses map onto theoretical constructs central to the extant literature on neighborhood effects). This strategy is adopted for several reasons. First, for measurement reasons, we believe that multivariate indices of underlying dimensions of neighborhood composition are more reliable than single-index measures. Second, this approach allows us to specify, conceptually and empirically, neighborhood dimensions that are relatively independent. Rather than ask, "What is the best measure of neighborhood disadvantage—the fraction poor, the fraction of families headed by women, the fraction of families with an income above thirty thousand dollars, or the fraction of prime-age males who are jobless?" we ask, "How are neighborhood factors organized, and what are their separate and combined effects on the family process and developmental outcomes of interest?"

Third, this strategy provides our network of cooperating independent research projects with a coherent, systematic framework in which to compare the nature of our six very different samples. Two of the data sets, the PSID and the NLSY, do not pose unusual challenges because they are national samples. A third sample is based on a multisite study of low-birth-weight babies. Three of the projects present more difficulties, since they were selected because they oversample from poor and minority communities (and contain more family and developmental process data than the two national samples). Since they are local samples, a comparative study using these data must be able to relate the neighborhood conditions in which the children and adolescents in these samples are raised to a nationally representative sample of neighborhoods. We do so by presenting nationally standardized means and variances on each of our neighborhood indices for all six samples analyzed in this volume.

Fourth, this approach permits a description of sample differences not only in means and variances but also in the organization of neighborhood variables. If the indices of neighborhood disadvantage are more highly interrelated in some samples than others, this fact affects our ability to ascertain independent effects.

Fifth and finally, we believe that this approach to the organization of neighborhood factors provides our network of researchers with the conceptual and analytic tools to examine systematically the effects of interactions or patterns among neighborhood indices across multiple data sets.

Other scholars may disagree with our approach. Historically and currently, some social scientists have believed that such an approach is dangerously atheoretical and risks combining conceptually unrelated elements into single dimensions. Such fears are not unfounded. Early attempts at empirically operationalizing and testing key features of social disorganization theory using a factorial ecology approach employed factor analyses inappropriately (not guided by theory, capitalizing on chance, and so on). (See Chow and Coulton [1992] and Sampson and Morenoff [vol. 2] for historical analysis of this issue.) But the social sciences have made considerable advances in the logic and mathematics for using such multivariate techniques, and several other modern researchers have taken a similar approach to examining the organization of neighborhood characteristics.

In the following sections, (1) the method and results of factor analyses of census data from a nationally representative sample of tracts, from which six internally coherent, theoretically interpretable, and reasonably independent dimensions emerge are described; (2) the other five data sets are compared with the nationally standardized means and variances on the factor scores and the correlations among the factor scores; and (3) the very different neighborhoods in which black and white children are raised are described with nationally representative data.

## FACTOR ANALYSES

Researchers have disagreed over which features of neighborhood socio-economic composition are the most important influences on the social norms and individual behavior of children, youth, and parents. Some have emphasized the concentration of poor, minority, female-headed families and the resulting lack of adult supervision and monitoring (Hogan and Kitigawa 1985). Others have focused on the absence of middle-class or high-status professionals and the resulting lack of role models (Crane 1991).[2] Still others have argued that joblessness (both in the macrostructure and in the immediate social milieu) is an especially important influence on the development of minority children, youth, and parents in urban ghettos because it precludes the rational planning of life (Wilson 1991b).

Researchers working in the tradition of social disorganization theory have suggested, in addition to socioeconomic factors, other neighborhood demographic compositional factors likely to influence child and adolescent development. For instance, following Shaw and McKay (1942), Sampson (1992; Sampson and Morenoff vol. 2) has argued that a high degree of ethnic heterogeneity and residential instability lead to an erosion of adult friendship networks and of a values consensus in the neighborhood. Coulton and colleagues (1993; Korbin and Coulton vol. 2) have argued that age and gender segregation in poor neighborhoods creates extreme child-care burdens for some communities. Indeed, social disorganization theory specifies that a number of community structural factors have differential effects on a range of community processes, which in turn affect child and adolescent outcomes.

In light of these considerations, our first concern was to examine the underlying organization of census-tract variables of neighborhood composition for evidence of the conceptual dimensions identified by previous theory and research. We identified thirty-four variables from census data that we considered potentially related to the social, economic, and demographic dimensions described in earlier research. To obtain a representative sample of census tracts, we turned to the PSID and drew a sample of all ten- to sixteen-year-olds (girls and boys) living in metropolitan areas as of 1980. We used this sample to maximize sample size and coordinate the location of the sample with the 1980 census. When appended to this sample, the tract-level data (drawn from roughly eighteen hundred tracts) provided a nationally representative and manageable number of observations for our factor analysis. We examined the intercorrelations among these thirty-four variables by submitting the data to a principal components analysis. Using scree and kaiser criteria as lower and upper bounds, we rotated between five, six, and seven factors (using both varimax and oblimin rotations) and then examined them for theoretical interpretability. The varimax and oblimin solutions yielded similar results, and the six-factor solution resulted in the lowest number of double-loaded variables and the most interpretable factors, in light of the extant literature on relevant neighborhood compositional factors. The results of the six-factor solution (varimax rotation) are presented in table 3.1.

The factor structure strongly resembles six conceptual dimensions of neighborhood composition identified from the socioeconomic, social disorganization, and social isolation literature just described. Using this factor analysis as a guide, we created six composite scores to represent these six underlying dimensions of neighborhood composition. We selected for inclusion in a composite score only those variables that loaded highly and reflected unambiguously the underlying conceptual dimension. Twenty-one of the original thirty-four variables were retained. The retained measures are noted with superscript letters in table 3.1.

In summary, we have found that it is possible to construct from census data multivariate tract-level factors of (1) low SES—poor, black, female-headed families; (2) high SES—high-income, educated, professional-managerial workers; (3) male joblessness; (4) ethnic diversity; (5) family concentration (crowded housing, young population); and (6) residential stability. However, because the effects of residential stability might well be curvilinear—with both high and very low rates of mobility indicating neighborhood problems (see also Korbin and Coulton vol. 2)—this factor was dropped from the set of neighborhood conditions used in our analyses.

TABLE 3.1 Principal Components Analysis of Census-Tract Variables Based on the PSID Sample: Varimax Rotation, Six Factors

| | Low SES | High SES | Male Joblessness | Ethnic Diversity | Family Concentration | Residential Stability |
|---|---|---|---|---|---|---|
| % of families with children headed by females | .89[a] | | | | | |
| % of non-Latino individuals who are black | .91[a] | | | | | |
| % of non-Latino individuals who are white | −.83[a] | | | | | |
| % of nonelderly individuals who are poor | .73[a] | .42 | | | | |
| % of families with children living as subfamilies | .69[a] | | | | | |
| Ratio of children to families with children | .65[a] | | | | | |
| Ratio of two-parent families to children | −.87[a] | | | | | |
| % of females aged 16–64 who are employed | −.68 | | | | | |
| % of males aged 16–64 who worked fewer than 26 weeks | .68 | | .56[c] | | | |
| % of workers in laborer or service occupations | .63 | .51 | | | | |
| % of families with incomes < $10,000 | .62 | .61 | | | | |
| % of adults unemployed | .60 | .41 | | | | |
| % of housing units that are rental | .53 | | | | | .47 |
| % of individuals aged 25+ with 13+ years of schooling | | −.89[b] | | | | |
| % of workers in executive/ professional occupations | | −.89[b] | | | | |
| % families with income > $30,000 | | −.87[b] | | | | |
| % of individuals aged 25+ with < 12 years of schooling | | .76 | | | | |
| Gini coefficient of family income | | .66 | | | | |
| % of individuals aged 16–19 and not in military with < 12 years of schooling | | .63 | | | | |
| % of housing units vacant | | .45 | | | | |
| % of males aged 16–64 not in labor force | | | .66[c] | | | |
| Number of family income categories used to calculate | | | | | | |

TABLE 3.1 *Continued*

| | Low SES | High SES | Male Joblessness | Ethnic Diversity | Family Concentration | Residential Stability |
|---|---|---|---|---|---|---|
| Gini coefficient | | | −.60 | | | |
| % females aged 16–64 employed 27+ weeks | | | −.54 | | .42 | |
| % of individuals aged 25+ with 12 years of schooling | | | −.43 | | | |
| % of foreign-born individuals | | | | .85[d] | | |
| % of Latino individuals | | | | .82[d] | | |
| Index of ethnic diversity | | | | .62[d] | | |
| % neither black, white, nor Latino | | | | .54[d] | | |
| Ratio of persons to occupied units | | | | | −.82[e] | |
| % of all individuals aged 0–17 | | | | | −.74[e] | |
| % of all individuals aged 65+ | | | | | .68[e] | |
| % of housing units in 5+ unit structures | | | | | .51 | |
| % of individuals aged 5+ who lived in the same dwelling 5 years ago | | | | | | .93 |
| % of individuals aged 5+ who lived in both the same house and country 5 years ago | | | | | | .80 |

[a] Measure used in the analysis as part of the low-SES factor.

[b] Measure used in the analysis as part of the high-SES factor.

[c] Measure used in the analysis as part of the male joblessness factor.

[d] Measure used in the analysis as part of the ethnic diversity factor.

[e] Measure used in the analysis as part of the family concentration factor.

Each of the remaining five dimensions of neighborhood composition is conceptually distinct and internally consistent. However, the dimensions often display substantial correlations with one another, particularly in the local-area samples in which variation across neighborhood characteristics was purposely limited in order to produce as large a sample of disadvantaged children and adolescents as possible.

Correlations based on the nationally representative PSID sample are presented in table 3.2. There are substantial correlations among these factors even in PSID data: −.62 between low SES and high SES and .49 between low SES and family concentration.

As indicated in the upcoming chapters, the limited variability in neighborhood conditions within several of the localized samples makes it difficult to obtain reliable estimates of the effects of all five neighborhood factors. In these cases we use a single neighborhood risk composite factor, which is the sum of the first three of our factors, scoring the high-SES factor negatively.

TABLE 3.2   Correlation Matrix of Factors Based on the PSID Sample

|  | Low SES | High SES | Male Joblessness | Ethnic Diversity |
|---|---|---|---|---|
| High SES | −.62 | | | |
| Male joblessness | .05 | −.06 | | |
| Ethnic diversity | .36 | −.15 | −.00 | |
| Family concentration | .49 | −.38 | .09 | .24 |

Note: In contrast to the signs of the measures in table 3.1, the high-SES factor is scaled so that higher values indicate higher SES, the male joblessness factor is scaled so that higher values indicate more male joblessness, and the family concentration factor is scaled so that higher values indicate more children and more crowded conditions.

## COMPARISON OF NEIGHBORHOOD CONDITIONS SAMPLED ACROSS DATA SETS

As just noted, one of the reasons we wished to create such neighborhood factor scores was to facilitate the comparative analyses that are at the heart of this broader collaborative research endeavor. By identifying and creating compositional factors, we can describe the neighborhoods involved in various samples using the nationally representative data as a standard of comparison.

To accomplish this goal, we took the following steps to standardize these factor scores:

1. Individual-item standardization of all of the variables in the five factors was performed by subtracting (PSID) sample means and dividing by (PSID) standard deviations. The PSID sample for this analysis was the same as that for the principal components analysis.

2. The items were added up within each factor by summing the $z$ scores obtained in step 1.

3. Finally, each factor was standardized by subtracting the mean factor score obtained in step 2 and dividing by the standard deviation of the factor score obtained in step 2.

These steps yield factor scores for this nationally representative sample of tracts with a mean of 0 and a standard deviation of 1. Thus, when neighborhood factor scores are constructed for other, less representative samples, the sample means and standard deviations and the intercorrelations among factor scores are directly interpretable in relation to a nationally representative sample of tracts.

Table 3.3 presents means for the five factor scores for each of the five samples employed in our comparative analyses. It may seem somewhat surprising that the PSID "All" means and standard deviations are not zeroes and ones, respectively. The difference is explained by the fact that the sample drawn to scale the factors was from 1980, while the analysis sample draws neighborhood data from between 1968 and 1984, with addresses prior to

TABLE 3.3    Means and Standard Deviations on Five Factors Across Analysis Samples

| Data Set and Subsample | Low SES | High SES | Male Joblessness | Ethnic Diversity | Family Concentration |
|---|---|---|---|---|---|
| IHDP—whites | −.16 | .04 | −.14 | .44 | −.57 |
| | (.67) | (.94) | (.88) | (1.38) | (1.03) |
| IHDP—blacks | 1.72 | −.91 | 1.27 | −1.32 | .14 |
| | (1.15) | (.63) | (1.25) | (2.67) | (1.07) |
| NLSY—whites | −0.23 | −0.44 | −0.17 | −0.20 | −0.12 |
| | (0.57) | (0.67) | (0.77) | (0.93) | (0.81) |
| NLSY—blacks | 1.19 | −0.80 | 0.11 | 0.19 | 0.90 |
| | (1.23) | (0.67) | (0.95) | (1.05) | (1.33) |
| Atlanta—blacks | 2.32 | −1.14 | 1.71 | −.39 | .50 |
| | (.84) | (.54) | (1.11) | (.39) | (.90) |
| NY-Washington- Baltimore—whites | −0.36 | −0.88 | 0.31 | 1.10 | −1.03 |
| | (0.52) | (0.42) | (0.51) | (1.04) | (0.54) |
| NY-Washington- Baltimore—blacks | 1.73 | −0.64 | 1.57 | 1.27 | 0.06 |
| | (0.70) | (0.78) | (0.99) | (1.03) | (0.94) |
| NY-Washington- Baltimore—Latinos | 1.12 | −1.10 | 1.40 | 2.84 | −0.04 |
| | (0.79) | (0.65) | (0.96) | (1.37) | (0.95) |
| Upstate New York—whites | .34 | −.53 | .05 | .46 | .60 |
| | (.83) | (.79) | (.83) | (.79) | (1.03) |
| Upstate New York—blacks | 1.51 | −.90 | .81 | 1.05 | .34 |
| | (.97) | (.59) | (1.01) | (.68) | (1.07) |
| PSID—all, aged 10–16 | .21 | −.48 | −.26 | .22 | −.19 |
| | (.90) | (.85) | (.71) | (.88) | (.88) |
| PSID—whites, aged 10–16 | −.15 | −.20 | −.23 | .22 | −.42 |
| | (.52) | (.90) | (.76) | (.92) | (.67) |
| PSID—blacks, aged 10–16 | 1.69 | −1.03 | .03 | .59 | .55 |
| | (1.00) | (.62) | (.76) | (.92) | (.97) |

1976 being matched to data from the 1970 census. Income, unemployment, and family concentration were somewhat lower in 1970 as compared with 1980, while neighborhood ethnic diversity was somewhat higher. The standard deviations are somewhat lower than unity in the PSID analysis sample, in part because the neighborhood data are averaged over a period of as long as seven years.

The low-birth-weight children who make up the IHDP sample live in somewhat worse neighborhoods than the adolescents in the representative PSID sample. Although also a national sample, the NLSY as well draws subjects from neighborhoods that are somewhat worse than subjects from the PSID. This is because the NLSY sample is made up of children in 1988 born to women who were fourteen to twenty-one years old in the study's first year (1979). All such children were born to young mothers, whose neighborhood characteristics are somewhat below average across the various dimensions of SES captured in our factor analyses.

The three local samples, consisting of children and adolescents from Atlanta (Spencer), upstate New York (Connell), and New York City, Baltimore, and Washington, D.C. (Aber) drew subjects from very low SES neighborhoods. The black children in the Atlanta sample are especially disadvantaged, scoring 2.3 standard deviations above the national mean on the low-SES factor. Furthermore, the Atlanta sample's poverty is more homogeneous than average, as indicated by the less-than-unity standard deviations on the low- and high-SES factors. We must keep in mind the conceptual and methodological implications of these differences in means of the factor scores when we discuss and interpret the results of our comparative analyses.

In summary, by standardizing these neighborhood indices on a nationally representative sample of tracts, it is possible to characterize other nonrepresentative samples of neighborhoods based on such features as their mean levels and variances, and on the internal consistency of the factors and the degree of correlation among them. Thus, the evidence that important variation among neighborhoods in their socioeconomic and sociodemographic composition can be captured on key theoretically defined dimensions permits our group (as well as other researchers) to begin to test empirically propositions from economic, sociological, and developmental theories of neighborhoods' effects.

## RACIAL DIFFERENCES IN NEIGHBORHOOD AND FAMILY CONDITIONS

The striking racial differences in neighborhood factor scores led us to estimate, using the PSID sample of adolescents, racial differences in the means on all of the component variables in each of the five factors (table 3.4). Since these data are drawn from a probability sample and weighted to adjust for differential selection probabilities and nonresponse, they constitute representative national estimates of the characteristics of the neighborhoods in which black and white adolescents reside.

Table 3.4 shows vast racial differences in most of the measures of neighborhood conditions. Relative to whites, black adolescents grow up in neighborhoods with three times as many neighbors who are poor (22.8 percent versus 7.5 percent) and only half as many families with incomes above thirty thousand dollars (12.5 percent versus 28.2 percent). The typical black child has 58.9 percent black neighbors, as compared with only 4.4 percent for the typical white child. There are roughly three times as many women heading families in the neighborhoods of black, as opposed to white, children (25.2 percent versus 8.9 percent). Somewhat surprisingly, racial differences in the extent of male joblessness in the neighborhood were more modest (16.3 percent for blacks versus 10.2 percent for white).

Before attaching undue importance to the very different neighborhood conditions under which black and white children are raised, it is important

TABLE 3.4    Means of White and Black Adolescents on Census-Tract Measures Used
in Neighborhood Factors, PSID Sample

| Factor | Census-Tract Measure | White Mean | Black Mean |
|---|---|---|---|
| Low SES | % of families with children headed by females | 8.9 | 25.2 |
| | % of non-Latino individuals who are black | 4.4 | 58.9 |
| | % of non-Latino individuals who are white | 92.3 | 39.1 |
| | % of nonelderly individuals who are poor | 7.5 | 22.8 |
| | % of families with children living as subfamilies | 3.9 | 9.1 |
| | Ratio of children to families with children | 2.4 | 2.9 |
| | Ratio of two-parent families to children | 0.75 | 0.52 |
| High SES | % of individuals aged 25+ with 13+ years of schooling | 25.0 | 14.1 |
| | % of workers in executive/professional occupations | 25.8 | 14.4 |
| | % families with income > $30,000 | 28.2 | 12.5 |
| Male joblessness | % of males aged 16–64 not in labor force | 10.2 | 16.3 |
| | % of males aged 16–64 who worked fewer than 26 weeks | 15.1 | 22.4 |
| Ethnic diversity | % of foreign-born individuals | 5.2 | 3.3 |
| | % of Latino individuals | 3.7 | 4.3 |
| | Index of ethnic diversity | 11.7 | 32.7 |
| | % neither black, white, nor Latino | 0.8 | 0.7 |
| Family concentration | Ratio of persons to occupied units | 2.8 | 3.7 |
| | % of all individuals aged 0–17 | 35.4 | 38.3 |
| | % of all individuals aged 65+ | 8.8 | 9.1 |

to keep in mind that very different *family*-level conditions prevail as well. To explore racial differences in SES at both family and neighborhood levels, a single indicator of low SES was chosen—family income below the official poverty line. A household's poverty status is based on a set of income thresholds that were developed in the 1960s and are adjusted each year for changes in the cost of living, using the consumer price index. In 1990, U.S. poverty thresholds for families of three, four, and five persons were $10,419, $13,359, and $15,792, respectively. Families with annual cash incomes, before taxes, that exceed these thresholds are considered "not poor," while families with incomes falling below them are "poor."

National patterns of family- and neighborhood-level poverty can be described with representative data from the PSID. Our analysis of the patterns of family- and neighborhood-level poverty spans 1979 to 1984 and is based on a sample of 409 black and 528 white children aged ten to thirteen in 1980. Our measure of neighborhood poverty is the fraction of the neighborhood's nonelderly population who were poor, averaged over the years between 1979 and 1984. (See Duncan, Brooks-Gunn, and Klebanov [1994] for similar analyses of younger children from the PSID.)

Measurement of income and poverty status during each year in the period between 1979 and 1984 in the PSID provides data for a variety of multiyear measures of family-level poverty (Duncan and Rodgers 1991). Here we simply count the number of years in which the child lived in a household with income below the poverty line. The distribution of the samples across these family- and neighborhood-level poverty measures is shown in table 3.5. Data are presented separately by race, with results for whites (actually, all non-blacks) in the top panel and blacks in the bottom.

A comparison of row totals shows large differences in the family poverty experiences of whites and blacks. Roughly 75 percent of white adolescents never lived in poor families; only 25 percent of black adolescents escaped poverty altogether. Poverty experiences are temporary for many more whites than blacks. Among ever-poor whites, only 25 percent were poor in five or six years. Among ever-poor blacks, more than 50 percent were poor all the time. Across the whole samples, only about 5 percent of whites were poor in at least five of the six years; 40 percent of black children and adolescents were poor that long.

Consistent with earlier tables, the longitudinal data presented in the column totals of table 3.5 show stark ethnic differences in neighborhood-level poverty as well. More than 60 percent of whites, but only 6 percent of blacks, lived in neighborhoods with few (that is, less than 10 percent) poor neighbors. Using neighborhood poverty rates in excess of 40 percent to define "ghetto" neighborhoods, the incidence of ghetto poverty among blacks is dramatically higher than for whites.

The interior of table 3.5 shows that nearly half of the blacks, but less than 10 percent of whites, who escape poverty at the family level encounter it (in

TABLE 3.5   Six-Year Family and Neighborhood Poverty Levels for White and Black Children, Aged Ten to Thirteen in 1980

| | Six-Year Average Fraction of Individuals in Neighborhood Who Were Poor | | | | | Total |
|---|---|---|---|---|---|---|
| Number of years family was poor | 0–10% | 10–20% | 20–30% | 30–40% | 40%+ | |
| White (n = 528) | | | | | | |
| None | 52.4 | 17.6 | 3.1 | 0.9 | 0.3 | 75.3% |
| 1–4 years | 7.5 | 8.7 | 1.8 | 0.2 | 0.0 | 17.9% |
| 5–6 years | 0.7 | 2.9 | 0.9 | 0.2 | 0.0 | 6.8% |
| White total | 60.6% | 29.2% | 5.8% | 1.3% | 0.3% | 100.0% |
| Black (n = 409) | | | | | | |
| None | 3.7 | 11.0 | 6.0 | 2.1 | 2.8 | 25.5% |
| 1–4 years | 1.0 | 9.2 | 10.3 | 3.8 | 9.5 | 33.7% |
| 5–6 years | 1.3 | 12.6 | 11.5 | 4.4 | 10.9 | 40.7% |
| Black total | 6.0% | 32.7% | 27.7% | 10.3% | 23.2% | 100.0% |

Source: Panel Study of Income Dynamics.

rates in excess of 20 percent) in their neighborhoods. The majority of white children, but less than 5 percent of black children, escape *both* family- and neighborhood-level poverty.

All in all, our look at multiyear patterns of poverty at the family and neighborhood levels magnifies the differences found in the more familiar single-year numbers. Most whites, but relatively few blacks, escape family-level poverty altogether. And among children in families that did manage to escape family-level poverty, relatively few whites, but most blacks, have substantial numbers of poor neighbors.

## SUMMARY AND CONCLUSIONS

Our use of data from six different data sets and our desire to generalize results across the six samples require that we adopt a common analytic framework. This framework involves a simple set of models with which researchers can provide descriptive associations between neighborhood characteristics and developmental outcomes, adjust those associations for the effects of correlated family-level influences, investigate whether family-process measures available in some of the data sets mediate the apparent neighborhood effects, estimate developmental models within resource-rich and resource-poor neighborhoods, and explore various threats to inferring causation from the adjusted correlations.

To test the effects of poor neighborhoods on the development of children and youth, we must operationalize variation in neighborhood characteristics in a conceptually and empirically sound way. This chapter also presents our theoretical and empirical approach to developing multiple-index measures of neighborhood structure and composition. We have been able to construct factors that represent important concepts from economic theory and social disorganization theory such as the concentrations of low-SES and high-SES neighbors and the levels of ethnic diversity and male joblessness in the neighborhood. Further, by standardizing measures of neighborhood conditions using a national norm generated from the PSID, we can compare and contrast the samples of neighborhoods from which our six data sets drew samples of subjects. The fruits of these efforts will be employed in subsequent chapters when the effects of neighborhood conditions (identically defined and measured) on outcomes at four distinct phases of development across several different data sets are reported.

Finally, race differences in neighborhood conditions of poverty and in the joint probability of experiencing persistent family poverty and neighborhood poverty are examined. The developmental contexts of the average black and white child are vastly different in contemporary America (Brooks-Gunn, Duncan, and Klebanov 1996). This fact, what Massey (1990) calls "American Apartheid," will influence our analytic strategy (all analyses will be conducted within race or ethnic group) and also our interpretation of results.

---

Work on this chapter was supported in part by grants from the National Institute of Mental Health (MH43084) and the Carnegie Corporation (B4850) awarded to Edward Seidman, J. Lawrence Aber, LaRue Allen, and Christina Mitchell. We express our appreciation to the adolescents and schools whose cooperation made this study possible.

## NOTES

1. In the case of the NLSY, the representativeness is of young mothers and of children born to those young mothers. In the case of the PSID, the representativeness is mothers and children of all ages.

2. Although Crane's neighborhood measure is of high-status workers, his interpretation is in the context of an "epidemic" model, in which the absence of such workers and the complementary presence of low-income neighbors may induce bad behavior.

# 4

# Neighborhood and Family Influences on the Intellectual and Behavioral Competence of Preschool and Early School-Age Children

*P. Lindsay Chase-Lansdale, Rachel A. Gordon,
Jeanne Brooks-Gunn, and Pamela K. Klebanov*

I n this chapter we examine neighborhood- and family-level effects on the functioning of preschool (three- and four-year-old) and early school-age (five- and six-year-old) children. We use data from the Children of the National Longitudinal Survey of Youth (NLSY), a survey of children based on a national survey of adolescents and young adults begun in 1979, and from the Infant Health and Development Program (IHDP), a large eight-site study of an early educational intervention for premature and low-birth-weight children and their parents.

## BACKGROUND

Developmentalists now recognize the importance of considering the ecological contexts of a growing child. Bronfenbrenner (1979) has long advocated for such an approach and has often used the contextual complexity of young children's worlds as an exemplar. Among the "ecosystems" or contexts central to preschoolers' and early school-age children's lives are the household, extended family, neighborhood, religious community, child-care setting, schools, and health system. In many of these contexts, both horizontal (that is, child–child) and vertical (that is, adult–child and older child–younger child) relationships blossom (Hartup 1989). While the family (parents, siblings, and extended family members) and the child-care setting have been considered important contextual contributors to the raising of children (see, for example, Brooks-Gunn and Chase-Lansdale 1991; Chase-Lansdale, Brooks-Gunn, and Zamsky 1994; Dunn 1983; Hayes, Palmer, and Zaslow 1990; Hofferth and Phillips 1991; Maccoby and Martin 1983; Stewart 1983), little research has examined the impact of the larger neighborhood environment on young children's development (but see Brooks-Gunn, Duncan et al. 1993; Chase-Lansdale and Gordon, 1996; Duncan, Brooks-Gunn, and Klebanov 1994).

Young children's encounters with contexts outside of the home begin slowly. In the earliest months of life, most children have somewhat limited contact with organized ecosystems outside the home, except for involvement with extended family, visits to health-care providers, or visits to a church or temple. However, mothers of infants are increasingly returning to the labor force, and infant day care is on the rise. About 17 percent of infants of working mothers were in center-based care in 1993 (Casper, 1996, 6). By the preschool years, significantly more children enter ecosystems outside the home through child-care participation. In 1993, 58 percent of mothers of preschool children were employed in the labor force (U.S. House of Representatives 1994, table 12-1). Thirty-nine percent of the three- to four-year-old children of these mothers were enrolled in center-based care or preschool, and 24 percent were cared for by a relative or nonrelative in a home other than their own (Casper 1996, 6). While much of this recent rise in child-care use for young children has been due to women's rising labor force participation, many young children are also exposed to contexts outside the home through preschool enrichment programs. For example, in 1993, an estimated 26 percent of three-year-olds and 41 percent of four-year-olds were enrolled in either publically or privately funded nursery school programs (Snyder 1996, 61).

Throughout the preschool period, the family is an important intermediary as young children venture into the neighborhood environment. Even when young children encounter contexts outside the home, such as through a trip to the neighborhood park or a visit to the local health clinic, parents limit and qualify the nature and extent of a child's experiences. Thus, especially for the youngest preschoolers, many influences of the neighborhood may operate through effects on the family context. Such indirect neighborhood effects are the focus of chapter 5.

The family remains a central force in children's lives during the first years of school, and many indirect effects of the neighborhood will continue to flow through the family. Yet, transitions to new contexts like kindergarten and first grade may result in increasingly direct effects of neighborhoods, at least some of which may be driven by interactions with adults and peers in these new contexts. In fact, 69 percent of children in the IHDP and 77 percent of children in the NLSY are enrolled in some form of regular schooling by age five or six. Furthermore, given children's increasing capabilities and desires for independence at the early school-age period, parents may allow children greater freedom in independent contacts with the neighborhood and with peers. In private time spent apart from parents in and near their own home settings (for example, a different room, hallways, front steps, or yards) or in visits to a friend's home, children are less beholden to the strict confines of parental decisions and supervision during contacts with their surroundings.

Still, parental perceptions of the risks and opportunities in the local community and of the child's maturity level will likely define the degree of *direct* exposure children have with their neighborhood. That is, just as some families may channel neighborhood effects, some families may serve as buffers, continually restricting direct exposure (Furstenberg 1993). For instance, in impoverished inner-city neighborhoods, young children may have differential exposure to physical danger, criminal activity, and drug use (Burton 1991; Ladner 1971). However, the choices that parents make in the face of such environmental dangers may also compromise development (Furstenberg 1993; Ladner 1971). Young children who must stay indoors for physical protection will likely have fewer opportunities for interactions with a range of peers and adults. Other parents with fewer resources of time, emotions, money, and social support may be less able to limit their children's exposure to environmental hazards. Moreover, some children in these families may "grow up quickly" with great responsibilities, concerns, and anxieties and with little time to devote to developmental tasks. In contrast, young children in impoverished suburban and rural areas may not be exposed to the daily physical dangers and anxieties found in some inner-city neighborhoods; however, some parents may be better than other parents at drawing on limited neighborhood resources to foster their children's development. Finally, in more affluent settings, parental effectiveness in identifying and accessing opportunities will influence the degree to which children can directly take advantage of more abundant neighborhood resources.

As children's contact with the neighborhood increases over the preschool and early school-age period, what mechanisms might underlie direct neighborhood effects? Past theoretical work has considered how neighborhoods might impact the lives of children and families, although most research has focused on older children and adolescents (for example, Crane 1991; Mayer and Jencks 1989; Wilson 1991a, 1991b). Five general frameworks can be used to organize these various theoretical approaches: (1) the *neighborhood resources* approach, which emphasizes the importance of public and private services in the neighborhood; (2) the *competition* approach, which focuses on how scarce resources must be sought and allocated; (3) the *collective socialization* approach, which examines how monitoring, supervising, and role modeling, not only in the family but within the larger neighborhood and community, influence children's development; (4) the *contagion* approach, which expects that the behavior of peers will greatly influence others' behavior; and (5) the *relative deprivation* approach, which suggests that children and family members evaluate how their personal situation is better or worse than their neighbors'.

We expect that direct neighborhood effects on young children will be first seen through the mechanisms of neighborhood resources and collective socialization. The presence of additional resources in the neighborhood may stimulate young children's development. For example, parks and libraries and a wide variety of children's programs, such as sports leagues and arts and crafts classes, supply ready opportunities for enriching experiences

outside the home. Other resources in the neighborhood, although not necessarily specifically targeted at children, may also provide a context that supports children's development. For example, avid police protection and
consequent lower levels of crime will likely facilitate families' and children's
visits with neighbors in streets, yards, and alleys and their use of local parks
and empty lots for recreation. In addition, the presence of accessible health
clinics and medical centers in the community may encourage regular check-
ups (Sampson 1992), thus fostering children's physical health and perhaps
also the early identification of developmental delays.

Collective socialization theories are based on the psychological literature on
parenting, supervision, and role models, as well as the sociological literature
on monitoring and social isolation. For example, Wilson (1991b) has posited
that living in neighborhoods in which families have few economic resources,
few individuals have jobs, few jobs are located in the neighborhood, and many
mothers are single may result in "social isolation." Furthermore, such neighborhoods may also be characterized by "social disorganization" (Sampson 1992;
Sampson and Groves 1989; Wilson 1994). These theories propose that
neighborhoods which are not isolated nor disorganized have high aggregate
levels of factors such as parental self-efficacy, emphasis on school and work
skills, and future orientation. In some such communities, neighbors may
encourage higher quality parenting and help supervise neighborhood children
(Garbarino and Crouter 1978; Garbarino and Sherman 1980). Among families
with young children, these parents might share ways to deal with persistent
temper tantrums, compare strategies for encouraging a child's budding talents,
or one parent might supervise a neighborhood outing to a nearby park.

The mechanisms of neighborhood resources and collective socialization
may become more prominent as children enter new child-care, preschool,
kindergarten, and formal school contexts over the preschool and early school-
age years. Here, children encounter a new set of adults, a greater range of
children, and self-selected friendships in classrooms. Not only will children
be exposed to new perspectives and supports from teachers and friends' parents, but their own parents may discover new social networks through the
child's enrollment in school and other organized activities (Steinberg 1989).
Through contact with other competent parents, a child's own parents may
gain new ideas about child rearing and ways of stimulating and supporting
their child's development. Finally, different children may create different
experiences in the same environment (Lerner 1982; Scarr and McCartney
1983). While the child's individual qualities may influence even the earliest
interactions with caregivers, during the early school-age period some children
will be more capable of eliciting and seeking out stimulating relationships and
experiences in these new contexts.

We anticipate that the effects of the final three mechanisms—contagion,
competition, and relative deprivation—will be less evident for preschool children but may begin to operate at the early school-age years as children come

into increasing contact with regular school contexts. Peers provide opportunities for children to deal with conflicts, disagreements, negotiations, and compromises and to express affection, consolation, and empathy. However, negative effects may occur as well. For instance, negative expectations and treatment by adults and teachers, as well as difficult interactions (like teasing and bullying) with peers, may lead some children not only to feel rejected but also to recognize what is lacking in their family and neighborhood. The effects of competition for scarce neighborhood resources may become stronger as parents try to enroll children in particular programs and schools with limited space. These competition effects may be accentuated in neighborhoods with a fairly dense concentration of young families.

As outlined in chapter 3, the SSRC Working Group has developed five measures of neighborhood characteristics, based on factor analyses of census-tract variables. The first two factors, the presence of impoverished and affluent neighbors, are seen as proxies for the mechanisms of neighborhood resources and collective socialization. Children and families living among fewer impoverished neighbors and more affluent neighbors are expected to have access to more of the benefits discussed earlier, such as parks, libraries, activities, health clinics, and local neighborhood support networks, as well as the constellation of factors associated with social organization in the community.

The third factor, male joblessness, may parallel the effects of impoverished neighbors, such as limited economic resources, strained mental health, and diminished parenting skills. In addition, the contrast of pervasive male joblessness in the neighborhood with larger societal values may become more salient when young children enter school. The fourth factor, the concentration of families within the neighborhood, may influence the degree to which families must compete for scarce resources. Furthermore, sheer crowdedness may potentiate feelings of anxiety and danger. Finally, the fifth factor, the diversity of ethnicity in the neighborhood, may provide opportunities either for young children's developing ethnic identity or for exposure to ethnic discrimination, depending to some degree on whether or not the majority of the neighborhood is of a similar or different racial and ethnic heritage as the child (see Chase-Lansdale and Gordon, 1996, for the application of a measure of the fraction of neighbors who are the same race as the child in a study of neighborhood effects on young children).

In sum, we expect both family- and neighborhood-level effects for preschool and early school-age children; however, direct neighborhood effects may be stronger in the early school age than in the preschool years. We expect further that the strongest and earliest direct neighborhood effects will be seen for the presence of impoverished and affluent neighbors. As early school-age children have broader exposure to contexts outside the home, especially through regular schooling, we anticipate we will also find effects of the concentration of families, level of male joblessness, and level of ethnic diversity in the neighborhood.

## METHOD AND DATA

As noted earlier, our analyses draw from the IHDP, a sample of primarily premature and low-birth-weight children, and the Children of the NLSY, a national survey of children.

### INFANT HEALTH AND DEVELOPMENT PROGRAM DATA SET

As detailed in the IHDP (1990) and Brooks-Gunn and associates (1992), the IHDP is an eight-site randomized clinical trial designed to test the efficacy of educational and family-support services and high-quality pediatric follow-up, offered in the first three years of life, in reducing the incidence of developmental delay in low-birth-weight (LBW), preterm infants. Six of the centers were located in large metropolitan areas with large populations of poor families, and two were located in metropolitan areas serving both urban and rural communities. The clinical trial and even the study's focus on LBW babies are incidental to our desire to understand the nature of neighborhood effects.[1] For our purposes, the most important feature of the data is the high-quality measurement of children's developmental outcomes; maternal mental health; and the family's structure, economic status, support systems, and home environment. The IHDP is a longitudinal data set, and assessments were conducted on the same children at age three and then age five.

Since infants chosen for inclusion in the study may not be representative of all infants, it is important to spell out the sample selection process. Infants weighing no more than 2,500 grams at birth and of thirty-seven weeks or less gestational age were screened for eligibility[2] if they were forty weeks postconceptional age between January 7, 1985, and October 9, 1985, and were born in one of eight participating medical institutions (see this chapter's acknowledgements). The research design included stratification by clinical site and into birth-weight groups (lighter-birth-weight preterm infants weighed 2,000 grams or less, and heavier-birth-weight preterm infants weighed 2,001 to 2,500 grams). Stratification assured a two to one balance of the lighter- to heavier-birth-weight group within each site.

Of the 1,302 infants who met enrollment criteria, 274 (21 percent) were eliminated because consent was refused, and 43 were withdrawn before entry into their assigned group. This resulted in a total sample of 985 infants, and attrition from this remaining sample was low—7 percent of the 985 infants at the thirty-six-month assessment (IHDP 1990). So that characteristics of the census tract or enumeration district in which the child resided could be attached to the data, the child's address at the time of randomization was geocoded. Ninety-one percent ($N = 895$) of the total sample of infants had addresses that were successfully matched to census tract or enumeration district. Finally, a sample of Hispanic children were excluded from these analyses, since the number of these children was small ($N = 105$ in the sample at the time of recruitment and 101 whose addresses could be geocoded).[3] This resulted in a final analytic sample of 793 subjects—489 (62 percent) African American and 304 (38 percent) white.

INITIAL STATUS AND DESIGN VARIABLES   The eight IHDP sites varied on a number of dimensions (see table 4.1 [Brooks-Gunn, McCarton, Casey, McCormick et al. 1994; IHDP 1990, table 2, 3037; McCarton, Brooks-Gunn, Wallace et al. 1997]); thus, seven dummy variables were created to control for study site.[4] Treatment status (*intervention* = 1, *follow-up* = 0) was also controlled.[5]

In addition, two initial status variables, the child's birth weight and neonatal health, were controlled because of their significant associations with child outcomes. That is, children born at lower birth weights (less than 2,500 grams) are at greater risk for school failure and low cognitive scores (Grunau 1986; Hoy, Bill, and Sykes 1988; Klebanov, Brooks-Gunn, and McCormick 1994b; Klein et al. 1985; McCormick 1989; Nickel, Forrest, and Lamson 1982; Vohr and Coll 1985) and behavior problems (Benasich, Brooks-Gunn, and McCormick forthcoming; Klebanov, Brooks-Gunn, and McCormick 1994a; Klein 1988; McCormick et al. 1992; McCormick, Gortmacker, and Sobol 1990) than normal-birth-weight children. Similarly, children who are sicker at birth also have lower cognitive scores (Klein et al. 1985; Scott et al. 1989) and more behavioral problems (Scott et al. 1989). Thus, regression models control for the child's birth weight (in grams)[6] and neonatal health index, a measure that standardized the length of stay for the neonatal hospitalization by the child's birth weight (Scott et al. 1989). The recorded neonatal stay was based on hospital discharge records.

CHILD OUTCOME MEASURES   We examined two broad domains of development—cognitive and behavioral functioning. At both age three and age five, receptive English vocabulary and verbal ability were measured using the Peabody Picture Vocabulary Test-Revised (PPVT-R; Dunn and Dunn 1981). The PPVT-R requires the child to indicate (by words or gestures) which of four pictures on a page best illustrates a vocabulary word the examiner says. In the IHDP, because three years of age is about the earliest age at which the test can be administered, the PPVT-R was censored at a score of 40 (that is, scores less than 40 were assigned a value of 40 for data analytic purposes). At age three, two children had censored scores, and at age five, thirty-seven children had censored scores.

In addition, cognitive functioning was tested at each age with a standard scale of intelligence: at age three, with the Stanford-Binet Intelligence Scale Form L-M, third edition, corrected for prematurity (Terman and Merrill 1973), and at age five, with the Wechsler Preschool and Primary Scale of Intelligence (WPPSI; Wechsler 1967), both of which are age appropriate. The Stanford-Binet is the most widely used intelligence test for three-year-olds (Anastasi 1988; Sattler 1988), and the WPPSI was developed for use with children

*(Text continues on page 88.)*

TABLE 4.1 Baseline Characteristics (Before Randomization) of the Primary Analysis Group

| Baseline Characteristic | Site* | | | | | | | |
|---|---|---|---|---|---|---|---|---|
| | Arkansas | Einstein | Harvard | Miami | Pennsylvania | Texas | Washington | Yale |
| Birth weight, g (mean ± SD) | | | | | | | | |
| Intervention group | 1861.0 ± 429.1 | 1785.3 ± 427.6 | 1741.2 ± 455.0 | 1727.1 ± 492.7 | 1920.9 ± 422.3 | 1754.3 ± 395.4 | 1810.6 ± 432.5 | 1947.8 ± 434.2 |
| Follow-up group | 1817.0 ± 437.1 | 1837.9 ± 420.9 | 1761.7 ± 466.0 | 1682.4 ± 586.3 | 1810.4 ± 466.8 | 1746.3 ± 440.9 | 1842.6 ± 455.8 | 1719.9 ± 504.3 |
| Gestational age, wk (mean ± SD) | | | | | | | | |
| Intervention group | 33.1 ± 2.3 | 32.6 ± 2.5 | 33.1 ± 2.8 | 32.6 ± 2.3 | 33.6 ± 2.7 | 32.6 ± 2.8 | 33.1 ± 2.5 | 33.3 ± 2.2 |
| Follow-up group | 33.0 ± 2.5 | 32.8 ± 2.5 | 32.7 ± 2.9 | 32.7 ± 2.6 | 33.7 ± 2.7 | 33.2 ± 2.8 | 33.5 ± 3.1 | 32.7 ± 3.0 |
| Neonatal Health Index‡ (mean ± SD) | | | | | | | | |
| Intervention group | 100.5 ± 16.4 | 104.2 ± 14.1 | 100.9 ± 14.2 | 103.0 ± 15.0 | 99.8 ± 15.8 | 98.4 ± 19.2 | 101.4 ± 15.9 | 97.3 ± 16.4 |
| Follow-up group | 99.7 ± 15.7 | 97.8 ± 16.5 | 99.6 ± 16.7 | 97.7 ± 16.3 | 100.1 ± 16.1 | 100.9 ± 13.9 | 99.2 ± 16.1 | 101.8 ± 15.4 |
| Maternal age, y (mean ± SD) | | | | | | | | |
| Intervention group | 23.3 ± 4.5 | 24.8 ± 6.1 | 26.4 ± 5.9 | 22.7 ± 6.1 | 24.3 ± 5.8 | 22.0 ± 6.0 | 26.3 ± 5.4 | 26.9 ± 5.9 |
| Follow-up group | 24.5 ± 5.9 | 25.7 ± 6.5 | 27.7 ± 5.7 | 22.7 ± 5.2 | 22.8 ± 5.7 | 21.4 ± 5.0 | 27.3 ± 5.7 | 25.7 ± 5.8 |
| Maternal education‡ (mean ± SD) | | | | | | | | |
| Intervention group | 1.8 ± 0.8 | 1.7 ± 0.9 | 2.2 ± 0.8 | 1.5 ± 0.7 | 1.7 ± 0.8 | 1.6 ± 0.6 | 2.1 ± 0.9 | 2.3 ± 0.8 |
| Follow-up group | 2.0 ± 0.8 | 1.8 ± 0.9 | 2.5 ± 0.7 | 1.5 ± 0.7 | 1.9 ± 0.8 | 1.4 ± 0.6 | 2.2 ± 0.8 | 2.3 ± 0.8 |

|  | | | | | | | | |
|---|---|---|---|---|---|---|---|---|
| Gender, % M | | | | | | | | |
| Intervention group | 47.9 | 50.0 | 48.9 | 52.3 | 47.9 | 49.0 | 49.0 | 54.3 |
| Follow-up group | 47.5 | 50.0 | 48.4 | 50.0 | 41.5 | 40.9 | 50.0 | 62.1 |
| Maternal race, % | | | | | | | | |
| Black | | | | | | | | |
| Intervention group | 54.2 | 41.3 | 40.0 | 77.3 | 95.8 | 69.4 | 23.5 | 26.1 |
| Follow-up group | 52.5 | 47.8 | 31.2 | 80.4 | 94.3 | 71.6 | 16.3 | 45.5 |
| Hispanic | | | | | | | | |
| Intervention group | 2.1 | 39.1 | 6.7 | 11.4 | 0.0 | 14.3 | 2.0 | 4.3 |
| Follow-up group | 0.0 | 40.2 | 6.5 | 14.3 | 1.9 | 14.8 | 2.5 | 1.5 |
| White/other | | | | | | | | |
| Intervention group | 43.7 | 19.6 | 53.3 | 11.4 | 4.2 | 16.3 | 74.5 | 69.6 |
| Follow-up group | 47.5 | 12.0 | 62.4 | 5.4 | 3.8 | 13.6 | 81.3 | 53.0 |

Note: From "Enhancing the Outcomes of Low-Birth-Weight, Premature Infants: A Multisite Randomized Trial by the Infant Health and Development Program." 1990. *Journal of the American Medical Association* 263(22):3037. Copyright 1990 by the American Medical Association. Reprinted with permission.

* For full names of sites, see the list of participating universities.

† Neonatal Health Index is a score standardized to a mean of 100, with high scores signifying better health (Scott, Bauer, Kraemer, and Tyson 1989).

‡ Maternal education is measured on a three-point scale, where 1 indicates less than high school graduate; 2, high school graduate; and 3, some college or more.

between the ages of four and six and a half years. The reliability of the three WPPSI measures of IQ—verbal IQ, performance IQ, and full-scale IQ—range from 0.93 to 0.96 (Sattler 1988). We focus here primarily on the WPPSI verbal IQ score.

The measurement of cognitive ability in young children is highly predictive of their later success in school. Preschool verbal ability (measured by the PPVT-R) is predictive of literacy scores as much as fifteen years later, even after controlling for the effects of educational, social, and economic well-being (Baydar, Brooks-Gunn, and Furstenberg 1993). Similarly, preschool cognitive and verbal ability are predictive of dropping out of high school (Brooks-Gunn, Guo, and Furstenberg 1993).

Behavioral functioning is measured in the IHDP by two standard, age-appropriate scales of behavioral competence: at age three, the Child Behavior Checklist for Ages 2–3 (CBCL/2–3; Achenbach, Edelbrock, and Howell 1987), a ninety-nine-item questionnaire; and at age five, the Revised Child Behavior Profile for Ages 4–5 (CBP/4–5; Achenbach and Edelbrock 1984), a 120-item questionnaire. The CBCL/2–3 has adequate reliability and validity (Achenbach, Edelbrock, and Howell 1987; Spiker et al. forthcoming). In both scales, mothers rate the degree to which statements are *not true* (0), *often true* (1), or *very true* (2) of their child's behavior. For three-year-olds, mothers are instructed to consider the child's behavior during the past two months; for five-year-olds, the time period is the past six months. Factor analyses of each scale have revealed two broad factors—internalizing (for instance, too fearful or anxious, unhappy, sad, or depressed) and externalizing (for example, destroys his or her own things; has temper tantrums or a hot temper). Higher scores on the CBCL/2–3 and CBP/4–5 indicate more behavior problems. Behavior problems reported as early as two years of age are highly correlated with reports in early childhood (Brooks-Gunn, Klebanov et al. 1993), which in turn are highly correlated with problems reported at school age (Duncan, Brooks-Gunn, and Klebanov 1994).

INDIVIDUAL AND FAMILY-LEVEL MEASURES    IHDP family-level independent variables used in the analysis are: the child's gender (coded *male* = 1, *female* = 0), race (*African American* = 1, *white* = 0), the mother's completed schooling (in years), whether the family was headed by the mother (*female headship* = 1, *other* = 0), maternal age at birth (*less than nineteen years* = 1, *other* = 0), maternal employment (two dummy variables—*full-time* = 1, *other* = 0; *part-time* = 1, *other* = 0, with *unemployed* as the comparison), and family income to needs (see description next paragraph). In addition, for five-year-olds, whether the child was in school (*in school* = 1, *not in school* = 0) is added as a control variable.[7]

The family's income was obtained in each of the three or five years of the child's life. Respondents were asked to provide an estimate of the total family income in a series of categories. For analyses, these categorical responses were reassigned with the midpoint of the interval.[8] Then, for each year, a family income-to-needs ratio was computed by dividing each household's income by the corresponding poverty threshold for a household of that size. By definition, an income-to-needs ratio of 1.0 indicates that a family's income is equal to the poverty threshold. For example, in 1991 children (as well as other family members) living in a four-person household whose income totaled $41,772 would have an income-to-needs ratio of 3.0 ($41,772/$13,924), and would be considered nonpoor for that year. Members of a four-person household with a total household income of only $6,962 would have an income-to-needs ratio of 0.5 and would be designated as poor. For analyses, income-to-needs ratios were averaged over the three or five years of the child's life (that is, when the child was one, two, and three years old; when the child was one, two, three, four, and five years old).

## CHILDREN OF THE NATIONAL LONGITUDINAL SURVEY OF YOUTH (NLSY)

SAMPLE    The Children of the NLSY includes over seven thousand children ranging in age from infancy through late adolescence who have been assessed bienially since 1986. (For a more detailed discussion of the Children of the NLSY, see Chase-Lansdale et al. [1991].) We restrict our analyses to children who were aged three or four (preschool) and aged five or six (early school age) in 1986.[9] It should be emphasized that unlike the IHDP data, which are longitudinal, the data presented here from the Children of the NLSY are cross-sectional. Thus, in the NLSY, the five- to six-year-olds are different children from the three- to four-year-olds, while the IHDP five-year-olds are the same children as the IHDP three-year-olds.

For these analyses, we select only those children whose usual residence is with their mothers (1,148 of 1,178 preschoolers; 883 of 919 early school-age children), and for consistency with the IHDP analytic sample, we exclude Hispanics. In addition, 10 preschoolers and 18 early school-age children whose family addresses, taken from the 1986 interview, could not be geocoded are omitted from these analyses. Thus, the sample for this chapter comprises 882 preschoolers (332 African American, 550 white) and 697 early school-age children (299 African American, 398 white).

The NLSY is one of a series of surveys, the National Longitudinal Surveys of Labor Market Experience (NLS), funded by the U.S. Department of Labor, whose central goal is to determine the causes and consequences of employment in the United States. The surveys are conducted by the National Opinion Research Center (NORC) at the University of Chicago, for the Center for Human Resource Research at the Ohio State University. The NLSY is a probability sample of over twelve thousand youth first assessed in 1979 when they were between the ages of fourteen and twenty-one. An untapped resource in the NLSY became apparent in the early 1980s: the children born to the female respondents. Assessment of these Children of the NLSY began in 1986 funded by the National Institute of Child Health and Human Development, the Foundation for Child Development, and the William T. Grant Foundation. Along with the annual NLSY questionnaires covering areas such as marital and fertility history, educational and labor force experience, income and assets, and health limitations, the biennial child supplements consist of assessments of the cognitive, socioemotional, and physical development of the child (Chase-Lansdale et al. 1991).

A major issue in planning for the Children of the NLSY involved how to balance the costs of such large-scale child assessments with the need for high-quality data. Extensive consultation with a technical advisory board including child assessment and child development experts and representatives of various funding agencies ensued. In considering various well-established measures, criteria for selection centered on issues including child–interviewer rapport and the ease of training nonpsychologist field personnel; testing conditions and sensitivity to cultural, racial, and economic diversity; the need for relatively brief assessments requiring little equipment; and the need to assess children from a wide age range on a broad set of dimensions. Several field tests followed, and final assessments were selected, sometimes "short forms" of well-established assessment batteries. (See also Baker and Mott [1989] for extensive discussion of the training of interviewers and fielding of the study.)

While the NLSY youth were representative of all U.S. fourteen- to twenty-one-year-olds in 1979, the children of female respondents in 1986 are not fully representative of all U.S. children. Rather, the children represent children born to a nationally representative sample of women aged twenty-one to twenty-eight years on January 1, 1986. In the 1986 wave, the Children of the NLSY respondents might be regarded as "the first 40 percent of child-bearing in a reasonably contemporary cohort of American women" (Baker and Mott 1989, 19). Thus, the oldest children in the 1986 wave have mothers who were younger at the child's birth. For example, all children over age eleven in 1986 were born to mothers aged eighteen or younger at the child's birth. Although still important, this predominance of young motherhood lessens for children who were younger in 1986. Below age six, less than half of children were born to teenage mothers. Thus, while representative of young mothers, the NLSY in 1986 is not representative of mothers across the full range of childbearing years.[10]

Finally, the appropriate sampling weights must be used to make statistics from the NLSY youth representative of all youth aged fourteen to twenty-one in 1979, and to make statistics from the Children of the NLSY, 1986 wave, representative of children born to women aged twenty-one to twenty-eight years on January 1, 1986. The sampling weights are required due to over-sampling of African American, Hispanic, and economically disadvantaged whites in the original NLSY to permit statistically reliable comparisons by race, ethnicity, and SES. The sampling weights also adjust for attrition and nonresponse to the child assessments (although not for differential non-response across particular assessments). Sampling weights are used in all analyses of the NLSY reported in this chapter.

CHILD OUTCOME MEASURES    As just discussed for the IHDP, we explored two broad domains of children's development—intellectual and behavioral functioning. The NLSY, like the IHDP, uses the Peabody Picture Vocabulary Test (PPVT)[11] to assess children's verbal ability (PPVT-R; Dunn and Dunn 1981). The PPVT-R was standardized on a nationally representative sample of forty-two hundred children sampled in 1979 (Dunn and Dunn 1981). While the NLSY assigned a zero to raw scores that are linked to a standard score below 40, we chose to substitute the actual standard score for these scores using the PPVT Supplementary Norms Table (Dunn and Dunn 1981). Only five preschool children and eight early school-age children had PPVT standard scores less than 40.

For preschoolers, we consider only verbal ability; but for early school-age children, two additional measures of the child's intellectual functioning are available—the Peabody Individual Achievement Tests (PIAT) of Reading Recognition and Mathematics (Dunn and Markwardt 1970). These PIAT tests are among the most widely used brief assessments of academic achievement (Sattler 1988). Reading recognition assesses a child's word recognition and pronunciation ability. Skills tapped include matching letters, naming names, and reading single words aloud. The child reads a word silently and then says it aloud. The PIAT Mathematics assessment measures a child's attainment in mathematics as taught in mainstream education. For young children, skills such as recognizing numbers are assessed. The child examines each problem and then points to or names one of four options as his or her answer. Both the PIAT Reading and PIAT Math assessments were normed in the late 1960s on a national sample of 2,887 kindergarten through twelfth-grade children (Dunn and Markwardt 1970). The revised version of the PIAT has not been administered in this sample.

Because the Children of the NLSY are disproportionately born to poor, young, minority mothers, their scores on these measures of intellectual functioning are expected to be somewhat lower than the national average. While the mean PPVT score for all NLSY children is substantially lower than the average PPVT score in the norming sample, both the PIAT Reading and PIAT Math scores of NLSY children are highly similar to their respective norming samples. This differential performance on the PIAT and PPVT assessments may be due to the difference of at least a decade between the creation of the norms (Baker and Mott 1989) or to some other factors.

Behavioral functioning in the Children of the NLSY was measured using the Behavior Problems Index (BPI), which was developed by Zill and Peterson to assess behavior problems in children aged four to seventeen years (see Baker, Keck, Mott, and Quinlan 1993; Peterson and Zill 1986). Thus, we have data on behavioral functioning for all early school-age children, but only for the four-year-old preschoolers. Items were drawn primarily from a measure of behavioral functioning used in the IHDP data set, the Child Behavior Checklist (Achenbach and Edelbrock 1981). The BPI consists of twenty-eight questions in which the mother indicates whether a statement is *often true, sometimes true,* or *not true* of her child's behavior over the past three months. The BPI was standardized using the National Health Survey of fifteen thousand respondents, and those norms were used to convert the NLSY raw scores to standard scores (Zill 1988, 1990). The mean of the NLSY ($x$ = 109 overall) is higher than the national average of 100.

As in the IHDP, we chose to focus on two broad bands of behavior problems—internalizing and externalizing problems. We drew on the national survey of problem behaviors by Achenbach and associates (1991) in constructing the internalizing and externalizing scales for the BPI. In their survey, Achenbach and colleagues developed a new measure, the ACQ (Achenbach, Conners, and Quay) Behavior Checklist by drawing items from sources similar to those used in developing the BPI. Indeed, although the BPI is a shorter scale, most BPI items correspond directly to items in the ACQ Behavior Checklist (see table 5.8.1 in Baker et al. 1993, 217–18; table 2 in Achenbach et al. 1991, 10–11). We identified seven internalizing (for example, unhappy, sad, or depressed; feels no one loves him or her; cries too much) and ten externalizing (for example, disobedient at home; bullies; has strong temper) items in the BPI.[12] We verified the two dimensions with an exploratory factor analysis of the seventeen items (data not shown). However, two externalizing items were asked only of children in school (namely, disobedient at school, has trouble getting along with teachers). For comparable measures between children who were in and out of school, we chose to omit these two items from the raw total used in these analyses.[13] Thus, the internalizing scale was computed as the simple sum of seven items, and the externalizing scale as the simple sum of eight items.[14] A higher score indicates a greater degree of problem behaviors. The two scales show adequate internal consistency levels (Cronbach's alpha of 0.62 for internalizing and 0.77 for the externalizing dimension).

INDIVIDUAL AND FAMILY-LEVEL MEASURES    Variables included in the analyses were the following: the child's gender (coded *male* = 1, *female* = 0), the child's age (months), race (*African American* = 1, *white* = 0), the mother's completed schooling as of May 1 in the survey year (in years; 0 to 18), whether the family was headed by the mother (*female headship* = 1; *mother married or cohabiting with a male partner* = 0). In addition, two dummy variables coded the mother's age at the birth of her first child and at the age of the study child (if not also the first child). In particular, the first dummy equaled 1 if the mother was age eighteen years or younger at the study child's birth (whether or not she had previously been a teen mother); the second dummy variable equaled 1 if the mother was eighteen or younger at an earlier birth but not at the study child's birth. Thus, a mother with a 0 on both variables was never a teenage mother. Maternal employment was coded using three dummy variables. The first variable indicated that the mother was working 1 to 19 hours during the survey week, the second that the mother was working 20 to 29 hours during the survey week, and the third that the mother was working 30 or more hours during the survey week. Mothers who were not working during the survey week were coded a 0 on all three variables. In addition, for early school-age children, whether the child was enrolled in regular school during the survey week was added as a control (1 = *child enrolled in school*; 0 = *child not enrolled in school*).

A family income-to-needs ratio was also used in these analyses. First, family income,[15] including income from an opposite-sex cohabiting partner, for each of the three, four, five, or six years of the child's life, was converted to 1986 dollars using the consumer price index (CPI). Then, the average family income was calculated over these three, four, five, or six years of the child's life.[16] Finally, the family income-to-needs ratio was calculated by dividing this average family income by the appropriate 1986 poverty threshold, given the number of adults and children in the family in 1986 (see discussion of IHDP family measures for an example).

While the IHDP is a sample of LBW preterm infants, only 8 percent of preschoolers and 7 percent of early school-age children in the NLSY weighed less than 2,500 grams at birth.

## RESULTS

### FIVE-FACTOR NEIGHBORHOOD MODEL

In the analyses in this chapter we are able to meet several conditions thought to be important when exploring neighborhood effects (Bronfenbrenner, Moen, and Garbarino 1984; Mayer and Jencks 1989; Steinberg 1989). For example, controlling simultaneously for several neighborhood qualities that are tapped through five factors allows us to test separate neighborhood effects. In addition, three interactions of individual-level and contextual variables are also pursued, whether the pattern of significant neighborhood effects differs by the age, race, and gender of the child, and we touch on possible nonlinear effects of neighborhoods.

Three sets of regressions were run for each measure of children's intellectual and behavioral functioning. The first set (model 1) includes only the five neighborhood factors. The second set (model 2) includes only the family-level measures of family structure, economic status, maternal characteristics, child's school status, race, and gender. The third set (model 3) then considers the neighborhood-level and family-level characteristics simultaneously.[17] These three sets of regressions were run for the total sample and by the racial and gender subgroups. Results for the subgroups control for either race or gender, depending on which subgroup is presented. In the following discussion, we focus primarily on the significance of neighborhood-level variables in the third model, noting results for the full sample on the first and second models. (The additional models are available from the authors upon request.)

PRESCHOOL CHILDREN

INTELLECTUAL FUNCTIONING IN THE FULL SAMPLE   Table 4.2 provides the effect of neighborhood-level characteristics on preschool children's (that is, three- and four-year-olds') intellectual functioning, without controlling for family-level characteristics. We find the greatest consistency across outcomes and data sets for the effect of impoverished neighbors, where children who live among more impoverished neighbors have lower IQ scores (IHDP) and lower PPVT scores (IHDP and NLSY). In the IHDP, the presence of affluent neighbors is related to higher IQ and PPVT scores, and increased ethnic diversity in the neighborhood is related to lower IQ scores. In contrast, in the NLSY, a higher concentration of families in the neighborhood is associated with lower PPVT scores.

When we examine family-level effects before controlling for neighborhood-level characteristics (see table 4.3), we find that in all models the family income-to-needs ratio and mother's education are associated with higher IQ scores (IHDP) and higher PPVT scores (IHDP and NLSY), and African American children have lower IQ scores (IHDP) and PPVT scores (IHDP and NLSY) than do white children.

TABLE 4.2   Effects of Neighborhood Characteristics on Children's Intellectual Functioning at Ages Three to Four

|  | IHDP Stanford Binet IQ Scores | IHDP PPVT Standard Scores | NLSY PPVT Standard Scores |
|---|---|---|---|
| Neighborhood factors |  |  |  |
| Low SES | −3.62* | −3.12* | −6.35* |
|  | (1.17) | (1.07) | (0.97) |
| High SES | 4.91* | 3.31* | −0.02 |
|  | (1.10) | (1.01) | (1.01) |
| Male joblessness | −0.01 | −0.62 | −1.12 |
|  | (0.95) | (0.87) | (0.81) |
| Family concentration | 0.45 | 0.61 | −1.61* |
|  | (0.69) | (0.63) | (0.70) |
| Ethnic diversity | −1.23* | −0.59 | −1.15 |
|  | (0.38) | (0.35) | (0.75) |
| $N$ | 681 | 627 | 785 |
| Adjusted $R^2$ | 0.28 | 0.29 | 0.16 |
| Mean of $Y$ | 88.87 | 87.79 | 92.12 |
| (Stnd. dev.) | (19.74) | (17.48) | (18.37) |

*Indicates coefficient is more than twice its standard error.

TABLE 4.3   Effects of Family Characteristics on Children's Intellectual Functioning at Ages
            Three to Four

| | IHDP<br>Stanford Binet<br>IQ Scores | IHDP<br>PPVT Standard<br>Scores | NLSY<br>PPVT Standard<br>Scores |
|---|---|---|---|
| Family characteristics | | | |
| Family income/needs | 3.52* | 2.65* | 2.28* |
| | (0.51) | (0.46) | (0.59) |
| Female head | 0.16 | 0.73 | 1.56 |
| | (1.36) | (1.24) | (1.50) |
| Mother's education | 1.12* | 0.78* | 1.97* |
| | (0.32) | (0.29) | (0.39) |
| Teenage mother at study | 1.20 | −3.45* | −0.93 |
| child's birth | (1.74) | (1.58) | (1.80) |
| Teenage mother at a pre- | | | −1.21 |
| vious birth (NLSY) | | | (1.57) |
| Mother's employment | | | |
| 30–39 hrs/week (NLSY) | 1.41 | 1.55 | −2.22 |
| or full-time (IHDP) | (1.42) | (1.29) | (1.25) |
| 20–29 hrs/week (NLSY) | 1.07 | 2.48 | −0.26 |
| or part-time (IHDP) | (1.70) | (1.55) | (1.98) |
| 1–19 hrs/week (NLSY) | | | −0.76 |
| | | | (2.26) |
| Child is African | −10.19* | −10.43* | −21.05* |
| American | (1.64) | (1.49) | (1.57) |
| Child is male | −2.28 | 0.84 | −3.10* |
| | (1.19) | (1.08) | (1.11) |
| Age in months | | | −0.07 |
| (NLSY) | | | (0.08) |
| N | 681 | 627 | 785 |
| Adjusted $R^2$ | 0.40 | 0.42 | 0.30 |
| Mean of Y | 88.87 | 87.79 | 92.19 |
| (Stnd. dev.) | (19.74) | (17.48) | (18.32) |

*Indicates coefficient is more than twice its standard error.

The joint models testing the neighborhood-level and family-level characteristics simultaneously (see table 4.4) find that only the positive effect between the presence of affluent neighbors and children's IQ scores (IHDP)
remains significant at the neighborhood level. In contrast, at the family level,
the effects of family income, mother's educational level, and the child's race
are significant in all models.

In terms of variance explained, we find that the neighborhood-level-alone
models explain approximately 50 percent to 70 percent as much variance as
the family-level-alone models. When the neighborhood-level and family-
level characteristics are run simultaneously, little additional variance is
explained over that in the family-level-alone models. However, the set of
neighborhood variables does contribute significantly to the model for the
NLSY ($F = 3.69$, $p = .003$).

TABLE 4.4    Effects of Neighborhood and Family Characteristics on Children's Intellectual Functioning at Ages Three to Four

| | IHDP Stanford Binet IQ Scores | IHDP PPVT Standard Scores | NLSY PPVT Standard Scores |
|---|---|---|---|
| Neighborhood factors | | | |
| Low SES | −0.09 | 0.10 | −1.51 |
| | (1.14) | (1.04) | (1.01) |
| High SES | 2.45* | 1.24 | 0.09 |
| | (1.04) | (0.95) | (0.94) |
| Male joblessness | 0.20 | −0.43 | −0.68 |
| | (0.87) | (0.79) | (0.74) |
| Family concentration | 0.71 | 0.83 | −1.16 |
| | (0.63) | (0.57) | (0.65) |
| Ethnic diversity | −0.58 | −0.07 | −1.32 |
| | (0.35) | (0.32) | (0.69) |
| Family characteristics | | | |
| Family income/needs | 3.12* | 2.42* | 2.30* |
| | (0.52) | (0.48) | (0.60) |
| Female head | −0.08 | 0.69 | 2.17 |
| | (1.36) | (1.24) | (1.51) |
| Mother's education | 1.01* | 0.75* | 1.85* |
| | (0.32) | (0.29) | (0.39) |
| Teenage mother at study child's birth | 1.10 | −3.38* | −1.06 |
| | (1.74) | (1.58) | (1.80) |
| Teenage mother at a previous birth (NLSY) | | | −1.37 |
| | | | (1.57) |
| Mother's employment | | | |
| 30–39 hrs/week (NLSY) or full-time (IHDP) | 1.51 | 1.51 | −2.04 |
| | (1.42) | (1.29) | (1.26) |
| 20–29 hrs/week (NLSY) or part-time (IHDP) | 0.89 | 2.33 | −0.32 |
| | (1.70) | (1.55) | (1.97) |
| 1–19 hrs/week (NLSY) | | | −0.67 |
| | | | (2.26) |
| Child is African American | −10.14* | −10.17* | −17.51* |
| | (1.83) | (1.67) | (1.88) |
| Child is male | −2.26 | 0.86 | −3.16* |
| | (1.19) | (1.08) | (1.11) |
| Age in months (NLSY) | | | −0.05 |
| | | | (0.08) |
| N | 681 | 627 | 779 |
| Adjusted $R^2$ | 0.41 | 0.42 | 0.31 |
| Mean of Y | 88.87 | 87.79 | 92.20 |
| (Stnd. dev.) | (19.74) | (17.48) | (18.37) |

*Indicates coefficient is more than twice its standard error.

INTELLECTUAL FUNCTIONING BY RACE    Table 4.5 presents the previous joint regression models from table 4.4, but conducted separately for African Americans and whites. At the neighborhood level, the link between the presence of affluent neighbors and children's IQ scores is evident only for white children in the IHDP. In addition, in the NLSY, we now find that a higher level

TABLE 4.5    Effects of Neighborhood and Family Characteristics on Children's Intellectual Functioning at Ages Three to Four, by Race

| | IHDP Stanford Binet IQ Scores | | NLSY PPVT Standard Scores | |
|---|---|---|---|---|
| | White | Black | White | Black |
| Neighborhood factors | | | | |
| Low SES | 2.15 | −0.79 | −1.54 | −0.76 |
| | (2.42) | (1.34) | (1.65) | (1.27) |
| High SES | 3.03⁺ | 1.12 | 0.38 | −0.98 |
| | (1.53) | (1.64) | (1.18) | (1.78) |
| Male joblessness | −2.03 | 1.10 | −1.20 | −0.27 |
| | (1.59) | (1.04) | (1.01) | (1.03) |
| Family concentration | −0.20 | 0.73 | −1.07 | −1.79 |
| | (1.13) | (0.80) | (0.88) | (0.94) |
| Ethnic diversity | −1.20 | −0.14 | −2.17* | 1.15 |
| | (0.94) | (0.41) | (1.01) | (1.03) |
| Family characteristics | | | | |
| Family income/needs | 2.88* | 2.66* | 2.73* | 0.64 |
| | (0.71) | (0.92) | (0.72) | (1.29) |
| Female head | 2.71 | −1.72 | 2.10 | 1.21 |
| | (2.91) | (1.52) | (2.06) | (2.05) |
| Mother's education | 1.47* | 0.37 | 1.56* | 2.04* |
| | (0.55) | (0.40) | (0.49) | (0.67) |
| Teenage mother at study | −0.69 | −0.13 | 0.15 | −4.44 |
| child's birth | (4.68) | (1.78) | (2.28) | (3.00) |
| Teenage mother at a pre- | | | −2.49 | 1.86 |
| vious birth (NLSY) | | | (2.04) | (2.44) |
| Mother's employment | | | | |
| 30–39 hrs/week (NLSY) or | 3.32 | 1.50 | −1.59 | −2.43 |
| full-time (IHDP) | (2.60) | (1.78) | (1.60) | (2.16) |
| 20–29 hrs/week (NLSY) or | 3.81 | −1.04 | 0.09 | −0.56 |
| part-time (IHDP) | (2.83) | (2.16) | (2.34) | (4.38) |
| 1–19 hrs/week (NLSY) | | | −1.40 | 3.88 |
| | | | (2.63) | (6.25) |
| Child is male | −0.88 | −2.80* | −3.11* | −2.92 |
| | (2.21) | (1.39) | (1.38) | (1.88) |
| Age in months (NLSY) | | | 0.07 | −0.45* |
| | | | (0.10) | (0.14) |
| N | 269 | 412 | 495 | 284 |
| Adjusted $R^2$ | 0.30 | 0.22 | 0.11 | 0.11 |
| Mean of Y | 100.11 | 81.86 | 96.62 | 74.36 |
| (Stnd. dev.) | (20.52) | (15.58) | (16.01) | (16.36) |

*Indicates coefficient is more than twice its standard error. ⁺indicates $t < 2.0$, but $p < .05$.

of ethnic diversity is associated with lower PPVT scores for white, but not African American, children. No significant neighborhood-level effects were found for children's PPVT scores in the IHDP (data not shown). In these same models, we again find positive effects of the family's income-to-needs ratio and mother's educational level across most outcomes.

INTELLECTUAL FUNCTIONING BY GENDER    In additional models conducted separated by child gender (controlling for both neighborhood and family-level characteristics), positive effects of affluent neighbors are found only in the IHDP and only for boys (for both IQ and PPVT scores; data not shown). In the NLSY, the presence of impoverished neighbors is significantly related to lower PPVT scores for girls, and the higher concentration of families is associated with lower PPVT scores for boys (data not shown).

BEHAVIORAL FUNCTIONING    Several significant effects are found between neighborhood-level variables and children's internalizing and externalizing problems in the models that jointly control for neighborhood and family-level characteristics (data not shown). However, these findings are often in unexpected directions and are not consistent across the two data sets. In the IHDP, children in the full sample, African American children, and girls show fewer internalizing problems as the level of male joblessness in the neighborhood increases. For African American children and girls, a similar effect is found for externalizing problems. In contrast, in the NLSY, higher levels of internalizing problems are associated with higher male joblessness in the neighborhood for the full sample and for whites. For African American children in the NLSY, greater ethnic diversity in the neighborhood is related to fewer internalizing problems. Finally, girls in the NLSY who live among more affluent neighbors have higher externalizing problems.

EARLY SCHOOL-AGE CHILDREN

The results of neighborhood-level regression models predicting early school-age children's (that is, five- and six-year-olds') intellectual functioning are found in table 4.6.[18] As for preschool children, we again find the most consistent significant effects across models for the presence of impoverished (five of six models) and affluent (six of six models) neighbors. In all cases, impoverished neighbors are associated with children's lower intellectual functioning, and affluent neighbors with children's higher intellectual functioning. These effects are also found for children's total and performance IQ scores in the IHDP (data not shown). In addition, in three models, ethnic diversity in the neighborhood is associated with lower intellectual functioning, namely, children's verbal IQ (IHDP) and PPVT scores (IHDP and NLSY).

Table 4.7 presents the results of regression models that include only the family-level variables. Here, as in the preschool years, we find that the family's income-to-needs ratio, mother's educational level, and child's race are significant in most models. For the early school-age children, we have added a control for the child's school enrollment, and children who are in school show higher reading recognition, mathematical achievement, and verbal ability in the NLSY.

TABLE 4.6    Effects of Neighborhood Characteristics on Children's Intellectual Functioning at Ages Five to Six

| | IHDP WPSSI Verbal IQ Scores | IHDP PPVT Standard Scores | NLSY PIAT Reading | NLSY PIAT Math | NLSY PPVT Standard Scores |
|---|---|---|---|---|---|
| Neighborhood factors | | | | | |
| Low SES | −4.38* | −5.81* | −0.31 | −2.82* | −5.71* |
| | (1.05) | (1.35) | (0.73) | (0.81) | (1.01) |
| High SES | 4.61* | 4.61* | 2.48* | 2.40* | 2.21* |
| | (0.99) | (1.28) | (0.81) | (0.88) | (1.09) |
| Male joblessness | 0.70 | −0.01 | −0.46 | 0.92 | 0.51 |
| | (0.85) | (1.10) | (0.60) | (0.66) | (0.83) |
| Family concentration | −0.56 | 0.10 | −0.33 | −0.18 | −1.20 |
| | (0.62) | (0.80) | (0.46) | (0.50) | (0.62) |
| Ethnic diversity | −1.60* | −2.00* | 0.14 | −0.90 | −2.93* |
| | (0.34) | (0.44) | (0.62) | (0.69) | (0.87) |
| N | 601 | 601 | 669 | 672 | 622 |
| Adjusted $R^2$ | 0.28 | 0.29 | 0.02 | 0.06 | 0.16 |
| Mean of Y | 90.41 | 81.69 | 107.34 | 101.06 | 95.44 |
| (Stnd. dev.) | (17.43) | (21.71) | (11.73) | (13.08) | (16.88) |

*Indicates coefficient is more than twice its standard error.

When we jointly consider the neighborhood- and family-level effects variables (see table 4.8), we find that the effect of impoverished neighbors drops out of all models. However, the presence of affluent neighbors remains significantly associated with children's higher verbal IQ (IHDP), reading recognition (NLSY), and PPVT scores (NLSY). In addition, the effects of ethnic diversity remain in the IHDP, with higher levels of neighborhood ethnic diversity associated with lower verbal IQ and verbal ability. Finally, a new effect appears in the NLSY: a greater concentration of families in the neighborhood is related to lower verbal ability. The family-level effects for mother's education, the child's race, the family's income-to-needs ratio, and the child's school enrollment remain as just described.

We again find that the family-only models explain a higher level of variance than do the neighborhood-only models (adjusted for the number of parameters in the model). In addition, little additional variance is explained in the combined neighborhood and family models than in the models with only family-level controls. In the NLSY, we find that the set of neighborhood variables contributes significantly to the full regression model only for children's verbal ability ($F = 3.67$, $p = .003$), but not for children's mathematical achievement or reading recognition.

INTELLECTUAL FUNCTIONING, BY RACE    The models that are conducted separately for African American and white children can be found in table 4.9. We find that greater ethnic diversity in the neighborhood is related to lower PPVT scores (IHDP and NLSY) and to lower verbal IQ scores (IHDP) for white, but

TABLE 4.7   Effects of Family Characteristics on Children's Intellectual Functioning at Ages Five to Six.

| | IHDP WPSSI Verbal IQ Scores | IHDP PPVT Standard Scores | NLSY PIAT Reading Recognition | NLSY PIAT Mathematics Scores | NLSY PPVT Standard Scores |
|---|---|---|---|---|---|
| Family characteristics | | | | | |
| Family income/needs | 3.13* | 3.88* | 1.87* | 0.83 | 0.97 |
| | (0.55) | (0.67) | (0.45) | (0.50) | (0.61) |
| Female head | −0.82 | −1.66 | 1.72 | 2.65* | 0.61 |
| | (1.34) | (1.61) | (1.05) | (1.16) | (1.44) |
| Mother's education | 1.50* | 1.42* | 1.08* | 0.90* | 2.01* |
| | (0.33) | (0.40) | (0.28) | (0.31) | (0.39) |
| Teenage mother at | −0.23 | 0.43 | 0.23 | −4.31* | −1.68 |
| study child's birth | (1.58) | (1.90) | (1.07) | (1.20) | (1.51) |
| Teenage mother | | | −2.30 | −2.97* | −0.20 |
| at a previous | | | (1.27) | (1.38) | (1.72) |
| birth (NLSY) | | | | | |
| Mother's employment | | | | | |
| 30–39 hrs/week | 1.67 | 3.35 | 1.10 | 0.90 | 0.22 |
| (NLSY) or full- | (2.00) | (2.40) | (0.90) | (1.01) | (1.26) |
| time (IHDP) | | | | | |
| 20–29 hrs/week (NLSY) | 1.92 | 3.13 | 0.54 | −0.62 | 0.61 |
| or part-time (IHDP) | (2.39) | (2.88) | (1.67) | (1.78) | (2.18) |
| 1–19 hrs/week (NLSY) | | | 4.85* | 1.74 | 6.53* |
| | | | (1.74) | (1.97) | (2.46) |
| Child is African American | −7.77* | −13.67* | −1.13 | −6.81* | −18.17* |
| | (1.57) | (1.89) | (1.09) | (1.20) | (1.50) |
| Child is male | −1.56 | −0.49 | −1.36 | −1.85* | −1.40 |
| | (1.03) | (1.36) | (0.83) | (0.92) | (1.14) |
| Age in months (NLSY) | | | −0.60* | −0.09 | −0.05 |
| | | | (0.08) | (0.09) | (0.11) |
| Child is in school | −0.69 | −0.17 | 8.14* | 8.92* | 4.98* |
| | (1.25) | (1.51) | (1.22) | (1.35) | (1.67) |
| N | 601 | 601 | 680 | 684 | 632 |
| Adjusted $R^2$ | 0.38 | 0.42 | 0.18 | 0.18 | 0.29 |
| Mean of Y | 90.41 | 81.69 | 107.27 | 101.02 | 95.30 |
| (Stnd. dev.) | (17.43) | (21.71) | (11.71) | (13.07) | (16.82) |

*Indicates coefficient is more than twice its standard error.

not African American, children. In addition, for white children in the NLSY, a higher concentration of families in the neighborhood is related to lower verbal ability, and the presence of affluent neighbors is associated with higher reading recognition scores. Again, the family-level variables are associated with intellectual functioning across both data sets.

INTELLECTUAL FUNCTIONING, BY GENDER   We ran models jointly controlling for neighborhood- and family-level characteristics separately for boys and girls

(Text continues on page 104.)

TABLE 4.8  Effects of Neighborhood and Family Characteristics on Children's Intellectual Functioning at Ages Five to Six

| | IHDP WPSSI Verbal IQ Scores | IHDP PPVT Standard Scores | NLSY PIAT Reading Recognition | NLSY PIAT Mathematics Scores | NLSY PPVT Standard Scores |
|---|---|---|---|---|---|
| **Neighborhood factors** | | | | | |
| Low SES | −1.72 | −1.40 | 0.12 | −1.19 | −0.03 |
| | (1.08) | (1.30) | (0.81) | (0.90) | (1.11) |
| High SES | 1.99* | 1.59 | 1.79* | 1.34 | 2.22* |
| | (1.00) | (1.21) | (0.76) | (0.84) | (1.01) |
| Male joblessness | 0.76 | −0.05 | −0.16 | 0.70 | −0.07 |
| | (0.82) | (0.99) | (0.56) | (0.63) | (0.77) |
| Family concentration | −0.29 | 0.47 | −0.53 | −0.33 | −1.57* |
| | (0.60) | (0.72) | (0.42) | (0.47) | (0.57) |
| Ethnic diversity | −1.10* | −1.31 * | 0.61 | −0.26 | −1.32 |
| | (0.34) | (0.40) | (0.58) | (0.65) | (0.81) |
| **Family characteristics** | | | | | |
| Family income/needs | 2.59* | 3.26* | 1.70* | 0.77 | 0.82 |
| | (0.57) | (0.69) | (0.46) | (0.51) | (0.62) |
| Female head | −0.88 | −1.73 | 1.49 | 2.96* | 0.55 |
| | (1.33) | (1.60) | (1.09) | (1.19) | (1.46) |
| Mother's education | 1.35* | 1.36* | 1.04* | 0.83* | 1.88* |
| | (0.33) | (0.40) | (0.29) | (0.32) | (0.40) |
| Teenage mother at study child's birth | −0.24 | 0.37 | 0.39 | −4.05* | −1.59 |
| | (1.57) | (1.89) | (1.09) | (1.22) | (1.51) |
| Teenage mother at a previous birth (NLSY) | | | −2.47 | −3.08* | −0.38 |
| | | | (1.28) | (1.39) | (1.72) |
| **Mother's employment** | | | | | |
| 30–39 hrs/week (NLSY) or full-time (IHDP) | 0.75 | 2.37 | 1.22 | 0.92 | −0.13 |
| | (1.99) | (2.40) | (0.91) | (1.02) | (1.27) |
| 20–29 hrs/ week (NLSY) or part-time (IHDP) | 0.72 | 1.43 | 0.28 | −0.82 | −0.13 |
| | (2.39) | (2.89) | (1.68) | (1.80) | (2.19) |
| 1–19 hrs/week (NLSY) | | 4.31* | 1.34 | 5.59* | |
| | | (1.75) | (1.98) | (2.46) | |
| Child is African American | −6.52* | −12.73* | −0.87 | −5.56* | −16.76* |
| | (1.72) | (2.08) | (1.31) | (1.44) | (1.81) |
| Child is male | −1.46 | −0.37 | −1.28 | −1.67 | −1.14 |
| | (1.12) | (1.35) | (0.84) | (0.93) | (1.15) |
| Age in months (NLSY) | | −0.62* | −0.11 | −0.08 | |
| | | (0.08) | (0.09) | (0.11) | |
| Child is in school | −0.80 | −0.24 | 7.93* | 9.12* | 4.97* |
| | (1.24) | (1.49) | (1.24) | (1.38) | (1.68) |
| *N* | 601 | 601 | 665 | 668 | 618 |
| Adjusted *R²* | 0.40 | 0.44 | 0.19 | 0.19 | 0.31 |
| Mean of *Y* | 90.41 | 81.69 | 107.33 | 101.05 | 95.41 |
| (Stnd. dev.) | (17.43) | (21.71) | (11.75) | (13.10) | (16.89) |

*Indicates coefficient is more than twice its standard error.

TABLE 4.9   Effects of Neighborhood and Family Characteristics on Children's Intellectual Functioning at Ages Five to Six by Race

| | IHDP WPPSI Verbal IQ Scores | | IHDP PPVT Standard Scores | |
|---|---|---|---|---|
| | White | Black | White | Black |
| **Neighborhood factors** | | | | |
| Low SES | −1.86 | −1.10 | −0.71 | −1.14 |
| | (2.31) | (1.30) | (2.53) | (1.66) |
| High SES | 2.10 | 1.76 | 2.83 | 1.00 |
| | (1.50) | (1.59) | (1.64) | (2.03) |
| Male joblessness | 1.22 | 0.66 | −0.27 | 0.83 |
| | (1.52) | (1.01) | (1.66) | (1.28) |
| Family concentration | −0.77 | −0.28 | 0.07 | −0.05 |
| | (1.10) | (0.76) | (1.21) | (0.97) |
| Ethnic diversity | −2.26* | −0.58 | −2.80* | −0.60 |
| | (0.89) | (0.40) | (0.97) | (0.51) |
| **Family characteristics** | | | | |
| Family income/needs | 2.82* | 2.02* | 2.98* | 3.28* |
| | (0.80) | (0.94) | (0.88) | (1.20) |
| Female head | 2.61 | −3.61* | 4.49 | −6.04* |
| | (2.42) | (1.61) | (2.65) | (2.05) |
| Mother's education | 1.34* | 1.02* | 1.17* | 1.24 |
| | (0.51) | (0.51) | (0.56) | (0.64) |
| Teenage mother at | 6.37 | −1.82 | 5.83 | −1.12 |
| study child's birth | (4.33) | (1.62) | (4.74) | (2.07) |
| Teenage mother at a previous birth (NLSY) | | | | |
| Mother's employment | | | | |
| 30–39 hrs/week (NLSY) | 2.86 | 0.27 | 3.17 | 2.96 |
| or full-time (IHDP) | (4.17) | (2.24) | (4.56) | (2.86) |
| 20–29 hrs/week (NLSY) | 5.62 | −0.98 | 5.38 | 0.48 |
| or part-time (IHDP) | (4.61) | (2.90) | (5.04) | (3.70) |
| 1–19 hrs/week (NLSY) | | | | |
| Child is male | −0.93 | −2.41 | −0.81 | −0.63 |
| | (2.10) | (1.33) | (2.30) | (1.70) |
| Age in months (NLSY) | | | | |
| Child is in school | −4.28 | 2.16 | −2.98 | 2.63 |
| | (2.28) | (1.50) | (2.50) | (1.91) |
| N | 228 | 373 | 228 | 373 |
| Adjusted $R^2$ | 0.32 | 0.13 | 0.30 | 0.16 |
| Mean of Y | 100.89 | 84.14 | 96.57 | 72.79 |
| (Stnd. dev.) | (18.13) | (13.57) | (19.70) | (17.61) |

TABLE 4.9 *Continued*

| NLSY PIAT Reading Recognition Scores | | NLSY PIAT Mathematics Scores | | NLSY PPVT Standard Scores | |
|---|---|---|---|---|---|
| White | Black | White | Black | White | Black |
| 0.76 | −0.33 | −1.20 | −0.69 | −0.26 | 0.58 |
| (1.48) | (0.96) | (1.66) | (1.06) | (1.99) | (1.38) |
| 2.61* | −1.22 | 2.04 | −0.56 | 2.27 | 1.18 |
| (0.99) | (1.47) | (1.10) | (1.59) | (1.30) | (2.11) |
| 0.26 | −1.34 | 1.07 | −0.60 | −0.25 | −0.43 |
| (0.77) | (0.79) | (0.87) | (0.88) | (1.05) | (1.14) |
| −0.74 | −0.24 | −0.68 | 0.42 | −1.52* | −1.18 |
| (0.56) | (0.70) | (0.63) | (0.78) | (0.74) | (1.03) |
| 1.04 | −0.70 | −0.41 | −0.68 | −2.60* | 0.38 |
| (0.92) | (0.75) | (1.03) | (0.84) | (1.25) | (1.12) |
| | | | | | |
| 1.83* | 1.15 | 0.84 | 0.81 | 0.46 | 2.59+ |
| (0.57) | (0.91) | (0.64) | (1.00) | (0.76) | (1.32) |
| 2.34 | −0.51 | 3.94* | 1.14 | 1.03 | 1.31 |
| (1.54) | (1.45) | (1.69) | (1.60) | (2.02) | (2.11) |
| 0.95* | 1.60* | 0.72 | 1.23* | 1.43* | 2.96* |
| (0.39) | (0.45) | (0.43) | (0.50) | (0.52) | (0.69) |
| −0.05 | 0.82 | −3.49* | −4.96* | −1.86 | −0.63 |
| (1.48) | (1.55) | (1.68) | (1.73) | (2.05) | (2.30) |
| −2.73 | −1.40 | −3.91* | −0.87 | −1.32 | 1.89 |
| (1.78) | (1.78) | (1.92) | (1.98) | (2.32) | (2.60) |
| | | | | | |
| 0.34 | 3.44* | 1.26 | 0.04 | −0.82 | 0.83 |
| (1.20) | (1.53) | (1.36) | (1.69) | (1.64) | (2.27) |
| 0.54 | 4.34 | −1.34 | 2.60 | −2.21 | 5.53 |
| (2.13) | (3.26) | (2.27) | (3.61) | (2.70) | (4.80) |
| 4.05 | 5.45 | 0.66 | 7.25 | 3.80 | 14.85* |
| (2.16) | (3.85) | (2.48) | (4.06) | (3.00) | (5.43) |
| −1.73 | 0.12 | −1.67 | −0.79 | −0.47 | −2.65 |
| (1.12) | (1.30) | (1.25) | (1.44) | (1.52) | (1.91) |
| −0.69* | −0.42* | −0.19 | 0.06 | −0.05 | −0.17 |
| (0.11) | (0.12) | (0.12) | (0.13) | (0.15) | (0.17) |
| 7.99* | 7.95* | 9.94* | 7.72* | 4.22 | 7.15* |
| (1.66) | (1.84) | (1.86) | (2.04) | (2.22) | (2.68) |
| 379 | 286 | 381 | 287 | 355 | 263 |
| 0.19 | 0.18 | 0.14 | 0.12 | 0.09 | 0.15 |
| 107.96 | 105.34 | 102.85 | 95.35 | 99.95 | 80.79 |
| (11.72) | (11.65) | (12.79) | (12.46) | (14.36) | (16.13) |

*Indicates coefficient is more than twice its standard error.

+ Indicates $t < 2.0$, but $p < .05$.

(data not shown). At the neighborhood level, higher levels of ethnic diversity in the neighborhood are related to lower total IQ and PPVT scores for both boys and girls in the IHDP. In addition, for boys, living among more affluent neighbors is associated with higher verbal ability in both the IHDP and NLSY. In the NLSY, boys' verbal ability and reading recognition are lower when they live among a greater concentration of families in the neighborhood, and girls' mathematical achievement is lower when they live among impoverished neighbors. Finally, while higher levels of male joblessness in the neighborhood are related to boys' lower reading recognition scores, male joblessness is related to girls' higher reading recognition and higher mathematical achievement.

BEHAVIORAL FUNCTIONING FOR THE FULL SAMPLE    Models regressing children's behavior problems onto the five neighborhood factors alone show only three significant effects (see table 4.10)—namely, in the NLSY, children in neighborhoods with higher levels of male joblessness and greater ethnic diversity exhibit greater internalizing problems, and denser family concentration relates to more externalizing problems.

The model predicting children's behavior problems using only the family-level variables is presented in table 4.11. In both the NLSY and IHDP, a higher family income-to-needs ratio is related to fewer externalizing problems, and mother's educational level is associated with fewer internalizing problems in both the IHDP and NLSY, as well as with fewer externalizing problems in the IHDP.

TABLE 4.10   Effects of Neighborhood Characteristics on Children's Behavioral Functioning at Ages Five to Six

|  | IHDP Achenbach Internalizing | IHDP Achenbach Externalizing | NLSY Behavior Problems Internalizing | NLSY Behavior Problems Externalizing |
|---|---|---|---|---|
| Neighborhood factors |  |  |  |  |
| Low SES | 0.05 | 0.30 | −0.13 | −0.10 |
|  | (0.68) | (0.63) | (0.13) | (0.17) |
| High SES | −0.64 | −0.53 | 0.27 | −0.02 |
|  | (0.65) | (0.60) | (0.14) | (0.19) |
| Male joblessness | 0.02 | 0.31 | 0.24* | 0.06 |
|  | (0.56) | (0.52) | (0.10) | (0.14) |
| Family concentration | 0.06 | 0.19 | 0.12 | 0.27* |
|  | (0.40) | (0.37) | (0.08) | (0.10) |
| Ethnic diversity | 0.17 | 0.29 | 0.23* | 0.18 |
|  | (0.22) | (0.21) | (0.11) | (0.14) |
| N | 642 | 642 | 685 | 688 |
| Adjusted $R^2$ | 0.00 | 0.01 | 0.02 | 0.01 |
| Mean of Y | 13.79 | 12.75 | 9.36 | 11.96 |
| (Stnd. dev.) | (9.56) | (8.88) | (2.04) | (2.69) |

*Indicates coefficient is more than twice its standard error.

TABLE 4.11   Effects of Family Characteristics on Children's Behavioral Functioning at Ages Five to Six

| Family characteristics | IHDP Achenbach Internalizing | IHDP Achenbach Externalizing | NLSY Behavior Problems Internalizing | NLSY Behavior Problems Externalizing |
|---|---|---|---|---|
| Family income/needs | −0.61 | −0.77* | −0.10 | −0.28* |
| | (0.36) | (0.33) | (0.08) | (0.11) |
| Female head | 2.06* | 1.35 | 0.27 | 0.09 |
| | (0.88) | (0.79) | (0.19) | (0.25) |
| Mother's education | −0.69* | −0.46* | −0.11* | −0.10 |
| | (0.22) | (0.20) | (0.05) | (0.07) |
| Teenage mother at study | −0.12 | 1.34 | −0.24 | 0.12 |
| child's birth | (1.04) | (0.93) | (0.20) | (0.26) |
| Teenage mother at a | | | −0.12 | 0.78* |
| previous birth (NLSY) | | | (0.23) | (0.30) |
| Mother's employment | | | | |
| 30–39 hrs/week (NLSY) | 1.31 | 0.82 | −0.31 | −0.19 |
| or full-time (IHDP) | (1.31) | (1.18) | (0.17) | (0.22) |
| 20–29 hrs/week (NLSY) | 1.81 | 1.74 | −0.29 | −0.05 |
| or part-time (IHDP) | (1.57) | (1.41) | (0.30) | (0.40) |
| 1–19 hrs/week | | | 0.67* | 0.20 |
| (NLSY) | | | (0.32) | (0.43) |
| Child is African American | −2.89* | −1.79 | −0.02 | −0.59* |
| | (1.03) | (0.93) | (0.20) | (0.26) |
| Child is male | −0.48 | 4.72* | −0.30 | 0.22 |
| | (0.74) | (0.67) | (0.15) | (0.20) |
| Age in months (NLSY) | | | 0.02 | 0.00 |
| | | | (0.01) | (0.02) |
| Child is in school | −0.03 | −0.17 | −0.40 | −0.60* |
| | (0.82) | (0.74) | (0.22) | (0.30) |
| N | 642 | 642 | 699 | 702 |
| Adjusted $R^2$ | 0.06 | 0.12 | 0.03 | 0.04 |
| Mean of Y | 13.79 | 12.75 | 9.35 | 11.96 |
| (Stnd. dev.) | (9.56) | (8.88) | (2.01) | (2.67) |

*Indicates coefficient is more than twice its standard error.

When we consider neighborhood- and family-level variables simultaneously (see table 4.12), we find that mothers in the NLSY report greater internalizing problems for children living among more affluent neighbors and greater externalizing problems when living in neighborhoods with a higher concentration of families. At the family level, several variables are significant in two models. The family's income-to-needs ratio is related to lower externalizing problems in both the IHDP and the NLSY. In addition, in the IHDP, mothers with higher educational levels report fewer internalizing and externalizing problems. In

TABLE 4.12   Effects of Neighborhood and Family Characteristics on Children's Behavioral Functioning at Ages Five to Six

| | IHDP Achenbach Internalizing | IHDP Achenbach Externalizing | NLSY Behavior Problems Internalizing | NLSY Behavior Problems Externalizing |
|---|---|---|---|---|
| Neighborhood factors | | | | |
| Low SES | 0.18 | 0.12 | −0.14 | 0.09 |
| | (0.72) | (0.65) | (0.15) | (0.20) |
| High SES | 0.36 | 0.25 | 0.29* | 0.13 |
| | (0.67) | (0.60) | (0.14) | (0.19) |
| Male joblessness | −0.01 | 0.26 | 0.20 | −0.05 |
| | (0.55) | (0.49) | (0.10) | (0.14) |
| Family concentration | −0.01 | 0.07 | 0.13 | 0.30* |
| | (0.40) | (0.36) | (0.08) | (0.10) |
| Ethnic diversity | 0.10 | 0.18 | 0.18 | 0.13 |
| | (0.22) | (0.20) | (0.11) | (0.14) |
| Family characteristics | | | | |
| Family income/needs | −0.63 | −0.73* | −0.10 | −0.30* |
| | (0.38) | (0.34) | (0.09) | (0.11) |
| Female head | 2.02* | 1.33 | 0.25 | 0.07 |
| | (0.89) | (0.80) | (0.20) | (0.26) |
| Mother's education | −0.71* | −0.47* | −0.09 | −0.10 |
| | (0.22) | (0.20) | (0.05) | (0.07) |
| Teenage mother at study | −0.11 | 1.33 | −0.18 | 0.11 |
| child's birth | (1.04) | (0.94) | (0.20) | (0.27) |
| Teenage mother at a | | | −0.12 | 0.82* |
| previous birth (NLSY) | | | (0.23) | (0.31) |
| Mother's employment | | | | |
| 30–39 hrs/week (NLSY) | 1.30 | 0.92 | −0.30 | −0.19 |
| or full-time (IHDP) | (1.33) | (1.19) | (0.17) | (0.22) |
| 20–29 hrs/week (NLSY) | 1.85 | 1.91 | −0.25 | 0.02 |
| or part-time (IHDP) | (1.60) | (1.43) | (0.30) | (0.40) |
| 1–19 hrs/week (NLSY) | | | 0.66* | 0.24 |
| | | | (0.33) | (0.43) |
| Child is African | −2.90* | −1.96 | −0.02 | −0.72* |
| American | (1.15) | (1.03) | (0.24) | (0.32) |
| Child is male | −0.49 | 4.69* | −0.31+ | 0.17 |
| | (0.75) | (0.67) | (0.16) | (0.21) |
| Age in months (NLSY) | | | 0.02 | 0.01 |
| | | | (0.01) | (0.02) |
| Child is in school | −0.05 | −0.20 | −0.45+ | −0.68* |
| | (0.83) | (0.74) | (0.23) | (0.30) |
| N | 642 | 642 | 681 | 684 |
| Adjusted $R^2$ | 0.05 | 0.11 | 0.04 | 0.05 |
| Mean of $Y$ | 13.79 | 12.75 | 9.35 | 11.95 |
| (Stnd. dev.) | (9.56) | (8.88) | (2.02) | (2.69) |

*Indicates coefficient is more than twice its standard error. + indicates $t < 2.0$, but $p < .05$.

the NLSY, children who are enrolled in school have fewer reported internalizing and externalizing problems. Finally, African American children are reported to have fewer internalizing problems in the IHDP and fewer externalizing problems in the NLSY, and males have more reported externalizing problems in the IHDP and fewer reported internalizing problems in the NLSY.

In terms of variance explained, while the magnitude of change in adjusted variance explained is still small, the contribution of the set of neighborhood factors is significant for both internalizing and externalizing problems in the NLSY ($F = 2.68$, $p = .021$; $F = 2.24$, $p = .049$).

BEHAVIORAL FUNCTIONING, BY RACE    Table 4.13 shows the results of models that jointly control for neighborhood- and family-level variables but are conducted separately by race. No neighborhood effects are significant in the IHDP. In the NLSY, higher levels of male joblessness in the neighborhood are related to greater reported internalizing and externalizing problems for African American children, and a greater concentration of families in the neighborhood is associated with more reported externalizing problems for white children.

At the family level, mother's educational level is associated with fewer reported internalizing and externalizing problems for whites in the IHDP and fewer internalizing problems for African American children in both the IHDP and NLSY.

BEHAVIORAL FUNCTIONING, BY GENDER    When we jointly consider neighborhood- and family-level separately for boys and girls (data not shown), no neighborhood-level effects are significant in the IHDP. In the NLSY, for boys, higher levels of male joblessness and ethnic diversity in the neighborhood are associated with more internalizing problems, but living among more neighbors who are impoverished is related to fewer internalizing problems for boys. For girls, the presence of more affluent neighbors is related to higher levels of reported internalizing and externalizing problems, and a higher concentration of families in the neighborhood is associated with more internalizing problems.

NONLINEAR EFFECTS

While we focus on linear effects of neighborhoods in these chapters, we also believe that nonlinear effects should be considered (see also chapter 9). Linear effects may underestimate neighborhood effects, overlooking potential threshold-like changes in the relationship along the distribution of a given neighborhood characteristic (Steinberg 1989; Mayer and Jencks 1989).

(Text continues on page 110.)

TABLE 4.13  Effects of Neighborhood and Family Characteristics on Children's Behavioral Functioning at Ages Five to Six, by Race

| | IHDP Achenbach Internalizing | | IHDP Achenbach Externalizing | | NLSY Behavior Problems Internalizing | | NLSY Behavior Problems Externalizing | |
|---|---|---|---|---|---|---|---|---|
| | White | Black | White | Black | White | Black | White | Black |
| Neighborhood factors | | | | | | | | |
| Low SES | -0.17 | 0.08 | -0.53 | 0.26 | -0.36 | -0.16 | -0.09 | -0.26 |
| | (1.35) | (0.93) | (1.19) | (0.86) | (0.28) | (0.17) | (0.36) | (0.25) |
| High SES | 0.37 | -0.52 | 0.50 | -0.53 | 0.27 | 0.22 | 0.06 | 0.24 |
| | (0.88) | (1.14) | (0.78) | (1.05) | (0.19) | (0.26) | (0.24) | (0.39) |
| Male joblessness | 0.91 | -0.44 | 1.26 | -0.35 | 0.16 | 0.32* | -0.29 | 0.51* |
| | (0.89) | (0.72) | (0.78) | (0.66) | (0.15) | (0.14) | (0.19) | (0.21) |
| Family concentration | 0.29 | -0.19 | -0.15 | 0.15 | 0.11 | 0.13 | 0.29* | 0.25 |
| | (0.65) | (0.55) | (0.57) | (0.50) | (0.11) | (0.13) | (0.13) | (0.19) |
| Ethnic diversity | -0.08 | 0.13 | -0.01 | 0.18 | 0.34 | 0.14 | 0.24 | 0.15 |
| | (0.52) | (0.29) | (0.46) | (0.26) | (0.17) | (0.14) | (0.22) | (0.21) |
| Family characteristics | | | | | | | | |
| Family income/needs | -0.31 | -1.12 | -0.60 | -0.94 | -0.12 | -0.10 | -0.40* | 0.04 |
| | (0.47) | (0.68) | (0.41) | (0.62) | (0.11) | (0.16) | (0.14) | (0.24) |
| Female head | 1.97 | 2.13 | 1.38 | 1.46 | 0.22 | 0.21 | -0.19 | 0.66 |
| | (1.42) | (1.16) | (1.25) | (1.06) | (0.29) | (0.26) | (0.36) | (0.38) |
| Mother's education | -0.66* | -0.89* | -0.58* | -0.49 | -0.08 | -0.16* | -0.09 | -0.20 |
| | (0.30) | (0.36) | (0.26) | (0.33) | (0.07) | (0.08) | (0.09) | (0.12) |

| | (1) | (2) | (3) | (4) | (5) | (6) | (7) |
|---|---|---|---|---|---|---|---|
| Teenage mother at study child's birth | -0.44 (2.54) | 1.46 (2.24) | 1.06 (1.07) | -0.26 (0.28) | 0.02 (0.27) | 0.20 (0.36) | -0.11 (0.41) |
| Teenage mother at a previous birth (NLSY) | -0.39 (1.17) | | | -0.25 (0.32) | 0.24 (0.32) | 0.88* (0.41) | 0.74 (0.47) |
| Mother's employment | | | | | | | |
| 30–39 hrs/week (NLSY) or full-time (IHDP) | -0.71 (2.44) | -0.91 (2.15) | 1.66 (1.48) | -0.36 (0.23) | -0.07 (0.27) | -0.06 (0.29) | -0.56 (0.40) |
| 20–29 hrs/week (NLSY) or part-time (IHDP) | -1.30 (2.70) | 0.66 (2.38) | 2.35 (1.92) | -0.21 (0.39) | -0.61 (0.58) | -0.03 (0.49) | 0.02 (0.87) |
| 1–19 hrs/week (NLSY) | | | | 0.67 (0.41) | 0.73 (0.66) | 0.31 (0.52) | -0.21 (0.98) |
| Child Is male | -0.51 (1.23) | 5.74* (1.09) | 4.00* (0.88) | -0.51* (0.21) | 0.26 (0.23) | -0.01 (0.27) | 0.67 (0.34) |
| Age in months (NLSY) | | | | 0.02 (0.02) | 0.03 (0.02) | 0.01 (0.03) | 0.01 (0.03) |
| Child is in school | 1.77 (1.34) | 1.27 (1.18) | -0.95 (0.99) | -0.59 (0.31) | -0.09 (0.32) | -0.76 (0.40) | -0.51 (0.48) |
| $N$ | 255 | 255 | 386 | 391 | 290 | 391 | 293 |
| Adjusted $R^2$ | 0.07 | 0.17 | 0.07 | 0.04 | 0.03 | 0.05 | 0.06 |
| Mean of $Y$ | 14.01 | 12.60 | 12.85 | 9.32 | 9.43 | 12.01 | 11.78 |
| (Stnd. dev.) | (9.66) | (8.99) | (8.82) | (2.06) | (1.91) | (2.62) | (2.91) |

*Indicates coefficient is more than twice its standard error.

Possible nonlinear effects of the presence of affluent neighbors were explored using piecewise linear regression applied to the early school-aged NLSY sample. Piecewise linear regression models possible "break-points" in the regression line, allowing the slope of the regression line to differ before and after these break-points. Possible break-points were modeled at the full-sample and within-race quartiles of the high-SES factor, which measures the presence of affluent neighbors. Thus, whether the presence of affluent neighbors is important only after a certain threshold concentration level is achieved or for only certain levels of concentration of affluent neighbors was explored.

We find that, while the linear model best explains the relation between the presence of affluent neighbors and children's PPVT scores for whites and males, a pattern of piecewise effects is important for understanding the relationship between the presence of affluent neighbors and children's verbal ability for African American children and females. (See figure 4.1 for an illustration of the effects).[19] In particular, for African American children and for females, the presence of affluent neighbors is related to higher PPVT scores only when there is a moderate concentration of affluent neighbors (that is, between –1.05 and –0.18 on the high-SES factor). In other words, for African American and for female children, PPVT scores and the presence of affluent neighbors are positively associated only when the concentration of affluent neighbors in the community is between the levels found for the twenty-fifth and seventy-fifth percentiles of the full sample.[20]

## DISCUSSION

In this chapter, we have considered direct neighborhood influences on young African American and white children in two large data sets. We anticipated that direct effects would be evident moreso for early school-age than for preschool children and that the earliest observed effects would involve proxies for the mechanisms of neighborhood resources and collective socialization.

### PRESCHOOL CHILDREN

Our central hypothesis—that preschool children would show few direct neighborhood effects—was supported. In the full sample, when the effects on cognitive outcomes of both neighborhood- and family-level characteristics were tested in the combined model, the positive link between the presence of affluent neighbors and children's IQ scores in the IHDP was the only significant neighborhood influence of the five neighborhood factors for three cognitive outcomes. For behavioral functioning, male joblessness was the only significant neighborhood factor. Yet, the findings are mixed, in that male joblessness was related to a decrease in internalizing problems

FIGURE 4.1   Illustration of Linear and Nonlinear Effects of the Presence of Affluent Neighbors on Children's Verbal Ability (PPVT Standard Scores): By Race and Sex.

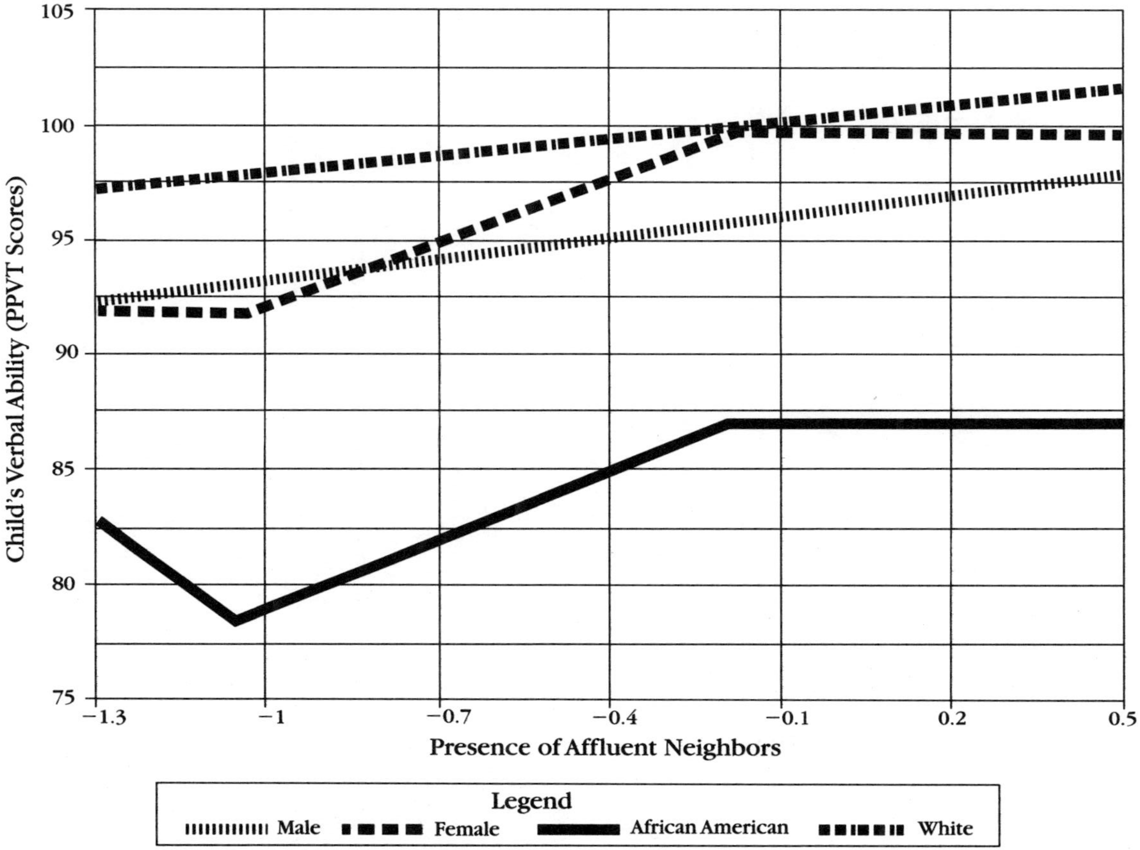

in the IHDP and an increase in internalizing behaviors, as would be expected, in the NLSY. For both cognitive and behavioral outcomes, family factors—specifically, family's income-to-needs ratio, mother's education, and race—accounted for most of the variance in all regression equations. All of these findings thus indicate that the family is the primary socializing unit for preschool children and that direct neighborhood influences on such young children, as measured by the five SSRC factors, are small or filtered by family experience.

Despite their relatively weak effects, the meaning of these few neighborhood factors should be addressed. The finding that the presence of affluent neighbors is positively related to three- and four-year-olds' performance on IQ tests (with family factors controlled) suggests the "neighborhood resource" framework as an explanatory mechanism. The greater availability of public and private services and community resources is likely to be related to a stronger economic base in a neighborhood characterized by higher levels of middle- and upper-income neighbors. Stimulation and opportunity for enrichment at the neighborhood level may be operating here, but again, we suggest this with caution, given only one significant effect of affluent neighbors.

Male joblessness at the neighborhood level may operate primarily through the mechanism of collective socialization, specifically through lower levels of role modeling, monitoring, and supervision (see, for example, Sampson 1992; Wilson 1991b). In the NLSY, these processes may explain the higher rates of internalizing problem behaviors for preschoolers, but one must question why externalizing problem behaviors are not affected. In addition, while the absence of role modeling, monitoring, and social disorganization constitute plausible ways in which male joblessness might erode adolescent development, more process-oriented research is needed to delineate the mechanisms by which joblessness is deleterious for preschoolers. In contrast, in the IHDP, male joblessness predicts fewer internalizing problems, an unexpected finding. These different effects across the two samples may be partially explained by the different sampling frames. However, these findings require more exploration and replication.

EARLY SCHOOL-AGE CHILDREN

Our argument that the transition to school ushers in an era of more direct exposure to neighborhood influences is partially supported by our findings. For both cognitive and behavioral outcomes, more neighborhood factors play a significant role in child development for children at this age than for preschoolers. However, again, the relative influence of neighborhood factors over family factors is modest. As with the preschool findings, most of the variance of the joint models is explained by family-level factors. In such joint models testing the relative impact of neighborhood and family-level characteristics, the presence of affluent neighbors is significantly related to children's PPVT scores (verbal ability) and reading recognition scores (PIAT) in the NLSY and to children's verbal IQ in the IHDP. In the NLSY, male joblessness was significantly related to higher levels of internalizing and externalizing problems among African American five- and six-year-olds, but not among white children. The concentration of families in the neighborhood was related to lower PPVT scores in the NLSY, but not in the IHDP. A final neighborhood factor, ethnic diversity, was related to lower verbal IQ scores and PPVT scores in the IHDP, but not in the NLSY. Notably, ethnic diversity was related to depressed intellectual functioning across the two data sets for white children, but not for African American children.

How do these findings add up? Our interpretation is one of cautious support for the role of different aspects of neighborhood environments in early school-age children's lives. The importance of more affluent neighbors in children's intellectual functioning is in keeping with the argument regarding resources and opportunities for enrichment previously outlined. Such opportunities may be found in the community at large, as well as in schools. Although it is possible to find strong schools in impoverished neighborhoods, the links between neighborhoods occupied by middle-income neighbors and adequate schools are more prevalent.

We do not find that the concentration of poverty in the aggregate seems to be deleterious, as would be predicted based on theory (Sampson 1992; Wilson 1991a, 1991b). This was not anticipated. However, male joblessness (Wilson 1994) does have negative consequences for African American children, suggesting the presence of such mechanisms as social disorganization, absence of role models, and lack of routine. In contrast, greater ethnic diversity in the neighborhood does not significantly affect African American children and negatively affects white children's intellectual functioning. Theory and evidence suggest that societal and individual ethnic congruence enhances the development of ethnic identity (Harris 1995; Tweed et al. 1990), which in turn is related to other aspects of healthy development (Spencer 1985, 1987). The lack of findings for African American children and for behavioral functioning are unexpected and may reflect the greater collinearity of neighbor factors for the African American children in our data sets (see Chase-Lansdale and Gordon 1996; note 26) and the need to consider other measures of young children's development of socioemotional competence and ethnic identity, among other factors.

Although the most consistent neighborhood effects for five- and six-year-olds involved the presence of affluent neighbors, this effect was not evident for all subgroups, especially for blacks and females. As others have suggested (Mayer and Jencks 1989; Steinberg 1989), neighborhood effects may operate in nonlinear patterns. Thus, we explored possible nonlinear effects in one set of models—the effects of affluent neighbors on PPVT scores of five- and six-year-olds in the NLSY. We found significant nonlinear effects for blacks and females, indicating that the presence of affluent neighbors has a beneficial effect on children's PPVT scores, but only within a moderate range (that is, between the twenty-fifth and seventy-fifth percentiles of the full-sample distribution of the factor capturing the presence of affluent neighbors). These results suggest a circumscribed effect for certain subgroups and may point toward potential hidden nonlinear effects of other variables. We speculate that in the most affluent neighborhoods (namely, those above the seventy-fifth percentile), there may be differential community resource allocation to females and African Americans. In addition, African American families may find it challenging to develop social networks in these affluent communities (Jarrett vol. 2; Tatum 1987). Future work will pursue nonlinear effects for other child outcomes.

This chapter has certain limitations. One concern is that neighborhood measures cannot be adequately distinguished from family measures, and thus neighborhoods may simply be a reflection of the families who come to live in certain neighborhoods. (See chapter 9 for a discussion of selection bias and unmeasured heterogeneity.) A second limitation is that the IHDP data set is primarily a sample of LBW, preterm infants. The developmental outcomes of LBW, preterm infants are somewhat lower than those of normal-birth-weight infants (Institute of Medicine 1985; McCormick 1985, 1989). However, while on average LBW infants have lower IQ scores and more behavior problems, the associations between family-level variables (such as sociodemographic characteristics, child-rearing attitudes, and home environment) and developmental outcomes are similar to those reported for normal-birth-weight infants (Brooks-Gunn, Klebanov, Liaw, and Spiker 1993, Drillien 1964; Dunn 1986; Gottfried 1984; Klebanov, Brooks-Gunn, and McCormick 1994b; McCormick et al. 1992). Based on these findings, we expect that the use of a LBW sample does not result in substantially different associations between neighborhood- and family-level variables and child outcomes, as compared to a normal-birth-weight sample with the same demographic characteristics. However, caution should be taken in generalizing the IHDP results to normal-birth-weight samples.

In addition, both the NLSY and IHDP are not fully representative of all U.S. children. As discussed in the methods section, the Children of the NLSY in 1986 are representative of children of young mothers (approximately the first 40 percent of a cohort's childbearing), and the IHDP sample includes LBW children from eight sites, six of which are located in large metropolitan areas with large poor populations and the other two in metropolitan areas that serve both urban and rural populations. The comparison of descriptive statistics in chapter 3 of this volume reveals the greater representation of families from neighborhoods with fewer affluent neighbors, more impoverished neighbors, higher levels of male joblessness, greater ethnic diversity, and higher levels of family concentration in these two data sets than the nationally representative PSID data set. Furthermore, descriptive analyses comparing the IHDP sample with the fully nationally representative Panel Study of Income Dynamics (PSID; see chapter 9) reveal the lower-than-average SES of the IHDP sample (Brooks-Gunn, Duncan, Klebanov, and Sealand 1993). Thus, while many of our results are consistent with our hypotheses about the impacts of neighborhood characteristics on young children's intellectual and behavioral functioning, these findings should be pursued in future studies using fully representative samples.

This chapter can be viewed as outlining a framework regarding potential neighborhood influences on young children. Further work should be conducted in order to understand the extent to which census-tract variables are proxies for ongoing neighborhood-level processes. While one conclusion to draw from our results is that family effects on children overshadow neighborhood effects, the potential remains for uses of census-tract variables that are different from the SSRC factors presented here and for examining additional characteristics, such as region and urbanicity, that may moderate neighborhood effects (see Chase-Lansdale and Gordon 1996). In addition, in-depth knowledge of neighborhood characteristics either from ethnographic studies (see Jarrett vol. 2) or from the refined observational methods of developmental psychology (see Spencer et al. vol. 2) is needed not only to understand mechanisms of neighborhood influences but also to pursue the bidirectional influences between families and their neighbors. Since the neighborhood effects net of family characteristics are modest in this chapter, we believe that a future focus on variation within neighborhoods is essential.

---

The analysis and writing of this chapter were supported by grants from the Russell Sage Foundation, the March of Dimes Foundation, the National Institute for Child Health and Human Development, the Committee on the Urban Underclass of the Social Science Research Council, the William T. Grant Foundation, the Smith Richardson Foundation, and the Rockefeller Foundation, whose generosity is appreciated. This work would not have been possible without authorization from the Bureau of Labor Statistics to draw on census tract level variables matched to the National Longitudinal Survey of Youth. We are especially grateful for the leadership and assistance of Michael R. Pergamit when he was Director of Longitudinal Research at the Bureau of Labor Statistics. The Infant Health and Development Program was supported by the Robert Wood Johnson Foundation; the Pew Charitable Trusts; the Bureau of Maternal and Child Health and Resources Development, HRSA, PHS, DHHS (MCJ-060515); and NICHD. The participating universities and site directors were Patrick H. Casey, M.D., University of Arkansas for Medical Sciences (Little Rock, AR); Cecelia M. McCarton, M.D., Albert Einstein College of Medicine (Bronx, NY); Marie McCormick, M.D., Harvard Medical School (Boston, MA); Charles R. Bauer, M.D., University of Miami School of Medicine (Miami, FL); Judith Bernbaum, M.D., University of Pennsylvania School of Medicine (Philadelphia, PA); Jon E. Tyson, M.D., and Mark Swanson, M.D., University of Texas Health Science Center at Dallas; Clifford J. Sells, M.D., and Forrest C. Bennett, M.D., University of Washington School of Medicine (Seattle, WA);

and David T. Scott, Ph.D., Yale University School of Medicine (New Haven, CT). The Longitudinal Study Office is directed by Cecelia McCarton and Jeanne Brooks-Gunn. The Data Coordinating Center is directed by James Tonascia and Curtis Meinert at the Johns Hopkins University, School of Hygiene and Public Health. We would especially like to thank T. R. Gross, the director of the National Study Office and C. Ramey, the director of the Program Development Office, of the Infant Health and Development Program. We would like to thank the Educational Testing Service, Division of Policy Research, for their continued support, as well as for the postdoctoral fellowship that Dr. Klebanov held. We would also like to thank the Population Research Center at the University of Chicago for support toward this project and a predoctoral fellowship funded by the National Institute of Child Health and Human Development to Rachel A. Gordon.

# NOTES

1. One-third of the infants were randomized to the intervention group and two-thirds to the follow-up group. The intervention program was initiated on discharge from the neonatal nursery and continued until thirty-six months. The services for infants in the intervention group consisted of home visits over the three years, an educational child-care program at a child-development center in the second and third years, and bimonthly parent-group meetings in the child's second and third years of life (Brooks-Gunn, Klebanov, Liaw, and Spiker 1993; Ramey, Bryant, Wasik, Sparling, Fendt, and LaVange in press). Pediatric surveillance was conducted for both groups (intervention and follow-up) who were seen seven times over the first three years.

2. Reasons for exclusion included the following: living more than a forty-five-minute drive to center-based care (46.9 percent); hospital discharge before or after the recruitment period (13.3 percent); a gestational age of greater than thirty-seven weeks (18.6 percent); or some other maternal or infant condition precluding participation in the intervention program (21.2 percent). In this last group, only sixty-one infants were excluded for health reasons, so this sample is not biased toward healthy low-birth-weight preterm infants.

3. Additionally, all tests were conducted in English, and a significant portion of the Hispanic children were bilingual. Bilingual children in the United States have lower scores on verbal ability tests conducted in English and Spanish than monolingual children in Spanish-speaking countries (Dunn 1986). Finally, Hispanic children were concentrated in three of the eight sites, rather than being distributed among the eight sites, as was the case for black and white children (Infant Health and Development Program 1990; McCarton, Brooks-Gunn, and Tonascia in press).

4. Regressions that included the seven dummy variables for the eight sites revealed only one significant site difference, with the Washington site differing from the Yale site on Achenbach internalizing behavior problem scores. However, once the probability values were adjusted for the number of site comparisons conducted, this result was nonsignificant.

5. There was a significant treatment effect for both cognitive and behavioral functioning at age three (IHDP 1990). However, both intervention and follow-up-only groups were included in the sample here because of sample size considerations. There were no interactions between initial status variables (namely, birth weight and neonatal health) and treatment status.

6. We ran regression models that included additive and neighborhood-interactive effects of birth weight to test whether being very low birth weight results in different associations between neighborhood- and family-level variables and child outcomes. Regression analy-

ses were run that omitted infants who weighed 1,000 grams or less. Our results indicate that the associations between neighborhood- and family-level variables and child outcomes remain unchanged. Moreover, the strength of the associations was essentially unchanged (results available from authors). Next, we ran a set of regressions that interacted birth weight with neighborhood-income-level variables and with family-income variables. None of these interactions were significant (results available from authors). These results suggest that the effects of neighborhood-level and family-level variables on child outcomes are not different for children at different points along the birth-weight distribution.

7. Gender, ethnicity, and maternal age were recorded at birth. For the three-year-old assessment period, maternal education, female headship, and maternal employment status were measured when the child was three years old, and the family income-to-needs ratio was averaged when the child was one to three years old. For the five-year-old assessment period, maternal education, female headship, and maternal em-ployment status were measured when the child was five years old, and the family in-come-to-needs ratios were averaged when the child was one to five years old. Child school enrollment status was measured when the child was five years old.

8. The categories in thousands of dollars were: < 5, 5–7.49, 7.5–9.9, 10–14.9, 15–19.9, 20–24.9, 25–34.9, 35–49.9, > 50. We assigned a value of 3.5 to respondents who reported an income in the first category and 65 to respondents who reported an income in the last category. The midpoint of the range was assigned to all other categories.

9. We combine three- and four-year-olds and five- and six-year-olds rather than restricting the analyses to just the three-year-old or five-year-old ages available in the IHDP to pro-duce an adequate sample size for analyses (that is, in the preschool and early school-age years, there are only approximately three hundred children per year of age).

10. This overrepresentation of young mothers decreases with each wave of the NLSY child assessments. By more recent survey waves, the sample of mothers is much more repre-sentative of the full range of childbearing years.

11. In the 1986 wave of the NLSY, the PPVT-R was assessed only in English.

12. As do Achenbach, Howell, Quay, and Conners (1991), we consider items dealing with social problems and hyperactivity as falling on neither the internalizing nor the external-izing dimension.

13. The correlation between the raw sum of externalizing items with and without these two items is $r = 0.98$.

14. The NLSY data are coded as 1 = *often true*, 2 = *sometimes true*, and 3 = *not true*. So that higher scores would be associated with more problem behaviors, we first reverse coded the items for each sub scale so that 1 = *not true*, 2 = *sometimes true*, and 3 = *often true*.

15. The key variable created by the NLSY by summing across various sources of income for all family members was used as a base to which an opposite-sex partner's reported income was added. For confidentiality, income variables with values that exceeded particular lim-its were truncated by the NLSY. For survey years 1979 to 1984, the upper limit was $75,000; and any income figures that were reported to be greater than $75,000 were truncated to $75,001. For survey years 1984 to 1986, the imposed ceiling was $100,000.

16. If family income was missing in a particular year, then the average was taken for just the years of the child's life with valid data.

17. In addition, in the IHDP, all regression models also included the initial status and control variables.

18. As noted earlier, the IHDP data are longitudinal, and analyses that control for develop-ment at age three (that is, age-five IQ regressions that control for age-three IQ, and age-

five behavior problem regressions that control for age-three behavior problems) reveal a similar pattern of results when neighborhood- and family-level variables are simultaneously controlled. Ethnic diversity is associated with lower IQ and verbal ability scores, while no neighborhood factors are associated with behavior problems. In addition, regressions that control for age-three IQ reveal that the presence of impoverished neighbors is associated with lower IQ scores.

19. The illustrations were created using the predicted values from the relevant regression models.

20. For both blacks and females, the presence of affluent neighbors is not related to PPVT scores above the full-sample seventy-fifth percentile. However, below the twenty-fifth percentile the pattern differs. For females, the presence of affluent neighbors is again unrelated to PPVT scores. For blacks, in neighborhoods that are below the full-sample twenty-fifth percentile, the presence of affluent neighbors is negatively related to PPVT scores.

21. University of Arkansas for Medical Sciences (Little Rock, AR), Albert Einstein College of Medicine (Bronx, NY), Harvard Medical School (Boston, MA), University of Miami School of Medicine (Miami, FL), University of Pennsylvania School of Meducine (Pennsylvania, PA), University of Texas Health Science Center at Dallas, University of Washington School of Medicine (Seattle, WA), Yale University School of Medicine (New Haven, CT).

# 5

# Are Neighborhood Effects on Young Children Mediated by Features of the Home Environment?

*Pamela K. Klebanov, Jeanne Brooks-Gunn,*
*P. Lindsay Chase-Lansdale, and Rachel A. Gordon*

O
ur goal in this chapter is to extend chapter 4's analyses in several ways in order to understand whether or not neighborhood of residence is linked to the actual environments of children's homes, not just to the family's income and educational resources. Following Coleman (1988) and Haveman and Wolfe (1994), we have begun to look at the family and community resources available to children (Brooks-Gunn 1996; Brooks-Gunn, Brown et al. 1995; Brooks-Gunn, Denner, and Klebanov 1995; Leventhal, Brooks-Gunn, and Kamerman 1997).

This chapter has three aims. The first is to look at how neighborhood composition is correlated with indicators in the home environment and cultural characteristics of the young children's mothers. Our measures include the cognitive stimulation provided to the child in the home, the physical environment of the home, the mother's warmth toward the child, the mother's mental health, the mother's coping style, and the social support received by the mother. Of these measures, the National Longitudinal Survey of Youth (NLSY) only has the cognitive stimulation one, while the Infant Health and Development Program (IHDP) has them all. We realize that our measures could be more numerous and perhaps more nuanced, but these analyses are a first step in explicating the mechanisms through which neighborhoods might influence young children. The mechanisms are all familial, as the family is the central socializing agent of the young child (Brooks-Gunn 1995). The question involves whether or not neighborhood indicators influence mothers' parenting, mental health, and social support.

The second aim of this chapter is to see whether or not the neighborhood effects on child outcomes reported in chapter 4 are mediated by the family-level process variables just specified. We expect that the mechanisms through which neighborhoods operate on young children are proximal, that is, they work through the family. The earlier chapter illustrated how neighborhood effects are reduced when family-level characteristics are included in regression equations. These results can be interpreted as net effects or as effects that operate through the family. In the case of the family income and parental income measures, the effects are usually characterized not as mediated effects but as compositional effects (that is, of the types of families that reside in certain neighborhoods). Here, whether or not the addition of the family-level process variables alters the strength of neighborhood effects is examined, the premise being that a reduction in the size of the beta coefficients indicates a mediating effect (Baron and Kenny 1986).

Our final aim is to go beyond examining mediated effects to explore a few likely moderated effects. The ways in which the family resource variables operate may differ as a function of the type of neighborhoods in which families reside. Family resources may influence child outcomes differently in resource-rich and resource-poor neighborhoods. This premise is examined via a series of separate analyses for these neighborhoods defined as resource rich and as resource poor, using the census-tract data reported in chapter 4.

## NEIGHBORHOODS AND YOUNG CHILDREN

As noted in chapter 4, larger environmental contexts such as neighborhoods may influence young children's lives in several different ways. These effects might be direct, as with observation of individual behavior within a neighborhood or the organization of a neighborhood. More likely, such influences might be indirect, as mediated through the family. Child-rearing attitudes, behaviors directed toward the child, explanations for behavior, observations of interactions within the household, organization and structure of the household, family routines, and parental feelings of competence all might be influenced by the neighborhood. And all of these familial factors have been shown to influence child outcomes (although variation occurs in the strength of associations between particular child outcomes and different family factors). However, few studies have actually looked at how neighborhoods influence parents, and in turn, how parents influence children.

The omission is partly due to the fact that most of the neighborhood literature has focused on teenagers, given the belief that contexts other than the family are more likely to influence teenagers' behavior than young children's behavior. Also, the effects of neighborhoods on parents, who then influence their children, are not hypothesized to be as salient for adolescents as for children (see Darling and Steinberg vol. 2). Indeed, it is likely that neighborhood effects on young children will be mediated through families, since most of their time is spent in the family setting and their interchanges with other contexts (such as child-care providers and friends) are managed by the family. We examine neighborhoods' effects on families by looking at the possibility that neighborhood effects on child outcome are mediated by family resources and by investigating the possibility that family resources are linked to child outcomes differently in resource-rich and resource-poor neighborhoods.

Most relevant to a discussion of neighborhoods, families, and young children is the work of Wilson (1991a, 1991b), who has not only examined structural changes but has discussed some of the familial processes that might result from living in certain neighborhoods. Wilson has posited that living in poor neighborhoods—neighborhoods in which few individuals have jobs, few jobs are located in the neighborhood, and many mothers are single—may result in what he has termed "social isolation."

Social isolation from mainstream jobs and lifestyles is thought to result in family practices that may be less conducive to the development of skills associated with school and work life. Wilson cited as examples of such skills: the organization and rhythm of family life, the emphasis on school and work skills, future orientation, routines, and parental self-efficacy. Affluent neighborhoods stress the importance of all of these practices. Neighborhood residence may influence such family characteristics, although to our knowledge few studies have tested this premise. Data from the IHDP have been analyzed to see whether or not neighborhood resources, specifically income, are associated with the home environment, maternal mental health, and social support (Klebanov, Brooks-Gunn, and Duncan 1994). These analyses differ from those presented here in several ways. First, only neighborhood income was examined, rather than a variety of neighborhood characteristics or clustered neighborhood characteristics.

Neighborhood poverty, rather than neighborhood affluence, was associated with lower maternal warmth and poorer physical environments, controlling for family income, maternal education, and race. Second, the analysis did not include as many family-level measures as are included in this chapter. For example, maternal employment is included in the regressions reported in this chapter. Third, the present chapter examines the effects of neighborhood characteristics on maternal characteristics and home environment independent of the effects of family income and maternal education. Figure 5.1 presents a theoretical model of how neighborhood and family resources might be linked (from Klebanov, Brooks-Gunn, and Duncan 1994, 443).

## METHODS

Characteristics of the sample were reported in chapter 4. Here, we describe the family-level process measures included in these analyses. These include parenting behavior, maternal mental health, social support, and behavioral coping.

In the IHDP, three aspects of parenting behavior were included in our analyses as possible mediators linking neighborhoods with child outcomes. The preschool version (ages three to six) of the Home Observation for Measurement of the Environment (HOME; Caldwell and Bradley 1984) is a fifty-five-item semistructured observation interview. The HOME inventory was administered when the child was three years old (corrected for prematurity) as a measure of the child's level of stimulation in the home environment.

FIGURE 5.1 Model of Neighborhood and Family Influences on Maternal Characteristics and Behavior

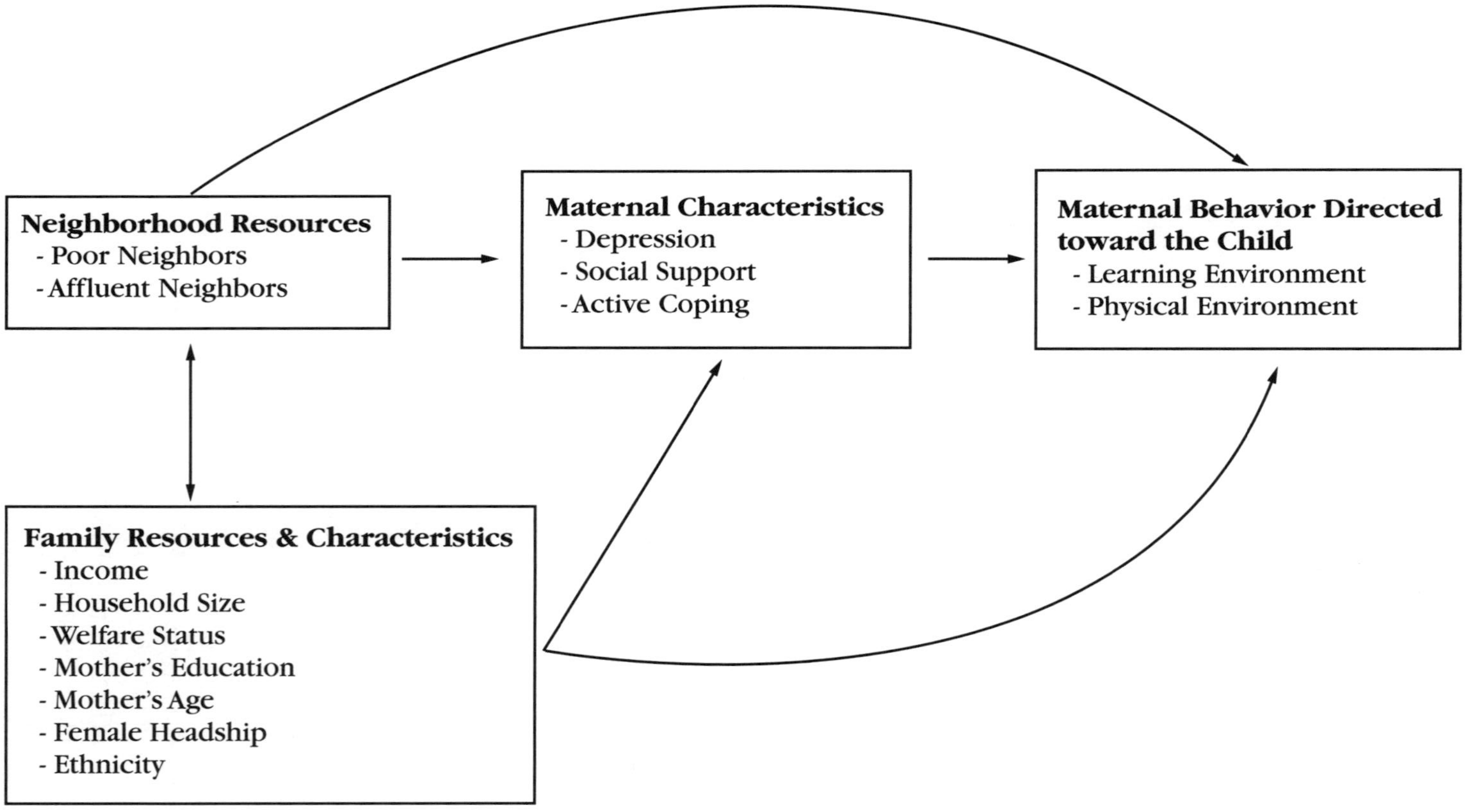

**Neighborhood Resources**
- Poor Neighbors
- Affluent Neighbors

**Maternal Characteristics**
- Depression
- Social Support
- Active Coping

**Maternal Behavior Directed toward the Child**
- Learning Environment
- Physical Environment

**Family Resources & Characteristics**
- Income
- Household Size
- Welfare Status
- Mother's Education
- Mother's Age
- Female Headship
- Ethnicity

Three subscales were used: (1) Provision of learning stimulation, which is a composite of the Learning, Academic, and Language stimulation and Variety in experience subscales (for example, the child has toys that teach color, size, shape or the child is encouraged to learn the alphabet and numbers; alpha = .87 for 32 items); (2) Physical environment (for example, outside play environment appears safe and the interior of the apartment is not dark or perceptually monotonous; alpha = .74 for 7 items); and (3) Warmth (for example, the parent caresses, kisses, or cuddles the child during the visit; alpha = .64 for 7 items). Reliability coefficients presented here are based only on the families in the follow-up-only group.

The Health and Daily Living Form, Revised Version (Moos et al. 1986) is a thirty-two-item self-report coping scale, developed for use with clinical populations and adolescents. Coping responses are classified into three domains, according to their method of coping: (1) active cognitive coping, (2) active behavioral coping, and (3) avoidance coping. Respondents indicate a recent stressful event and rate the frequency with which they use thirty-two coping responses, using a scale from 0 (*no*) to 3 (*yes, fairly often*). The reliability of this measure ranges from .60 to .74 for nonclinical adult populations, with the highest reliability for active behavioral coping, the form of coping examined here (for example, talked with a friend about the problem, made a plan of action and followed it).

The General Health Questionnaire (GHQ; Goldberg 1978) taps depression, somatization, and anxiety dimensions. A total score based on recording the responses to values from 0 to 3 (see Goldberg 1972) results in a total score from 0 to 36. The twelve-item version of the GHQ was used.

Social support was assessed using six vignettes adapted from Cohen and Lazarus (1977). These vignettes, pretested and used in the Central Harlem Study, have good discriminant validity (McCormick et al. 1987; McCormick et al. 1989). For each vignette, whether help can be expected from people living within the household and from those outside the household is determined by *yes* (1) or *no* (0) responses. Scores range from 0 to 12. A variety of questions about the availability of support are presented: including ones about the availability of support if the respondent needs to go out unexpectedly, is laid up for three months with a broken leg, needs help making an important decision, has a serious personal problem, needs to borrow money in an emergency, or has someone with whom to enjoy a free afternoon.

Only one family-level process scale was available from the Children of the NLSY. The HOME inventory was used in the NLSY (Baker and Mott 1989). Instead of the full HOME inventory (Caldwell and Bradley 1984), a short form was used (labeled the HOME-SF). Age-specific versions were developed to assess children's home environments. The preschool form was used for three- to five-year-olds. Both maternal report and interviewer observations are included—fifteen of the former and twelve of the latter for the preschool form (see Sugland et al. 1995).

In these analyses, only one HOME-SF subscale was included, and it assessed the quality of the child's home learning environment. We chose the HOME-SF Cognitive Stimulation subscale to assess the quality of the child's home learning environment. The Cognitive Stimulation subscale taps items like those on the Learning Stimulation and subscales of the full HOME inventory, which are used in the IHDP data (for example, the number of books the child has of his or her own; whether an adult in the home has helped the child learn the numbers, alphabet, colors, shapes, and sizes). Internally normed standard scores were calculated by the NLSY within a single year of age (mean = 100, standard deviation = 15). The Cognitive stimulation subscale shows good internal consistency (alpha = .69 for three-, four-, and five-year-olds in 1986). Unfortunately, the NLSY Warmth subscale, which would correspond to the IHDP Warmth subscale, did not meet adequate internal consistency levels to permit its use in analyses in this chapter (alpha = 0.49 for three-, four-, and five-year-olds in 1986).

## RESULTS

### NEIGHBORHOOD EFFECTS ON FAMILY-LEVEL PROCESSES

The results of the regressions examining the effects of neighborhoods on family-level process variables as measured when the children were three to four years of age are presented in table 5.1 (results for the HOME inventory Learning and Physical Environment subscales from IHDP at age three and the Children of the NLSY Cognitive Stimulation subscale, which is a composite of Learning subscales, at ages three to four and ages five to six). Table 5.2 presents results for maternal mental health, social support, and maternal warmth from the HOME inventory at age three for the IHDP. No significant regression coefficients were found for behavioral coping, so these data are not presented in table 5.2.

Within the IHDP—net of family income, maternal education, race, maternal age, and maternal employment—neighborhood characteristics were associated with all three aspects of the home environment. Living in poor neighborhoods and residing in ethnically diverse neighborhoods were each associated with less cognitively stimulating homes. At the family level, lower family incomes, one-parent households, and lower maternal education are correlated with less cognitively stimulating homes.

In the IHDP, the presence of low-SES neighbors was correlated with worse physical home environment, and the presence of ethnically diverse neighbors was associated with less maternal warmth. Less-poor families, more-educated mothers, and employed mothers had homes with higher-quality physical environments. Maternal warmth was correlated with maternal education and with ethnicity (white mothers being rated as warmer), net of all other effects.

*(Text continues on page 128.)*

TABLE 5.1   Effects of Neighborhood Factors and Family Characteristics on Maternal Parenting Behavior at Ages Three to Four and Five to Six

| | IHDP—Age 3 HOME Learning Environment | IHDP—Age 3 HOME Physical Environment | NLSY—Ages 3–4 HOME-SF Learning Environment | NLSY—Ages 5–6 HOME-SF Learning Environment |
|---|---|---|---|---|
| Neighborhood factors | | | | |
| Low SES | -1.07* | -0.24* | -0.18 | 0.09 |
| | (0.35) | (0.12) | (0.85) | (1.10) |
| High SES | -0.06 | -0.02 | -1.20 | 2.29* |
| | (0.32) | (0.11) | (0.77) | (1.01) |
| Male joblessness | 0.36 | -0.10 | -1.87* | -0.10 |
| | (0.27) | (0.09) | (0.63) | (0.75) |
| Family concentration | 0.23 | 0.002 | -0.36 | 0.57 |
| | (0.19) | (0.07) | (0.53) | (0.56) |
| Ethnic diversity | -0.41* | -0.04 | -0.45 | -0.75 |
| | (0.11) | (0.04) | (0.58) | (0.77) |
| Family characteristics | | | | |
| Family income/needs | 0.82* | 0.24* | 3.15* | 2.08* |
| | (0.16) | (0.06) | (0.50) | (0.60) |
| Female head | -1.12* | -0.09 | 0.64 | -1.78 |
| | (0.42) | (0.15) | (1.23) | (1.44) |
| Mother's education | 0.44* | 0.11* | 1.67* | 1.54* |
| | (0.10) | (0.03) | (0.32) | (0.38) |
| Teenage mother at study child's birth | 0.30 | -0.25 | -3.09* | 0.56 |
| | (0.53) | (0.19) | (1.47) | (1.54) |
| Teenage mother at a previous birth (NLSY) | | | -2.54* | 0.00 |
| | | | (1.29) | (1.65) |

(Table continues on p. 126.)

TABLE 5.1 Continued

|  | IHDP—Age 3 HOME Learning Environment | IHDP—Age 3 HOME Physical Environment | NLSY—Ages 3–4 HOME-SF Learning Environment | NLSY—Ages 5–6 HOME-SF Learning Environment |
|---|---|---|---|---|
| Mother's employment |  |  |  |  |
| 30–39 hrs./week (NLSY) or full-time (IHDP) | 0.76 | 0.36* | -0.47 | 0.07 |
|  | (0.43) | (0.15) | (1.03) | (1.21) |
| 20–29 hrs./week (NLSY) or part-time (IHDP) | 0.91 | 0.30 | 0.51 | 4.92* |
|  | (0.52) | (0.18) | (1.68) | (2.20) |
| 1–19 hrs./week (NLSY) |  |  | -2.21 | 4.14 |
|  |  |  | (1.84) | (2.30) |
| Child is African American | -2.69* | -0.20 | -5.30* | -5.02* |
|  | (0.56) | (0.20) | (1.55) | (1.75) |
| Child is male | 0.36 | -0.06 | -0.63 | -0.13 |
|  | (0.36) | (0.13) | (0.91) | (1.11) |
| Age in months (NLSY) |  |  | 0.09 | 0.09 |
|  |  |  | (0.07) | (0.11) |
| N | 634 | 634 | 795 | 619 |
| Adjusted $R^2$ | 0.45 | 0.28 | 0.23 | 0.14 |
| Mean of Y | 21.17 | 5.33 | 101.21 | 100.60 |
| (Stnd. dev.) | (6.03) | (1.85) | (14.42) | (14.56) |

*Indicates coefficient is more than twice its standard error.

TABLE 5.2 Effects of Neighborhood Factors and Family Characteristics on Maternal Warmth, Social Support, and Mental Health at Age Three (IHDP)

| | IHDP HOME Warmth | IHDP Social Support | IHDP Depression |
|---|---|---|---|
| Neighborhood factors | | | |
| Low SES | -0.22 | -0.09 | 0.17 |
| | (0.12) | (0.17) | (0.35) |
| High SES | -0.16 | -0.46* | 0.02 |
| | (0.11) | (0.16) | (0.32) |
| Male joblessness | -0.02 | -0.17 | -0.11 |
| | (0.09) | (0.13) | (0.26) |
| Family concentration | 0.04 | -0.06 | -0.22 |
| | (0.07) | (0.09) | (0.19) |
| Ethnic diversity | -0.14* | -0.13* | 0.02 |
| | (0.04) | (0.05) | (0.11) |
| Family characteristics | | | |
| family income/needs | 0.07 | 0.21* | -0.13 |
| | (0.06) | (0.08) | (0.16) |
| Female head | -0.24 | -1.90* | 0.05 |
| | (0.14) | (0.21) | (0.42) |
| Mother's education | 0.06* | -0.04 | 0.04 |
| | (0.03) | (0.05) | (0.10) |
| Teenage mother at study child's birth | -0.34 | 0.70* | 0.70 |
| | (0.18) | (0.26) | (0.53) |
| Teenage mother at a previous birth (NLSY) | | | |
| Mother's employment | | | |
| 30–39 hrs./week (NLSY) or full-time | 0.22 | 0.63* | -1.01* |
| | (0.15) | (0.21) | (0.43) |
| 20–29 hrs./week (NLSY) or part-time | 0.06 | 0.19 | -1.50* |
| | (0.18) | (0.26) | (0.52) |
| 1–19 hrs./week (NLSY) | | | |
| Child is African American | -0.55* | 0.40 | -1.24* |
| | (0.20) | (0.28) | (0.56) |
| Child is male | 0.08 | -0.01 | 0.48 |
| | (0.13) | (0.18) | (0.36) |
| N | 634 | 646 | 646 |
| Adjusted $R^2$ | 0.16 | 0.18 | 0.04 |
| Mean of Y | 5.09 | 10.51 | 21.69 |
| (Stnd. dev.) | (1.70) | (4.73) | (5.87) |

*Indicates coefficient is more than twice its standard error.

Maternal mental health was not associated with neighborhood characteristics, although it was correlated with ethnicity (African American mothers were depressed) and maternal employment (employed mothers were less depressed). Residing in ethnically diverse neighborhoods was linked to lower social support, as was residing in more affluent neighborhoods. Poor families, female-headed families, older mothers, and unemployed mothers reported less social support.

Results for the Children of the NLSY indicate that, controlling for family-level variables (income, education, age, and employment), male joblessness—not the presence of low–socioeconomic status (SES) neighbors or the existence of ethnic diversity—is associated with lower Cognitive Stimulation HOME scores for the three- to four-year-olds. Low family income is associated with a lower-quality home environment, as was found in the IHDP. However, for the five- to six-year-olds in the Children of the NLSY, the presence of high-SES neighbors was associated with better home environments.

## NEIGHBORHOOD EFFECTS AS MEDIATED BY FAMILY-LEVEL PROCESSES

Tables 5.3 and 5.4 present the results of the analyses investigating the effects of psychosocial family resources on child outcomes at ages three and four (table 5.3) and ages five and six (table 5.4). These analyses examine the question of whether or not the neighborhood effects are mediated through family-level processes. If so, then one might expect the regression coefficients for the neighborhood variables to be reduced (see tables 4.3, 4.7, and 4.9) when the family resource variables are entered.

## RESULTS FOR PRESCHOOL CHILDREN

The neighborhood effects reported in chapter 4 are likely to be mediated through their effects on the family, as postulated by Wilson (see figure 5.1). Our second aim is to see whether or not the maternal characteristics and home environment as measured in the NLSY and the IHDP mediate the reported neighborhood effects. The outcomes for the preschoolers are presented in table 5.3. As noted in chapter 4, high SES was associated with child IQ—not low SES, ethnic diversity, or male joblessness (as was found for home environments as the outcome in IHDP). Thus, it comes as no surprise that the neighborhood effect for child cognitive outcome is not mediated by family-level processes. In the IHDP, high SES is still associated with child IQ scores, even after entering the family-level process variables. At the same time, better learning environments and maternal mental health are associated with higher IQ scores, net of neighborhood effects, family income, maternal education, and family structural characteristics. By far the stronger of the two effects is for the home learning environment, where the coefficient exceeds its standard error by a factor of ten. Thus, little evidence exists that family processes, in

(*Text continues on page 133.*)

TABLE 5.3   Effects of Neighborhood Factors, Family Characteristics, and Maternal Characteristics on Developmental Outcomes at Ages Three to Four

| | IHDP Stanford-Binet IQ Score | IHDP PPVT-R Standard Scores | IHDP Achenbach Externalizing Behavior Problems | NLSY PPVT-R Standard Scores | NLSY Externalizing Behavior Problems |
|---|---|---|---|---|---|
| **Neighborhood factors** | | | | | |
| Low SES | 1.27 | 1.17 | 0.12 | -1.63 | 0.19 |
| | (1.10) | (1.03) | (0.82) | (1.02) | (0.25) |
| High SES | 2.46* | 1.30 | -0.90 | 0.20 | 0.41 |
| | (1.00) | (0.94) | (0.75) | (0.92) | (0.23) |
| Male joblessness | -0.43 | -0.91 | -0.87 | -0.20 | 0.26 |
| | (0.83) | (0.78) | (0.62) | (0.75) | (0.19) |
| Family concentration | 0.34 | 0.54 | -0.61 | -0.82 | 0.05 |
| | (0.60) | (0.56) | (0.45) | (0.63) | (0.16) |
| Ethnic diversity | -0.05 | 0.29 | -0.16 | -1.20 | 0.01 |
| | (0.34) | (0.32) | (0.26) | (0.69) | (0.17) |
| **Family characteristics** | | | | | |
| Family income/needs | 2.10* | 0.78 | -0.39 | 0.84 | -0.19 |
| | (0.52) | (0.46) | (0.38) | (0.60) | (0.16) |
| Female head | 1.24 | 0.65 | -0.30 | 2.27 | 0.20 |
| | (1.39) | (1.30) | (1.04) | (1.51) | (0.36) |
| Mother's education | 0.48 | 0.33 | -0.21 | 1.02* | 0.01 |
| | (0.31) | (0.29) | (0.23) | (0.39) | (0.10) |
| Teenage mother at study child's birth | 0.72 | -3.75* | 2.42 | -0.38 | -0.13 |
| | (1.68) | (1.57) | (1.25) | (1.78) | (0.41) |
| Teenage mother at a previous birth (NLSY) | | | | -1.29 | -0.65 |
| | | | | (1.55) | (0.40) |
| **Mother's employment** | | | | | |
| 30–39 hrs./week (NLSY) or full-time | 0.46 | 1.41 | -0.29 | -1.91 | 0.44 |
| | (1.37) | (1.29) | (1.02) | (1.24) | (0.31) |
| 20–29 hrs./week (NLSY) or part-time | -0.63 | 1.37 | -0.39 | -1.31 | -0.51 |
| | (1.64) | (1.54) | (1.22) | (1.96) | (0.63) |
| 1–19 hrs./week (NLSY) | | | | -1.21 | -0.01 |
| | | | | (2.23) | (0.53) |

(Table continues on p. 130.)

TABLE 5.3 *Continued*

| | IHDP Stanford-Binet IQ Score | IHDP PPVT-R Standard Scores | IHDP Achenbach Externalizing Behavior Problems | NLSY PPVT-R Standard Scores | NLSY Externalizing Behavior Problems |
|---|---|---|---|---|---|
| Child is African American | -6.88* (1.80) | -8.72* (1.65) | 1.66 (1.34) | -15.65* (2.23) | -1.30* (0.53) |
| Child is male | -2.63* (1.14) | 0.88 (1.06) | 2.10* (0.85) | -3.16* (1.10) | 0.55 (0.29) |
| Age in months (NLSY) | | | | -0.07 (0.08) | 0.07 (0.04) |
| **Maternal characteristics** | | | | | |
| HOME learning environment 36 mos. (IHDP)/36–59 mos. (NLSY) | 1.41* (0.14) | 1.14* (0.13) | -0.30* (0.11) | 0.40* (0.04) | -0.03* (0.01) |
| HOME physical environment 36 mos. (IHDP) | -0.56 (0.37) | 0.41 (0.35) | -0.96* (0.28) | | |
| HOME warmth 36 mos. (IHDP) | -0.14 (0.39) | -0.70 (0.37) | 0.09 (0.29) | | |
| Depression 36 mos. (IHDP) | -0.26* (0.12) | -0.12 (0.11) | 0.45* (0.09) | | |
| Moos active Behavioral coping 36 mos. (IHDP) | -0.05 (0.10) | -0.17 (0.09) | 0.13 (0.08) | | |
| Social support 36 mos. (IHDP) | -0.09 (0.26) | -0.46 (0.24) | -0.29 (0.19) | | |
| *N* | 634 | 610 | 634 | 715 | 380 |
| Adjusted $R^2$ | 0.50 | 0.46 | 0.18 | 0.37 | 0.04 |
| Mean of *Y* | 88.87 | 87.79 | 25.26 | 92.77 | 12.29 |
| (Stnd. dev.) | (19.74) | (17.48) | (11.48) | (18.19) | (2.75) |

*Indicates coefficient is more than twice its standard error.

130

TABLE 5.4 Effects of Neighborhood Factors, Family Characteristics, and Maternal Characteristics on Developmental Outcomes at Ages Five to Six

| | IHDP WPPSI Verbal IQ Score | IHDP PPVT-R Standard Scores | IHDP Achenbach Externalizing Behavior Problems | NLSY PPVT-R Standard Scores | NLSY PIAT Reading Scores | NLSY Externalizing Behavior Problems | NLSY Internalizing Behavior Problems |
|---|---|---|---|---|---|---|---|
| Neighborhood factors | | | | | | | |
| Low SES | -0.54 (1.03) | 0.003 (1.25) | -0.13 (0.67) | -0.30 (1.18) | 0.43 (0.86) | 0.05 (0.21) | -0.10 (0.16) |
| High SES | 2.16* (0.95) | 1.72 (1.16) | 0.10 (0.62) | 1.72 (1.06) | 1.51 (0.80) | 0.20 (0.19) | 0.38* (0.15) |
| Male joblessness | 0.33 (0.78) | -0.50 (0.95) | 0.26 (0.51) | 0.18 (0.80) | -0.17 (0.59) | -0.05 (0.14) | 0.18 (0.11) |
| Family concentration | -0.62 (0.56) | 0.05 (0.69) | 0.16 (0.37) | -1.61* (0.59) | -0.81 (0.44) | 0.32* (0.11) | 0.15 (0.08) |
| Ethnic diversity | -0.65* (0.32) | -0.83* (0.39) | 0.07 (0.21) | -1.19 (0.84) | 0.43 (0.60) | 0.12 (0.15) | 0.20 (0.11) |
| Family characteristics | | | | | | | |
| Family income/needs | 1.52* (0.56) | 2.03* (0.68) | -0.32 (0.36) | 0.57 (0.63) | 1.51* (0.47) | -0.25* (0.11) | -0.04 (0.09) |
| Female head | -0.55 (1.28) | -1.35 (1.55) | 0.90 (0.83) | 0.76 (1.55) | 2.29* (1.15) | 0.15 (0.27) | 0.23 (0.21) |
| Mother's education | 0.81* (0.32) | 0.67 (0.40) | -0.35 (0.21) | 1.41* (0.41) | 0.82* (0.30) | -0.03 (0.07) | -0.05 (0.06) |
| Teenage mother at study child's birth | 0.11 (1.50) | 1.01 (1.83) | 1.07 (0.97) | -1.55 (1.58) | 0.21 (1.14) | -0.05 (0.28) | -0.18 (0.21) |
| Teenage mother at a previous birth (NLSY) | | | | -0.77 (1.78) | -2.26 (1.35) | 0.83* (0.31) | -0.14 (0.24) |
| Mother's employment | | | | | | | |
| 30–39 hrs./week (NLSY) or full-time | -0.99 (1.89) | 0.54 (2.30) | 1.13 (1.22) | -0.43 (1.32) | 1.36 (0.96) | -0.24 (0.23) | -0.37* (0.18) |
| 20–29 hrs./week (NLSY) or part-time | -0.64 (2.27) | 0.13 (2.77) | 1.86 (1.47) | -1.07 (2.32) | -0.48 (1.76) | 0.58 (0.42) | -0.01 (0.32) |
| 1–19 hrs./week (NLSY) | | | | 4.03 (2.52) | 3.39 (1.81) | 0.38 (0.44) | 0.71* (0.34) |

(Table continues on p. 132.)

TABLE 5.4  Continued

| | IHDP WPPSI Verbal IQ Score | IHDP PPVT-R Standard Scores | IHDP Achenbach Externalizing Behavior Problems | NLSY PPVT-R Standard Scores | NLSY PIAT Reading Scores | NLSY Externalizing Behavior Problems | NLSY Internalizing Behavior Problems |
|---|---|---|---|---|---|---|---|
| Child is African American | -3.62* | -9.64* | -1.78 | -16.07* | -0.85 | -0.93* | -0.26 |
| | (1.67) | (2.03) | (1.08) | (1.92) | (1.40) | (0.33) | (0.26) |
| Child is male | -1.92 | -0.85 | 4.50* | -0.37 | -0.87 | 0.18 | -0.27 |
| | (1.06) | (1.29) | (0.68) | (1.20) | (0.88) | (0.21) | (0.16) |
| Age in months (NLSY) | | | | -0.03 | -0.66* | 0.00 | 0.03 |
| | | | | (0.12) | (0.09) | (0.02) | (0.02) |
| Child is in school | -0.88 | -0.58 | -0.18 | 4.26* | 8.27* | -0.44 | -0.55* |
| | (1.18) | (1.44) | (0.76) | (1.77) | (1.32) | (0.32) | (0.24) |
| Maternal characteristics | | | | | | | |
| HOME learning environment 36 mos. (IHDP)/5 or 6 yrs. (NLSY) | 1.16* | 1.28* | -0.17* | 0.19* | 0.14* | -0.03* | -0.03* |
| | (0.13) | (0.16) | (0.08) | (0.05) | (0.03) | (0.01) | (0.01) |
| HOME physical environment 36 mos. (IHDP) | -0.35 | 0.03 | -0.49* | | | | |
| | (0.35) | (0.43) | (0.23) | | | | |
| HOME warmth 36 mos. (IHDP) | 0.20 | 0.06 | -0.06 | | | | |
| | (0.37) | (0.45) | (0.24) | | | | |
| Depression 36 mos. (IHDP) | -0.08 | -0.20 | 0.32* | | | | |
| | (0.11) | (0.14) | (0.07) | | | | |
| Moos active behavioral coping 36 mos. (IHDP) | 0.05 | 0.14 | 0.18* | | | | |
| | (0.09) | (0.12) | (0.06) | | | | |
| Social support 36 mos. (IHDP) | -0.36 | -0.55* | -0.07 | | | | |
| | (0.23) | (0.28) | (0.15) | | | | |
| N | 585 | 585 | 585 | 554 | 595 | 611 | 608 |
| Adjusted $R^2$ | 0.48 | 0.50 | 0.16 | 0.33 | 0.21 | 0.08 | 0.07 |
| Mean of Y | 90.41 | 81.69 | 12.75 | 95.60 | 107.51 | 11.93 | 9.34 |
| (Stnd. dev.) | (17.43) | (21.71) | (8.88) | (16.77) | (11.83) | (2.66) | (2.05) |

*Indicates coefficient is more than twice its standard error.

particular the home learning environment, mediate the association between affluent neighbors and children's intelligence test scores.

The results from Children of the NLSY analyses present a different picture. As indicated in table 5.1, the level of male joblessness was associated with a lower-quality home environment. The quality of the learning environment is associated with PPVT-R scores, similar to what was found for the IHDP (table 5.3). However, adding the home learning environment to the models results in the neighborhood family concentration and ethnic diversity effects dropping out of the model (as well as the family income effect). In one sense, these findings may indicate a mediator effect. However, the fact that only male joblessness was correlated with HOME scores makes us more circumspect in interpreting this result.

As noted earlier, there were few findings for the IHDP regarding the behavior problems measures. Indeed, the addition of the six family process variables to the model shown in table 4.3 does not alter the (nonsignificant) neighborhood findings. However, better home learning, home physical environment, and maternal mental health scores were associated with lower internalizing and externalizing scores on the behavior problem scale at age three in the IHDP (results are not shown in table 5.3; see Brooks-Gunn, Klebanov, and Liaw 1995b). Boys were more likely to be reported as having externalizing problems; but no neighborhood–home mediated effect was found.

In the Children of the NLSY, findings were somewhat different. While the earlier models as discussed in chapter 4 were generally not significant, the addition of home learning alters the neighborhood findings. In particular, male joblessness is positively associated and ethnic diversity negatively associated with internalizing behaviors on the BPI. For externalizing problems, the presence of affluent neighbors is associated with problems. As in the IHDP, higher-quality home environments were correlated with lower rates of internalizing and externalizing behavior problems, and Externalizing problems were higher in males.

RESULTS FOR SCHOOL-AGE CHILDREN

High SES was associated with verbal IQ at age five in the IHDP (table 4.7). Adding in the family-level processes does not alter this effect (table 5.4). Ethnic diversity was also correlated with verbal IQ at age five; however, adding in family-level processes resulted in the neighborhood factor becoming less significant. The ratio between the unstandardized coefficient to the standard error drops from about a factor of three when controlling only for neighborhood and family income and structural variables for both verbal IQ and PPVT-R to about a factor of two when the family process variables are added to the regression. Therefore, the negative effect of ethnically diverse neighbors is in part mediated by the family process variables, specifically the quality of the home learning environment. Specifically, residing in an ethnically diverse neighborhood is associated with worse learning environments, which in turn affect children's verbal ability two years later (figure 5.2).

FIGURE 5.2   Two Models of Neighborhood and Family Influences on Child Development
Outcomes, Ages Five to Six

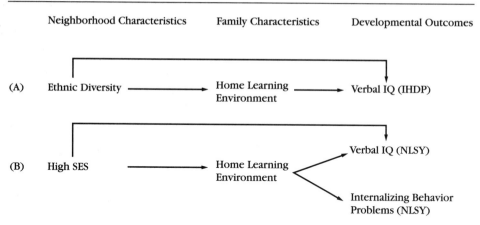

Likewise, evidence of mediation is found in the Children of the NLSY sample of five- and six-year-olds. As noted in chapter 4, residence in high-SES neighborhoods was associated with better reading scores on the PIAT and higher PPVT-R verbal ability scores, and family neighborhood concentration was associated with PPVT-R scores (table 4.7). Controlling for the home learning score results in a decrease in the association between high-SES neighbors and the PIAT and the PPVT-R scores. At the same time, the quality of the home environment is linked to reading and verbal ability. These findings suggest that the association between high-SES neighbors and school and cognitive outcomes is mediated by the quality of the home environment (figure 5.2). Similar findings are not revealed for the family concentration neighborhood measure.

No effects of family process resources as mediating the effects of neighborhoods on children's behavior problems were found in the IHDP. However, for the Children of the NLSY at ages five to six, the existence of high SES neighbors was associated with fewer internalizing behavior problems (table 4.9). Controlling for home learning results in a drop in the regression coefficient for high-SES neighbors (table 5.4), and home learning is associated with fewer internalizing problems. Again, evidence for a mediated model is found in the Children of the NLSY: high-SES neighbors are associated with better learning environments, which in turn are linked to fewer internalizing behavior problems (figure 5.2).

FAMILY PROCESS IN RESOURCE-RICH AND RESOURCE-POOR NEIGHBORHOODS

The final aim is to see whether or not family-level processes are linked to child outcomes differently as a function of neighborhood type. This issue is addressed by examining moderator effects rather than mediator effects. Indeed, what may be important is the interaction of neighborhood and family, rather than the indirect effects of neighborhoods as being mediated through the family (see figure 5.2). These analyses are less focused on explaining the overall neighborhood effects than on looking at subgroups of families or differential family effects in different contexts. Thus, these analyses represent the type Bronfenbrenner (1979) favored in his ecosystem model.

For these analyses, we constructed a composite neighborhood factor composed of the sum of the low-SES, high-SES, and male joblessness factors (see chapters 3 and 4). Higher scores indicated worse neighborhood conditions. Neighborhoods with scores less than 0 were considered resource rich; those with scores of 0 or above were considered resource poor. These scores were based on the national scores on these three factors, rather than the sample-specific scores (that is, based on data derived from the PSID; see chapter 3). Consequently, somewhat fewer families were in resource-rich neighborhoods in each sample, given that both the IHDP and the NLSY samples are more disadvantaged than the national PSID sample. In the IHDP at age three, 175 families resided in resource-rich neighborhoods versus 456 in resource-poor neighborhoods. At age five, 153 families resided in resource-rich neighborhoods versus 408 in resource-poor neighborhoods (numbers based on those with IQ data).

In both resource-rich and resource-poor neighborhoods, low family income and low-quality home learning environment were associated with age three IQ and PPVT-R (table 5.5). Black children had lower scores in both types of neighborhoods. Several other variables were associated with cognitive outcomes in the resource-poor neighborhoods—specifically, gender (girls having higher IQ scores in the poor neighborhoods) and maternal age (children of teenage parents having lower PPVT scores).

Similar to the IHDP findings, low-quality home learning environments were associated with lower PPVT-R scores in both resource-rich and resource-poor neighborhoods in the Children of the NLSY. However, family income did not reach significance in either regression. Also comparable was the finding that black children had lower verbal scores in both types of neighborhoods. Two family-level variables were associated with residence in a resource-poor neighborhood. Specifically full-time maternal employment was associated with lower scores, and maternal education was associated with higher scores. In addition, boys in resource-rich neighborhoods had lower IQ scores than girls in such neighborhoods, in contrast to the IHDP findings.

Interestingly, interactions between ethnicity and home learning were found in both samples. Specifically, in resource-rich neighborhoods black, but not white, children benefited from high-quality home learning environments in the IHDP. Whites were more likely to benefit from high-quality learning environments than blacks in resource-poor neighborhoods in both samples. In addition, in the IHDP, children in resource-poor neighborhoods were likely to have higher IQ scores if their mothers had more education and higher family incomes.

Quality of home environment as measured at age three in the IHDP was predictive of full-scale IQ and the PPVT-R at age five in both resource-rich and resource-poor neighborhoods (table 5.6). Also, higher maternal education was associated with higher IQ scores in resource-poor neighborhoods. An interaction between quality of learning environment and maternal education in resource-poor neighborhoods indicated that the effect of quality of home environment was greater for more-educated mothers. Being in school at the time of the age-five assessment was associated with lower IQ scores in the resource-rich neighborhoods.

The interactions between quality of learning environment and family characteristics indicated that the effect of quality of learning was more pronounced for children in families with more income in both types of neighborhoods. Similarly, the effects of home environment were stronger for white children (who are more likely to reside in families with higher incomes). These effects were seen in both types of neighborhoods.

The IHDP findings for the PPVT-R scores, as opposed to the full-scale IQ scores at age five, differ somewhat. Having a better quality of learning environment, being white, and being from a higher-income family were linked to higher verbal ability scores in both types of neighborhoods. Only two interactions were seen: better quality of home was associated with higher PPVT-R scores for whites, but not blacks, in resource-poor neighborhoods. Girls were more influenced by provision of cognitive stimulation than boys in resource-rich neighborhoods.

The NLSY results for the PPVT-R and the PIAT are as follows. In the resource-poor neighborhoods, children of more-educated mothers, children with better home environments, and white children had higher verbal scores (PPVT-R). Being in school had positive effects in resource-rich neighborhoods. One interaction was seen, in that less educated mothers were more affected by better home environments than were more educated mothers in the resource-rich neighborhoods (in direct contrast to the IHDP findings for IQ scores).

The PIAT scores were associated with quality of home and being in school in both types of neighborhoods. Maternal education was associated with better performance in resource-poor neighborhoods, and more family income was linked to higher PIAT scores in resource-rich neighborhoods. No interactions between family characteristics and home learning were found.

## DISCUSSION

These results discussed in this chapter partially support Wilson's thesis that residence in poor neighborhoods may detrimentally affect the family, specifically parenting behavior. Mothers in such neighborhoods exhibited less cog-

*(Text continues on page 141.)*

TABLE 5.5  Effects of Family Characteristics on Children's Developmental Outcomes at Ages Three to Four, by Neighborhood Resource

| | IHDP Stanford-Binet IQ Scores | | IHDP PPVT-R Standard Scores | | NLSY PPVT-R Standard Scores | |
|---|---|---|---|---|---|---|
| | Resource Rich | Resource Poor | Resource Rich | Resource Poor | Resource Rich | Resource Poor |
| Family characteristics | | | | | | |
| Family income/needs | 1.84* | 1.91* | 1.46* | 1.88* | 0.49 | 0.82 |
| | (0.84) | (0.69) | (0.72) | (0.67) | (0.90) | (0.83) |
| Female head | 1.99 | 0.76 | 2.57 | 1.26 | -0.30 | 2.49 |
| | (3.03) | (1.42) | (2.61) | (1.38) | (2.63) | (1.86) |
| Mother's education | 0.70 | 0.17 | 0.94 | 0.06 | 0.69 | 1.37* |
| | (0.68) | (0.34) | (0.59) | (0.33) | (0.59) | (0.57) |
| Teenage mother at study | 4.39 | -0.18 | 0.37 | -4.31* | -1.16 | -0.33 |
| child's birth | (5.67) | (1.69) | (4.87) | (1.63) | (2.90) | (2.29) |
| Teenage mother at a | | | | | -0.47 | -2.09 |
| previous birth (NLSY) | | | | | (2.64) | (1.92) |
| Mother's employment | | | | | | |
| 30–39 hrs./week (NLSY) | -2.05 | 2.40 | -0.83 | 2.29 | 0.17 | -3.35* |
| or full-time | (2.93) | (1.55) | (2.52) | (1.50) | (2.05) | (1.62) |
| 20–29 hrs./week (NLSY) | 0.85 | -1.60 | -1.24 | 2.32 | 0.09 | -2.07 |
| or part-time | (3.25) | (1.88) | (2.80) | (1.82) | (3.04) | (2.62) |
| 1–19 hrs./week (NLSY) | | | | | -0.19 | -3.26 |
| | | | | | (3.16) | (3.35) |
| Child is African American | -8.46* | -4.12* | -9.75* | -5.78* | -21.00* | -16.64* |
| | (3.75) | (1.88) | (3.23) | (1.82) | (3.63) | (1.86) |
| Child is male | -2.46 | -3.67* | 1.09 | -0.47 | -3.48* | -2.49 |
| | (2.40) | (1.28) | (2.06) | (1.24) | (1.76) | (1.43) |
| Age in months (NLSY) | | | | | 0.03 | -0.11 |
| | | | | | (0.13) | (0.11) |

(Table continues on page 138.)

TABLE 5.5  *Continued*

| | IHDP Stanford-Binet IQ Scores | | IHDP PPVT-R Standard Scores | | NLSY PPVT-R Standard Scores | |
|---|---|---|---|---|---|---|
| | Resource Rich | Resource Poor | Resource Rich | Resource Poor | Resource Rich | Resource Poor |
| HOME learning environment | 1.89* | 1.13* | 0.98* | 0.80* | 0.04* | 0.04* |
| | (0.32) | (0.13) | (0.28) | (0.13) | (0.01) | (0.01) |
| Interaction: learning × income/needs[a] | -0.09 | 0.24* | 0.12 | 0.02 | -0.01 | -0.00 |
| | (0.18) | (0.10) | (0.15) | (0.10) | (0.01) | (0.00) |
| Interaction: learning × mother's education[a] | 0.33 | 0.21* | 0.19 | 0.17* | -0.00 | -0.01 |
| | (0.26) | (0.05) | (0.23) | (0.04) | (0.00) | (0.01) |
| Interaction: learning × child is African American[a] | 2.10* | -1.73* | 2.23* | -2.00* | -0.02 | -0.02* |
| | (0.70) | (0.37) | (0.59) | (0.36) | (0.03) | (0.01) |
| Interaction: learning × child is male[a] | -0.54 | 0.02 | -0.40 | -0.20 | 0.00 | -0.01 |
| | (0.60) | (0.24) | (0.51) | (0.23) | (0.01) | (0.01) |
| $N$ | 175 | 456 | 175 | 432 | 260 | 455 |
| Adjusted $R^{2b}$ | 0.47 | 0.40 | 0.42 | 0.37 | 0.27 | 0.34 |
| Mean of $Y$ | 100.26 | 84.36 | 98.02 | 83.30 | 98.59 | 87.71 |
| (Stnd. dev.) | (20.82) | (17.25) | (17.03) | (15.72) | (16.19) | (18.34) |

*Indicates coefficient is more than twice its standard error.

[a] Interactions control for the effects of family characteristics. One interaction term per regression model; total of four models run per dependent variable.

[b] For regression model without interaction term.

TABLE 5.6  Effects of Family Characteristics on Children's Developmental Outcomes at Ages Five to Six, by Neighborhood Resource

| | IHDP WPPSI IQ Scores | | IHDP PPVT-R Standard Scores | | NLSY PPVT-R Standard Scores | | NLSY PIAT Reading Scores | |
|---|---|---|---|---|---|---|---|---|
| | Rich | Poor | Rich | Poor | Rich | Poor | Rich | Poor |
| Family characteristics | | | | | | | | |
| Family income/needs | 0.35 | 1.27 | 1.97* | 1.99* | −0.33 | 1.09 | 2.19* | 0.97 |
| | (0.77) | (0.78) | (0.95) | (0.95) | (0.91) | (0.88) | (0.81) | (0.59) |
| Female head | −3.75 | −0.64 | −1.50 | −1.47 | −0.26 | 1.58 | 5.53* | 0.85 |
| | (2.18) | (1.54) | (2.69) | (1.87) | (2.62) | (1.93) | (2.40) | (1.24) |
| Mother's education | 0.64 | 1.70* | 0.19 | 0.98 | 0.80 | 1.41* | 0.39 | 1.01* |
| | (0.46) | (0.44) | (0.56) | (0.54) | (0.64) | (0.54) | (0.57) | (0.35) |
| Teenage mother at study child's birth | 4.43 | 0.46 | 11.06* | −0.71 | −2.45 | −2.40 | −2.91 | 1.07 |
| | (4.13) | (1.66) | (5.10) | (2.02) | (2.66) | (1.98) | (2.34) | (1.27) |
| Teenage mother at a previous birth (NLSY) | | | | | −1.45 | −1.31 | −1.64 | −2.36 |
| | | | | | (2.94) | (2.25) | (2.64) | (1.53) |
| Mother's employment | | | | | | | | |
| 30–39 hrs./week (NLSY) or full-time | 0.34 | −0.04 | 3.84 | 0.67 | −1.17 | 0.45 | 1.68 | 1.00 |
| | (3.92) | (2.20) | (4.84) | (2.68) | (2.00) | (1.79) | (1.78) | (1.14) |
| 20–29 hrs./week (NLSY) or part-time | −0.81 | 1.69 | 5.04 | 0.42 | −1.14 | 0.64 | −0.84 | 0.10 |
| | (4.21) | (2.78) | (5.20) | (3.37) | (3.87) | (2.96) | (3.66) | (1.96) |
| 1–19 hrs./week (NLSY) | | | | | 7.31* | 1.43 | 7.94* | −0.64 |
| | | | | | (3.55) | (3.56) | (2.98) | (2.37) |
| Child is African American | −4.27 | −3.55 | −9.29* | −7.98* | −15.58* | −17.18* | 2.09 | −1.14 |
| | (2.86) | (1.93) | (3.53) | (2.35) | (3.25) | (1.90) | (2.95) | (1.23) |
| Child is male | −3.19 | −2.12 | −1.41 | −1.88 | 0.47 | −1.08 | 0.85 | −1.74 |
| | (1.83) | (1.32) | (2.25) | (1.61) | (1.85) | (1.56) | (1.65) | (1.01) |
| Age in months (NLSY) | | | | | −0.07 | 0.02 | −0.65* | −0.66* |
| | | | | | (0.20) | (0.15) | (0.18) | (0.10) |

(Table continues on p. 140.)

TABLE 5.6  *Continued*

| | IHDP WPPSI IQ Scores | | IHDP PPVT-R Standard Scores | | NLSY PPVT-R Standard Scores | | NLSY PIAT Reading Scores | |
|---|---|---|---|---|---|---|---|---|
| | Rich | Poor | Rich | Poor | Rich | Poor | Rich | Poor |
| Child is in school | -4.02* | 1.15 | -5.15* | 1.42 | 12.98* | -2.03 | 11.29* | 6.71* |
| | (2.00) | (1.45) | (2.47) | (1.76) | (2.87) | (2.25) | (2.58) | (1.48) |
| HOME learning environment | 2.00* | 1.08* | 1.91* | 1.16* | 0.01 | 0.02* | 0.02* | 0.01* |
| | (0.26) | (0.14) | (0.32) | (0.17) | (0.01) | (0.01) | (0.01) | (0.00) |
| Interaction: learning × income/needs[a] | 0.42* | 0.24* | -0.16 | -0.16 | 0.00 | 0.00 | -0.00 | 0.00 |
| | (0.13) | (0.11) | (0.17) | (0.14) | (0.01) | (0.00) | (0.00) | (0.00) |
| Interaction: learning × mother's education[a] | c | 0.28* | c | 0.09 | -0.02* | -0.00 | 0.00 | 0.00 |
| | | (0.09) | | (0.12) | (0.01) | (0.01) | (0.01) | (0.00) |
| Interaction: learning × child is African American[a] | -1.29* | -1.42* | 1.12 | -1.01* | -0.00 | -0.00 | 0.00 | -0.00 |
| | (0.53) | (0.39) | (0.66) | (0.48) | (0.02) | (0.01) | (0.02) | (0.01) |
| Interaction: learning × child is male[a] | -1.42* | -0.04 | -1.33 | -0.51 | 0.02 | 0.01 | -0.01 | -0.01 |
| | (0.46) | (0.24) | (0.58) | (0.29) | (0.02) | (0.01) | (0.01) | (0.01) |
| N | 153 | 408 | 153 | 408 | 190 | 364 | 196 | 399 |
| Adjusted $R^{2}$[b] | 0.57 | 0.35 | 0.57 | 0.33 | 0.30 | 0.30 | 0.19 | 0.22 |
| Mean of Y | 103.07 | 86.90 | 96.76 | 76.02 | 100.31 | 92.05 | 109.61 | 106.01 |
| (*Stnd. dev.) | (16.48) | (16.20) | (20.33) | (18.32) | (14.75) | (17.35) | (12.44) | (11.16) |

*Indicates coefficient is more than twice its standard error.

[a] Interactions control for the effects of family characteristics. One interaction term per regression model; total of four models run per dependent variable.

[b] For regression model without interaction term.

[c] Interaction term not entered in regression model because of tolerance limitations.

140

nitive stimulation and their homes were in worse physical condition than those mothers not residing in such neighborhoods, based on the IHDP data set. These findings were net of family income and other family characteristics. The comparable analyses for the Children of the NLSY did not reveal such an effect, although male joblessness was linked to lower-quality home environments. Whether or not these differences are due to sample composition or the use of the short versus full form of the HOME inventory is not known. (See Baker et al. [1993] and Sugland et al. [1995] for a discussion of the differences in predictive power of the short and full HOME in these two study populations.) However, these findings do suggest that socialization or contagion might account for the fact that home environments are of lower quality in poor neighborhoods. At the same time, this effect was due to the presence of poor neighbors, not the absence of affluent neighbors, as was described in chapter 4 for child cognitive outcomes.

Living in an ethnically diverse neighborhood was associated with lower-quality learning environments, as well as lower maternal warmth and lower social support. Ethnographers have written about the potentially negative effects of living in ethnically heterogeneous neighborhoods, if these neighborhoods are generally poor. Whether or not such effects would be due to relative deprivation, housing segregation, lack of agreed-upon norms and sanctions, or some other mechanism is not known. Also, these effects might vary as a function of ethnicity. Social support may be lower if distrust of neighbors is high in integrated neighborhoods. And maternal warmth may be less if mothers feel that they must prepare their children to reside in a harsher environment (that is, if ethnic conflict, whether real or imagined, is high) or if generally they are feeling uncomfortable (that is, they may be less warm to everyone, including their children). Examples in terms of impoverished neighborhoods, not ethnically heterogeneous neighborhoods, are provided by Coulton and Pandey (1992), Jarrett (vol. 2), Korbin and Coulton (vol. 2), and McLoyd (1990a).

Social support was also lower in families residing in affluent neighborhoods. Such social isolation may be due to psychological barriers (networks being less neighborhood focused) and physical barriers (large lots, security, fences). Also families residing in affluent settings might be comparing themselves to their neighbors, who might be perceived as having more access to child care and other forms of support, so that the diminished support is due to relative comparisons.

FAMILY PROCESSES AS A MEDIATOR OF NEIGHBORHOOD EFFECTS

We expected that many of the neighborhood effects reported in chapter 4 might operate through a series of family processes. Wilson (1991a, 1991b) has suggested a number of processes that might be influenced by neighborhood residence and which, in turn, might influence children. However, the measures available in the IHDP and NLSY are somewhat different from those considered by most scholars investigating neighborhood effects. The available measures, however, have been shown to predict child outcomes in small-scale developmental studies. Of most relevance are the three measures of home environment—home learning, home physical environment, and maternal warmth. These have been measured in numerous studies and have been conceptualized as critical for child development (Bradley et al. 1989, 1994; Berlin et al. 1995; Brooks-Gunn and Chase-Lansdale 1995; Brooks-Gunn, Klebanov et al. 1995; Sugland et al. 1995). In any case, our analyses are limited in that many relevant constructs of importance to families have not been conceptualized or measured (Brooks-Gunn, Klebanov et al. 1995).

We hypothesized that even at the preschool age the presence of affluent neighbors might have an indirect, rather than a direct, effect on children. Residing in neighborhoods with many affluent families may set positive norms for parenting that others emulate and that reinforce sanctions against certain types of parenting, although no evidence on young children in neighborhoods exists on this question, to our knowledge. Residing in a neighborhood with many affluent neighbors might result in more dense and possibly satisfying social support networks and less stress, which might be reflected in high social support and low maternal depression, factors that often are associated with enhanced child outcomes. However, little evidence exists of mediator effects for the children aged three to four.

One limitation of the analyses presented here is that the family process variables selected for inclusion were chosen for studies not specifically focused on neighborhood effects. Consequently, the constructs available may not be those most relevant to neighborhood effects on families. For example, we have no measures of supervision or monitoring, family organization, consistency in routines, or parental self-efficacy (Sampson and Groves 1993; Sampson and Laub 1994). Instead, we have cognitive stimulation in the home, maternal mental health, social support, and coping style, all of which have been hypothesized to be important for young children's development. Whether or not they are influenced by neighborhood residence is an unanswered question.

In contrast, mediated effects were more pronounced for the children in early elementary school. These effects were found for both samples, and the family mediator was the same in each, namely, the home learning environment. The positive effects of residing in a high-SES neighborhood on higher achievement and verbal ability scores and lower behavior problem scores were mediated by quality home learning environments in the Children of the NLSY. The negative effects of residing in an ethnically diverse neighborhood on verbal scores were offset in part by high-quality home learning in the IHDP. These findings provide support for the mechanisms as postulated by Wilson (1994) and Sampson (1992; Sampson and Morenoff vol. 2).

We are left with several questions, though. Why are the high-SES neighborhood effects mediated through home learning in one sample but not the other?

We are puzzled by this finding, especially since the link between high-SES neighborhood and child cognitive outcome was found in both samples. One possibility is that the two samples differ on neighborhood composition. Another factor might be the use of a different HOME measure in the two studies.

Second, why are mediated effects seen at the early elementary school age but not the preschool age? Perhaps the lack of mediated effects at the earlier age is really a developmental phenomenon—that is, neighborhood effects are less likely to be evidenced at the preschool age and are less consistent across data sets. Perhaps more neighborhood effects (and more mediation) are seen as children begin to spend more time outside of their homes. In both samples the majority of children were in kindergarten or, in the case of the Children of the NLSY, in first grade. Even those five-year-olds not in kindergarten were likely to be in preschool or prekindergarten. Mothers themselves may spend more time with other children and mothers as their children become older, so that their own parenting is more influenced by those outside of the family. Such speculations, however, await other studies of these two age groups.

FAMILY PROCESSES AS A MODERATOR OF NEIGHBORHOOD EFFECTS

Perhaps most noteworthy in the moderator analyses is the fact that the effect of the home environment is found across age groups, measures, samples, and resource-rich and resource-poor neighborhoods. Thus, the home learning effect is not dependent on the form of the scale used (short form in the NLSY and full form in the IHDP), nor is it age dependent (keeping in mind our restricted age range of three to six years). One might have hypothesized that home learning would be more important in resource-poor than in resource-rich neighborhoods, although this is not the case. We believe that these findings, although speculative, indicate the importance of home learning for young children, both in terms of verbal ability and school achievement. We anticipate that these links would become less strong throughout the middle childhood and early adolescent years, as more time is spent in school and with peers, although home learning effects would not disappear entirely (Baydar, Brooks-Gunn, and Furstenberg 1993; Brooks-Gunn, Guo, and Furstenberg 1993).

The second salient set of findings has to do with the interactions between quality of home environment and family characteristics in each of the neighborhood types. In resource-poor neighborhoods, white children were more likely to benefit from better home environments than were black children. This was true across samples at age three and in IHDP, but not NLSY, at age five.[1]

Why would the learning environment make less of a difference for black children than for white children in resource-poor neighborhoods? Among the possibilities are the following. First, black children, on average, lived in poorer neighborhoods than did white children. Even in the resource-poor neighborhood group, blacks were in worse neighborhoods than whites in the poor-neighborhood group (Duncan, Brooks-Gunn, and Klebanov 1994). Because of these differentials, black children may be less able to profit from better home environments. Second, the black families are more likely to experience stressful and negative life events than the white families, *even after controlling for family income*. For example, in the IHDP, we have examined the effects of cumulative risks on child outcomes in poor and nonpoor families (Brooks-Gunn, Klebanov, and Liaw 1995b; Liaw and Brooks-Gunn 1994; Brooks-Gunn et al. 1995). When comparing black and white children from poor families, the black children are more likely to experience low maternal education, low maternal verbal ability scores, maternal depression, persistent poverty, neighborhood poverty, parental unemployment, and low social support. Black families in resource-poor neighborhoods may be worse off than white families in resource-poor neighborhoods, just as they are worse off even when we are looking only at families below the poverty line. Third, the distributions of IQ and PPVT-R scores differ for the blacks and whites in both samples, as do the distributions of HOME scores. Measurement error is more likely with truncated distributions (Lord and Novick 1968).

Regardless of the reason, the fact that black children living in resource-poor neighborhoods may not benefit as much from better home environments is troubling from a policy viewpoint. If this finding is replicated, then it raises the following issue: Will programs and services based on enhancing the home environment be least effective for black children living in resource-poor neighborhoods? A more positive view is that this finding highlights the need for more attention to community-level, rather than just family-level, interventions. Would interventions have to alter the resources in the neighborhood as well as the family to make a difference in children's lives? Clearly, many individuals running and evaluating community-based programs would argue just that (see Brown and Richman vol. 2; Korbin and Coulton vol. 2).

Other moderator effects were seen, although results were less consistent across samples, ages, and measures. Effects were moderated by family income and maternal education such that children with more income benefited more from better learning environments in both types of neighborhoods in the IHDP, but not for the Children of the NLSY. Maternal education had a similar effect in the IHDP, but only for resource-poor neighborhoods. A similar argument to that posed for black families in poor neighborhoods may also be put forth for children whose mothers are less educated and whose families have less income. Again, such data speak to the importance of considering both neighborhood and family resources when developing or planning services.

In conclusion, neighborhood effects on preschool children were less likely to operate through parental behaviors or psychosocial resources in the family, using the IHDP and the Children of the NLSY data sets, than expected. However, evidence for such effects becomes stronger as children enter school. These data support Wilson's (1991a, 1991b) thesis. More sensitive measures of family processes (that is, those likely to be important in a neighborhood context) are needed. Additionally, moderator effects were also found. Interestingly, the effects were more likely to occur in resource-poor, rather than resource-rich, neighborhoods. Finally, children from more-advantaged families were more likely to benefit from the provision of learning experiences in the home than children from less-advantaged families in resource-poor neighborhoods, suggesting the need to integrate family-level and neighborhood-level interventions.

---

The analysis and writing of this chapter were supported by grants from the Russell Sage Foundation, the March of Dimes Foundation, the Foundation for Child Development, the National Institute for Child Health and Human Development Research Network on Child and Family Well-Being (NICHD), the Social Science Research Council Underclass Committee, and the Rockefeller Foundation, whose generosity is appreciated. The Infant Health and Development Program was supported by the Robert Wood Johnson Foundation; the Pew Charitable Trusts; the Bureau of Maternal and Child Health and Resources Development, HRSA, PHS, DHHS (MCJ-060515); and NICHD. The participating universities and site directors were Patrick H. Casey, M.D., University of Arkansas for Medical Sciences (Little Rock, AR); Cecelia M. McCarton, M.D., Albert Einstein College of Medicine (Bronx, NY); Marie McCormick, M.D., Harvard Medical School (Boston, MA); Charles R. Bauer, M.D., University of Miami School of Medicine (Miami, FL); Judith Bernbaum, M.D., University of Pennsylvania School of Medicine (Philadelphia, PA); Jon E. Tyson, M.D., and Mark Swanson, M.D., University of Texas Health Science Center at Dallas; Clifford J. Sells, M.D., and Forrest C. Bennett, M.D., University of Washington School of Medicine (Seattle, WA); and David T. Scott, Ph.D., Yale University School of Medicine (New Haven, CT). The Longitudinal Study Office is directed by Cecelia McCarton, Marie McCormick, and Jeanne Brooks-Gunn. The Data Coordinating Center is directed by James Tonascia and Curtis Meinert at the Johns Hopkins University, School of Hygiene and Public Health. We also would like to thank R. T. Gross, the director of the National Study Office, and C. Ramey, the director of the Program Development Office of the Infant Health and Development Program. Finally, we thank the Educational Testing Service, Division of Policy Research, for the postdoctoral fellowship Dr. Klebanov held.

## NOTES

1. Additionally (and as expected, given previous literature), blacks had lower scores than did whites. See Brooks-Gunn, Klebanov, and Duncan (in press) for a discussion of the reasons for these findings in the IHDP. See Crane (unpublished) for a similar discussion for the Children of the NLSY.

$$6$$

# Neighborhood and Family Factors Predicting Educational Risk and Attainment in African American and White Children and Adolescents

*Bonnie L. Halpern-Felsher, James P. Connell, Margaret Beale Spencer,
J. Lawrence Aber, Greg J. Duncan, Elizabeth Clifford,
Warren E. Crichlow, Peter A. Usinger, Steven P. Cole,
LaRue Allen, and Edward Seidman*

I n American society, individual development during early and middle childhood largely depends on events occurring at home and in school (Entwisle and Alexander 1992, 1993). As children develop, they spend less time with adults and more time with their friends. Adolescence, in particular, is a time when many activities take place outside the home and when youth are presumably subjected to more extrafamilial influences than at any previous time (Brown 1990; Csikszentmihalyi, Larson, and Prescott 1977). In this chapter we explore the extent to which neighborhood composition and family characteristics are associated with school outcomes using several separate data sets of African American and white males and females representing three age periods: middle childhood, early adolescence, and middle adolescence.

## EDUCATIONAL RISK AND ATTAINMENT

Reviews of the psychological, sociological, and educational literature reveal numerous studies exploring associations between *family* economic background and academic performance (Vito 1993). For example, quantitative research has found family poverty, ethnicity, and household composition to be associated with academic achievement (Alexander and Entwisle 1989; Chase-Lansdale and Brooks-Gunn 1995; Danziger and Danziger 1995; Duncan and Brooks-Gunn 1997; Entwisle and Hayduk 1982; Huston 1991; Huston, Garcia-Coll, and McLoyd 1994; McLanahan and Sandefur 1994; Neisser 1986). Patterson, Kupersmidt, and Vaden (1990) found that the best predictors of academic achievement were family income level and ethnicity, with gender and household composition also making significant contributions. Their results suggest that being African American, male, or from low-income or single-parent homes increases the risk of poor elementary school performance. In their longitudinal study, Entwisle and Alexander (1992) examined the extent to which poverty, family structure, and the racial composition of schools explained obtained differences between black and white elementary students' mathematics scores. Their multiple regression analyses revealed that family economic status was clearly an important variable in accounting for these differences, but that family structure was not (see also Korenman, Miller, and Sjaastad 1995; Smith, Brooks-Gunn, and Klebanov forthcoming).

In addition to studies exploring the effect of family resources on children's and adolescents' school performance and behavior, Wilson's (1987) theory has sparked a renewed and growing interest in understanding how *neighborhoods* affect academic achievement. Wilson's theory states, among other things, that the social isolation of poor blacks in the inner cities amplifies social ills associated with poverty, such as school failure and delinquency. As discussed in earlier chapters in this volume and by Jencks and Mayer (1990), neighborhoods can influence children's and adolescents' development in many ways. In this chapter, we restrict our empirical examination to associations between neighborhood composition and educational outcomes.

Few quantitative studies exist that seek to document neighborhood effects on educational or any other developmental outcomes in middle childhood. However, these effects have been studied in preschool-age children (see, for example, Brooks-Gunn, Duncan et al. 1993; Duncan, Brooks-Gunn, and Klebanov 1994), and a substantial body of literature exists on the effects of neighborhoods on adolescents' academic success (Brooks-Gunn, Duncan et al. 1993; Clark 1992; Crane 1991; Dornbusch, Ritter, and Steinberg 1991). For example, Crane (1991) tested epidemic models using data from a special linked family-tract cross-sectional file from the 1970 census-based PUMS file. Consistent with those models, he found highly nonlinear effects of neighborhood quality on adolescent educational outcomes. Dropping out of high school was very likely to occur among individuals, whether black or white, living in neighborhoods with extremely small numbers (5 percent or fewer) of workers in the neighborhood holding professional or managerial jobs. Apart from neighborhoods in this extreme category, however, there was little evidence that neighborhood characteristics mattered. Crane's estimates of sex-specific effects for black and white youth showed significant (and also nonlinear) effects for black males, but not females, residing in the largest cities.

The epidemic model's power to describe patterns of neighborhood effects is called into question by Clark's (1992) failure to replicate Crane's (1991) results using similar data from the 1980 census. Although Clark found that several measures of neighborhood resources predict males' high school dropout status, she failed to find substantial evidence of *nonlinear* effects.

Brooks-Gunn, Duncan, and colleagues (1993) examined the impact of neighborhoods, singly and in concert with family-level variables, on school leaving (and out-of-wedlock childbearing) among adolescent females using data from the Panel Study of Income Dynamics (PSID). In an attempt to distinguish between the effects of poor and affluent neighbors, they included distinct indicators of the presence or absence of low- and high-income neighbors. They found that (1) neighborhood effects were often statistically significant and at times rivaled family effects; (2) to the extent that economic characteristics of neighborhoods affected child development (IQ measures), the *absence* of affluent neighbors seemed much more important than the *presence* of low-income neighbors (findings that support models of collective socialization rather than epidemic); and (3) associations between neighborhood variables and adolescent outcomes were stronger in white females than in blacks and, particularly, economically *dis*advantaged adolescent females. The latter results appear to run counter to the hypothesis that the co-occurrence of minority status and growing up in disadvantaged families makes these children particularly vulnerable to neighborhood effects. However, these same results could suggest that poor African American females have, by necessity, adapted more effectively to these adverse conditions than have their less disadvantaged, white peers.

Clark's (1992) analysis of 1980 census data on adolescent males' school-dropout status replicated many of the findings of Brooks-Gunn, Duncan, and colleagues (1993) for their PSID sample of adolescent females. After controlling for family-level characteristics, Clark found that several indicators of economically well-off neighbors are significant predictors of school dropout, but that black youth appear to benefit less from affluent neighbors than do white youth. In contrast to Brooks-Gunn and colleagues, however, Clark found evidence that the number of poor neighbors is a significant predictor of dropout status, although the size of the detrimental effect of poor neighbors is estimated to be considerably less than the size of the beneficial effect of affluent neighbors.

Dornbusch, Ritter, and Steinberg (1991) examined the effects of census-based neighborhood characteristics on schooling outcomes, but they used a smaller and much more localized sample than Brooks-Gunn, Duncan, and associates (1993), Clark (1992), or Crane (1991). An advantage of the Dornbusch data is that it contains measures of family processes (namely, parenting style, parental involvement, decision making, and reaction to grades). The principal neighborhood measure used in these studies is composed of indicators of both neighbors with high socioeconomic status (SES) and those with low SES, and thus it does not provide tests of the theoretically important distinction between low- and high-SES neighbors. Dornbusch and colleagues (1991) found that neighborhood SES is a highly significant predictor of self-reported grades, even after controlling for family structure and parental schooling. In contrast to the studies just cited, they found somewhat stronger effects of neighborhood SES for blacks than for whites. They did not report whether the effects of neighborhood SES were different for the males and females in their samples. Family *process* variables accounted for relatively small fractions of the effects of the neighborhood variables for both ethnic groups (see also Darling and Steinberg vol. 2).

Also noteworthy is a study by Garner and Raudenbush (1991), who used data from a sample of adolescents in one education authority in Scotland in the mid-1980s, with area data taken from the 1981 Census of Population. Neighborhood quality was measured by a "deprivation score," a previously developed index of twelve economic, demographic, and housing measures formed from census data. Using hierarchical linear modeling methods to estimate their model, they found a negative and highly significant effect of the neighborhood deprivation score on completed schooling. They did not report whether the effects of neighborhood deprivation interacted with either the adolescents' sex or family SES.

Taken as a whole, the existing literature on neighborhood effects confirms the presence of these effects on educational risk and attainment. However, this literature produces little consistent evidence as to *which* children and adolescents might be most susceptible to neighborhood influences and does not explore, in any detail, the processes whereby gender and ethnic subgroups of adolescents may be differentially adapting to these neighborhood conditions. Crane's (1991) evidence appears to suggest that black males are most susceptible to the epidemic effects of bad neighbors, but Clark (1992) did not replicate this result using more recent census data. Both Clark, for males, and Brooks-Gunn, Duncan, and colleagues (1993), for females, provided evidence that black adolescents are *least* affected by the collective socialization and institutional benefits of affluent neighbors.

This chapter reports on associations between family economic risk, neighborhood composition, and educational outcomes in white and black male and female children and adolescents. We are particularly interested in examining whether and how neighborhood and family conditions influence these outcomes in different gender, age, and ethnic groups.

## METHODS

### SAMPLES

The samples and measures used to assess the effects of neighborhood and family conditions on educational outcomes will be discussed next.

MIDDLE CHILDHOOD  A single middle-childhood sample was used in this study. Data were obtained from all white and black students from four elementary schools in an upstate New York urban school district during the 1990–1991 academic year (grades three through five at the time of data collection) who had complete student records ($N = 1,040$). These elementary school students ranged in age from eight to eleven years, with a mean age of 9.8 years ($SD = 1.1$) and a mean grade level of 4.3 ($SD = .80$).

EARLY ADOLESCENCE   Three data sets examining the influence of family and neighborhood conditions on early adolescents' school outcomes were used in these analyses. The Atlanta youth were drawn from a larger sample of 562 students (386 boys, 166 girls) participating in a longitudinal project exploring the Promotion of Academic Competence (Project PAC). In the larger study, students were randomly selected from the enrollment lists of four public middle schools (grades six to eight). The students ranged in age from 11 to 16 years, with a mean age of 13.1 years ($SD = 1.1$). Only data collected in the first wave during the 1989 to 1990 school year were included in the current study, resulting in 346 black subjects (237 males, 109 females). No white youth were included in the larger study.

The New York City/Baltimore/Washington, D.C. (NYC/B/DC) early adolescence sample is a subsample of subjects participating in the Adolescent Pathways Project (see Seidman 1991). The larger project consisted of 1,333 adolescents (561 boys, 772 girls) who participated in an accelerated longitudinal study looking at the development of adaptation and maladaptation of youth living in high-risk communities in the three urban communities. Data were collected during the spring of 1988 or the spring of 1989. Subjects were sampled from elementary and junior high or middle high schools (grades five or six) and middle schools or high schools (grades eight or nine) that were predominantly African American, Latino, or white and had a minimum of 60 percent to 80 percent of the student body eligible for reduced-price or free lunches. The current analyses were on the 669 subjects (134 white males, 129 black males, 175 white females, 231 black females) with complete data on the variables used in this study. The age range for the students was 10 to 16 years, with a mean age of 12.3 years ($SD = 1.6$).

The New York early adolescent sample included all black and white students in an upstate New York urban school district in the 1989 to 1991 academic year (grades six to eight) who had complete student records ($N = 3,406$). These students ranged in age from 12 to 15 years, with a mean age of 13.1 years ($SD = 1.0$). Subjects were part of a large, multiethnic longitudinal study of urban students' academic motivational processes.

MIDDLE ADOLESCENCE   Two middle adolescence data sets were used in this study. The PSID is an ongoing longitudinal survey of U.S. households begun in 1968 by the Survey Research Center of the University of Michigan (Hill 1992). Low-income families were initially oversampled in the PSID, but weights have been developed and are used throughout our analyses to adjust for both the differential initial sampling probabilities and for differential nonresponse that has arisen since the beginning of the study. The PSID sample used in this study consists of 3,395 adolescents observed between the ages of sixteen and twenty-one. Given that the data span 1968 to 1991, the oldest cohort in the sample was age sixteen in 1968, while the youngest cohort was age sixteen in 1985. All but the oldest cohort were observed in the PSID at ages younger than sixteen. In forming family- and neighborhood-level measures, we averaged all of the available information between ages ten and sixteen.

The single-district New York sample of middle adolescents was drawn from the same upstate New York urban school district that produced samples just discussed. This sample consists of 1,797 students attending district schools during the 1987 to 1988 academic year who had complete student records. Only students fifteen years or older and in high school were included in this sample. These students ranged in age from fifteen to twenty ($X = 15.6$, $SD = .84$) and ranged from ninth to twelfth grade ($X = 10.0$, $SD = 1.0$) at the time of data collection.

## MEASURES

NEIGHBORHOOD CHARACTERISTICS   Neighborhood characteristics were measured for all data sets using 1980 census-tract data. Five neighborhood composition factors were used in these analyses: (1) concentration of neighbors with low SES, (2) concentration of neighbors with high SES, (3) ethnic diversity, (4) family concentration (density), and (5) concentration of jobless males (see chapter 3). Based on the variance accounted for by these factors and their interpretability as indices of risk, using Wilson's (1987) work on defining underclass neighborhoods, we aggregated three of the indices to form the composite variable: (1) low SES (high concentration of family and individual poverty), (2) low concentration of high-SES residents, and (3) high levels of male joblessness. As described earlier, a common metric for each factor was created that represented standard deviation units away from the average of a nationally representative sample of neighborhoods in the PSID data set (chapter 3).

FAMILY CHARACTERISTICS   For all three New York samples, the sole family characteristic variable was family economic risk, which was measured using information obtained from school records on the eligibility of subjects for the free or reduced-price lunch program (Entwisle and Astone 1994; but see Hauser [forthcoming] for limitations of this measure). Eligibility for free or reduced-price lunch is determined by federal guidelines.[1] Families were considered to be economically at risk only when target subjects' siblings (where applicable) were also coded as eligible for free or reduced-price lunches and where eligibility was stable over a three-year period.

For the Atlanta middle adolescence sample, the family characteristic variables included family income, family structure, and mother's education. Family income was assessed from parental reports of family income. These figures were then transformed into an index based on family size and federal poverty guidelines. A dichotomous variable indexing family structure was created, with subjects who reported living with their mother without a male caregiver coded as *single female–headed family* and other family configurations coded as *other*. Mother's highest level of completed education was coded in number of years of education (for example, *high school diploma* = 12, *college degree* = 16).

The NYC/B/DC sample included two family variables. Students reports of family labor market participation and automobile ownership were used to create a family risk index. Also, a family structure variable was created, with subjects who reported living with their mother without a male caregiver coded as *single female–headed family* and other family configurations coded as *other*.

PSID family-level independent variables used in the analyses included (1) mother's completed schooling, in years; (2) the fraction of years between ages ten and sixteen in which the family was headed by the mother; (3) the calendar year in which the sample adolescent turned sixteen; and (4) family economic status, obtained by dividing each family's income by its corresponding poverty threshold.[2]

EDUCATIONAL OUTCOMES    Educational risk behavior in the New York single middle childhood sample was assessed using an adaptation of the Five-Flag Identification System (Crichlow and Vito 1989). For these children, a flag was assigned when (1) yearly attendance was below 82 percent; (2) national percentile scores on standardized achievement tests were below 38 percent for math and below 37 percent for reading, or when one of these scores was below 15 percent; (3) two or more instructional days were lost due to suspension; (4) the student was one or more years older than the average student at the same grade level, or there was recommendation for retention but the parents refused; or (5) the student moved often or the parents or teachers requested child services, such as for psychological testing or counseling. A similar educational risk behavior measure was used for the middle and late adolescent New York samples, with the only exception being that flag 5 was replaced by the criterion that two or more core courses (English, math, social studies, or science) were failed in the past academic year.

For the Atlanta sample, the composite total national percentile ranking (NPR) from the Iowa Test of Basic Skills from the 1988 to 1989 academic year was the educational outcome measure. Combined reading and math standardized test scores from either the 1987 to 1988 or 1988 to 1989 academic year were used as the educational outcome measure for the NYC/B/DC sample. The dependent variable in the PSID was a continuous measure of years of completed schooling, typically ascertained when the individual was in his or her mid-twenties.

# RESULTS

Before turning to the specific study results, the data analytic strategy used across all data sets is described. Following the description, the results are first presented within age periods: middle childhood, early adolescence, and middle adolescence. Then, age-group differences in the extent to which neighborhood and family conditions are associated with children's and adolescents' school outcomes are described using only the three New York data sets.

## DATA ANALYTIC STRATEGY

Table 6.1 displays the sample characteristics of neighborhood risk, family characteristics, and school outcome variables for each of the data sets. For all data sets, effects of neighborhood risk on the educational outcomes were first tested by linear regression analysis in which the neighborhood composite variable (concentration of high-SES neighbors, low-SES neighbors, and male joblessness) was used to predict school outcomes both without (first columns in each table) and with (second columns) controls for family economic risk or the other family characteristics. Use of this neighborhood composite variable (versus the five separate indices) reduces the variable-to-subject ratio and creates a more reliable neighborhood composite. Next, the five individual neighborhood risk indicators were simultaneously entered into a regression equation both without (first columns) and with (second columns) the family variables.

## MIDDLE CHILDHOOD

Results indicate that the composite neighborhood risk variable predicted educational outcomes only for the white males and females, and only when family economic risk was not included in the equation. Neighborhood risk was not a significant predictor of school risk behavior for the black sample. Family economic risk, as measured by eligibility for the free or reduced-price lunch program, was not associated with educational risk behavior for any of the subsamples (see table 6.2).

In examining the unique influence of each of the five neighborhood indices on school risk behavior (see table 6.3), the regression analyses revealed that, for the white males, the presence of high-SES neighbors was associated with lower educational risk behavior. However, this indicator was no longer significant once family economic risk was added to the equation. For the black males, the concentration of jobless males in the students' neighborhoods predicted a higher number of flags, even when controlling for family economic risk. Family economic risk was not associated with educational risk behavior for either male subsample. None of the neighborhood or family factors predicted school risk behaviors in either the white or the black female subsamples.

TABLE 6.1  Sample Demographic Information

| | White Males | White Females | African American Males | African American Females |
|---|---|---|---|---|
| New York sample Middle childhood | | | | |
| N | 101 | 94 | 414 | 431 |
| Neighborhood risk[a] | 1.52 | 1.62 | 4.59 | 4.60 |
| | (2.29) | (2.43) | (2.41) | (2.18) |
| Family economic risk[b] | .62 | .58 | .83 | .82 |
| School outcomes[c] | .81 | .59 | 1.10 | .89 |
| | (1.04) | (.90) | (1.09) | (.96) |
| New York sample Early adolescence | | | | |
| N | 638 | 607 | 1,025 | 1,136 |
| Neighborhood risk[a] | .12 | .06 | 2.83 | 2.92 |
| Family economic risk[b] | (2.02) | (2.05) | (2.38) | (2.93) |
| School outcomes[c] | .96 | .81 | 1.98 | 1.54 |
| | (1.29) | (1.14) | (1.54) | (1.42) |
| Atlanta sample Early adolescence | | | | |
| N | — | — | 237 | 109 |
| Neighborhood risk[a] | — | — | 5.27 | 4.89 |
| | — | — | (2.24) | (2.62) |
| Family income/needs | — | — | 1.04 | 1.25 |
| | — | — | (0.88) | (1.09) |
| School outcomes[d] | — | — | 37.52 | 46.98 |
| | — | — | (25.33) | (26.91) |
| NYC/B/DC sample Early adolescence | | | | |
| N | 134 | 175 | 129 | 231 |
| Neighborhood risk[a] | .86 | .80 | 3.59 | 4.15 |
| | (1.02) | (1.08) | (2.13) | (2.13) |
| Family economic risk[e] | −.25 | −.25 | .08 | .02 |
| | (.51) | (.54) | (.60) | (.61) |
| School outcomes[f] | .15 | .37 | .15 | .07 |
| | (.85) | (.86) | (.79) | (.80) |
| New York sample Middle adolescence | | | | |
| N | 275 | 204 | 653 | 665 |
| Neighborhood risk[a] | .92 | .96 | 3.02 | 3.40 |
| | (2.20) | (2.03) | (2.33) | (2.31) |
| Family economic risk[b] | .43 | .46 | .63 | .64 |
| School outcomes[c] | 1.61 | 1.63 | 2.37 | 2.02 |
| | (1.40) | (1.37) | (1.69) | (1.40) |

TABLE 6.1   *Continued*

|  | White Males | White Females | African American Males | African American Females |
|---|---|---|---|---|
| PSID sample | | | | |
| Middle adolescence | | | | |
| N | 785 | 821 | 858 | 931 |
| Neighborhood risk[a] | −.11 | −.06 | 3.66 | 3.78 |
|  | (1.82) | (1.77) | (2.17) | (2.14) |
| Family income/needs | 3.18 | 3.23 | 1.40 | 1.37 |
|  | (1.91) | (1.97) | (.91) | (.82) |
| School outcomes[g] | 13.4 | 13.2 | 12.0 | 12.4 |
|  | (2.4) | (2.3) | (1.9) | (1.9) |

[a] Mean (and standard deviation) of the three-variable neighborhood risk composite in standard deviation units based on national norms for the PSID (chapter 3).

[b] Proportion of subjects eligible for the free or reduced-cost lunch program.

[c] Represents average number of "flags" for each group.

[d] Represents average score on the Iowa Test of Basic Skills.

[e] Based on students' reports of family labor market participation and automobile ownership.

[f] Represents average score on the reading/math composite.

[g] Represents years of completed schooling.

The overall predictive power of the demographic variables measured in the full model was very small for all middle childhood subgroups (see table 6.3). For the white sample, the combined $R^2$ for the full equation, including family economic risk, did not exceed 6 percent. For the black sample, 1 percent and 2 percent of the variance in educational risk behavior was accounted for by the demographic variables for the male and female subjects, respectively.

## EARLY ADOLESCENCE

Neither the three-factor neighborhood risk composite or the family variables were consistent predictors of school outcomes for the Atlanta or NYC/B/DC early adolescent samples (tables 6.4 and 6.5). Neighborhood risk significantly predicted scores on the Iowa Test of Basic Skills for the African American females in the Atlanta data set, but only when family economic risk was not included in the model. Mother's education, but not family income, predicted African American males' and females' test scores. For the NYC/B/DC sample, neighborhood risk predicted reading and math scores, both with and without family characteristics in the equation, for the white females. Only for the white females was family poverty associated with lower reading and math scores. In contrast to the findings from the Atlanta and NYC/B/DC data sets, the neighborhood risk composite was a consistent and robust predictor of school out-

*(Text continues on page 158.)*

TABLE 6.2  Effects of Neighborhood Composite and Family Characteristics on School Outcomes: New York Middle Childhood Sample

| | White Males | White Males | Black Males | Black Males | White Females | White Females | Black Females | Black Females |
|---|---|---|---|---|---|---|---|---|
| Neighborhood characteristics | | | | | | | | |
| Composite neighborhood factors (low SES, high SES, and male joblessness combined) | .09* (.04) | .07 (.05) | .03 (.02) | .03 (.02) | .09* (.04) | .06 (.04) | .00 (.02) | .00 (.02) |
| Family characteristics | | | | | | | | |
| Eligible for reduced-price/ free lunch | — | .25 (.22) | — | .10 (.14) | — | .33 (.19) | — | .07 (.12) |
| N | 101 | 101 | 414 | 414 | 94 | 94 | 431 | 431 |
| Adjusted $R^2$ | .04 | .04 | .00 | .00 | .05 | .07 | .00 | .00 |
| Mean of $Y$[a] | .81 | .81 | 1.10 | 1.10 | .59 | .59 | .89 | .89 |
| (Stnd. dev.) | (1.04) | (1.04) | (1.09) | (1.09) | (.90) | (.90) | (.96) | (.96) |

*Indicates coefficient is at least twice its standard error.

[a] School outcomes are represented by the average number of "flags" for this group.

TABLE 6.3  Effects of Neighborhood Characteristics and Family Characteristics on School Outcomes: New York Middle Childhood Sample

| | White Males | White Males | Black Males | Black Males | White Females | White Females | Black Females | Black Females |
|---|---|---|---|---|---|---|---|---|
| **Neighborhood characteristics** | | | | | | | | |
| Low SES | -.15 | -.16 | -.02 | -.02 | .29 | .27 | -.17 | -.17 |
| | (.21) | (.21) | (.12) | (.12) | (.18) | (.18) | (.09) | (.09) |
| High SES | -.44* | -.41 | .15 | .15 | -.26 | -.25 | .03 | .03 |
| | (.20) | (.21) | (.17) | (.17) | (.18) | (.18) | (.15) | (.15) |
| Male joblessness | .05 | .03 | .24* | .23* | -.31 | -.32 | .13 | .13 |
| | (.19) | (.20) | (.11) | (.11) | (.23) | (.23) | (.08) | (.08) |
| Family concentration | .00 | .00 | -.12 | -.11 | -.01 | .02 | .05 | .04 |
| | (.14) | (.14) | (.09) | (.09) | (.14) | (.14) | (.08) | (.08) |
| Ethnic diversity | .09 | .09 | .07 | .08 | .11 | .05 | .09 | .09 |
| | (.16) | (.16) | (.07) | (.07) | (.15) | (.15) | (.06) | (.06) |
| **Family characteristics** | | | | | | | | |
| Eligible for reduced-price/ free lunch | — | .19 | — | -.09 | — | .28 | — | .05 |
| | | (.26) | | (.14) | | (.20) | | (.11) |
| *N* | 101 | 101 | 414 | 414 | 94 | 94 | 431 | 431 |
| Adjusted *R²* | .04 | .04 | .01 | .01 | .05 | .06 | .02 | .02 |
| Mean of *Y*ᵃ | .81 | .81 | 1.10 | 1.10 | .59 | .59 | .89 | .89 |
| (Stnd. dev) | (1.04) | (1.04) | (1.09) | (1.09) | (.90) | (.90) | (.96) | (.96) |

*Indicates coefficient is at least twice its standard error.

ᵃ School outcomes are represented by the average number of "flags" for this group.

TABLE 6.4   Effects of Neighborhood Composite and Family Characteristics on School Outcomes: Atlanta Early Adolescence Sample

| | African American Males | African American Males | African American Females | African American Females |
|---|---|---|---|---|
| **Neighborhood factors** | | | | |
| Neighborhood risk factor | −.38 | −.21 | −1.74* | −1.05 |
| | (.63) | (.74) | (.87) | (.97) |
| **Family characteristics** | | | | |
| Family income/needs | — | 2.96 | — | 1.13 |
| | | (2.08) | | (2.64) |
| Female head | — | .41 | — | 5.63 |
| | | (3.47) | | (5.32) |
| Mother's education | — | 1.84* | — | 3.72* |
| | | (.76) | | (.96) |
| Grade six | — | −2.52 | — | 11.72* |
| | | (4.05) | | (5.65) |
| Grade seven | — | (2.72) | — | (.46) |
| | | (4.20) | | (6.85) |
| $N$ | 237 | 237 | 109 | 109 |
| Adjusted $R^2$ | .00 | .03 | .02 | .16 |
| Mean of $Y$[a] | 37.52 | 37.52 | 46.98 | 46.98 |
| (Stnd. dev.) | (25.33) | (25.33) | (26.91) | (26.91) |

*Indicates coefficient is at least twice its standard error.

[a] School outcomes are represented by the average score on the Iowa Test of Basic Skills.

comes for all four subgroups in the New York early adolescence data set; and family economic risk was associated with white males' and females' school risk behavior (table 6.6).

Tables 6.7, 6.8, and 6.9 display the results from the regression analyses using the five separate neighborhood indicators and the family characteristic variables for the three early adolescence data sets. Results from the Atlanta sample suggest that male joblessness is associated with black males' test scores, and black females' test scores were higher in neighborhoods with a higher concentration of middle-class neighbors (but only without the family variables in the model). Mothers' education was an independent predictor of both black males' and females' test scores. Concentration of neighbors with low SES was the only neighborhood factor to predict the reading and math composite for subjects (for only the white females) in the NYC/B/DC sample. Family poverty was also associated with white females' school outcomes. For the New York sample, white males benefited from a higher concentration of middle-class neighbors, and both black males and white females had poorer school outcomes when residing in areas with a higher concentration

(Text continues on page 161.)

TABLE 6.5  Effects of Neighborhood Composite and Family Characteristics on School Outcomes: NYC/B/DC Early Adolescence Sample

| | White Males | White Males | Black Males | Black Males | White Females | White Females | Black Females | Black Females |
|---|---|---|---|---|---|---|---|---|
| Neighborhood characteristics | | | | | | | | |
| Composite neighborhood factors (low SES, high SES, and male joblessness combined) | .08 (.08) | -.08 (.08) | .05 (.04) | .06 (.04) | -.16* (.06) | -.16* (.07) | -.03 (.03) | -.03 (.03) |
| Family characteristics | | | | | | | | |
| Poverty | — | .5 (.18) | — | -.06 (.15) | — | -.36* (.16) | — | .01 (.11) |
| No father | — | -.07 (.32) | | -.06 (.20) | | .45 (.26) | | -.14 (.15) |
| N | 134 | 134 | 129 | 129 | 175 | 175 | 231 | 231 |
| Adjusted $R^2$ | .00 | .01 | .01 | .01 | .03 | .05 | .00 | .00 |
| Mean of $Y$[a] | .15 | .15 | .15 | .15 | .37 | .37 | .07 | .07 |
| (Stnd. dev.) | (.85) | (.85) | (.79) | (.79) | (.86) | (.86) | (.80) | (.80) |

*Indicates coefficient is at least twice its standard error.

[a] School outcomes are represented by the average score on the reading-math composite.

TABLE 6.6  Effects of Neighborhood Composite and Family Characteristics on School Outcomes: New York Early Adolescence Sample

| | White Males | White Males | Black Males | Black Males | White Females | White Females | Black Females | Black Females |
|---|---|---|---|---|---|---|---|---|
| Neighborhood characteristics composite neighborhood factors (low SES, high SES combined) | .16* (.02) | .13* (.02) | .06* (.02) | .06* (.02) | .11* (.02) | .08* (.02) | .07* (.02) | .07* (.02) |
| Family characteristics eligible for reduced-price/free lunch | — | .54* (.11) | — | .12 (.10) | — | .50* (.10) | — | .14 (.09) |
| N | 638 | 638 | 1025 | 1025 | 607 | 607 | 1136 | 1136 |
| Adjusted $R^2$ | .06 | .09 | .01 | .01 | .04 | .07 | .02 | .02 |
| Mean of $Y$[a] | .96 | .96 | 1.98 | 1.98 | .81 | .81 | 1.54 | 1.54 |
| (Stnd. dev.) | (1.29) | (1.29) | (1.54) | (1.54) | (1.14) | (1.14) | (1.42) | (1.42) |

*Indicates coefficient is at least twice its standard error.

[a] School outcomes are represented by the average number of "flags" for this group.

TABLE 6.7   Effects of Neighborhood Characteristics and Family Characteristics
on School Outcomes: Atlanta Early Adolescence Sample

| | African American Males | African American Males | African American Females | African American Females |
|---|---|---|---|---|
| Neighborhood factors | | | | |
| Low SES | −6.49 | −6.00 | −.70 | −5.52 |
| | (3.88) | (4.48) | (5.36) | (5.83) |
| High SES | −2.01 | −.38 | 11.19* | 8.51 |
| | (3.73) | (4.27) | (5.59) | (6.11) |
| Male joblessness | −3.65* | −4.23* | 2.98 | 4.50 |
| | (1.75) | (2.00) | (2.60) | (2.83) |
| Family concentration | −1.19 | −1.05 | −3.84 | .33 |
| | (1.71) | (1.95) | (2.63) | (2.94) |
| Ethnic diversity | 1.40 | 1.44 | −3.21 | −4.88 |
| | (6.72) | (7.66) | (7.72) | (8.29) |
| | | | | |
| Family characteristics | | | | |
| Family income/needs | — | 2.23 | — | 1.03 |
| | | (2.09) | | (2.63) |
| Female head | — | .06 | — | 6.81 |
| | | (3.47) | | (5.33) |
| Mother's education | — | 2.07* | — | 3.74* |
| | | (.76) | | (.99) |
| Grade six | — | −2.27 | — | 12.42* |
| | | (4.04) | | (5.67) |
| Grade seven | — | 2.80 | — | 2.76 |
| | | (4.19) | | (6.98) |
| | | | | |
| $N$ | 237 | 237 | 109 | 109 |
| Adjusted $R^2$ | .01 | .04 | .06 | .18 |
| Mean of $Y$[a] | 37.52 | 37.52 | 46.98 | 46.98 |
| (Stnd. dev.) | (25.33) | (25.33) | (26.91) | (26.91) |

*Indicates coefficient is at least twice its standard error.

[a] School outcomes are represented by the scores on the Iowa Test of Basic Skills.

of jobless males. Family economic risk predicted school outcomes for the white males and females.

For the most part, the predictive power of the full model tested was small for these three samples of early adolescents (see tables 6.7 to 6.9). For the Atlanta sample, the $R^2$ was .04 for the black males and .18 for the black females. The larger predictive power for the females appears to be due to the family characteristic variables, and not the neighborhood indicators. $R^2$s for the subjects in the NYC/B/DC sample were .03, .04, .04, and .01 for the white and black males and females, respectively. The corresponding values for the New York sample were .10, .02, .07, and .02.

(Text continues on page 164.)

TABLE 6.8  Effects of Neighborhood Characteristics and Family Characteristics on School Outcomes: NYC/B/DC Early Adolescence Sample

| | White Males | White Males | African American Males | African American Males | White Females | White Females | African American Females | African American Females |
|---|---|---|---|---|---|---|---|---|
| **Neighborhood characteristics** | | | | | | | | |
| Low SES | .02 | .02 | .05 | .04 | -.37* | -.37* | -.01 | -.02 |
| | (.19) | (.19) | (.18) | (.19) | (.16) | (.16) | (.14) | (.14) |
| High SES | -.28 | -.30 | .03 | .02 | .15 | .11 | -.02 | -.02 |
| | (.22) | (.22) | (.20) | (.20) | (.17) | (.17) | (.13) | (.13) |
| Male joblessness | -.05 | -.06 | .07 | .07 | .02 | .03 | -.04 | -.05 |
| | (.19) | (.19) | (.13) | (.13) | (.07) | (0.7) | (0.7) | (.07) |
| Crowding/age structure | -.13 | -.13 | .02 | .02 | -.02 | -.04 | .02 | .02 |
| | (.16) | (.16) | (.14) | (.15) | (.14) | (.14) | (.10) | (.10) |
| Ethnic diversity | .12 | .12 | -.05 | -.04 | .08 | .05 | -.11 | -.10 |
| | (.08) | (.08) | (.10) | (.10) | (.15) | (.15) | (.11) | (.11) |
| **Family characteristics** | | | | | | | | |
| Poverty | — | .06 | — | -.03 | — | -.36* | — | .04 |
| | | (.18) | | (.16) | | (.16) | | (.12) |
| No father | — | -.08 | — | .04 | — | .46 | — | -.18 |
| | | (.32) | | (.22) | | (.26) | | (.16) |
| N | 134 | 134 | 130 | 130 | 176 | 176 | 229 | 229 |
| Adjusted $R^2$ | .00 | .03 | .03 | .04 | .02 | .04 | .01 | .01 |
| Mean of $Y$[a] | .15 | .15 | -.16 | -.16 | .37 | .37 | -.06 | -.06 |
| (Stnd. dev.) | .85 | .85 | .80 | .80 | .86 | .86 | .80 | .80 |

*Indicates coefficient is at least twice its standard error.

[a] School outcomes are represented by the average score on the reading/math composite.

TABLE 6.9 Effects of Neighborhood Characteristics and Family Characteristics on School Outcomes: New York Early Adolescence Sample

| | White Males | White Males | African American Males | African American Males | White Females | White Females | African American Females | African American Females |
|---|---|---|---|---|---|---|---|---|
| Neighborhood factors | | | | | | | | |
| Low SES | .10 | .05 | -.08 | -.08 | .11 | .05 | -.01 | -.01 |
| | (.12) | (.12) | (.09) | (.09) | (.11) | (.11) | (.08) | (.08) |
| High SES | -.33* | -.29* | .07 | .08 | -.10 | -.05 | -.17 | -.17 |
| | (.08) | (.08) | (.12) | (.12) | (.08) | (.08) | (.10) | (.10) |
| Male joblessness | .21 | .19 | .26* | .26* | .24* | .21* | .10 | .09 |
| | (.11) | (.10) | (.10) | (.10) | (.09) | (.09) | (.08) | (.08) |
| Family concentration | -.08 | -.07 | -.01 | -.01 | -.11 | -.08 | -.02 | -.02 |
| | (.06) | (.06) | (.06) | (.06) | (0.6) | (.05) | (.05) | (.05) |
| Ethnic diversity | -.15 | -.12 | .06 | .06 | -.04 | -.02 | .11 | .10 |
| | (.10) | (.10) | (.07) | (.07) | (.09) | (.09) | (.06) | (.06) |
| Family characteristics | | | | | | | | |
| Eligible for reduced-price/ free lunch | — | .52* | — | .12 | — | .48* | — | .13 |
| | | (.11) | | (.10) | | (.10) | | (.09) |
| N | 638 | 638 | 1025 | 1025 | 607 | 607 | 1136 | 1136 |
| Adjusted $R^2$ | .07 | .10 | .01 | .02 | .04 | .07 | .02 | .02 |
| Mean of $Y$[a] | .98 | .98 | 1.98 | 1.98 | .81 | .81 | 1.54 | 1.54 |
| (Stnd. dev.) | (1.29) | (1.29) | (1.54) | (1.54) | (1.14) | (1.14) | (1.42) | (1.42) |

*Indicates coefficient is at least twice its standard error.

[a] School outcomes are represented by the average number of "flags" for this group.

163

MIDDLE ADOLESCENCE

With only one exception, the neighborhood risk composite significantly predicted educational risk behavior, both with and without the family variables,
for all subgroups of middle adolescent subjects in the PSID and New York data
sets. Neighborhood risk was no longer significant once the family variables
were added to the model only for the white females from the New York data
set. Family economic risk was a significant, unique predictor of school behavior for all subsamples (see tables 6.10 and 6.11).

In examining the results from the analyses using the separate neighborhood indices, the presence of higher-income neighbors predicted more years
of schooling and lower frequency of risk behavior for the white males in both
the PSID and New York samples, and for the white and black females in the
PSID sample. The black males and females from the PSID sample appeared
to benefit from ethnic diversity in the neighborhood. Finally, concentration
of males without jobs in the neighborhood predicted black males' school
behavior from the New York sample when family economic risk was not in
the equation (tables 6.12 and 6.13).

For the PSID data set, adjusted $R^2$s for the full model are .24 and .26 for the
white males and females, respectively, and .08 and .11 for the black males and
females. For the New York data set, $R^2$s are .10 and .16 for the white males
and females, respectively, and .02 both for the black males and females.

As significant as some of the neighborhood factors were for the PSID data,
the family-level characteristics were more important. The addition of the
family-level measures more than doubled the explanatory power of the
regressions. Family income and maternal schooling were highly significant
predictors of completed schooling for all four subgroups; family structure
appeared to matter most for black males.

AGE-GROUP DIFFERENCES

The three New York data sets will be used to illustrate age-group differences in
the extent to which neighborhood and family characteristics are associated with
males' and females' school-outcomes in middle childhood to early adolescence,
and in middle adolescence. The three New York samples were chosen because
the students' demographic profiles are comparable, very similar instrumentation
exists in all three data sets, and all students are from the same metropolitan area.

Figure 6.1 depicts the effects that the neighborhood composition variable
has on black and white students' school outcomes across the three age groups
(middle childhood, early adolescence, and middle adolescence), and figure 6.2
displays the results using family economic risk. Neighborhood risk and family
economic risk were not significant, unique predictors of school outcomes in
middle childhood for either males or females (the bivariate relationship

(Text continues on page 169.)

TABLE 6.10 Effects of Neighborhood Composite and Family Characteristics on School Outcomes: PSID Middle Adolescence Sample

| | White Males | | Black Males | | White Females | | Black Females | |
|---|---|---|---|---|---|---|---|---|
| Neighborhood factors | | | | | | | | |
| Neighborhood risk composite | -.42* | -.12* | -.12* | -.08* | -.50* | -.16* | -.12* | -.09* |
| | (.05) | (.05) | (.03) | (.03) | (.05) | (.05) | (.03) | (.03) |
| Family characteristics | | | | | | | | |
| Family income/needs | | .30* | | .16* | | .28* | | .17* |
| | | (.04) | | (.06) | | (.04) | | (.06) |
| Female head | | -.30 | | -.32 | | -.14 | | .03* |
| | | (.27) | | (.14) | | (.25) | | (.13) |
| Mother's education | | .23* | | .09* | | -.16* | | .16* |
| | | (.04) | | (.03) | | (.05) | | (.03) |
| $N$ | 785 | 785 | 858 | 858 | 821 | 821 | 931 | 931 |
| Adjusted $R^2$ | .07 | .22 | .02 | .07 | .11 | .25 | .02 | .09 |
| Mean of $Y$[a] | 13.4 | 13.4 | 12.0 | 12.0 | 13.2 | 13.2 | 12.4 | 12.4 |
| (Stnd. dev.) | (2.4) | (2.4) | (1.9) | (1.9) | (2.3) | (2.3) | (1.9) | (1.9) |

*Indicates coefficient is at least twice its standard error.

[a] School outcomes are represented by the years of completed schooling.

165

TABLE 6.11 Effects of Neighborhood Factors and Family Characteristics on School Outcomes: New York Middle Adolescence Sample

| | White Males | | African American Males | | White Females | | African American Females | |
|---|---|---|---|---|---|---|---|---|
| Neighborhood characteristics | | | | | | | | |
| Neighborhood risk | .16* | .13* | .07* | .07* | .17* | .07 | .07* | .06* |
| composite | (.04) | (.04) | (.02) | (.03) | (.05) | (.05) | (.02) | (.02) |
| Family characteristics | | | | | | | | |
| Eligible for the free/ | | .36* | | .13 | | .96* | | .26* |
| reduced-price lunch | | (.18) | | (.12) | | (.20) | | (.11) |
| $N$ | 275 | 275 | 653 | 653 | 204 | 204 | 665 | 665 |
| Adjusted $R^2$ | .06 | .08 | .01 | .02 | .06 | .16 | .01 | .02 |
| Mean of $Y$[a] | 1.61 | 1.61 | 2.37 | 2.37 | 1.63 | 1.63 | 2.02 | 2.02 |
| (Stnd. dev.) | (1.40) | (1.40) | (1.69) | (1.49) | (1.37) | (1.37) | (1.40) | (1.40) |

*Indicates coefficient is at least twice its standard error.

[a] School outcomes are represented by the average number of "flags" for this group.

166

TABLE 6.12 Effects of Neighborhood Characteristics and Family Characteristics on School Outcomes: PSID Middle Adolescence Sample

| | White Males | | African American Males | | White Females | | African American Females | |
|---|---|---|---|---|---|---|---|---|
| **Neighborhood characteristics** | | | | | | | | |
| Low SES | .03 | −.02 | −.17 | −.14 | −.36 | .06 | .22 | .10 |
| | (.21) | (.20) | (.10) | (.11) | (.20) | (.18) | (.11) | (.11) |
| High SES | .93* | .43* | .14 | .06 | .86* | .38* | .72* | .51* |
| | (.11) | (.11) | (.12) | (.13) | (.10) | (.10) | (.13) | (.13) |
| Male joblessness | .05 | .19 | −.03 | .06 | −.04 | .04 | −.13 | .03 |
| | (.15) | (.15) | (.08) | (.09) | (.14) | (.09) | (.10) | (.10) |
| Family concentration | −.13 | −.14 | −.08 | −.08 | .00 | .04 | .08 | .12 |
| | (.09) | (.09) | (.06) | (.06) | (.09) | (.09) | (.12) | (.07) |
| Ethnic diversity | −.12 | .06 | .20* | .24* | .10 | .18 | .23* | .18 |
| | (.11) | (.11) | (.09) | (.09) | (.12) | (.11) | (.08) | (.08) |
| **Family characteristics** | | | | | | | | |
| Family income/needs | — | .27* | — | .22* | — | .26* | — | .14* |
| | | (.05) | | (.06) | | (.04) | | (.06) |
| Female head | | .27* | | .22* | | .26* | | .00 |
| | | (.05) | | (.06) | | (.04) | | (.14) |
| Mother's education | .23* | | .09* | | .24* | | .16* | |
| | (.04) | (.04) | (.04) | (.03) | (.04) | (.03) | (.03) | (.03) |
| N | 785 | 785 | 858 | 858 | 821 | 821 | 931 | 931 |
| Adjusted $R^2$ | .11 | .24 | .03 | .08 | .14 | .26 | .05 | .11 |
| Mean of $Y$[a] | 13.4 | 13.4 | 12.0 | 12.0 | 13.2 | 13.2 | 12.4 | 12.4 |
| (Stnd. dev) | (2.4) | (2.4) | (1.9) | (1.9) | (2.3) | (2.3) | (1.9) | (1.9) |

*Indicates coefficient is at least twice its standard error.

[a] School outcomes are represented by the average years of schooling for this group.

TABLE 6.13   Effects of Neighborhood Characteristics and Family Characteristics on School Outcomes: New York Middle Adolescence Sample

| | White Males | | African American Males | | White Females | | African American Females | |
|---|---|---|---|---|---|---|---|---|
| Neighborhood characteristics | | | | | | | | |
| Low SES | -.13 | -.14 | .12 | .12 | .22 | .09 | .03 | .05 |
| | (.18) | (.18) | (.11) | (.11) | (.20) | (.19) | (.11) | (.11) |
| High SES | -.37* | -.32* | .01 | .02 | -.03 | .02 | -.20 | -.21 |
| | (.16) | (.14) | (.14) | (.14) | (.15) | (.14) | (.13) | (.13) |
| Male joblessness | .19 | .15 | .17 | .15 | .34* | .16 | -.08 | .05 |
| | (.19) | (.19) | (.11) | (.11) | (.16) | (.16) | (.10) | (.10) |
| Family concentration | .15 | .15 | -.13 | -.14 | -.06 | -.05 | -.07 | -.07 |
| | (.10) | (.10) | (.08) | (.08) | (.12) | (.11) | (.08) | (.08) |
| Ethnic diversity | -.08 | -.08 | .15 | .15 | -.07 | .04 | -.02 | .00 |
| | (.16) | (.16) | (.09) | (.09) | (.17) | (.16) | (.08) | (.08) |
| Family characteristics | | | | | | | | |
| Eligible for the free/ reduced-price lunch | | .32 | | .14 | | .96* | | .23 |
| | | (.18) | | (.12) | | (.20) | | (.12) |
| $N$ | 275 | 275 | 653 | 653 | 204 | 204 | 665 | 665 |
| Adjusted $R^2$ | .09 | .10 | .02 | .02 | .07 | .16 | .02 | .02 |
| Mean of $Y^{a}$ | 1.61 | 1.61 | 2.37 | 2.37 | 1.63 | 1.63 | 2.02 | 2.02 |
| (Stnd. dev.) | (1.40) | (1.40) | (1.69) | (1.69) | (1.37) | (1.32) | (1.40) | (1.40) |

*Indicates coefficient is at least twice its standard error.

[a] School outcomes are represented by the average number of "flags" for this group.

FIGURE 6.1   Age Differences in Effects of Neighborhood Composition on Educational Risk from Middle Childhood to Middle Adolescence (New York Samples Only)

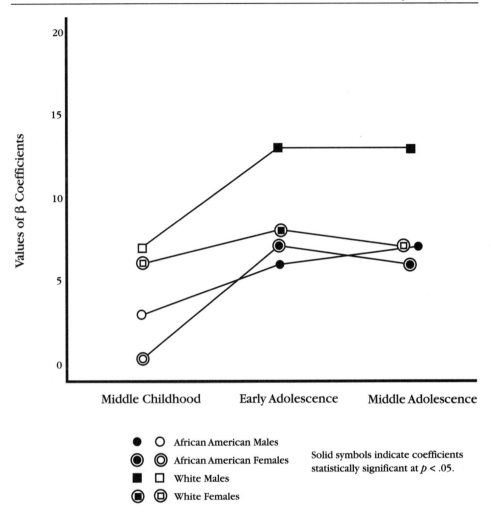

between neighborhood risk and school outcomes was significant for the white males and females when family economic risk was not included in the model). Neighborhood risk became increasingly more predictive for males, with the largest jump in effects observed from middle childhood to early adolescence (standardized parameter estimates increased from .07 to .13 for the white males and .03 to .06 for black males). The magnitude of the effects for white males remained higher across all age groups than for the black males.

Neighborhood risk also became a significant predictor of females' school outcomes during early adolescence, with the largest increase in effect observed for the black females, for whom the standardized parameter esti-

FIGURE 6.2   Age Differences in Effects of Family Economic Risk on Educational Risk
from Middle Childhood to Middle Adolescence (New York Samples Only)

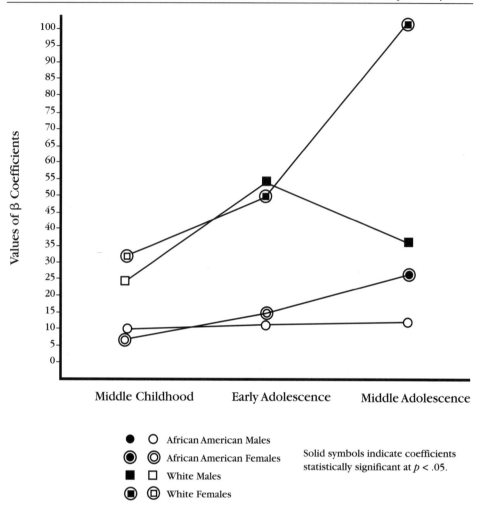

mates increased from .00 to .07. Neighborhood risk remained a significant
predictor of school risk for the black females from early to middle adolescence. The magnitude of effects for white females over the three age periods
was .06, .08, and .07, demonstrating little change in neighborhood effects for
this group over time.

Developmental trends were also noted in family characteristics' influence
on school risk behavior for the black and white males and females (figure
6.2). Family characteristics had no significant effect on school outcomes in
middle childhood for any of the four subgroups. Family economic risk
remained insignificant for black males' school outcomes and did not emerge

as significant for black females until middle adolescence. In contrast, family economic risk became a strong predictor of white males' and females' school outcomes in early and middle adolescence. Although parameter estimates decreased from early to middle adolescence (from .54 to .36), these effects remained significant. The effects of family economic risk were particularly strong for the white females, whose parameter estimates increased from .33 in middle childhood to .96 in middle adolescence.

## DISCUSSION

Replicating the work of Brooks-Gunn, Duncan, and colleagues (1993) and Clark (1992), but contradicting findings from Dornbusch, Ritter, and Steinberg (1991), we found family and neighborhood variables to be more tightly linked to outcomes for the white males and females than for the black youth. These results suggest several possible interpretations. As discussed in chapter 9, the distribution of family and neighborhood characteristics (such as the percentage of high-SES neighbors) is sharply different in mean levels across these two ethnic groups. These differences have led us to question whether there are adequate thresholds of these neighborhood concentration variables to produce strong effects on school outcomes in the African American samples.

A second interpretation posits that outcomes such as those assessed in this study are "allocated" differently across ethnic groups, not only in frequency but also on the basis of different criteria. For example, school suspensions show mean level differences between ethnic groups, with black students receiving many more suspensions than white students from the same schools (Crichlow and Vito 1989). Halpern-Felsher (1994) has suggested that cultural mismatches between minority urban students, especially black males, and their typically white teachers may lead both to more suspensions and other disciplinary actions and to less behaviorally referenced application of these disciplinary measures toward these students than toward white students. This mismatch hypothesis is consistent with the lower association found in this study between student demographic characteristics and school outcomes in the African American samples than in the white samples.

Age-group differences in the effects of neighborhood and family risk on school outcomes were observed. The neighborhood risk composite and family economic risk had no unique effect on educational outcomes in the middle childhood group. However, these variables were related to school outcomes in white females in the NYC/B/DC early adolescent samples and in early and middle adolescents in the New York and PSID samples. These developmental trends were further illustrated using the three New York samples, as depicted in figures 6.1 and 6.2. Results suggest that neighborhood composition (in this case, the concentration of high-SES neighbors, low-SES neighbors, and jobless males) is more strongly associated with school risk behaviors in adolescence than in middle childhood. These developmental findings are particularly true for white and African American males. Family economic risk also becomes a more important factor in predicting school outcomes across the entire age range for females and, from middle childhood to early adolescence, for white males.

The results showing weak associations between neighborhood and family economic risk to educational outcomes for the middle childhood sample suggest that these composition variables are not, by themselves, strongly associated with children's educational risk behavior. These findings encourage us to look elsewhere for sources of variation that affect school performance and adjustment, such as the quality of elementary education in neighborhood schools. Other sources of neighborhood variation that may indirectly affect children's educational outcomes are discussed in chapter 7.

The emergence of stronger neighborhood and family effects on educational outcomes in the early adolescent group are consistent with the fact that adolescents spend more time away from home than do younger children and are therefore exposed to more nonfamilial influences, such as positive and negative adult role models, employment opportunities, and same-age and older peer groups. The dramatic increase in the salience of family economic resources as predictors of educational outcomes for females suggests that with the developmental transition from childhood to adolescence, females (both white and black) become more susceptible to the effects of economic hardship on their families. Quantitative studies of these issues by McLoyd (1990b) and qualitative research by Fine and Zane (1989) offer suggestions for how these adolescent females may experience trade-offs between the demands of family responsibilities exacerbated by poverty and the responsibilities incurred as they make the transition to middle school and high school during this same period (see Conger, Conger, and Elder forthcoming).

In addition to the findings involving family economic risk and neighborhood composition, the individual neighborhood variables also predicted adolescents' school outcomes. White male adolescents did better in school when there were more middle-class residents and fewer low-SES residents in their neighborhoods. These results support the findings from Brooks-Gunn, Duncan, and colleagues (1993) and Clark (1992) that pressure from high-SES neighbors positively influences students' school outcomes, especially for white youth. However, as discussed in chapter 9, this positive effect of high-SES neighbors may also extend to black youth when those neighbors are themselves African American.

African American males were negatively influenced by the concentration of jobless males in their neighborhoods. These results are consistent with Crane's (1991) finding that black males are most affected by poorer neighbors and with Wilson's (1987) hypothesis that the most corrosive element of the urban underclass experience for youth is joblessness.

The lack of complete cross-sample replication of these findings may be attributed to the sample constraints imposed by the designs of the larger studies from which the subjects for these analyses were drawn. With the exception of the PSID, these studies were designed to examine sources of variation of academic achievement *within* samples of poor, mostly minority children and adolescents. Thus, investigating effects of variation in either neighborhood risk or family economic conditions on educational outcomes was not a priority of the larger sampling frame. In fact, compressed ranges on both of these constructs were expected and obtained and, we believe, contributed to the weak neighborhood effects in these samples relative to the PSID sample.

Despite these imposed constraints, our findings did support the presence of neighborhood effects on educational outcomes in the New York and PSID samples. Results from these samples indicate that neighborhood and family conditions are each uniquely associated with educational outcomes, with these associations varying by age, gender, and ethnicity. Some theoretical propositions are offered to explain these variations, but further theoretical and measurement efforts to examine how neighborhoods affect developmental trajectories differently in these groups are still needed. Chapter 7 contains a discussion of possible mechanisms whereby neighborhood composition and other characteristics could affect the school success of urban children and adolescents.

---

This article was supported in part by a grant from the Maternal and Child Health Bureau MCJ000978A. Data used from the New York sample were collected while James P. Connell was a W. T. Grant Foundation Faculty Scholar. We thank our colleagues from the Social Science Research Council for their valuable discussion of the study results and their feedback on the chapter. Work on this chapter was supported in part by grants from the National Institute of Mental Health (MH43084) and the Carnegie Corporation (B4850) awarded to Edward Seidman, J. Lawrence Aber, LaRue Allen, and Christina Mitchell. We express our appreciation to the adolescents and schools whose cooperation made this study possible.

## NOTES

1. According to the figure for the 1990–1991 academic year, a family of two is eligible for free lunch if the annual income is less than $10,946 and for a reduced-price lunch if the annual income is greater than $10,946 but less than $15,577. For a family of four, the free-lunch figure is $16,510 and the reduced-price figure is $23,495.

2. Incomes and poverty thresholds are averaged over the seven-year period between ages ten and sixteen. U.S. poverty thresholds are based on a set of income thresholds that were developed in the 1960s and are adjusted each year for changes in the cost of living, using the Consumer Price Index. In 1990, U.S. poverty thresholds for families of three, four, and five persons were $10,490, $13,359, and $15,792, respectively. Families with annual cash incomes, before taxes, that exceed these thresholds are considered "not poor," while families with incomes falling below them are "poor." The ratio of income-to-poverty threshold (called here the "income-to-needs ratio") serves as a measure of individuals living in a four-person household whose income totaled $40,077. They would have income-to-needs ratios of 3.0 ($40,077/$13,359).

# 7

# How Neighborhoods Affect Educational Outcomes in Middle Childhood and Adolescence: Conceptual Issues and an Empirical Example

*James P. Connell and Bonnie L. Halpern-Felsher*

I n this chapter we build on the data presented in chapter 6 to raise a set of conceptual issues regarding the ways that neighborhoods could influence educational outcomes across the developmental span from middle childhood to later adolescence. First, we briefly describe the developmental backdrop against which the influences of neighborhood characteristics may emerge. We then describe a recently developed general model of these influences and use this model to help generate a series of specific hypotheses concerning potential pathways from neighborhood characteristics to educational outcomes during childhood and adolescence. We also present an empirical example that tests one particular set of hypotheses. Finally, we discuss the limitations of current neighborhood research in relation to the conceptual issues raised in this chapter, and we suggest ways to overcome these limitations in future studies of neighborhood effects on children's and adolescents' educational outcomes.

## DEVELOPMENTAL ISSUES

Biological changes marking the transition to adolescence—namely, the onset of puberty and menarche—are well documented, and these changes transform the physical and psychological capacities and concerns of youth (Crockett and Petersen 1993). The social implications of these changes for youths are less well documented but no less important. As youths move from childhood to adolescence, the changing physical personae of male and female youths result in different patterns of expectations and social exchange among same-age and younger peer groups. Peer perceptions that a young teenager is ready for sexual activity, substance use, employment, and other adult behavioral patterns are more likely when that teenager is more physically mature (Magnusson, Stattin, and Allen 1985). In addition, the growth spurt and other postpubertal physical characteristics of young males result in cognitive, emotional, and behavioral responses from nonfamilial adults in schools and in neighborhood settings that markedly differ from those given to prepubertal males. According to Spencer and her colleagues (Spencer, Swanson, and Cunningham 1991; Spencer and Markstrom-Adams 1990), these shifting responses of adults are amplified dramatically for minority male youths and can have important influences on these youths' experiences and behaviors in these settings.

Psychological changes are occurring during this period as well. As children move toward and through adolescence, they are drawing firmer and more complicated conclusions about their own personal capacities, both in relation to others' capabilities and in relation to meeting personal and societal expectations now and in the future (Graber, Brooks-Gunn, and Petersen forthcoming). "What's important for me to do?" and "How well am I doing it?" are key questions youth begin to ask at the outset of this period and often answer by the end of it. These changes in the need and ability to "make meaning" of personal experiences are perhaps the key psychological transitions occurring across this age period (see chapter 6).

The grist for meaning making is interaction with adults and peers and observation of their behaviors and interactions. With increasing symbolic capacities, the meaning youths make of these experiences deepens and broadens across this age period—from isolated reactions to events, to bundling experiences together into coherent stories that can precondition reactions to subsequent events, to the development of meaning structures that can shape and sustain broad behavior patterns in the future.

As youths move from childhood to and through adolescence, the interpersonal and institutional opportunities for meaning making change dramatically. Interpersonally, youths spend less time with parents and more time in independent activities with peers as playmates and workmates, and as potential intimate partners. Other important transitions in interpersonal relationships occur as young adolescents' exposure to and involvement in social institutions change. For example, experiences in middle school and, for some youths', involvement with social services and law enforcement agencies give early adolescents their first exposure to bureaucratic and, in many case, impersonal structures. Youths experience adults who know very little about them and who can exert direct, frequent control over them. Young adolescents participate more independently in neighborhood institutions, such as voluntary youth-serving organizations, churches, and some social services. At the end of this period, young people can and do work.

For youths living in poverty, a disproportionate number of whom are minority youths, the formation of beliefs about themselves, their capacities, and their future is fueled by different sets of experiences than those of more-advantaged youths. The role models available, the messages conveyed to youth about their potential by these role models and by the majority culture, the physical conditions of their neighborhoods and schools, and, more generally, the availability of positive supports from familial and nonfamilial adults can greatly influence youths' perceptions (Connell, Aber, and Walker 1995; Public/Private Ventures 1995). These different patterns of support make it more difficult for these youths to emerge from this period able to initiate and regulate productive, socially desirable behavior.

With the transitions to middle school and high school occurring over this period, there is increasing variability and lability in youth's trajectories of academic performance (Connell and Furman 1984; Harter, Whitesell, and Kowalski 1992; Simmons et al. 1987; Simmons, Carlton-Ford, and Blyth 1987). Again, transitions from elementary to middle and high school are more problematic for urban youths (Seidman et al. 1994). For some youths' difficulties with school become chronic, and their persistence becomes more predictive of longer-term employment and economic difficulties.

Changes in all of these domains are normative for this age period, but the experience and exact timing of these changes can vary dramatically for youths' living in different communities and for youths from different ethnic groups (see Seidman 1991; Seidman et al. 1994). Comparative research is sorely needed on these timing and process issues and is now being pursued in various qualitative studies (for example, Burton 1991; Burton, Allison, and Obeidallah 1995; Jarrett 1994, vol. 2). Research on ethnic groups other than African Americans is needed as well. In the next section, we attempt to push this research agenda forward by describing a set of hypotheses concerning how neighborhood characteristics can influence developmental outcomes, particularly in the education domain, among urban children and adolescents.

## CONCEPTUAL FRAMEWORK REGARDING NEIGHBORHOODS' EFFECT ON ADOLESCENT OUTCOMES

We can use existing theory and research (and intuition) to generate hypotheses about how neighborhood characteristics, broadly conceived, could shape the developmental trajectories of youths' outcomes. In this chapter, we focus on youths' capacity to be productive in school from ages ten to sixteen. Connell and colleagues (1995) recently presented a conceptual framework for examining these issues (see figure 7.1), and we summarize this framework's neighborhood and community dimensions before presenting our specific hypotheses.

Connell and associates (1995) hypothesized that four dimensions of community and neighborhood have direct and indirect associations with various outcomes in urban adolescents, including educational, economic, social or interpersonal, and citizenship outcomes. These interrelated dimensions are (1) physical conditions and demographic characteristics, (2) economic opportunity structure, (3) institutional capacities, and (4) social exchange and sym-

FIGURE 7.1 Model Depicting Hypothesized Relations Among Community Dimensions, Social Mediators, Developmental Processes, and Desired Outcomes in Young Adulthood

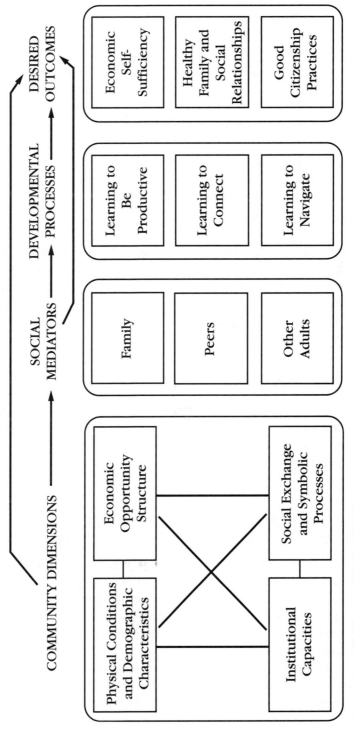

Source: Connell, Aber, and Walker (1995).

177

bolic processes. These dimensions are of particular interest because they are potentially amenable to intervention. Connell and associates (1995) described these four dimensions as follows.

1. *Physical conditions and demographic characteristics*. The physical conditions and demographic characteristics of neighborhoods include the economic, racial, educational, and social characteristics of the residents; the relative location of the major subgroups of residents who differ in those respects; and the physical presentation, structure, safety, accessibility, and habitability of the neighborhood.

2. *Economic opportunity structure*. Important aspects of the economic opportunity structure include the industrial composition, the location of the jobs, and the overall demand for labor.

3. *Institutional capacities*. In this context, institutional capacities encompass the concentration and quality of institutions and organizations that support healthy youth development. For example, direct supports include the quality of the basic educational and child-care organizations, plus the concentration, accessibility, and quality of churches and of cultural, recreational, and service organizations such as Boys and Girls Clubs, Little Leagues, and YMCAs. Indirect supports involve, for example, the degree to which the community's political, social, and economic institutions help adult caregivers provide resources to their youths.

4. *Social exchange and symbolic processes*. Again, from our youth development perspective, these processes include the formation of dense friendship networks among adults; the articulation of and support for common values about child and youth development; the monitoring and supervision of youths, especially by nonparental adults; and mutual accountability among adults on behalf of youths.

## HOW CAN URBAN NEIGHBORHOODS AFFECT YOUNG ADOLESCENTS' EDUCATIONAL OUTCOMES?

For this illustrative discussion, we focus on only one of the three developmental processes in Connell and associates' (1995) model—learning to be productive. We consider how neighborhood dimensions could affect educational productivity between the ages of ten and sixteen as measured by school performance measures (grades, test scores, and retention) and school adjustment measures (suspensions and attendance). Each of these educational outcomes may be differentially influenced by neighborhood characteristics, but in this initial discussion we treat them as equivalent. In fact, these outcomes are moderately to highly correlated in most samples we have investigated (see, for example, Connell, Spencer, and Aber 1994; Connell et al. 1995).

The following set of hypotheses is neither definitive nor exhaustive, but it does represent a broader set of pathways than we can now test with available data.

1. Neighborhood variation in the concentration of positive and negative, culturally matched role models (for example, the concentration of high school graduates and older youths attending school in the neighborhood versus the concentration of high school dropouts and idle school-aged youths) could affect the educational outcomes of the community's youths.

   The earlier discussion of developmental issues directed us to look for where early to late adolescents get information that helps them make meaning of their experiences. Over the past thirty years, the role of vicarious learning has been well documented in the psychological literature (for example, Bandura 1971, 1977). A clear implication of this long history of work is that the modeling of specific behaviors and patterns of behavior powerfully shapes individual learning. This effect is even more powerful when the role model is perceived to be similar to the individual but of higher status because of age or other attributes. This first hypothesis is grounded in this literature and recognizes the domain specificity of these effects as well. For example, we expect individual-level educational outcomes to be more strongly associated with neighborhood concentration of individuals with particular levels of educational attainment and behavioral attributes than with the percentage of residents who are members of a particular ethnic or racial group. While ethnicity or race could be seen as a causal factor contributing to educational attainment of individuals in a particular neighborhood, we believe that the educational status of these individuals is the more proximal causal variable in the model.

2. As indicated in Connell and associates' (1995) model, neighborhoods vary in the opportunities for employment for their residents and the concentration of residents employed. Wilson (1987) and others have argued that the perceived opportunities for work and the exposure to the regularities of work encourage youths to stay in school and perform well. To the extent that these neighborhood characteristics affect youths' perceptions of opportunities and exposure to working individuals, they could affect youths' motivation to stay in school and therefore influence their educational outcomes. We can further hypothesize that youths are even more powerfully motivated to stay in school and do well when they see adults involved in meaningful work either in their local or their surrounding areas and see these adults' educational attainments as contributing to their getting good jobs, keeping these jobs, and advancing their employment status.

3. Many elementary schools and some middle schools are neighborhood schools. When this is the case, characteristics of the neighborhood in which these schools are located could affect the quality of schooling received by students, ultimately influencing their educational outcomes.

   At least two mechanisms could account for these links between the physical and social conditions of neighborhoods and the quality of education received in the neighborhood-based schools. The first mechanism is economic. In most states, school funding is based primarily on local tax revenues. If schools in a particular geographic area (for example, a small district or a subdistrict) are funded according to that area's tax base, then the quality of the housing stock will affect these revenues and presumably the quality of education available for residents. If the area's physical and social conditions are perceived negatively by potential commercial investors, the commercial tax base could also be negatively affected, leading to less revenue for the schools.

   Demographic characteristics of neighborhoods can also affect economic mediators, which in turn can affect the educational quality of neighborhood schools. Because poor, single-parent families and jobless males are cash poor, they are hard pressed to support local commercial enterprises (such as stores or services), making these areas less likely to attract commercial enterprises that generate tax revenue.

   Another mediator through which physical and demographic characteristics of neighborhoods can affect the quality of educational services provided to children and youths involves the quality of the staff interacting with adults in the neighborhood-based schools. Even within a relatively poor school district, the physical and demographic characteristics of the district's neighborhoods could vary considerably. Demographic variation in the residents' educational levels could affect the qualifications of the proximate employment pool from which to draw nonteaching and teaching staff. Perceptions of the neighborhood's crime rate, accessibility, and physical characteristics could also determine the attractiveness of the school to potential staff living *outside* the neighborhood. Seniority systems in most large school districts allow more-experienced staff to choose where they will teach within the district. Accordingly, more-senior staff may be drawn to more "attractive" neighborhoods, leaving a less-experienced pool of teachers for the schools located in less desirable neighborhoods. To the extent that such variation in staff experience affects the quality of education received in these different neighborhoods, students' educational performance could vary as well.

4. Neighborhoods vary in the concentration and quality of educationally supportive institutions, such as churches and voluntary youth-serving organizations, and in their concentration of organized activities that undermine

school engagement, such as illegal economies and gang activity. The balance of these pulls and pushes on youths' school attendance could affect their educational outcomes.

The institutional capacities to support youth development vary widely between affluent and poor neighborhoods and even between working-class and poor neighborhoods (chapter 8). As Connell and colleagues (1995, 98) pointed out, "The institutions that provide 'primary services' to youth—Boys and Girls Clubs, Little Leagues, YMCAs, etc.—are typically less represented, with fewer resources, in poorer neighborhoods. This scarcity of institutional capacity, coupled with the schools' low resources, means that youth often are without attractive, organized and positive activities for most of their weekdays, evenings, and weekends." In posing this hypothesis, we suggest that researchers not only examine the concentration and quality of these educationally supportive and positive opportunities for youths but also estimate the "counterweight" of undermining and distracting activities available for youths in their immediate and surrounding neighborhoods. For example, the concentration and virulence of gang activities, the opportunities for profit in the neighborhood's illegal economies, antisocial norms, and the number of attractive venues for youth idleness could offset the presence of positive opportunities and supports such as those just described. Therefore, we recommend that the balance and dynamics of these pushes and pulls toward youth engagement in school be assessed in order to test this hypothesis.

5. If parental economic and emotional stress is a function of neighborhood conditions, and if the economic stress decreases neighborhood and individual levels of parental involvement with the schools and with the youths' educational efforts, youths' educational outcomes could be compromised. Questions persist about the direction and relative strength of causal relationships between individual- and neighborhood-level measures of poverty. Do neighborhood conditions make residents poorer and thereby less able to support their children's educational efforts? Or, by virtue of their poverty, are poorer individuals and families forced to migrate and remain in low-resource neighborhoods, which could compound, but may not cause, their reduced capacity to support their children's educational efforts? As noted in chapter 10, this conceptual debate and the associated methodological controversy over how to estimate these relative causal influences are complex and will not be resolved easily (see also Furstenberg and Hughes vol. 2; Sampson and Morenoff vol. 2).

6. Neighborhoods vary in the density of adult friendship networks, the networks' degree of value consensus about youths, and the networks' monitoring of youths (Sampson and Groves 1989). To the extent that these neighborhood characteristics are also associated with nonfamilial adults

encouraging neighborhood youths to avoid truancy and stay in school, they could be associated with more positive educational outcomes (see Darling and Steinberg vol. 2).

We have drawn on Wilson's (1993) work in formulating this hypothesis. He provided some needed nuance to the simpler hypothesis that social isolation of households and families in poorer neighborhoods is what leads to poorer outcomes for their youths, and he pointed out that social integration alone will not produce positive youth outcomes. Instead, social integration built around shared high expectations for youths and shared commitments to monitoring and mentoring youths toward mainstream behavior and accomplishments are necessary ingredients as well.

7. Neighborhood variation in institutional capacities to support parents' efforts to raise their youths could affect the youths' educational success. Neighborhoods with more competent nonfamilial adults in recreational, church, child-care, and educational settings who can reinforce positive— or, in some cases, offset negative—parenting practices should have higher concentrations of educationally successful youths. These neighborhood-based supports for caregivers include direct instruction, as well as positive role modeling of parenting skills. (See Connell et al. [1995] for a more detailed profile of these neighborhood supports.)

To test these seven hypotheses, additional measurement work on both the community dimensions themselves and the mediators of their effects will be required. In some cases, data-analytic strategies other than the ordinary least squares regression techniques used to test our simple direct effects models will be called for as well. We discuss these future directions at the conclusion of this chapter.

## EMPIRICAL EXAMPLE

In the following empirical example, taken from a recent publication (Connell et al. 1995), we examine one set of hypotheses about how neighborhood risk (measured by the neighborhood composite risk index used in previous chapters) affects psychological variables included in a motivational model developed by Connell and his colleagues (Connell 1990; Connell and Wellborn 1991). The motivational variables have been established as proximal predictors of students' educational outcomes in previous research (Connell, Spencer, and Aber 1994). This empirical example also explores possible gender differences in the pathways through which neighborhood demographic composition may affect educational outcomes in minority urban youths, as well as the strength of the effects.

## HYPOTHESES

Based on quantitative and qualitative studies (see, for example, chapter 6) of neighborhood and family effects on urban adolescents' development, we expected to find both direct and indirect effects of neighborhood risk and family poverty on males' and females' educational outcomes, with effects of neighborhoods stronger in males and family effects stronger in females. The specific psychological mediators included in the model, shown in figure 7.2, are drawn from theory and research on urban students' engagement and disaffection (see, for example, Connell et al. 1995; Connell, Spencer, and Aber 1994; Connell and Wellborn 1991).

## SAMPLE

Subjects were 736 junior high school students (grades seven to nine at initial assessment in the fall of 1987) from an upstate New York urban school district. Half of the subjects in the sample ($N = 363$) had been identified as eligible for participation in five programs for at-risk youths being conducted in the school district. These programs were initiated in the fall of 1987. Students were considered eligible for these programs if they received three or more "flags" from the Five-Flag Identification System (Crichlow and Vito 1989). Students selected for the program were then matched with other at-risk youths from their same school who had received three or more flags but who were not participating in the program. The other half of the sample ($N = 373$) was selected as a comparison group for the entire at-risk sample. These students were selected to match the at-risk group by school, grade level, ethnicity, and gender. The comparison students had to have received either none or only one flag in order to be selected for this group.

Only the African American students who had complete and usable survey data were used in this study, yielding a total of 443 subjects (225 males, 218 females), equally split between students eligible and not eligible for the at-risk programs. Chi-square tests revealed no significant differences on any of the demographic characteristics between this subsample and the total African American sample. Sample demographic information for the current sample is shown in table 7.1.

## MEASURES

*Neighborhood risk* was measured using the composite index used throughout this volume—a single index that averaged three neighborhood composition factors: (1) the percentage of low-SES neighbors, (2) the percentage of jobless males, and (3) the additive inverse of the percentage of high-SES neighbors. A common metric for each factor was created that represented standard deviation units away from the average of a nationally representa-

FIGURE 7.2 Model Depicting the Hypothesized Relations Among the Contextual, Psychological, and Educational Outcome Variables

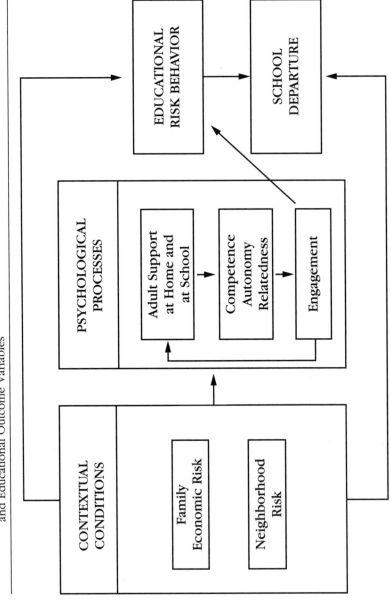

*Source:* Connell, Halpern-Felsher et al. (1995).

TABLE 7.1     Sample Demographic Information

|  | Males | Females |
|---|---|---|
| N | 225 | 218 |
| Neighborhood risk[a] | 3.60 (2.16) | 4.00 (2.12) |
| Family economic risk[b] | .84 | .90 |

[a] Mean (and standard deviation) of the three-variable neighborhood risk composite in standard deviation units based on national norms of PSID data (Duncan and Aber this volume).

[b] Proportion of subjects eligible for the free/reduced-cost lunch program.

tive sample of neighborhoods developed by Duncan and his colleagues on the Panel Study of Income Dynamics (PSID) data set (chapter 3).

*Family economic risk* was assessed using information obtained from school records. Eligibility of the student's family for the free or reduced-price lunch program was used as a marker of family poverty. Eligibility for free or reduced-price lunches is determined by federal guidelines.[1] Validity checks on the poverty measure were conducted. Families were considered to be economically at-risk only when the target students' siblings (where applicable) were also coded as eligible for free or reduced-price lunches and where eligibility was stable over a three-year period.

The Research Assessment Package for Schools–Student Report (RAPS-S; Connell, Pierson, and Wellborn 1992) was used to assess the psychological variables included in the model (see table 7.2 for sample items). The RAPS-S, a 204-item student-report questionnaire, was used to tap the psychological constructs shown in figure 7.2. The questionnaire was administered to groups of between fifteen and thirty-five students. Research assistants read the items aloud while at least one monitor from the research team moved around the room to answer students' questions and encourage focus on the items. Students were asked to respond to the questions in a Likert-type format. Items tapping each of the constructs were interspersed throughout the questionnaire. Students were told that they could choose not to respond to any of the questions they found objectionable. This version and subsequent versions of the RAPS-S have been administered to over ten thousand urban students, and the instrument's psychometric properties have been found to be adequate to excellent within these samples.

Three dimensions of *perceived adult support*, at home and at school, are included in the RAPS-S survey: perceived structure, autonomy support, and involvement. *Perceived structure* is the quality and legitimacy of the information students receive about educational expectations and consequences from adults in their families and schools. *Perceived autonomy support* refers to adults at home and in school involving students in important decisions and providing connections between work in school and students' own personal

TABLE 7.2   Research/Assessment Package for Schools: Student Report

### Variable Definition and Sample Items

### Perceived Adult Support

*Adult involvement*

Parents and teachers show interest in, are knowledgeable about, and put time and effort into students' learning, while also communicating positive affect.

*Sample items:*
- My parents like to talk to me about school.
- My parents know a lot about what happens to me in school.
- My teacher cares about how I do in school.
- My teacher doesn't seem to have enough time for me.

*Adult autonomy support*

Parents and teachers provide voice and choice for students in important school-related decisions, take students' perspective, and help students draw connection between school learning and students' current and future life.

*Sample items:*
- My parents talk about connections between schoolwork and things in my life.
- When it comes to school, my parents try to control everything I do.
- My teacher lets me decide things for myself.
- My teacher thinks what I say is important.

*Adult structure*

Parents and teachers set expectations and standards that are clear and optimally challenging and deliver consequences that are fair, affirming, and useful.

*Sample items:*
- My parents make it clear what they expect of me in school.
- I know how my parents will act if I don't do my homework.
- The rules in my classroom are clear.
- My teachers' expectations for me are way off base.

### Developmental Needs

*Competence*

Students report that they have control over positive and negative academic outcomes, they know effective strategies for producing or avoiding these outcomes, and they have the capacities to execute these strategies.

*Sample items:*
- Trying hard is the best way for me to do well in school.
- I don't know what it takes to get good grades in school.

*Autonomy*

Students report that they do their schoolwork because it is interesting and/or personally important to them versus because they fear failure or external consequences.

*Sample items:*
- I do my classwork because I want to understand the subject.
- I do my homework because I'll get in trouble if I don't.

TABLE 7.2     *Continued*

*Relatedness to self*
    Students experience emotional security and satisfaction with self.

    *Sample items:*
    • When I think about myself, I feel important.
    • I wish I liked myself better.

*Relatedness to others*
    Students experience optimal connection and emotional security with teachers and other students.

    *Sample items:*
    • When I'm with my teacher, I feel happy.
    • I wish my teacher would spend more time with me.

Engagement

Students report behaviors and emotions that reflect commitment to and interest in academic endeavors.

    *Sample items:*
    • When I'm in school, I feel happy.
    • I read books, even when they are not assigned.
    • When I'm in class, I just act as if I'm working.
    • I pay attention in class.

goals. Finally, *perceived involvement* refers to the students' experience of adults at home and in school dedicating psychological resources to them in terms of interest, attention, and emotional support. The three dimensions were combined to create the *adult support at home* and *adult support at school* variables.

Three sets of *developmental needs* are also assessed by the RAPS-S survey. *Perceived competence* refers to students' perceptions of their strategies and capacities for achieving success and avoiding failure in school (Skinner, Wellborn, and Connell 1990). *Perceived autonomy* is operationalized using subjects' endorsements of different reasons for why they do schoolwork and homework. These reasons are then combined into four subscales that tap styles of self-regulation, which vary in degree of perceived autonomy (Connell and Ryan 1987; Ryan and Connell 1989). Students' *perceived relatedness* in school is assessed by asking subjects to rate the emotional quality of their experience with significant social partners in the school setting—teachers and classmates in this study (Connell and Wellborn 1991). Scores for each of the three self-system variables were computed for use in the path analyses.

The RAPS-S survey items tapping students' school *engagement* include reports of behavior, emotion, psychological orientation, and reactions to challenge in the classroom. Subscale scores on these variables were combined into a single score for use in the analyses.

*Educational risk behavior* was assessed using the Five-Flag Identification System developed by Crichlow and Vito (1989). In this system, a flag was assigned when (1) yearly attendance was below 82 percent; (2) national percentile scores on standardized achievement tests were below 38 percent for math and below 37 percent for reading, or when one of these scores was below 15 percent; (3) two or more instructional days were lost due to suspension; (4) two or more courses (English, math, social studies, or science) were failed in the past academic year; or (5) the student was two or more years older than the average student at the same grade level. Selection of the variables included in the composite and the established cutoff values were based on analysis of historical records of students who left school before graduation, as predicted by a set of approximately fifty indicators of risk behavior. The five markers in the Five-Flag composite showed unique and significant contributions to the prediction of school departure (Crichlow and Vito 1989). These findings were consistent with other studies of school departure among urban students. For the current study, the variable *time 1 educational risk behavior* is the number of flags the student received as of June 30, 1987. The variable *time 2 educational risk behavior* is the number of flags the student received as of June 30, 1988.

*School departure* was assessed from school records and is a dichotomous variable. A value of one was assigned when the student records indicated departure from school because of being sent to reform school, being sent to a youth home, completing an employment certificate, attending evening school for vocational training only, being pregnant, having health problems, completing military service, being overage, or entering a job corps. Students who had left under any of these conditions and who had not returned by the spring of 1991 were considered to have left school before graduating. Students still in school and students who left school under conditions other than those just listed (such as going to another school within or outside the district, graduating, or moving out of the district to a known destination) received a code of zero.

## RESULTS

Ordinary least squares path analysis was used to examine linkages among the family and neighborhood context, adult support, developmental needs, and school outcomes variables. To test the model adequately using the available longitudinal data, we introduced several modifications of traditional path analytic strategies. In the first equation, the adult support at home and at school variables were regressed separately on neighborhood risk, family economic risk, and time 1 educational risk behavior. In the second equation, each of the developmental needs variables was regressed on the adult support variables and the three independent variables included in the first equation. In the third equation, engagement was regressed on the developmental needs variables and all of the independent variables included in the first two equations. In the fourth equation, time 2 educational risk behavior was regressed on engagement, the neighborhood and family risk variables, developmental needs, and adult support variables, with these latter two sets of variables residualized with respect to time 1 educational risk behavior. In the final equation, leaving school before graduation was regressed on time 2 educational risk behavior, plus all of the independent variables used in the fourth equation.

The strategy of residualizing the adult support variables and the developmental needs variables for the final two regression equations precluded the necessity of estimating equations in which time 1 and time 2 educational risk behavior were both included. This strategy was considered both theoretically appropriate, given that there were no hypotheses concerning change from time 1 to time 2 educational risk behaviors, and pragmatically necessary, given the mathematical and logical dependency of various components of the two risk behavior composites.[2]

The correlational results suggest that, consistent with our hypotheses, family economic risk and neighborhood risk influence males' and females' perceptions of adult support and school outcomes in different ways. For the males, significant correlations were obtained between time 2 educational risk behavior and neighborhood risk ($r = .13$, $p < .05$) and family economic risk ($r = .19$, $p < .001$). The point biserial correlations between these contextual variables and school departure were $r = .21$ ($p < .001$) and $r = .12$ ($p < .05$), respectively. For the females, correlations between neighborhood risk and time 2 educational risk behavior and neighborhood risk and school departure were nonsignificant ($rs = .01$ and $-.05$). Family economic risk significantly correlated with time 2 educational risk behavior ($r = .13$, $p < .05$) and with school departure ($r = .16$, $p < .01$).

Contrary to our hypothesis, nonsignificant correlations were found between neighborhood risk and adult support at home and at school for both the males and females, between family economic risk and home support for the males, and between family economic risk and school support for the females (see table 7.3). However, the correlation between family economic risk and school support was significant and, unexpectedly, positive ($r = .18$, $p < .01$) for the males. For females, family economic risk and support at home were significantly negatively related ($r = -.17$, $p < .01$).

Path analyses were conducted separately for males and females, and the results are presented in figure 7.3 and table 7.4 for males and figure 7.4 and table 7.5 for females. The results of the path analyses supported many of the hypothesized paths in the motivational model (Connell et al. 1995). In this chapter, only results pertinent to neighborhood and family economic risk are discussed.

For the males, the path analyses revealed a direct, unmediated path from neighborhood risk to school departure, suggesting that males from neighborhoods with lower concentrations of disadvantaged neighbors and jobless

*(Text continues on page 195.)*

TABLE 7.3 Correlations Among Variables Used in the Analyses for the Male and Female Subjects

| Males[a] | Support at Home | Support at School | Competence | Autonomy | Relatedness | Engagement |
|---|---|---|---|---|---|---|
| Time 1 | | | | | | |
| educational risk | -.02 | -.18*** | -.24**** | -.05 | -.16** | -.14** |
| Neighborhood risk | .03 | .10 | .05 | -.01 | .03 | .03 |
| Family economic risk | -.04 | .18*** | .06 | .05 | .09 | .13** |
| Support at home | — | .15** | .21**** | .17*** | .14** | .16*** |
| Support at school | .15** | — | .37**** | .22**** | .46**** | .54**** |
| Competence | .21**** | .37**** | — | .39**** | .44**** | .50**** |
| Autonomy | .17*** | .22**** | .39**** | — | .18*** | .26**** |
| Relatedness | .14** | .46**** | .44**** | .18*** | — | .58**** |
| Engagement | .17*** | .54**** | .50**** | .26**** | .58**** | — |
| Time 2 | | | | | | |
| educational risk | .05 | -.17*** | -.30**** | -.04 | -.19*** | -.19*** |
| School departure | .07 | -.09 | -.07 | -.02 | -.13** | -.17*** |
| Females[b] | | | | | | |
| Time 1 | | | | | | |
| educational risk | -.04 | -.13** | -.32**** | -.12* | -.18*** | -.15** |
| Neighborhood risk | .00 | -.02 | -.07 | -.02 | .02 | .03 |
| Family economic risk | -.17*** | .03 | -.09 | -.03 | -.04 | -.01 |
| Support at home | — | .23**** | .28**** | .12* | .27**** | .31**** |
| Support at school | .23**** | — | .30**** | .26**** | .52**** | .51**** |
| Competence | .28**** | .30**** | — | .39**** | .52**** | .53**** |
| Autonomy | .12* | .26**** | .39**** | — | .21*** | .37**** |
| Relatedness | .27**** | .52**** | .52**** | .21*** | — | .62**** |
| Engagement | .31**** | .51**** | .53**** | .37**** | .62**** | — |
| Time 2 | | | | | | |
| educational risk | -.11 | -.14* | -.34**** | -.13* | -.19** | -.20*** |
| School departure | -.12* | -.11* | -.15** | -.02 | -.08 | -.09 |

[a] $N = 225$. [b] $N = 218$.

* $p < .10$. ** $p < .05$. *** $p < .01$. **** $p < .001$.

FIGURE 7.3 Results from Path Analyses Showing Relations Among the Contextual, Psychological, and Educational Outcome Variables for the African American Males (*N* = 225)

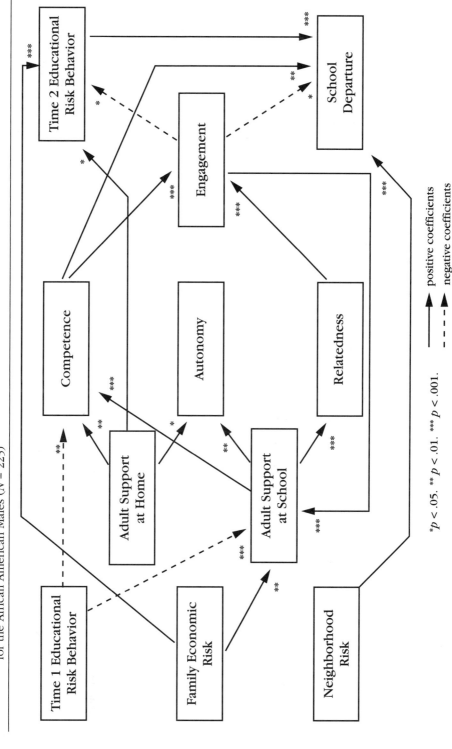

*p < .05. ** p < .01. *** p < .001.

*Source:* Connell, Halpern-Felsher et al. (1995).

TABLE 7.4  Parameter Estimates and Standard Errors from Path Analyses for African American Males

| | Support at Home | Support at School | Competence | Autonomy | Relatedness | Engagement | Time 2 Education Risk | School Departure |
|---|---|---|---|---|---|---|---|---|
| **Time 1** education risk | -.01 (.02) | -.09* (.03) | -.04* (.01) | .00 (.02) | -.02 (.02) | .01 (.01) | — | — |
| Family economic risk | -.07 (.10) | .31* (.11) | .04 (.06) | .04 (.08) | .04 (.07) | .05 (.05) | .99* (.29) | -.05 (.07) |
| Neighborhood risk | .01 (.02) | .03 (.02) | .00 (.01) | -.01 (.01) | .00 (.01) | -.01 (.01) | .04 (.05) | .04* (.01) |
| Support at home | — | — | .10* (.04) | .11* (.05) | .06 (.05) | .01 (.03) | .21* (.10) | .01 (.02) |
| Support at school | — | — | .17* (.04) | .13* (.05) | .31* (.04) | .17* (.03) | -.04 (.13) | .01 (.03) |
| Competence | — | — | — | — | — | .25* (.06) | -.60 (.38) | .25* (.10) |
| Autonomy | — | — | — | — | — | .03 (.05) | .15 (.11) | -.01 (.03) |
| Relatedness | — | — | — | — | — | .28* (.05) | .19 (.30) | -.03 (.08) |
| Engagement | — | — | — | — | — | — | -.92* (.39) | -.22* (.10) |
| **Time 2** educational risk | — | — | — | — | — | — | — | .16* (.02) |
| $R^2$ | .01 | .07** | .18 | .05 | .21 | .47 | .09 | .33 |

$N = 225$. *indicates coefficient is at least twice its standard error.

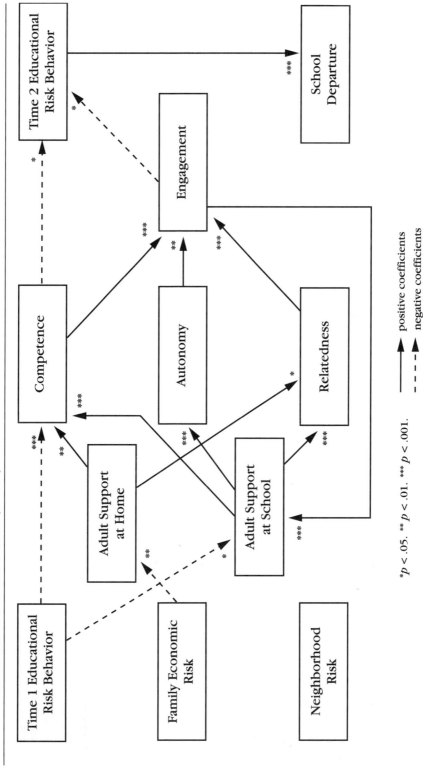

FIGURE 7.4   Results from Path Analyses Showing Relations among the Contextual, Psychological, and Educational Outcome Variables for the African American Females (*N* = 218)

*p < .05. ** p < .01. *** p < .001.

*Source:* Connell, Halpern-Felsher et al. (1995).

TABLE 7.5   Parameter Estimates and Standard Errors From Path Analyses for African American Females

| | Support at Home | Support at School | Competence | Autonomy | Relatedness | Engagement | Time 2 Education Risk | School Departure |
|---|---|---|---|---|---|---|---|---|
| Time 1 educational risk | -.01 (.02) | -.06* (.03) | -.06* (.01) | -.03 (.02) | -.03 (.02) | .01 (.01) | — | — |
| Family economic risk | -.28* (.11) | .11* (.15) | .00 (.06) | -.01 (.10) | -.05 (.09) | .03 (.06) | .50* (.31) | .09 (.09) |
| Neighborhood risk | .00 (.01) | .00 (.02) | .00 (.01) | .00 (.01) | .01 (.01) | .01 (.01) | .00 (.05) | .00 (.01) |
| Support at home | | — | .14* (.04) | .05 (.06) | .14* (.05) | .07 (.04) | .02 (.10) | -.02 (.03) |
| Support at school | | — | .10* (.03) | .15* (.05) | .33* (.04) | .12* (.03) | .02 (.11) | -.02 (.03) |
| Competence | — | — | | | | .27* (.07) | -.80* (.40) | .06 (.11) |
| Autonomy | — | — | | | | .12* (.04) | .06 (.10) | .03 (.03) |
| Relatedness | — | | | | | .28* (.05) | .33 (.29) | .05 (.08) |
| Engagement | — | | | | | | -.74* (.36) | -.06 (.10) |
| Time 2 educational risk | — | | | | | | | .13* (.02) |
| $R^2$ | .02 | .01 | .21 | .06 | .30 | .50 | .04 | .16 |

$N$ = 218. *indicates coefficient is at least twice its standard error.

males and higher concentrations of middle-class neighbors have a higher probability of remaining in school beyond their eleventh year. In contrast to the results for the males, no effects of neighborhood risk on educational outcomes were obtained for the females.

Although neighborhood effects were not mediated through the model variables, family economic risk was found to predict adolescents' school outcomes directly and indirectly. Consistent with the correlational findings, the path analyses revealed that, for males, the effect of family economic risk on adult support was counterintuitive, with students from poorer families reporting higher levels of support from adults in the school setting than students from more economically advantaged homes. The direct path from family economic risk to time 2 educational risk behavior indicates that African American male adolescents from less economically disadvantaged families showed less educational risk behavior in early high school. For the female adolescents, family economic risk negatively influenced females' perceptions of adult support at home. That is, African American females from poorer families experienced their parents as less supportive and less involved in their educational endeavors than did females from less-poor families.

## DISCUSSION

In this chapter, we suggested theoretical and empirical strategies for examining *how* neighborhoods can influence children's and adolescents' educational outcomes, and seven hypotheses were offered. Data were then presented that test a version of one of these hypotheses—that the influence of neighborhood factors on youths' school performance is mediated through adult support experienced by the youths.

Although many components of the hypothesized model were supported (see Connell et al. 1995), the expected pathways from neighborhood characteristics to student reports of parent and teacher support were not found, indicating that these particular psychological variables might not mediate the effects of neighborhood composition on educational outcomes in this sample of urban, African American adolescents. Instead, a direct, unmediated link from neighborhood risk to males' school departure was found. No link from neighborhood risk to any of the model variables was obtained for the female adolescents.

For males, the results suggest that some pathways outside of the psychological processes measured in this study shape males' educational outcomes. Connell and colleagues (1995) pointed to the "world of the streets" as an important influence on African American males' identities and decision making (see also Sullivan 1989). A critical aspect of the "streets" not assessed in this set of measures is the peer culture. Adolescents spend approximately twice as much time with peers as they spend with their parents or other adults (Brown 1990; Csikszentmihalyi, Larson, and Prescott 1977; Savin-Williams and Berndt 1990). Accordingly, peers become a major source of socialization and development for adolescents (Clasen and Brown 1985; Youniss and Smollar 1985). To the extent that peers reside within the same neighborhood, they are exposed to similar neighborhood processes that could affect their school performance, such as positive and negative role models, perceived employment and educational opportunities, youth idleness, and opportunities for involvement in illicit activities. Accordingly, peers may be a proximal influence on males' school performance and adjustment, with the effect of the neighborhood characteristics being mediated through this peer system.

The direct path from neighborhood risk to school departure for the males also suggests that we may need to disaggregate the neighborhood composite indicator and explore how each particular neighborhood variable may be influencing males' achievement. Earlier analyses of this data set suggested that the concentration of young adult males who had not graduated from high school was the single most significant (negative) predictor of young adolescent males' risk behavior in school.

In the model tested in this chapter, neighborhood risk and family economic risk are included in the regression equations simultaneously. Therefore, neighborhood- and family-level variables are "competing" to explain the variance in the adult support variables. The predictive relations between neighborhood- and family-level variables are not estimated in these models. For example, the availability of jobs within the neighborhoods and the access to transportation for employment outside of the immediate area can directly affect a family's economic status. Neighborhoods also vary in their concentration of child-care services, churches, and nonfamilial adults who can support and assist parents. Since economically impoverished families typically reside in similarly disadvantaged neighborhoods, they are more likely to be without these supports than are more middle-class families. Parents experiencing these stressors may be forced to allocate less time and attention to their children, resulting in these adolescents reporting lower support from their families for their school-related activities (see McLoyd [1990b] for a similar argument). Chapter 9 contains a discussion of how misspecification of effects such as these could lead to underestimates of neighborhood effects.

Additionally, many urban adolescent young women, who, compared to their male counterparts, spend more time at home than out in the neighborhood, are often expected to assist with household chores and child care. Because these young women are relied on at home, they could perceive their families as less encouraging of their school efforts. The negative path from family economic risk to adult support at home for the females is consistent with this hypothesis.

The effect of family economic risk on males' achievement was also mediated by adult support—in this case, teachers' support. However, this path was
unexpectedly positive, suggesting that males from less economically disadvantaged families report experiencing lower levels of adult support at
school than do adolescent males from poorer families. In another study
(Halpern-Felsher and Connell 1995), a similar counterintuitive result was
obtained, with males from poorer neighborhoods reporting higher levels of
teacher support. These studies suggest that it is African American children and
adolescents from less economically distressed families or neighborhoods,
who perceive their teachers as less supportive. Two interpretations are
offered. First, males from economically distressed families and neighborhoods
may feel safer and more supported in their school environment than in other
environments. Alternatively, Halpern-Felsher (1994) argued, the cultural mismatch between the predominantly middle-class, white, female teachers and
these minority adolescent males may lead some teachers to hold similar and
low expectations for all minority students. Accordingly, African American
males, who expect and receive high levels of involvement and support from
adults in their homes and neighborhoods but do not receive comparable levels of support from their teachers, perceive their teachers more negatively.
(See also Connell et al. [1995] for a more detailed argument).

The empirical findings presented in this chapter highlight the need to
develop additional markers of neighborhood dimensions (other than demographic composition) that can affect the everyday lives not only of the adolescents but also of the adults living and working with them. Many of these
variables are included in the broader model shown in figure 7.1 and are
embedded in the set of hypotheses offered earlier, including the employment
opportunities in the students' proximal and distal neighborhoods; the competence, continuity, and connectedness of adults in the youths' neighborhood; and the neighborhood's balance of supportive formal and informal
institutions versus distracting or counterproductive institutions and networks.

The findings also point to the enormous gap in our empirical representation of processes *mediating* neighborhood effects on adolescent outcomes.
This data set, while relatively rich in psychological and interpersonal predictors of educational outcomes, was restricted to school-focused beliefs and
experiences of these youths. Broader assessments of adolescents' ability to
be productive and connected and to navigate outside the school setting were
not included. Similarly, while students' school-related experiences with
familial and nonfamilial adults were assessed by the survey instrument
employed, other familial processes important to these adolescents' development were not included, such as sibling characteristics, home responsibilities, physical conditions at home, and educational resources in the home
environment.

We also need to increase our understanding of the extent to which
neighborhood conditions influence parents' economic and emotional re-

sources, which may in turn affect parents' allocation of support to their children. Similarly, we need to understand the link between variation in neighborhood conditions and the pool of teachers within these neighborhood schools. For example, levels of neighborhood crime, even if not created by the residents themselves, can deter the more senior and competent teachers from electing employment in these areas. An examination of teachers within these neighborhood schools with respect to SES, race or ethnicity, and training may further explain the counterintuitive association between family economic risk and higher teacher support reported by the males in this sample.

Given the rudimentary nature of our work in this area and the relatively immature state of the study of neighborhood effects on youth development, these "errors of omission" are not surprising, nor is the predictive weakness of mediator models that we have generated from our initial forays. But we remain optimistic. The field's repertoire of theory, measures, and data analytic strategies is growing and is being brought to bear on hypotheses such as those offered earlier in this chapter. We believe stronger results will be forthcoming from these studies, and with these stronger results will come more compelling implications generated for the burgeoning public and private investment in place-based, youth-focused intervention. Addressing conceptual issues such as those raised in this chapter about how neighborhoods affect the development of poor children and adolescents is crucial if these initiatives are to be rationally designed and effectively implemented.

---

This research is part of a larger collaborative effort funded by the Russell Sage Foundation, the William T. Grant Foundation, and the Smith Richardson Foundation under the direction of the Social Science Research Council's Committee on the Urban Underclass. Data used in this study were collected while the first author was a W. T. Grant Foundation Faculty Scholar. The authors thank the students and staff from the participating school district for their willingness to participate in this research. Requests for reprints should be sent to: James P. Connell, Director, Institute for Research and Reform in Education, 710 Glengarry Road, Philadelphia, PA 19118.

## NOTES

1. According to the figure for the 1990–1991 academic year, a family of two is eligible for free lunch with an annual income less than $10,946, and for a reduced-cost lunch with an annual income greater than $10,946 but less than $15,577. For a family of four, the free-lunch figure is $16,510 and the reduced-cost-lunch figure is $23,495.

2. For example, both time 1 and time 2 risk behavior include whether the student is one or more years older than the average student in his or her grade level, an attribute whose value remains constant once it occurs. Similarly, achievement test data from the preceding year stays in the student's records if the student has not taken the current year's tests. Therefore, the same score for achievement could be included in the time 1 and time 2 risk

behavior composite. This logical and mathematical dependency between the two waves of measurement creates an artificially high correlation between the variables that distorts any interpretation of findings emerging from equations in which both variables are included. However, by residualizing the key variables expected to be influenced by earlier risk behavior, the mediators' unique effects on subsequent indicators of risk can be estimated.

# 8

# Neighborhood and Family Influences on Young Urban Adolescents' Behavior Problems: A Multisample, Multisite Analysis

*Margaret Beale Spencer, Steven P. Cole,*
*Stephanie M. Jones, and Dena Phillips Swanson*

For American youth, the transition from late childhood to early adolescence represents a confluence of biological, psychological and social changes. These changes and transitions between the ages of ten and sixteen years are largely independent of ethnicity, economic resources, contextual risk, and unique neighborhood characteristics. This study examines urban African American youth in poor, distressed neighborhoods. It was designed to examine individual differences in coping, adaptation, and mental health among youth in high-risk environments. Thus, the selected measures address positive microcontext, coping and identity. In addition, we examine differences in processes and outcomes between youth in somewhat risky and extremely risky neighborhoods. We address the following questions: Are the effects of processes dampened by living in extreme situations? Are others exacerbated? Accordingly, our goal in this chapter is to use two data sets to explore how mental health outcomes are affected by neighborhood and family influences and how these outcomes are predicted and moderated by specific measures of coping and identity processes.

As with other developmental periods represented in this volume, the early adolescent period lends itself to a range of hypotheses regarding how neighborhood characteristics affect the development of youth. Unfortunately, little research has been conducted on neighborhood effects generally or on early adolescent youth living in high-risk urban environments. Even the data available in our initial studies presented in this volume are rudimentary at best—both in terms of neighborhood measures and, particularly in this chapter, relative to the samples available for study.

Nettles and Pleck (1994) noted that more contemporary investigations of black adolescents have now focused attention on an examination of mechanisms that undergird competence development and psychologically healthy outcomes. In their review, poverty was linked to increased rates of behavioral and academic problems during childhood and adolescence. They also noted, however, an improvement in high school graduation rates for blacks (64 percent), which exceeded that of Latinos (52 percent), although both remained behind that of whites (78 percent). Similarly, Nettles and Pleck reported that overall school dropout rates dropped from 32 percent in 1973 to 20 percent in 1983. However, dropout rates were inconsistent with employment statistics. They noted, for example, that the Latino dropout rate was higher than the rate for blacks, yet blacks continued to have higher unemployment rates than other groups. In general, studies of urban African American adolescents suggest inconsistencies. They also underscore the need to search for underlying mechanisms and contextual characteristics that might contribute to variations in normative adolescent struggles, particularly among impoverished youth.

Normal adolescent development involves strong foundational needs that (1) are associated with normative biological shifts, (2) require important ego transformations that are linked to changes in cognitive abilities and coping responses, and, in general, (3) represent processes that do not function independently of context. Many foundational needs have their roots in the biological challenges emanating from within (see, for example, Lerner 1982). Other needs, however, interact with social expectations, in conjunction with developmental tasks, and demonstrate equally strong pressures from without (Havighurst 1953). White (1959, 1960) and others have contended that the biologically based human need for mastery and competence is of critical concern for low-resource youth and families. As a multifaceted construct, competence also represents important affective outcomes such as a sense of self-efficacy (Spencer 1985; Spencer, Swanson, and Cunningham 1991; White 1959, 1960).

The emerging biological and psychological capacities of youth permit new emotional experiences and patterns of behavior, which, in this culture, are often manifested in personal experimentation and behavioral lability. These emerging capacities also potentiate risk behavior and mental health syndromes that can have important long-term implications. For youth in high-risk environments the stakes are even higher. Opportunities for risky experimentation and the lack of opportunities for constructive expression of emerging identities and capacities lead to higher incidents of risk behavior and poorer mental health outcomes (Nettles and Pleck 1994). The basic and broader cross-species need for mastery and competence is viewed by White (1959, 1960) and others as biologically based and of critical concern for low-resource youth and families, irrespective of available supports required for making competence needs a reality. Biologically based competence motivation is present for all and is accompanied by a sense of efficacy, which is an important affective outcome (White 1960). In sum, as a multifaceted construct, competence notions also represent affective products (White 1959, 1960) that are less often associated with psychological mediators as predictors (see reviews by Spencer 1985, Spencer, Swanson, and Cunningham 1990).

The psychologically sensitive adolescent period requires that youth cope with expectations for mastery independent of the actual structural nature of the context, the availability of resources, and the degree of risk. Both behavioral problems and poor mental health are expected outcomes for many youth. Family and neighborhood characteristics, more than other variables, can lessen or exacerbate such problems among early adolescents. The generalized risks for youth can be heightened by the interactive influences of race or ethnicity, gender, and chronic poverty. We are trying to integrate the complex normative processes of adolescent coping and identity formation with economic, and often contextual, risk factors and thereby better understand the relationships among (1) neighborhood and family context, (2) psychological processes of coping and identity, and (3) mental health outcomes for African American urban adolescents.

To explore research on how neighborhood conditions affect this population of youth, we present results from two independent data sets collected in urban school settings. Both include census-tract-level indices of neighborhood characteristics, along with indicators of youth mental health.

As indicated elsewhere in this volume, the two data sets, although conceptually linked, emphasize at least two distinct theoretical perspectives on human development: identity and cultural-ecological theories (Ogbu 1985; Spencer 1985; Spencer and Markstrom-Adams 1990) and developmental risk (DR) research (Allen, Aber, and Leadbeater 1990; Allen, Leadbeater, and Aber 1994). As noted elsewhere (Connell, Spencer, and Aber 1994), the overlapping modeling across perspectives suggests that social contexts help shape individuals' beliefs about themselves in particular culturally sensitive endeavors, such as school. Importantly, these beliefs result in coping strategies and identity processes that represent important aspects of normative cognitive processes that are unavoidable (Spencer 1985).

The parallel theoretical perspectives that represent the two data sets share important characteristics. First, identity and cultural-ecological and developmental risk perspectives emphasize "meaning making" as a critical process that evolves transactionally in multiple settings and strongly influences the etiology of risk and resilience in youth. Nevertheless, each perspective represents an undergirding theoretical point of view specific to the particular data set.

A second shared characteristic is the conceptualization of self-system processes as dynamic (that is, interactive), rather than static, traits. Third, there is a shared assumption about the influence of transactions between social context experiences and an individual's actions. Finally, the two perspectives share the view that within groups of youth who live in high-risk communities, specific predictors (such as coping, identity, and few negative life events) provide more accurate interpretations of particular results (such as behavioral problems) than do traditional pathology-driven models (see, for example, Kardiner and Ovesey 1951).

The findings summarized in this chapter result from analyzing cross-project data on youth in high-risk environments. As suggested by figure 8.1, we have generated several possible mechanisms for how neighborhoods might affect mental health outcomes of two types. One type of outcome, referred to as "internalizing" by Achenbach and Edelbrock (1981), includes tendencies to become anxious, fearful, depressed, and paranoid and to feel shy, disliked, teased, and so on. Another type of outcome, termed "externalizing," represents tendencies to engage in antisocial behavior, including aggression, vandalism, stealing, disobedience, school skipping, and extreme anger. The overall approach taken represents the type of collaborative and applied research strategy generally believed to be missing from the developmental literature.

## METHOD

The description for the New York City/Baltimore/Washington sample is provided and is followed by the Atlanta-based project.

### SUBJECTS AND SAMPLE

Two independent samples were examined in this study. All participants are African American early adolescents who are participating in larger longitudinal studies.

The New York City/Baltimore/Washington, D.C. (NYC/B/DC) sample was drawn from subjects participating in the Adolescent Pathways Project, an accelerated longitudinal study of youth living in high-risk communities in Baltimore, Washington, D.C., and New York City (Seidman 1991). The total project sample consists of 1,431 adolescents (561 boys, 772 girls; 27 percent black, 23 percent white, 38 percent Latino, and 12 percent other/unspecified). Data were collected from students attending elementary and junior high or middle schools that were predominantly black, Latino, or white and had a minimum of 60 percent of the student body eligible for reduced-price or free lunches. Within each school, all students in the grade prior to the transition to junior high or middle school (grades five and six) or high school (grades eight or nine) were recruited. The age range for these subjects was 10 to 16 years, with a mean age of 12.3 years ($SD = 1.6$). For this study, 360 African American subjects (129 boys, 231 girls) with a complete set of demographic information, questionnaire responses, and mental health outcomes are included.

The Atlanta subjects were drawn from a larger sample of 562 subjects (396 boys, 166 girls) participating in a longitudinal project that explores identity and coping processes in the prediction of competence and resiliency among African American youth (Promotion of Academic Competence Project, PAC) (Spencer 1988). In this larger study, students were randomly selected from the enrollment lists of four public middle schools (grades six to eight). Par-

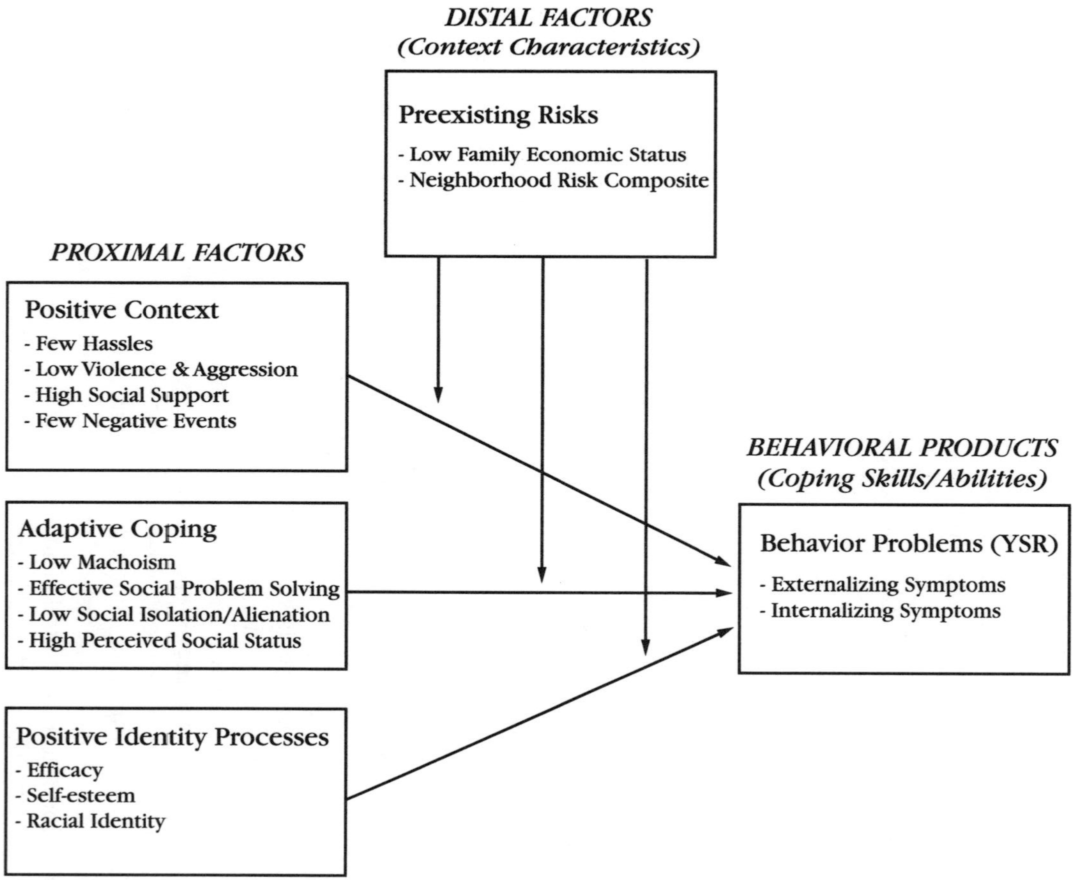

FIGURE 8.1  Contextual and Psychological Influences on Behavioral Outcomes

ticipant schools represented two contiguous school systems' highest rate of free/reduced-cost lunch participation. The students ranged in age from 11 to 16 years, with a mean age of 13.1 years ($SD = 1.1$). Although five years of data on adolescents and their parents have been completed to date, only data collected in the first wave during the 1989–90 school year were included in the current study. Of the larger sample, 531 students (368 males, 163 females) with a complete set of demographic information, questionnaire responses, and mental health outcomes are included in this study.

## MEASURES AND MEASUREMENT STRATEGIES

The measures used in this study include ones on (1) individual and family demographics, (2) neighborhood risk, (3) identity processes, and (4) mental health outcomes. Individual and family demographic variables for the NYC/B/DC data set include gender (*male* = 0, *female* = 1), a family-level poverty index, and family structure. The family-level poverty index was created using student reports of family labor market participation and automobile ownership. The family structure variable was created by coding subjects who reported living with their mother without a male caregiver as *single female–headed family* and other family configurations as *other*. In addition, an employment variable was used where employment was measured as two full-time jobs in the household, one full-time and one part-time job, one full-time or two part-time jobs, or no job. For the Atlanta sample the individual and family demographic variables include gender (*male* = 0, *female* = 1), family income, family structure, and mother's education. Family income was assessed using parental (interview) reports of family income. These figures were transformed into an index based on family size and federal poverty guidelines. The family structure variable was created in the same manner as for the NYC/B/DC data set. Mother's education was used as an additional indicator of family risk, with highest level of mother's completed education coded as number of years of education (for example, *high school diploma* = 12, *college degree* = 16).

For the moderator analyses, the family economic variables from each data set were standardized and combined to form "good family economy" composite variables. High scores indicated better family economy.

Neighborhood risk was measured using 1980 tract data that had previously been attached to the larger data sets in the two longitudinal studies. A principal components analysis of thirty-five census-tract variables was conducted on the Panel Study of Income Dynamics (PSID) data set, as well as the NYC/B/DC data. The principal components analysis revealed six neighborhood composition factors: (1) concentration of neighbors with low socioeconomic status (SES), (2) concentration of neighbors with high SES, (3) ethnic diversity, (4) family concentration (density), (5) concentration of jobless males, and (6) residential stability (see chapter 3). For this study, only relations between the first five neighborhood indicators and the youth outcomes were explored.

Additionally, these factors were used to form a neighborhood risk composite variable. Based on the variance accounted for by these factors and their interpretability as indices of risk using Wilson and his colleague's work on defining underclass neighborhoods (Wilson 1987), we aggregated three of the six indices to form one neighborhood composite variable (neighborhood risk factor) for this study: (1) low SES (high concentration of family and individual poverty), (2) low concentration of high-SES residents, and (3) high levels of male joblessness. A common metric for each factor was created that represented standard deviation units away from the average of a nationally representative sample of neighbors developed by Duncan and his colleagues on the Panel Study of Income Dynamics (PSID) (chapter 3). A higher value on the neighborhood risk factor indicates higher risk.

QUESTIONNAIRE RESPONSES

In both research sites, surveys were administered to groups of between twenty-five and thirty-three subjects in school classrooms. Also, for the Atlanta sample, other protocols were obtained in one-on-one sessions with, for the most part, same-race interviewers. The two sets of questionnaires differed in format. They generally consisted of statements that were rated either on Likert-type scales by the subjects or on forced-choice formats that varied by the context of the items. The complete protocols were reviewed by the investigators individually and as a group to identify sets of items that would be theoretically consistent with the general constructs (positive context, adaptive coping, and positive identity). An expanded theoretical model of the one presented in figure 8.1 is described in detail elsewhere (Spencer 1995). The elaborated model describes possible mechanisms for resilient and adverse outcomes, and the ideas are consistent with other research reported elsewhere (see Spencer 1986).

MEDIATIONAL CONSTRUCTS   The positive context construct is represented by four variables for the NYC/B/DC data set. They are neighborhood hassles, total social support, neighborhood cohesion, and negative life events. Neighborhood hassles is a composite of selected items (including noisy neighborhood, being scared by someone in your neighborhood, and so on) from the twenty-eight-item Daily Hassles Scale (Rowlison and Felner 1988). Total social support is a composite of items from a modified version of the Social Support Rating Scale (Cauce, Felner, and Primavera 1982). Neighborhood cohesion is a composite of nine items (including "I fit in with my neighbors," "I like living in my neighborhood," "things in my neighborhood have gotten worse," and so on) adapted from the Neighborhood Cohesion Instrument developed by Buckner (1986). Negative life events is a nineteen-item adaptation of the Life Events Checklist (Johnson 1986; Johnson and

McCutcheon 1980) describing negative events in four life domains: personal events, family problem events, school events, and friend events.

For the Atlanta data set the positive context construct is represented by a similar, but not identical, set of measures: daily hassles, social support, dangers, social status, self-esteem, life satisfaction, machismo, racial identity, and negative life events.

Adaptive coping and positive identity (API) were both composites of the machismo hypermasculinity scale (Mosher and Sirkin 1984), the Hare Self-Esteem/School subscale (Hare 1977), self-efficacy items, and the Racial Attitude Identity Scale (Parham and Helms 1981). Adaptive coping includes low machoism, effective social problem solving, low social isolation/alienation, and high perceived social status. Positive identity processes include efficacy, self-esteem, and racial identity. The API and class preparation were also incorporated in positive identity for the NYC/B/DC sample. The Atlanta sample additionally extracted from the Intellectual Achievement Responsibility Scale (Crandall, Katkovsky, and Crandall 1965) and the Life Satisfaction Scale (Conte and Salamon 1982).

Mental health outcomes include externalizing and internalizing behavior scores for both the NYC/B/DC and Atlanta data sets. The NYC/B/DC externalizing and internalizing scores were created from a subset of items from a thirty-eight-item short-form adaptation of Achenbach and Edelbrock's (1987) Youth Self Report (YSR). The YSR is a 118-item instrument designed to assess, in a standardized format, eleven- to eighteen-year-olds' reports of their own competencies and behavior problems. Fourteen items composed the internalizing scale for both males and females. The externalizing scale consisted of ten items for the males and nine for the females. Internalizing refers to the youth's experience of confusion, low self-esteem, and so on and is described as an assessment of personality problems. Externalizing items include youth's reports of disobedience, antisocial behavior, temper tantrums, and so forth and represent an assessment of conduct problems.

In addition, for the NYC/B/DC sample, an antisocial behavior measure was used. This measure assessed the students' experience with alcohol and with delinquency behaviors (for example, stealing, intimidation of others, forced entry). For the moderator analyses, a third mental health outcome variable—psychological symptoms—was created by averaging thirty-six of the YSR items for girls and thirty-eight for boys.

The YSR was also used to create the internalizing and externalizing scales for the Atlanta sample. Because the full YSR was used in the Atlanta sample and the internalizing and externalizing scales were scored using Achenbach and associates' (1991) approach, these scales are more reliable than those used in the NYC/B/DC data set. In accordance with Achenbach and colleagues' (1991) approach, the internalizing and externalizing scores were calculated by summing across the scale items for the Atlanta sample, whereas scale items were averaged in the NYC/B/DC data set. For the moderator analyses, the total YSR variable was added as a third score.

## RESULTS

Our strategy for presenting the results is to first report "direct" effects of neighborhood characteristics on internalizing and externalizing behaviors, both with and without statistical controls for family demographics. We then present the results of analyses testing the moderating influence of neighborhood characteristics on the relationship between Positive Context, Adaptive Coping, and Positive Identity and adolescent mental health outcomes.

### DIRECT EFFECTS OF NEIGHBORHOOD CHARACTERISTICS

Since initial data analyses suggested consistent patterns in general, analyses were run separately for boys and girls. Neither the neighborhood composite risk variable nor the family demographic characteristics predicted internalizing or externalizing behavior for any subgroup (African American males and females) in the NYC/B/DC or Atlanta data sets. Some significant findings were obtained using the separate neighborhood factors. These effects, however, disappeared once the family demographic characteristics were added to the equation.

Because the neighborhood risk composite did not predict the mental health outcomes in these two data sets, an exploration of the indirect paths through which neighborhood risk can influence behavioral and emotional adjustment was not conducted.

### MODERATING INFLUENCE OF NEIGHBORHOOD RISK

To test the influence of neighborhood risk as a moderator, the neighborhood composite variable (low SES + low concentration of high-SES residents + high levels of male joblessness) was divided within gender into two groups via a median split, resulting in four groups (high-risk females, low-risk females, high-risk males, low-risk males). A dichotomous neighborhood risk variable was created, with the lower-risk group coded as 1 and the higher-risk group coded as 2. Table 8.1 presents ranges, means, standard deviations, and sample sizes for the four neighborhood risk groupings and for the dichotomous neighborhood risk variable.

For the Atlanta sample, because of the larger number of male subjects, it was possible to divide the sample into thirds on the risk composite. The bottom third was designated as low-risk boys and the top third grouping was labeled as high risk.

Correlations were computed between several predictor constructs and the mental health outcomes for the four extreme risk groups by data set to ascer-

TABLE 8.1   Mean Census Scores, by Site and Level of Risk

| PAC | | | | |
|---|---|---|---|---|
| **All Females (Median Census Score = 1.914; M = 1.631)** | | | | |
| | Census Score | | | |
| Group (Risk Level) | Range | Mean | SD | N |
| Low risk (bottom half) | −.79–1.53 | 0.94 | 0.63 | 82 |
| High risk (top half) | 1.91–3.63 | 2.31 | 0.44 | 84 |
| **All Males (Median Census Score = 1.914; M = 1.756; n = 386)** | | | | |
| | Census Score | | | |
| Group (Risk Level) | Range | Mean | SD | N |
| Low risk (bottom third) | −.80–1.45 | 0.86 | 0.52 | 108 |
| High risk (top third) | 2.09–3.60 | 2.51 | 0.37 | 133 |
| Pathways | | | | |
| **All Females (Median Census Score = 1.441; M = 1.375)** | | | | |
| | Census Score | | | |
| Group (Risk Level) | Range | Mean | SD | N |
| Low risk (bottom half) | −1.28–1.44 | 0.86 | 0.54 | 86 |
| High risk (top half) | 1.47–2.98 | 1.90 | 0.40 | 84 |
| **All Males (Median Census Score = 1.338; M = 1.212)** | | | | |
| | Census Score | | | |
| Group (Risk Level) | Range | Mean | SD | N |
| Low risk (bottom half) | −.72–1.33 | 0.64 | 0.51 | 53 |
| High risk (top half) | 1.35–2.90 | 1.78 | 0.36 | 53 |

tain whether the correlations between predictors and outcomes looked different in "higher-" and "lower-ranked" neighborhoods. Tables 8.2 and 8.3 present the results of these correlations for the NYC/B/DC and Atlanta data sets, respectively. Using Fisher's $r$ to $z$ transformations, we tested correlations to see whether any of the results were significantly different from each other for the low- and high-risk groups by gender.

Correlations that are significantly different from each other for the high- and low-risk groups are as follows for the NYC/B/DC data set (see table 8.2): for females, negative life events with psychological symptoms, and coping and negative life events with externalizing; for males, negative life events with internalizing behavior. There are no significant differences in correlations with mental health outcomes between male and female high- and low-risk groups for neighborhood hassles, total social support, neighborhood cohesion, or positive identity.

Correlations that are significantly different from each other for the high- and low-risk groups in the Atlanta data set are as follows (see table 8.3): for females, negative life events and positive identity with total YSR, and

TABLE 8.2    Results of Correlations Between Process Constructs and Mental Health Outcomes—NYC/B/DC

| | Females | | | | | |
|---|---|---|---|---|---|---|
| | Low-Risk Neighborhoods | | | High-Risk Neighborhoods | | |
| | PSY | INT | EXT | PSY | INT | EXT |
| Neigh. hass. | .222* | .207 | .051 | .234* | .112 | .146 |
| Social support | −.092 | −.207 | .027 | .025 | −.035 | .065 |
| Neigh. cohes. | −.131 | −.178 | −.061 | −.178 | −.178 | −.010 |
| Neg. life ev. | −.428[a] | −.296** | −.355**[a] | −.186[a] | −.085 | −.190[a] |
| Adapt. coping | −.292** | −.248* | −.272**[a] | −.058 | −.170 | .042[a] |
| Pos. identity | −.406*** | −.405*** | −.325*** | −.397*** | −.397*** | −.279*** |

| | Males | | | | | |
|---|---|---|---|---|---|---|
| | Low-Risk Neighborhoods | | | High-Risk Neighborhoods | | |
| | PSY | INT | EXT | PSY | INT | EXT |
| Neigh. hass. | .261 | .263 | −.002 | .212 | .142 | .188 |
| Social support | .054 | .129 | −.090 | −.006 | −.025 | −.034 |
| Neigh. cohes. | −.006 | −.079 | −.069 | −.056 | −.025 | −.059 |
| Neg. life ev. | −.352** | −.178 | −.314*[a] | −.408** | −.414**[a] | −.273 |
| Adapt. coping | −.243 | −.299* | −.161 | −.190 | −.282* | −.093 |
| Pos. identity | −.264 | −.396* | −.123 | −.346* | −.497*** | −.049 |

* = $p < .05$, ** = $p < .01$, *** = $p < .001$
[a] Indicates that correlation coefficients are significantly different from each other in high-risk versus low-risk neighborhoods.

internalizing and externalizing behavior; for males, social status with total YSR and externalizing behavior (although neither is significant).

Based on the results of the correlations, regressions were run within gender, with the outcome regressed on the following independent variables: the dichotomous neighborhood risk variable, the selected identity process variables, and the interaction of the neighborhood risk variable and the identity process variables. These regressions were then rerun including the "good family economy" variables as controls. The results of these regressions are presented in tables 8.4 and 8.5.

For the NYC/B/DC data set there is a significant interaction between Adaptive Coping and neighborhood risk on externalizing behavior for females, with Adaptive Coping negatively associated with externalizing behavior in the context of low neighborhood risk (see figure 8.2). For males there is a significant interaction between negative life events and neighborhood risk on internalizing behavior, with negative life events negatively related to internalizing behavior in the context of low neighborhood risk (see figure 8.3). Three significant interactions emerged in the Atlanta data set. The interaction between Positive Identity and neighborhood risk on total YSR, externalizing and internalizing behaviors is significant for girls, so that in all cases a

TABLE 8.3  Results of Correlations Between Process Constructs and Mental Health Outcomes—Atlanta

| | Females | | | | | |
|---|---|---|---|---|---|---|
| | Low-Risk Neighborhoods | | | High-Risk Neighborhoods | | |
| | YSR | INT | EXT | YSR | INT | EXT |
| Neigh. Hass. | −.276** | −.269* | −.258* | −.279** | −.203 | −.271* |
| Social Support | .030 | .009 | −.056 | .044 | .076 | −.044 |
| Neigh. Dangers | −.179 | −.181 | −.072 | −.087 | −.123 | −.041 |
| Social Status | −.344*** | −.264* | −.325*** | −.088 | −.047 | −.164 |
| Neg. Life Ev. | −.445***a | −4.85***a | −.378***a | −.173a | −.180a | −.203a |
| Adapt. Coping | −.316** | −.284** | −.323*** | −.069 | −.051 | −.135 |
| Pos. Identity | −.507***a | −.498***a | −.404***a | −.243*a | −.248*a | −.218*a |

| | Males | | | | | |
|---|---|---|---|---|---|---|
| | Low-Risk Neighborhoods | | | High-Risk Neighborhoods | | |
| | YSR | INT | EXT | YSR | INT | EXT |
| Neigh. Hass. | −.249* | −.319*** | −.255** | −.132 | −.095 | .188* |
| Social Support | .062 | .023 | .042 | −.061 | −.077 | −.043 |
| Neigh. Dangers | −.089 | −.071 | −.087 | −.084 | −.075 | −.034 |
| Social Status | .187a | .092 | .241*a | −.118a | −.146 | −.130a |
| Neg. Life Ev. | −.352*** | −.339*** | −.361*** | −.379** | −.326*** | −.339*** |
| Adapt. Coping | −.034 | −.130 | −.125 | −.230** | −.212* | −.253** |
| Pos. Identity | −.481*** | −.512*** | −.370*** | −.490*** | −.497*** | −.480*** |

$* = p < .05$, $** = p < .01$, $*** = p < .001$

[a] Indicates that correlation coefficients are significantly different from each other in high-risk versus low-risk neighborhoods.

stronger negative relationship exists between positive identity and the three mental health outcomes for the lower-risk group than for the higher-risk group (see figures 8.4, 8.5, and 8.6). All five significant interactions held after controlling for family demographic characteristics.

## DISCUSSION

For the current set of analyses, no direct effects of neighborhood on individual outcomes are apparent for the NYC/B/DC and Atlanta samples. For this reason, the major analytic activity for this chapter became the exploration of possible moderating effects on a process construct (for example, positive identity, positive context, or adaptive coping) with mental health outcome measures (for example, internalizing or externalizing behavior) for neighborhoods designated as low- or high-risk in two geographically different data sets. Accordingly, the basic question explored was whether or not there was a moderating effect of neighborhood characteristics (that is, low or high risk) on the relationship between specific process constructs (that is, positive con-

TABLE 8.4   Results of Regression Analyses of the Effects of Process Constructs and Family Characteristics on Mental Health Outcomes—NYC/B/DC

| | Females | | | |
|---|---|---|---|---|
| | YSR | YSR | EXT | EXT |
| *Demographics/risk* | | | | |
| Good fam. econ. | | −.00 (.03) | | −.04 (.03) |
| Neigh. risk | −.04 (.08) | −.03 (.08) | −.00 (.09) | .00 (.09) |
| *Process constructs* | | | | |
| Neg. life events | −.01 (.02) | −.02 (.03) | −.04 (.03) | −.04 (.03) |
| Positive identity | | −.38 (.16)* | −.43 (.17)** | |
| *Interactions* | | | | |
| Neg. life × neigh. | −.02 (.03) | −.01 (.02) | .01 (.02) | .01 (.02) |
| Identity × neigh. | | | .20 (.10)* | .23 (.10)* |
| *N* | | | | |
| Adj. $R^2$ | .07 | .07 | .07 | .08 |

| | Males | |
|---|---|---|
| | INT | INT |
| *Demographics/risk* | | |
| Good fam. econ. | | −.02 (.04) |
| Neigh. risk | −.26 (.12)* | −.26 (.12)* |
| *Process constructs* | | |
| Neg. life events | .49 (.03) | .05 (.03) |
| *Interactions* | | |
| Neg. life × neigh. | −.05 (.02)* | −.06 (.02)* |
| *N* | | |
| Adj. $R^2$ | .09 | .09 |

βs and their standard errors are presented.

text, adaptive coping, and positive identity) and adolescent mental health outcomes (that is, internalizing and externalizing). The findings suggested the importance of realistically contextualizing the actual meaning of *low risk* versus *high risk* for the samples included.

As indicated in the methods section, median splits were used for both males and females by individual data sets to create lower-risk (bottom half) and higher-risk (top half) group designations. However, as evident from table 8.1, the Atlanta sample means for the high-risk designation groups, independent of gender, appear more extreme than the parallel designated high-risk groupings for the NYC/B/DC sample. Similarly, the mean scores for low-risk groupings by gender for the two samples show some variation. Mean listings in table 9.1 indicated what, in fact, the sampling strategies intended.

*(Text continues on page 216.)*

TABLE 8.5 Results of Regression Analyses of the Effects of Process Constructs and Family Characteristics on Mental Health Outcomes—Atlanta

### Females

| | YSR | YSR | EXT | EXT | INT | INT |
|---|---|---|---|---|---|---|
| *Demographics/risk* | | | | | | |
| Good fam. econ. | | -4.6 (2.8) | | -1.3 (.91) | | -1.1 (1.1) |
| Neigh. risk | -9.9 (4.0)* | -8.8 (4.6) | -1.26 (1.3) | -.96 (1.5) | -5.4 (1.6) | -5.2 (1.9)** |
| *Process constructs* | | | | | | |
| Neg. life events | -34.8 (19.1) | -36.9 (21.6) | -5.2 (6.2) | -5.8 (7.0) | -19.1 (7.6)* | -19.7 (8.7)* |
| Positive identity | -40.8 (8.9)*** | -44.1 (10.2)*** | -9.8 (2.9)*** | -10.8 (3.3)*** | -15.8 (3.5)*** | -16.6 (4.1)*** |
| *Interactions* | | | | | | |
| Neg. life × neigh. | 9.5 (13.4) | 1.3 (15.1) | -.74 (4.3) | -.20 (4.9) | 6.5 (5.4) | 7.0 (6.1) |
| Identity × neigh. | 17.5 (5.5)** | 18.8 (6.2)** | 4.1 (1.8)* | 4.6 (2.0)* | 6.7 (2.2)** | 7.0 (2.5)** |
| *N* | | | | | | |
| Adj. $R^2$ | .24 | .25 | .15 | .15 | .27 | .26 |

### Males

| | YSR | YSR | EXT | EXT |
|---|---|---|---|---|
| *Demographics/risk* | | | | |
| Good fam. econ. | | 4.2 (4.0) | | 1.6 (1.3) |
| Neigh. risk | 3.5 (5.0) | -4.2 (6.0) | 1.3 (1.6) | .95 (1.7) |
| *Process constructs* | | | | |
| Social status | 6.6 (9.1) | 6.0 (9.6) | 3.9 (2.9) | 3.6 (3.1) |
| *Interactions* | | | | |
| Social status × neigh. | 47.7 (8.0) | -4.2 (6.0) | -2.5 (1.8) | -2.3 (1.9) |
| *N* | | | | |
| Adj. $R^2$ | -.01 | -.01 | -.00 | -.00 |

*Note*: βs and their standard errors are presented.

FIGURE 8.2   Females (NYC/B/DC): Externalizing Mean Scores, by Risk and Coping

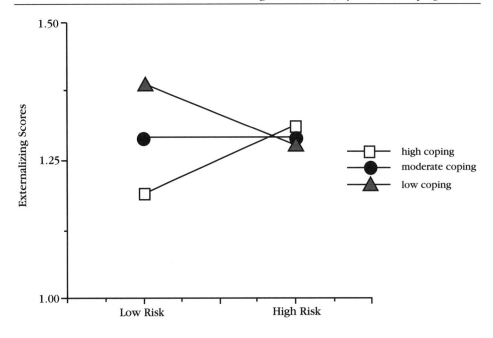

FIGURE 8.3   Males (NYC/B/DC): Internalizing Mean Scores, by Risk and Level of Negative Life Events

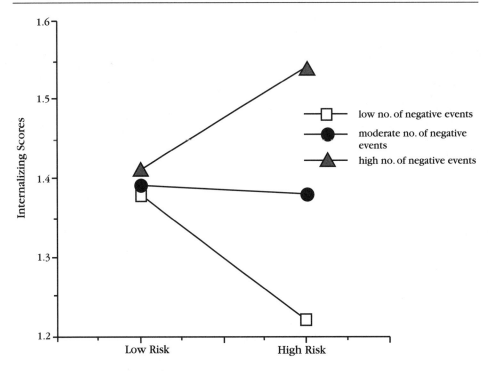

FIGURE 8.4    Females (Atlanta):  Internalizing Mean Scores, by Level of Risk and Identity

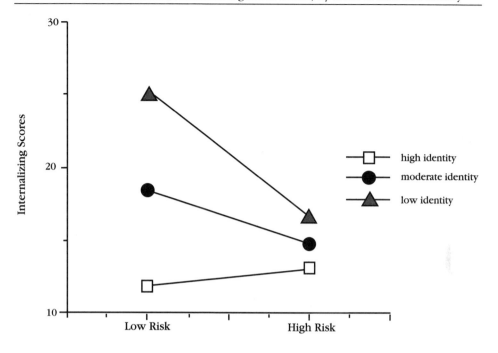

FIGURE 8.5    Females (Atlanta):  Externalizing Mean Scores, by Level of Risk and Identity

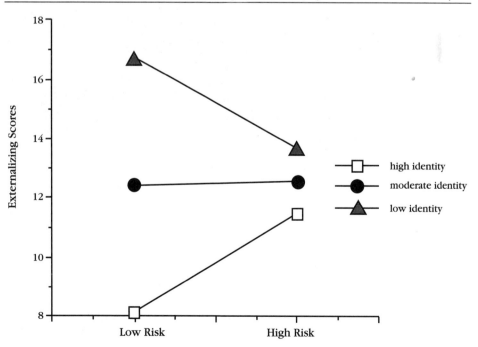

FIGURE 8.6   Females (Atlanta): YSR (Total) Mean Scores, by Level of Risk and Identity

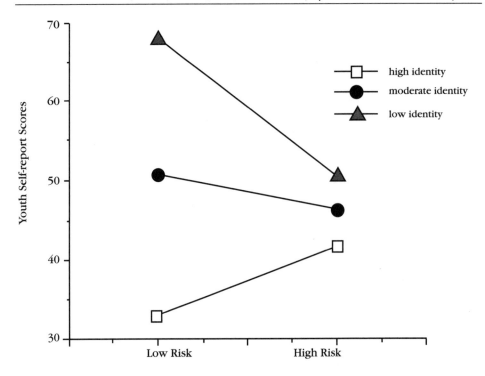

If one is sampling for high-risk subjects and sampling from the most economically destitute schools, subsequent designations of low risk are relative to the specific sample and may mean something quite different for a labeled low-risk sample obtained from a national sample or from a randomly stratified local sample. Accordingly, the parallel, although different, results (that is, process constructs) obtained for NYC/B/DC and Atlanta are not surprising. In fact, the Atlanta sample was 2.5 *SD* units below the nation's average neighborhood poverty level. Given the project's interest in resiliency, the Atlanta sample was randomly selected from the most economically disadvantaged schools of one particular school system. In sum, although the analyses presented used the term *low* risk, more realistic or accurate labels for *low risk* and *high risk* should probably be *relative (high) risk* and *extreme risk*, respectively.

For each data set, the finding that neighborhood characteristics of risk moderate the relationship between project-specific process constructs (such as positive identity and adaptive coping) and an adolescent mental health outcome was not surprising. For NYC/B/DC for girls only, level of risk moderated adaptive coping processes with externalizing problem behavior. As illustrated in figure 8.2, high levels of coping for girls were associated with less problem behavior outcomes, although only for those female subjects living in relatively lower-risk environments. No direct effects were evident between coping and externalizing behavior for those females living under the highest-risk conditions. Data for NYC/B/DC male subjects (see figure 8.3) indicated that neighborhood risk moderated the relationship between negative life events and internalizing behavior problem outcomes. High levels of negative life events were more thoroughly associated with internalizing problems for adolescent males in the highest-risk neighborhoods.

For Atlanta male adolescents, there were no moderated effects by risk level between the process constructs and either of the three mental health outcomes. However, there was a more consistent story between positive identity processes and adolescent mental health outcomes for girls, although the effect was significant only for those living in so-called low-risk situations (see figures 8.4, 8.5, and 8.6). The process construct (that is, positive identity) and mental health measures were significantly moderated by neighborhood risk level for girls. Positive identity apparently is protective of mental health only for those girls who live in low-risk environments.

The two sets of findings suggest different opportunities for prevention and intervention efforts. On the one hand, for girls, enhancing coping skills or promoting more positive identity processes may help only those who live in low or, more accurately, less extremely high risk neighborhoods. As evident from figures 8.4, 8.5, and 8.6, enhancing positive identity for girls living in extremely high risk environments, was not significant; the findings suggest that the anticipated or desired effect, although singularly inadequate, was heading in the expected direction: (high) positive identity with better mental health outcomes. This is not the case for girls in terms of coping and mental health (refer to figure 8.2).

Although there was only one set of significant results for African American males, the finding is important and in the expected direction: fewer (less extreme) negative life events is associated with better mental health (fewer internalizing problems) in the most distressed neighborhoods. Relative to prevention and intervention, the finding may well indicate that boys require more protection from adverse circumstances in the most extreme neighborhood conditions. The implications for sex-role development and male socialization are especially salient because boys more often receive peer and media reinforcement for hypermasculine responses to threats or adversity.

In summary, the findings raise more questions than they answer. However, they suggest different neighborhood risk experiences for males and females and different process constructs for each. With the Atlanta youth, the findings suggest the same process construct, although applicable to one gender group alone. Finally, the pattern of findings and lack of effects suggest that for extremely impoverished samples, *risk* may be an inadequate term for describing the high-risk experiences of such youth. When studying so-called high-risk groups, researchers may find traditional linear models (that is, ones that identify low-, moderate-, and high-risk groups) conceptually flawed or inadequate. Perhaps researchers need to examine risk as something that increases exponentially, rather than linearly along a continuum. Such a change in focus might help researchers and policy makers better understand individuals' and neighborhoods' problems and help them determine the optimal type and amount of support needed.

---

Funding for the research conducted in Atlanta was made available to the first author from the Spencer, Ford, and W. T. Grant Foundations, the Commonwealth Fund, and the Social Science Research Council. Work on this chapter was supported in part by grants from the National Institute of Mental Health (MH43084) and the Carnegie Corporation (B4850) awarded to Edward Seidman, J. Lawrence Aber, LaRue Allen, and Christina Mitchell. We express our appreciation to the adolescents and schools whose cooperation made this study possible.

# 9

# Conceptual and Methodological Issues in Estimating Causal Effects of Neighborhoods and Family Conditions on Individual Development

*Greg J. Duncan, James P. Connell, and Pamela K. Klebanov*

D rawing causal inferences from data such as ours is fraught with hazards. For our specific task—the estimation of the causal effects of
neighborhoods on children's development—the list of possible
sources of bias is long indeed. As discussed in earlier chapters, various concerns involving measurement issues may mean that our estimates understate
the true causal effects of neighborhoods on children and adolescents (see
also Korbin and Coulton vol. 2; Sampson and Morenoff vol. 2; Tienda 1991).
A separate set of concerns could be raised over the structure of the causal
models we choose to estimate, many of which may lead our estimates to
misrepresent causal effects. These possible problems, the conceptual and
methodological issues they raise, and possible methods for addressing them
empirically are the subjects of this chapter.

## CONCERNS WITH MODEL SPECIFICATION

We consider six possible deficiencies in our causal models, each of which
raises thorny conceptual and empirical issues unique neither to the work represented in this volume nor to the study of neighborhoods per se. In fact,
many of these issues arise in any empirical effort to isolate causal influences
on behavior. Our list is not meant to be exhaustive. We hope it will point
toward crucial next steps in understanding the nature of neighborhood
effects and in informing policies aimed at promoting beneficial neighborhood
environments for children and adolescents. We begin with a brief summary
of each of the six possible problems.

### MODERATORS OF NEIGHBORHOOD EFFECTS

The empirical strategy followed in our quantitative analyses is based on very
simple mediated models in which developmental outcomes are presumed

to be additive functions of family conditions and neighborhood factors. It is possible that important interactions between family and neighborhood conditions and between these variables and other moderators of their effects at the individual and more macro levels have been omitted. Additive models are estimated *within* demographically defined subgroups—by age, race, gender and, in some cases, family economic status—and this approach allows for the effects of neighborhood to differ across these subgroups. Some of our models are estimated separately within low-SES and high-SES neighborhoods. However, demographic and census-based neighborhood variables are, at best, crude markers for the full range of contextual conditions that could buffer or exacerbate neighborhood conditions' effects on development (see, for example, Bronfenbrenner 1977; Furstenberg and Hughes vol. 2; Sampson and Morenoff vol. 2). These potential moderators of neighborhood effects include other dimensions of neighborhoods themselves, as well as family and individual characteristics associated with what Bronfenbrenner refers to as "microsystems" (Connell, Aber, and Walker 1994; Darling and Steinberg vol. 2).

## SELECTION BIAS

A second concern is with possible selection bias resulting from the fact that families have some degree of choice regarding the neighborhoods in which they live. If important unmeasured characteristics of families lead them both to choose certain kinds of neighborhoods and to have children with different developmental trajectories, then the apparent effects of neighborhoods on these trajectories that we estimate in our simple models could either over- or understate true effects. With the exception of Evans, Oates, and Schwab (1992), whose work deals with the effects of school context, none of the existing studies of neighborhood effects has addressed the important selection issue (Tienda 1991).

Although one can readily imagine selection-bias stories involving neighborhoods, it is difficult to predict the likely direction in which the selection process might bias estimates of neighborhood influences. For example, Mayer (personal communication with the authors) suggested a scenario in which parents either choose two jobs and use the extra income to get into better neighborhoods or choose a single-earner strategy and stay in poorer neighborhoods but attempt to make up for the poorer location's deficiencies through mothers spending more time with their children. In this scenario, omitting measures of parental time with children leads to a *downward* bias in the effects of neighborhoods estimated from our simple models.

However, parents especially *ill*-equipped to handle bad neighborhoods probably are most likely to live in them because these parents lack the (partly unmeasured) wherewithal to move to better neighborhoods. In this case, the coincidence of a poor neighborhood and the children's poor developmental outcomes results from these parents' inability to avoid either, thus leading to an *over*estimation of current neighborhood conditions' effects. Conversely, parents who effectively promote their children's developmental success may find their neighborhood choices dominated by considerations of developmental consequences. If this capacity is not captured in measured parental characteristics, then the coincidence of positive developmental outcomes for their children and living in a better neighborhood would be misattributed to current neighborhood conditions and lead to an overestimation of neighborhood effects (Klebanov, Brooks-Gunn, and Duncan 1994).

In terms of the causal models, selection-bias problems can be thought of as a case of omitted variables. Failure to include the unmeasured parental characteristics leads to biased parameter estimates of the neighborhood context's influence.

## TRANSACTION MODELS OF NEIGHBORHOOD EFFECTS

A third concern is based on insights from transaction models of human development (Sameroff and Chandler 1975), which emphasize not only that individuals create and shape their own environments (for example, by deciding where to live) but also that characteristics of individuals and families (such as income, living arrangements, and decision making) are *shaped by* social and physical contexts such as neighborhoods. Our models assume that neighborhoods affect children. If neighborhoods affect parents as well, then our models understate the total effects of neighborhoods by ignoring the possibility that neighborhoods influence parental characteristics (Sampson and Morenoff vol. 2; Wilson 1987).

It is easy to imagine how neighborhoods might affect parents. For example, persistent residence in a neighborhood with high levels of crime, low levels of economic opportunity, weak marriage pools, and poor transportation can erode and eventually dissipate the competence and commitment of single mothers to seek employment in that neighborhood, to marry, or to move to a neighborhood where they can find work and provide safe activities outside the home for their children (Korbin and Coulton vol. 2). On the more positive side, opportunities provided by a neighborhood's job-training and job-placement programs, social services, community-based organizations, or informal social networks may enhance a single mother's opportunities to take these positive steps for her children.

Hypotheses such as these lead us to question our methods of estimating the relative contribution of neighborhood, family, and individual characteristics as they affect individual outcomes. The models estimated in this volume's empirical chapters control for family economic conditions and family structure as part of the estimation of neighborhood's effects. Included in these family conditions are any prior effects of neighborhood on these family characteristics.

Statistical controls for family characteristics in our additive models reduce our estimates to those of neighborhood influences on *child* development that are uncorrelated with neighborhood influences on *family* development. To the extent that neighborhoods do affect aspects of family development that in turn affect child development, our controls for family income, family structure, and other family-level characteristics produce an *under*estimation of neighborhood effects.

STATISTICAL SUPPRESSION OF NEIGHBORHOOD EFFECTS

A fourth source of concern is that effects of neighborhood variables on child and adolescent outcomes may be underestimated owing to suppression effects from other, unmeasured variables. In this case there is a spurious *lack* of correlation between neighborhood and outcomes, and the "true" relationship is revealed only when suppressor variables are included in the analysis. Suppression may account for why the expected positive relationship between the presence of high-SES neighbors and positive educational and cognitive outcomes was not found in our minority samples. If the high-SES neighbors of minority sample members are predominantly white, then their presence in minority neighborhoods may engender resentment rather than increase levels of neighborhood resources and provide positive role models for minority youth—factors that Wilson (1987) and others have cited as benefiting youth development. This relation between resentment and presence of high-SES (white) neighbors in minority groups may then suppress the positive relations between this neighborhood characteristic and positive outcomes in these groups.

THRESHOLD EFFECTS

Fifth, there is concern that neighborhood effects may not be linear across the entire range of neighborhood conditions. Perhaps there are "threshold" levels of low- or high-SES neighbors or of ethnic diversity beyond which certain neighborhood conditions matter, but before which they do not. This possibility is complicated by the fact that the minority subsamples in our studies have very compressed ranges of neighborhood conditions. For example, consistent with data on housing segregation presented by Massey (1993), data presented in chapter 3 show that even in the case of our two national samples, disproportionately few African American families reside in neighborhoods with high concentrations of affluent neighbors. This could truncate the within-group variance of these variables and attenuate their possible relationships with developmental outcomes. In data presented in this volume, this problem may account for the much stronger positive effects of high-SES neighbors in advantaged white samples than in black samples. Later in this chapter we explore this possibility further.

## HIERARCHICAL MODELS

Finally, the models we estimate use data from three levels. Developmental outcomes—our dependent variables—are measured for individual children and adolescents. Family environments of children are assessed using family-level measures such as family income and mother's completed schooling. And our census-based neighborhood factors are measured at the neighborhood, or census-tract, level. Measures from all three levels are combined in our ordinary least squares (OLS) regression models without regard to the level at which they are measured.

A great deal of methodological work during the past twenty years has been devoted to the development and estimation of hierarchical linear models (HLMs) by educational psychologists, multilevel models by sociologists, and random-coefficient models by econometricians. (See Bryk and Raudenbush [1992] for a discussion of these models in different disciplines and an exposition of HLMs.) These models account explicitly for the hierarchical nature of the data involved and, in so doing, provide more efficient estimates of model parameters at all levels. An important question raised by these models is whether our OLS-based approach produces misleading results about the nature and statistical significance of neighborhood- and family-level effects.

We argue that the data from the six studies presented in this volume are not typical for an HLM application and that other techniques are more useful to adjust our estimates for our samples' clustering of observations at the individual and family levels within neighborhoods. The usual application of HLMs is to data in which individuals (such as students) are clustered within units (such as schools), and the characteristics of a given unit (for instance, school-level average SES) are estimated from the group of individuals within the given unit (for instance, surveyed students within a given school). Efficient estimation of these models requires substantial numbers of individuals observed within the higher-level unit to provide adequate estimates of the higher-level unit's characteristics (Bryk and Raudenbush 1992).

Although some of the data sets used in our analyses contain observations on several children living within the same neighborhood, we never construct neighborhood-level measures by aggregating information obtained from our child or parental interviews, but instead rely on well-measured neighborhood-count data obtained from the decennial census. (See the chapter by Darling and Steinberg [vol. 2] for an example of the aggregative approach.) We accept the limitations of the decennial population census as a sole source for our neighborhood measures. However, coefficient estimates of the effects of census-based measures are not biased by our OLS-based estimation methods.

Clustering observations within neighborhoods does produce serial correlation in our samples, however, because observations sampled from a given neighborhood are apt to be more alike than observations drawn randomly from the population. Serial correlation does not bias coefficients but does inflate standard errors. Our OLS-based estimates of standard errors thus understate true standard errors and may cause us to pronounce a neighborhood-based measure statistically significant when, in fact, it is not. We use a survey sampling-error program to show that the properly computed standard errors in the PSID sample of whites are increased relatively little (10 percent to 20 percent) when compared with sampling errors obtained under the assumption of simple random sampling, while the adjustments for blacks are much larger.

## EMPIRICAL ILLUSTRATIONS

We now illustrate empirical strategies for addressing four of the first five sets of concerns raised in the previous section. We leave unaddressed in this chapter the first issue of possible moderators of neighborhood effects.[1] Our goal in this section is not to perform the definitive analyses to address these issues (no analysis will ever be definitive, and progress on most of these issues will require additional data collection), but we hope to illustrate how these issues might be approached in future work.

### SELECTION BIAS

How should the effects of selection bias best be gauged? The ideal situation would be one in which families were randomly assigned to neighborhoods. Rosenbaum and associates (1993) have come closest to these ideal conditions by using data from an unusual quasi experiment involving low-income black families from the Gautreaux housing project in Chicago. As noted in chapter 1, nearly four thousand families were involved in a subsidized program that arranged for private housing, much of it in Chicago suburbs, but some of it in the city of Chicago itself. Since participants were assigned to the first available housing and were not allowed to choose between city and suburb, their locations approached the experimental ideal of randomized assignment. Using this small and somewhat selective sample, Rosenbaum reported an impressive series of differences, both in the employment outcomes for adults and in developmental outcomes for their children, for the families assigned to the suburban locations. This experiment provides strong evidence that selection effects should not be expected to wipe out the effects of neighborhood conditions on developmental outcomes.

Evans, Oates, and Schwab (1992) adopted a model-based strategy to investigate selection bias. Their dependent variables were high school completion and out-of-wedlock teen childbearing, and their neighborhood variable was the average SES of the student body. When they ignored selection issues and regressed their outcomes on student-body SES and family-level controls, they found highly significant, beneficial effects of high student-body SES. However, when they estimated a two-equation model, with the first equation regressing student-body SES on characteristics of the metropolitan area in which the student resided and the second regressing the developmental outcomes on *predicted* student-body SES, the effects of student-body SES disappeared.

It is helpful to lay out a model in which the selection issue is included explicitly as part of a model of neighborhood effects. A simple representation of a model for the developmental outcomes, parental characteristics, and neighborhood quality of child $i$ is as follows:

$$(9.1)\quad \text{OUTCOME}_i = f_1\ (\text{DEM}_{Ci},\ \text{DEM}_{Pi},\ \text{PARENTING}_{Pi},\ \text{NEIGHBOR}_i) + u_i$$

In this equation,

$\text{OUTCOME}_i$ is the level of a developmental outcome (for example, IQ, behavior problems, high school completion) for the $i^{th}$ child

$\text{DEM}_{Ci}$ are demographic characteristics (age, sex, cohort, and race or ethnicity) of the $i^{th}$ child

$\text{DEM}_{Pi}$ are demographic and economic characteristics of the parental generation (maternal education, number of children, family structure, and income) for the $i^{th}$ child

$\text{PARENTING}_{Pi}$ are unobserved characteristics of the parents (for example, concern for their children's development) that affect developmental outcomes

$\text{NEIGHBOR}_i$ are characteristics of the neighborhood in which the $i^{th}$ child lives

$u_i$ is an error term that captures the effects of all other influences on the developmental outcomes

A key problem with most existing studies (including our earlier chapters) is that they estimate equation 9.1 and ignore the implications of the process by which parents are sorted into good and bad neighborhoods. Suppose certain parents are particularly concerned with the development of their children (that is, have high values on PARENTING) but that this special concern could not be measured. If that special concern promoted child development *and* led parents to choose higher-quality neighborhoods *and* is not captured by their income and other measured characteristics, then neighborhood effects estimated in our models will reflect both "true" (causal) effects of neighborhoods and the spurious effect of unmeasured parental characteristics.

There are two approaches to address this problem. The preferred approach is to locate data that measure the crucial omitted variables. Child development data sets such as the Infant Health and Development Program (IHDP) contain fairly sophisticated measures of parental characteristics, including, for example, an assessment of the home learning environment provided by parents (see chapters 4 and 5). Controls for such measures in equation 9.1 can help reduce the omitted-variable bias. We first employ this strategy to attempt to solve the problem. Unfortunately, one never knows how much of the bias is eliminated with this method, since it is always possible to think of still more unmeasured variables.

A second strategy for a consistent estimation of equation 9.1 is to replace NEIGHBOR with an instrumental variable for NEIGHBOR that is purged of NEIGHBOR's spurious correlation with PARENTING.[2] The trick for making this work is to identify a variable that is highly correlated with NEIGHBOR but is not highly correlated with the unobservable component of PARENTING. In effect, the first step in the instrumental variable procedure regresses NEIGHBOR on this variable and other exogenous regressors, calculates a predicted value of NEIGHBOR from the estimated regression relationship, and then uses the predicted, rather than the actual, value of NEIGHBOR in estimating equation 9.1.

Following an idea proposed by Gottschalk (1995), we use as instruments characteristics of the neighborhood of the mother's residence *after* child *i* (as well as all of *i*'s siblings) have left the parental home. Our argument is that as long as a child is present in the household of the mother, then the mother's choice of neighborhood reflects both her own preferences and her preferences based on concern about the effect of neighborhood quality on her children. After her children have left home, the mother's choice of neighborhood presumably no longer reflects her concern for the effect of the neighborhood on children. The persistent component of neighborhood selection that is based on her own preferences ensures that there will be a positive correlation between the future neighborhood and NEIGHBOR. The shifting basis for neighborhood choice after children have left home should produce a low correlation between future neighborhood characteristics and the unobserved component of PARENTING. Thus, the conditions for the instrumental variables approach would appear to be satisfied.

ADJUSTING FOR SELECTION BIAS THROUGH EXPLICIT CONTROLS FOR TYPICALLY UNMEASURED PARENTAL CHARACTERISTICS  We can illustrate the first approach by including in equation 9.1 measures of parental characteristics that are typically omitted from models of neighborhood effects. The IHDP data set is well suited for this purpose, since it includes the Home Observation for Measurement of the Environment (HOME) inventory, as well as measures of maternal coping, depression, and social support (Bradley et al. 1989, 1994; Brooks-Gunn, Klebanov, and Liaw 1995a; Klebanov, Brooks-Gunn, and Duncan 1994; Liaw and Brooks-Gunn 1994).

Our analysis of IHDP data uses IQ at thirty-six months as the developmental outcome and includes a standard set of SES background measures (mother's schooling, family income/needs, mother's age at the child's birth, and ethnicity) and measures of the child (birth weight, an index of neonatal health, and gender) (Brooks-Gunn, McCarton, et al. 1994; IHDP 1990). We include as typically unmeasured background parental characteristics the following: (a) HOME-scale assessments of the learning and physical environments and of maternal warmth, (b) coping, (c) maternal depression, and (d) social support.

To review:

1. The HOME (Bradley and Caldwell 1984) preschool version (for ages three to six) is a fifty-five-item semistructured observation interview. In our case, the HOME scale was administered when the child was thirty-six months of age (corrected for prematurity) as a measure of the child's level of stimulation in the home environment. Three subscales were used here: Provision of Learning Stimulation, which is a composite of the learning, academic, and language stimulation and variety in experience subscales; the Physical Environment (outside play environment appears safe, interior of apartment not dark or perceptually monotonous); and Warmth (parent caresses, kisses, or cuddles child during visit).

2. The Health and Daily Living Form, revised version (Moos et al. 1986) is a thirty-two-item self-reported coping scale, developed for use with clinical populations and adolescents. Respondents indicate a recent stressful event and rate the frequency with which they use various coping responses. We focus on the most active form of coping, behavioral coping.

3. The General Health Questionnaire (Goldberg 1972, 1978) taps depression, somatization, and anxiety dimensions. A total score, based on recoding the twelve responses to values from 0 to 3, results in a total score from 0 to 36.

4. Social support was assessed when the child was thirty-six months of age, using six vignettes (for example, the respondent needs to go out unexpectedly, is laid up for three months with a broken leg, needs help making an important decision, or has a serious personal problem) adapted from Cohen and Lazarus (1977) and McCormick and associates (1987).

It seems likely that the HOME subscales, especially the learning environment, reflect characteristics of parents that are likely simultaneously to affect developmental outcomes and to tap dimensions of child-related parental concerns that may well carry over into choice of neighborhood. Thus, they constitute very promising candidates to test for omitted-variable bias in equation 9.1. By the same token, the measures of maternal depression and social support may influence developmental outcomes *and* affect a mother's ability to avoid ending up in a neighborhood that is unhealthy for her children's development.

Our empirical strategy is very simple and involves estimation of equation 9.1 with and without controls for the HOME and maternal characteristics. Regression results are presented in table 9.1, in which columns show coefficients and standard errors from three separate OLS multiple regressions. The regression in the first column includes the six neighborhood factors plus controls for birth weight, the neonatal health index, and (not reported in the table) treatment-group status and site dummies. The regression in the second column adds typical family- and individual-level control variables. In the third column the regression adds the six typically unmeasured HOME environment and maternal characteristics. If the latter constitute powerful omitted variables, then we would expect to see the explanatory power of the neighborhood-level predictors decline substantially when the HOME and maternal characteristics are entered into the regression.

The first column shows the power of the neighborhood factors in the absence of controls for family-level differences. Low SES is associated with lower IQs, while high SES has the opposite-sign association. Ethnic diversity also has a negative association with thirty-sixth-month IQs (see chapters 4 and 5).

A comparison of the first two columns shows that the introduction of controls for conventional family-level and individual measures reduces most of these associations to below conventional levels of statistical significance. As was clear in the analysis presented in chapter 5 on early childhood, only high SES retains its significant association. Most of the family-level measures themselves are fairly powerful predictors of thirty-sixth-month IQs.

What happens when typically unmeasured parental characteristics are added to the equation? As shown in the third column, there is very little change. Although the HOME Learning environment and maternal depression are significant predictors of child IQ, their inclusion causes only a very small drop in the estimated effect of the high-SES neighborhood factor. The overall picture of neighborhood effects changes very little; in both cases only the high-SES factor is a significant predictor of thirty-six-month IQs. Thus, along with the Gautreaux experiment's findings, the "measure the unmeasured" approach to gauging selection bias does not appear to produce evidence of important biases in the simpler models used in earlier chapters.

ADJUSTING FOR SELECTION BIAS WITH INSTRUMENTAL VARIABLES    As just summarized, our instrumental-variables approach to the selection-bias problem involves locating a suitable instrument for NEIGHBOR in equation 9.1. Characteristics of the *future* neighborhoods of the mother, measured after all of her children have left home, arguably qualify. The mother's own neighborhood preferences will induce a positive correlation between characteristics of her neighborhoods before and after her children have left home. But since her children are no longer living with her, the mother's choice of new neighborhood is unlikely to give weight to the possible effects of those neighborhood characteristics on child development.[3]

TABLE 9.1 Effects of Neighborhood on IQ with and Without Typically Unmeasured Parental Characteristics—IHDP Data

| | Dependent Variable: IQ at 36 Months | | |
|---|---|---|---|
| Neighborhood factors | | | |
| Low SES | −3.62* | .004 | 1.28 |
| | (1.15) | (1.13) | (1.09) |
| High SES | 4.91* | 2.74* | 2.62* |
| | (1.09) | (1.03) | (0.99) |
| Male joblessness | −.01 | .15 | −.35 |
| | (.94) | (.86) | (.83) |
| Family | .45 | .71 | .28 |
| concentration | (.68) | (.62) | (.60) |
| Ethnic diversity | −1.23* | −.59 | −.06 |
| | (.38) | (.35) | (.34) |
| Typically unmeasured characteristics | | | |
| Home learning | | | 1.44* |
| | | | (.14) |
| Home physical | | | −.52 |
| | | | (.37) |
| Home warmth | | | −.16 |
| | | | (.39) |
| Depression | | | −.25* |
| | | | (.12) |
| Social support | | | −.11 |
| | | | (.24) |
| Coping | | | −.04 |
| | | | (.10) |
| Family characteristics | | | |
| Family | | 2.40* | 1.63* |
| income/needs | | (.44) | (.44) |
| Mother's education | | 1.26* | .53 |
| | | (.31) | (.30) |
| Black | | −10.86* | −6.75* |
| | | (1.77) | (1.75) |
| Teen mother? | | 1.27 | .83 |
| | | (1.72) | (1.66) |
| Child characteristics | | | |
| Birth weight (grams) | .004* | .003* | .003* |
| | (.001) | (.001) | (.001) |
| Neonatal index | .04 | .11* | .09* |
| | (.04) | (.04) | (.04) |
| Male | | −2.22 | −2.71* |
| | | (1.18) | (1.13) |
| N | 698 | 698 | 640 |
| R² | .28 | .40 | .50 |
| Mean (and stnd. dev.) | 88.87 | 88.87 | 88.87 |
| of dependent variable | (19.74) | (19.74) | (19.74) |

Note: All regressions include seven dummy variables for site and a dummy variable measure of treatment versus control status.

* indicates coefficient is more than twice its standard error.

No instrumental variable is perfect, and mother's future neighborhood is no exception. A first problem is that inertia may cause mothers to remain in the same neighborhood after children leave home, blocking the process by which preference changes should lead through residential mobility to neighborhoods better matched to the new set of preferences. Second, neighborhood characteristics may reflect important unobserved permanent features of *family*-level characteristics such as permanent family SES or mother's latent ability. Thus, the apparent effect of current neighborhood characteristics on child development may really reflect the impact of permanent family SES on development. Our ability to average family-level measures such as income over periods as long as seven years should go a long way in alleviating this problem.

With these cautions in mind, we use the PSID to illustrate the instrumental-variables approach, since its "following rules" call for continuing interviews with the mothers after the children have left the parents' residence. The panel period was not long enough to provide such information about all of the adolescents included in the analysis described in chapter 6. In fact, we could obtain the necessary data for only about one-third (1,246 out of 3,703) of the adolescents. Thus, we must also address the issue of whether the subsample that could be used for the instrumental-variables procedure differed from our larger analysis sample.

To keep things manageable, we focused on a single neighborhood dimension—high SES. We first looked to see whether the relationship between high SES (measured between ages ten and sixteen) and completed schooling differed between the subsamples of adolescents for whom information about the characteristics of the future neighborhoods of the mothers were and were not available. We did this by creating a dichotomous variable equaling one if the needed information was missing and zero if in fact the future-neighborhood characteristics were observed. We added this variable, plus the interaction between this variable and high SES (measured between ages ten and sixteen) into an OLS regression of completed schooling on high SES (measured between ages ten and sixteen), family income/needs between ages ten and sixteen, mother's education, and the fraction of time between ages ten and sixteen spent in a mother-only family. With this specification, the coefficient on the dichotomous "neighborhood missing" variable indicates whether the level of schooling differed between the missing and nonmissing subsamples, while the coefficient on the interaction variable indicates whether the relationship between high SES and completed schooling differed between the two subsamples.

We found no evidence of such differences for either white males or black males. For white females, there was no evidence of a difference in level, but there was some evidence (the coefficient on the interaction was significant at the 6 percent level) that the effect of high SES on completed schooling was about half as large for the missing-data group as for the group for whom mother's future neighborhood information was measured successfully. More significant differences showed up in the sample of black females. Both the level of completed schooling and the effect of the high-SES factor on completed schooling were significantly lower for the missing-data group. These findings suggest caution in interpreting the instrumental-variables results for black women, since the analysis subset used for the instrumental-variables analysis appears unusually sensitive to high-SES neighborhood effects.

Our instrumental-variables estimates are presented in table 9.2. Results from three equations are shown in the table for each of the four race and sex analysis groups. For purposes of comparison, we include, in the first column, results from an OLS regression of completed schooling on the High-SES factor and family-level controls (all of which are measured during adolescence). Estimates from this regression differ from those presented in chapter 6 because they are estimated on the smaller samples and include only the single high-SES neighborhood factor rather than all five factors or the three-variable neighborhood risk composite.

The second column details results from the first stage of the instrumental-variables procedure in which the adolescence-based neighborhood measure of high-SES is regressed on the high-SES factor measured for the mother after the point at which all children have left home, as well as on other exogenous variables. Results show uniformly strong associations between future-neighborhood SES and past-neighborhood SES.

The third column shows results from the second stage of the instrumental-variables procedure in which the predicted value of the high-SES factor is included in the completed schooling model. Somewhat surprisingly, the instrumental-variables procedure produces a uniformly significant set of estimated neighborhood effects across all four subgroups. Consistent with the theoretical discussion given earlier, there are several alternative interpretations to these results. The most optimistic, from the point of view of improving estimates of neighborhood effects, is that these estimates have been purged of selection bias and that the results presented in chapter 6 understate the true effect of affluent neighbors. An alternative explanation is that the instrumental-variables approach has purged NEIGHBOR of measurement error, but not of selection-bias problems. Replications of this kind of analysis are needed to increase our confidence that we have solved the selection-bias problem using the instrumental-variables approach.

## TRANSACTION MODELS

The preceding strategies help us estimate the extent to which individual and family characteristics may play a role in determining where people live. The transactional perspective forces us to recognize that even such seemingly exogenous family characteristics as economic status and structure may be molded by the kinds of neighborhoods in which families have resided. Once

TABLE 9.2  An Instrumental-Variables Approach to Adjusting for Selection Bias

| | | White Males | | | White Females | | | Black Males | | | Black Females | | |
|---|---|---|---|---|---|---|---|---|---|---|---|---|---|
| | | OLS | IV-First Stage | IV-Second Stage | OLS | IV-First Stage | IV-Second Stage | OLS | IV-First Stage | IV-Second Stage | OLS | IV-First Stage | IV-Second Stage |
| Neighborhood factors | High SES of adolescent | .23 (.17) | | | .59* (.13) | | | .24 (.16) | | | .79* (.16) | | |
| | High SES of mother | | .79* (.03) | | | .75* (.04) | | | .57* (.04) | | | .80* (.04) | |
| | Instrument for high SES of adolescent | | | .34* (.21) | | | .71* (.19) | | | .61* (.23) | | | .90* (.20) |
| Family characteristics | Family income/needs | .48* (.08) | .04* (.02) | .46* (.09) | .32* (.06) | .06* (.02) | .30* (.07) | .22* (.10) | .11* (.03) | .13 (.10) | .36* (.13) | .04 (.03) | .32* (.14) |
| | Mother's education | .15* (.05) | .01 (.01) | .14* (.05) | .20* (.05) | .02 (.01) | .19* (.05) | .02 (.04) | -.02 (.01) | .01 (.04) | .10 (.05) | -.02 (.01) | .10 (.05) |
| | Female head | .84 (.47) | -.07 (.09) | .85 (.47) | 1.28* (.41) | -.01 (.11) | 1.29* (.41) | -.04 (.23) | .06 (.07) | -.13 (.23) | .16 (.24) | -.02 (.06) | .14 (.25) |
| | Constant | 10.14* (.63) | -.48* (.12) | 10.34* (.67) | 9.93* (.57) | -.56* (.15) | 10.17* (.62) | 11.87* (.52) | -.70* (.15) | 12.57* (.61) | 11.89* (.56) | -.27 (.14) | 12.08* (.60) |
| Dependent variable | | Schooling | High SES of Adolescent | Schooling | Schooling | High SES of Adolescent | Schooling | Schooling | High SES of Adolescent | Schooling | Schooling | High SES of Adolescent | Schooling |
| | $N$ | 355 | 355 | 355 | 383 | 383 | 383 | 241 | 241 | 241 | 267 | 267 | 267 |
| | $R^2$ | .20 | .75 | .20 | .28 | .65 | .28 | .07 | .60 | .08 | .29 | .73 | .28 |

*Indicates coefficient is more than twice its standard error.

Source: Panel Study of Income Dynamics.

232

we recognize this possibility, it is clear that there is a need to expand our data-collection and data-analytic strategies beyond our current approaches. The six data sets represented in this volume did not include the kind of longitudinal data on neighborhood conditions, family characteristics, and developmental outcomes that would allow analysis of reciprocal effects or any modeling of earlier neighborhood effects on current family conditions. In addition, with our data-analytic strategy neighborhood and family characteristics were entered into regression equations simultaneously; we did not attempt to estimate effects of neighborhoods on developmental outcomes that are indirect *through* family conditions.

From the perspective of testing a transactional model of neighborhood and family effects on developmental outcomes, the limitations of our data and our current analytic framework pose just as difficult an inferential challenge as do the previously mentioned possibilities of selection effects. However, the results of the Gautreaux experiment discussed earlier bear directly on a key premise of the transaction model, in that both family economic conditions and child outcomes were *better* in the resource-rich suburban neighborhoods, suggesting that neighborhoods do indeed affect family and individual outcomes. Short of mounting another such experiment and compiling longitudinal data on neighborhood and family conditions, as well as child outcomes, we can at least model our cross-sectional data with the possibility of transactional processes being represented.

In the interest of offering some rudimentary quantitative strategies for advancing our understanding of these issues, we have specified a model in the top half of figure 9.1 that incorporates not only a key element of the full transaction model (that is, neighborhood conditions affecting family economic resources) but also the set of typically unmeasured variables included in our selection-effects model (table 9.1). In this model, we specify an indirect effect of the neighborhood factors on developmental outcomes through family income and an indirect effect of income on these same outcomes through the home environment, social support, coping, and maternal depression. The regression equations used to test this model also estimate direct effects of neighborhood on the HOME and maternal mediators and on developmental outcomes, and of income on the developmental outcomes.

We estimate the model with data from the IHDP. To heighten the precision of our estimates of the neighborhood effects, we adjust for characteristics—race and gender—that are completely exogenous to past or current neighborhood effects. The model is estimated in cross-sectional form, assigning to neighborhoods all of the causal "credit" arising from the cross-sectional correlation between neighborhood characteristics and family income. This will clearly overstate the true causal influence of these neighborhood variables to the extent that family income influences them, but it is useful to conduct these analyses in order to set some initial estimates of the magnitude of these neigh-

FIGURE 9.1   Partial Model of Transactional Process, with Coefficients and Standard Errors Taken from Table 9.3

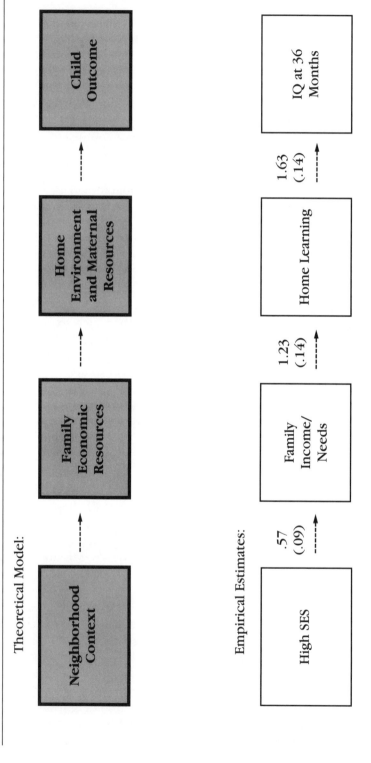

borhood variables' influence on family economic conditions and to look at more unbiased estimates of their total effects (direct and indirect) on developmental outcomes.

The results of OLS regressions for the various paths in the model are presented in table 9.3. The first column uses size-adjusted family income as the dependent variable and shows that two of the neighborhood factors—high SES and ethnic diversity—are statistically significant predictors of family economic well-being, with the former stronger than the latter. This suggests that families in neighborhoods with few high-income neighbors and more ethnic diversity are in greater economic distress. In regressions using the HOME and maternal characteristics as dependent variables, neighborhood factors show only sporadic direct effects: Low SES shows a detrimental effect on both the home learning and physical environment, high SES has an unexpected detrimental effect on social support, and ethnic diversity is detrimental to home learning and warmth (see Klebanov, Brooks-Gunn, and Duncan 1994).

However, as predicted by the transactional model, substantial indirect effects of neighborhood resources on child outcomes (in this case, IQ at thirty-six months) were obtained with family income and home learning acting as the mediating processes. This indirect effect is highlighted in figure 9.1. This indirect pathway suggests that the presence of high-SES neighbors (perhaps a marker for a tighter local labor market, greater educational opportunities for adults, better transportation, and better child care) predicts higher levels of family income, which in turn predicts a richer learning environment for the child that is associated with higher performance on intelligence tests. Each of the regression coefficients in this pathway is at least six times its standard error. These results suggest that while other path models could plausibly be fit to these same data, the data are consistent with the hypothesis that neighborhood conditions directly affect levels of family economic resources, which in turn affect child outcomes through their effects on the home learning environment.[4]

## UNDERESTIMATING NEIGHBORHOOD EFFECTS DUE TO SUPPRESSION EFFECTS

A persistent finding in our reduced-form model of neighborhood effects is that black males do not seem to benefit from affluent neighbors or family economic resources as much as other groups do. We presented some evidence from the upstate New York middle-childhood and adolescent samples that this lack of prediction might be due to a suppression effect (chapters 6 and 8).[5] We have also discussed another suppression effect that could account for these findings: high-SES neighbors who are predominantly white could create a cultural mismatch with minority youth, such as that hypothesized by Connell, Aber, and Walker (1994), to be operating in the school setting. This mismatch in the neighborhood could then result in less intense and effective patterns of

TABLE 9.3 A Cross-Sectional Version of the Transactions Model—IHDP Data

| | | | | Dependent Variable | | | | |
|---|---|---|---|---|---|---|---|---|
| | Family Income/Needs at 36 Months | HOME Learning | HOME Physical | HOME Warmth | Coping | Social Support | Depression | IQ at 36 Months |
| **Neighborhood factors** | | | | | | | | |
| Low SES | .02 (.10) | -1.13* (.36) | -.27* (.12) | -.23 (.12) | -.37 (.43) | -.03 (.18) | .12 (.34) | 1.48 (1.13) |
| High SES | .57* (.09) | .06 (.32) | .04 (.11) | -.14 (.11) | .19 (.39) | -.55* (.16) | .01 (.31) | 2.81* (1.03) |
| Male joblessness | -.10 (.07) | .28 (.27) | -.13 (.09) | -.04 (.09) | -.20 (.32) | -.26 (.14) | -.02 (.26) | -.54 (.86) |
| Family concentration | .03 (.05) | .18 (.20) | -.01 (.07) | .03 (.07) | .16 (.24) | -.01 (.10) | -.24 (.19) | .21 (.62) |
| Ethnic diversity | -.06* (.03) | -.43* (.11) | -.05 (.04) | -.15* (.04) | .02 (.13) | -.11 (.06) | .01 (.11) | .02 (.35) |
| **Family process** | | | | | | | | |
| Home learning | | | | | | | | 1.63* (.14) |
| Home physical | | | | | | | | -.54 (.38) |
| Home warmth | | | | | | | | -.33 (.40) |
| Depression | | | | | | | | -.05 (.10) |
| Social support | | | | | | | | -.17 (.25) |
| Coping | | | | | | | | -.30* (.13) |

TABLE 9.3 *Continued*

|  | | Dependent Variable | | | | | | |
|---|---|---|---|---|---|---|---|---|
|  | Family Income/Needs at 36 Months | HOME Learning | HOME Physical | HOME Warmth | Coping | Social Support | Depression | IQ at 36 Months |
| Family characteristics | | | | | | | | |
| Family income/Needs |  | 1.23* | .33* | .15* | .25 | .40* | -.18 | 1.50* |
|  |  | (.14) | (.05) | (.05) | (.16) | (.07) | (.13) | (.47) |
| Black | -1.15* | -2.68* | -.20 | -.50* | -1.12 | .02 | -1.31* | -6.44* |
|  | (.14) | (.55) | (.19) | (.19) | (.66) | (.28) | (.53) | (1.77) |
| Child characteristics | | | | | | | | |
| Male | .07 | .34 | -.04 | .06 | .60 | .02 | .44 | -2.87* |
|  | (.10) | (.37) | (.13) | (.12) | (.44) | (.19) | (.36) | (1.16) |
| N | 699 | 641 | 641 | 641 | 679 | 679 | 679 | 641 |
| $R^2$ | .42 | .40 | .24 | .15 | .05 | .06 | .03 | .46 |
| Mean (and stnd. dev.) of dependent variable | 1.91 | 21.17 | 5.33 | 5.09 |  |  |  | 88.87 |
|  | (1.76) | (6.03) | (1.85) | (1.70) |  |  |  | (19.74) |

*Indicates coefficient is more than twice its standard error. All regressions include seven dummy variables for site.

adult–youth communication (job networking, role modeling) than could be expected between these youth and, for example, black middle-class neighbors.

To conduct a rudimentary test of this hypothesis, we created the interaction between the high-SES factor and the fraction of individuals in the neighborhood who are black, under the assumption that more blacks in the neighborhood increases the chances that high-SES neighbors will be black as well.[6] These interaction variables were added to the PSID, the age-three IQ regression model in the IHDP data set, and the age-four to -five PPVT regression model in the NLSY. Estimated coefficients in the IHDP and NLSY sample were uniformly insignificant, both for the whole sample and for the black and white subsamples (results not shown), suggesting that there are no important suppression effects of this kind for young children.

The addition of a high-SES × percentage black interaction variable to the PSID-based analyses of completed schooling presented in chapter 6 produced a highly significant coefficient on the interaction variable for the subsample of black males and an insignificant coefficient for all other groups (table 9.4, columns 1, 4, 7, and 10). The sign of the coefficient on the interaction for black males is positive, which is consistent with the hypothesis that affluent neighbors benefit black males only if the affluent neighbors are themselves black.

The coefficient on the (noninteracted) high-SES variable in this same regression allows us to estimate the effects of high-SES neighbors on black males in neighborhoods in which there are virtually no other blacks. In this case, the coefficient implies that high-SES neighbors are detrimental, lending some support to the hypothesis that black youth resent these high-SES white neighbors and reject the mainstream values and behaviors they present. However, this result is based on a very small number of cases and represents a linear extrapolation from blacks living in different circumstances.

We pushed this result a little further by breaking up the high-SES factor into its three components—high family income, college-level education levels, and professional/managerial occupations (results not shown). Interestingly, the interaction of these three components with the percentage of black neighbors produces significant coefficients only for the schooling and occupational components, and not for the income component. It is tempting to read these results as favoring educational and occupational role-model explanations rather than resource-based explanations of why high-SES neighborhoods are beneficial.

From a substantive perspective, these results suggest that affluent neighbors enhance black males' educational attainment only if those neighbors are themselves black; and when combined with the upper New York State data, they provide initial evidence that a cultural mismatch between minority youth and potential adult role models may undermine these role models' effectiveness. These additional analyses have also shown that recognition of suppression effects can be useful in this research area.

TABLE 9.4  Alternative Specifications for Effects of Neighborhood Measures on Completed Schooling

| | White Males | | | White Females | | | Black Males | | | Black Females | | |
|---|---|---|---|---|---|---|---|---|---|---|---|---|
| Neighborhood factors | | | | | | | | | | | | |
| Low SES | .17 | .31 | .25 | .09 | .02 | −.09 | .09 | −.05 | −.12 | .07 | .11 | .05 |
| | (.29) | (.22) | (.20) | (.23) | (.20) | (.19) | (.12) | (.11) | (.10) | (.15) | (.12) | (.11) |
| High SES | .39* | .41* | | .37* | .38* | | −.38* | .08 | | .59* | .43* | |
| | (.11) | (.11) | | (.10) | (.10) | | (.18) | (.13) | | (.16) | (.14) | |
| Male joblessness | −.04 | .01 | −.02 | −.07 | −.04 | −.13 | −.08 | .50* | −.06 | −.11 | −.52* | −.10 |
| | (.14) | (.15) | (.14) | (.13) | (.14) | (.13) | (.08) | (.19) | (.08) | (.94) | (.21) | (.09) |
| Family concentration | −.09 | −.10 | −.10 | .07 | .06 | .05 | −.02 | −.06 | −.09 | .12 | .12 | .09 |
| | (.09) | (.09) | (.09) | (.08) | (.08) | (.08) | (.07) | (.06) | (.06) | (.07) | (.07) | (.07) |
| Ethnic diversity | −.04 | −.06 | −.04 | .16 | .17 | .19 | .09 | .12 | .24* | .21* | .24* | .18* |
| | (.11) | (.11) | (.10) | (.11) | (.11) | (.11) | (.10) | (.10) | (.09) | (.09) | (.08) | (.08) |
| High SES × % black | −.002 | | | .007 | | | .009* | | | −.003 | | |
| | (.009) | | | (.009) | | | (.003) | | | (.003) | | |
| Male joblessness × % black | | −.007 | | | −.006 | | | −.008* | | | .006* | |
| | | (.006) | | | (.009) | | | (.003) | | | (.003) | |
| High-SES spline 1 | | | .60* | | | .02 | | | −.28 | | | −.27 |
| | | | (.21) | | | (.19) | | | (.16) | | | (.18) |
| High-SES spline 2 | | | −.38 | | | .66* | | | 1.18* | | | 2.41* |
| | | | (.32) | | | (.30) | | | (.44) | | | (.38) |
| Constant | 10.15* | 10.22* | 10.37* | 9.76* | 9.75* | 9.36* | 11.42* | 11.62* | 11.25* | 11.12* | 11.06* | 10.57* |
| | (.43) | (.43) | (.46) | (.38) | (.38) | (.42) | (.32) | (.32) | (.33) | (.31) | (.31) | (.31) |
| N | 785 | 785 | 785 | 821 | 821 | 821 | 858 | 858 | 858 | 931 | 931 | 931 |
| $R^2$ | .22 | .22 | .22 | .26 | .26 | .26 | .08 | .08 | .08 | .10 | .10 | .14 |

* Indicates coefficient is more than twice its standard error. All regressions control for the following family-level measures: family income/needs, female headship, and mother's education.

*Source:* Panel Study of Income Dynamics.

239

## THRESHOLD EFFECTS

Our next empirical illustration also addresses our consistent finding of less-powerful neighborhood effects in black samples. In the previous section we discussed how suppression effects may help explain this finding. We also noted earlier that we are concerned about how threshold effects and the truncation of range on certain neighborhood characteristics within subgroups may reduce these variables' predictive power in these groups. These considerations led us to conduct further analyses, using the PSID sample, on the high-SES neighborhood factor. In the first set we were guided by the hypothesis that affluent neighbors will benefit youth if a critical mass of them reside in the neighborhood—a situation that may be rare in neighborhoods where large concentrations of black youth live. To examine this hypothesis, we tested the linearity of the effect of the high-SES factor within the four ethnic and gender subgroups. For these analyses, we set the threshold at the overall national average.

To investigate the possible nonlinear effects of the high-SES factor on educational attainment, we fit a piecewise linear (spline) function, allowing for separately sloped line segments to be fit to the subsamples with below- and above-average (national) values on the high-SES factor. A spline function is implemented by defining the first segment ("High-SES spline 1" in table 9.4) to equal the original high-SES factor and the second "High-SES spline 2" to take on positive values of the high-SES factor and take the value of zero otherwise (recall that the high-SES factor is scaled so that its [national] mean equals zero). For interpretive purposes, algebraic manipulation reveals that the coefficient on high-SES spline 1 shows the effect of high SES up to the point where high SES equals zero. The coefficient on high-SES spline 2 shows the increase (if positive) or decrease (if negative) in slope for the segment of the regression line corresponding to positive values of high SES.

The results show that for three of the four groups (white males are the exception), the effect of additional high-SES neighbors is significantly greater in neighborhoods with higher-than-average numbers of affluent families. In other words, for both black subgroups and for white females, additional high-SES neighbors do not help much if there are not many such neighbors around. However, once a threshold is reached, additional high-SES neighbors are a significant help, even for black males.

While we believed the hypothesis to be applicable to all subgroups, we were especially concerned with the black samples, where lower overall levels of income and housing segregation patterns have resulted in a disproportionate number of these individuals living in neighborhoods below the hypothetical threshold—neighborhoods where they will presumably not benefit from the presence of these neighbors. The results of these additional analyses suggest that this concern was justified: in neighborhoods with low concentrations of high-SES neighbors (such as those where disproportionate numbers of black youth live), having a few more middle-class neighbors will not help. No such thresholds were detected in either the IHDP or NLSY young-children samples (results not shown).

## ACCOUNTING FOR THE DATA'S HIERARCHICAL NATURE

The fact that our data sets contain measures drawn from three levels—the individual, the family, and the neighborhood—raises questions about the appropriateness of using OLS techniques to estimate our models.[7] In effect, OLS techniques ignore the data's hierarchical nature and assume that our observations are drawn randomly from our target populations. In fact, observations in all of our data sets are clustered within neighborhoods. What implications does this clustering have for the appropriateness of our OLS techniques?

It is useful to discuss the statistical issues within the context of a simple model. Taking the example of child IQ as our outcome of interest, maternal schooling (MOMED) and neighborhood-level socioeconomic status (NSES) as the independent variables of interest,[8] we can characterize the simple regression models used in earlier chapters in terms of a single equation at the individual level:

$$(9.2) \quad IQ_{ij} = \alpha + \beta_1 MOMED_{ij} + \beta_2 NSES_j + u_j + v_{ij}$$

In this equation,

subscript $i$ references individuals

subscript $j$ references neighborhoods

$u_j$ is the error term associated with the neighborhood

$v_{ij}$ is the error term associated with the individual child

There are various sampling and estimation strategies for obtaining the "best" estimates of the $\beta_1$ and $\beta_2$ parameters of equation 9.2. The approach should be dictated by whether the research questions guiding the study are primarily focused on (a) how differences *between* neighborhoods affect outcomes or (b) how differences between either families or individuals affect outcomes *within* neighborhoods.[9] In terms of equation 9.2, the choice depends on the relative analytical importance of the $\beta_1$ and $\beta_2$ parameters and the nature of the error terms $u_j$ and $v_{ij}$.

A statistical literature focusing on the "within" versus "between" distinction has arisen over the past twenty years (Bryk and Raudenbush 1992; Greene 1993; Sampson and Morenoff vol. 2). As a general characterization, the various estimators developed in this literature can be placed along a spectrum, with a within-neighborhood estimator falling at one extreme and a between-neighborhood estimator falling at the other extreme.[10]

The "within" estimator applies OLS to the regression of the deviation of each child's IQ from his or her own neighborhood-specific mean IQ on the deviation form of all independent variables. In the case of MOMED, the deviation form is the difference between each child's MOMED and neighborhood-average MOMED. But in the case of neighborhood-level NSES, the difference between each child's NSES and the neighborhood-average NSES is always zero. The same logic applies to the neighborhood-level error term $u$. Thus, both NSES and $u$ drop out of the within estimator equation, leaving:

$$(9.3) \quad IQ_{ij} - IQ_{.j} = \beta_1(MOMED_{ij} - MOMED_{.j}) + v_{ij} - v_{.j}$$

where the $.j$ notation on IQ, MOMED, and $v$ indicates the neighborhood-wide average value of those measures in the sample. The within estimator is especially valuable if one is interested in estimating the effects of family-level measures such as MOMED, since the differencing purges family-level measures of their possibly confounding correlations with both measured and unmeasured neighborhood-level conditions.

The "between" estimator applies OLS to the regression of the sample-mean IQ for each neighborhood to the sample-mean MOMED and census-based NSES for that neighborhood, that is, the regression:

$$(9.4) \quad IQ_{.j} = \alpha + \beta_1 MOMED_{.j} + \beta_2 NSES_j + u_j + v_{.j}$$

Note that there is no $.j$ associated with the $NSES_j$ measure, since in our case $NSES_j$ comes from the decennial census and not from the sample observations themselves. The number of cases with which equation 9.4 is estimated is equal to the number of neighborhoods rather than the number of individual children.

OPTIMAL SAMPLE DESIGNS   Suppose, as is true in our case, that the analytic goal is optimal estimation of the neighborhood effect $\beta_2$. Suppose further that the neighborhood-level measure NSES contains no measurement error and that there is no omitted-variables problem at the neighborhood level (that is, the error term $u_j$ is uncorrelated with the observed neighborhood measure $NSES_j$). The zero-measurement-error assumption in reasonable in our case, since we rely on data from the decennial census.[11] As with any regression-based analysis, the reasonableness of the omitted-variable assumption should be given careful thought. Solutions to the omitted-variable problem in this context boil down to finding a convincing instrumental variable that purges NSES of its correlation with $u_j$—a difficult task for any analysis.

Under these assumptions, the most efficient way of estimating $\beta_2$ would be OLS regression using data from a sampling scheme in which one child per neighborhood is selected.[12] Such a sampling scheme maximizes the dispersion of NSES in the sample and represents the between-neighborhood end of the estimator spectrum.[13] The selection of a single observation per neighborhood eliminates possible problems of serial correlation in $v_{ij}$ arising because two sampled observations in the $j^{th}$ neighborhood usually resemble one another more than two observations chosen randomly from the population. Such serial correlation does not bias the estimate of $\beta_2$, but it does render it less efficient than an estimate based on an independent, one-observation-per-neighborhood sampling scheme. In the absence of serial correlation, OLS techniques are appropriate.

By shifting our research emphasis from between-neighborhood differences in child IQ to within-neighborhood differences (for example, how a mother's SES affects her child's IQ, net of possible neighborhood influences), the emphasis on optimal parameter estimation shifts from the $\beta_2$ parameter to the $\beta_1$ parameter in equation 9.2. As we make this change in research emphasis, sampling schemes based on multiple observations per neighborhood become more appealing. Multiple observations support the within-neighborhood estimator by purging the estimated effects of family-level measures such as MOMED of their possible correlations with both measured and unmeasured neighborhood-level conditions. At the extreme of this sampling strategy would be all subjects sampled within a single neighborhood, thus completely controlling for neighborhood conditions. A clear cost of a sampling scheme providing multiple observations per neighborhood is, of course, suboptimal (or, in the extreme, no possible) estimation of the between-neighborhood effect on child IQ, since the clustering of subjects within neighborhoods reduces the number of neighborhoods sampled and most likely their dispersion. As already discussed, clustering also causes standard errors of neighborhood coefficients to be underestimated by standard regression packages that ignore serial correlation and assume simple random sampling.

Measurement error at the neighborhood level is another possible rationale for selecting multiple observations per neighborhood. Suppose, as is often the case in school-based-sample applications, that our measures of neighborhood-level conditions were calculated from sample observations within each neighborhood rather than from the decennial census. Greater measurement error in an independent variable generally biases downward the estimated effect of that variable (Bound et al. 1994).

Multiple observations per neighborhood would be an advantage here, since the additional observations within a neighborhood produce a more precise estimate of the neighborhood-level measure. The optimal sampling scheme in such a case is not completely at the within-estimator end of the spectrum, however, since a scheme in which the entire sample was selected within a single neighborhood would provide no variability in the neighborhood measure itself. But as noted earlier, measurement-error arguments such as these are not relevant for our situation, since we rely on neighborhood-level data from the decennial census rather than from the sample itself. Census-based neighborhood measures are calculated from responses of hundreds or, in some cases, thousands of households residing in the neighborhood to questions posed in the census forms.

OPTIMAL ESTIMATORS FOR OUR SAMPLES     The actual samples producing the data for our analyses range from national and multisite designs containing relatively few observations per neighborhood (PSID, IHDP, NLSY) to local designs containing many more observations per neighborhood (Upstate New York, Atlanta, Adolescent Pathways). In terms of our sampling discussion, our national and multisite samples are well suited for the estimation of neighborhood effects because they contain very few observations per neighborhood (roughly two, on average) and therefore provide nearly maximal dispersion in neighborhood characteristics.[14]

But OLS techniques are not entirely appropriate for the estimation of equation 9.2 with the national and multisite samples, since OLS techniques ignore the serial correlation that arises from the fact that some neighborhoods—and, in the case of studies like the PSID, families—in the sample produce multiple observations. Techniques such as generalized least squares (from which HLM draw their essential features) that rely on within-neighborhood sample variability are not feasible solutions for the serial-correlation problem, since the national and multisite samples contain too few observations per neighborhood to implement them, and extensive geographic mobility in their longitudinal data renders the definition of a child's "neighborhood" problematic.

A feasible method for correcting standard errors for serial correlation is to employ the replication-based methods developed by sampling statisticians to adjust for the nonindependence of observations in most national surveys. Some clustering makes sense in national surveys because it helps interviewers avoid excessive travel costs. In effect, these techniques recognize the groupings of families within neighborhood and, in the case of the PSID and NLSY, siblings within families, employed in the initial sampling design of the survey and make adjustments for the fact that observations clustered within wave 1 neighborhoods and families are more likely to share common characteristics than observations drawn at random from the population.

In the case of the PSID, most of the data used in this book are drawn from interviews taken ten or more years after the first wave. Since nearly one-quarter of American families with children move every year, there is considerable "unclustering" of families with time. However, if families move within the same neighborhoods or to new neighborhoods that are similar to their old ones, then observations originally clustered within the same neighborhood will continue to be clustered with respect to neighborhood characteristics and, as a consequence, will not be as different from one another as would two observations drawn at random from the population.

Since the PSID data also contain sibling observations, an analogous clustering problem exists at the family level: even though one adolescent's family income and structure can differ markedly from those of his or her siblings, by and large two siblings have more similar family backgrounds than do two individuals drawn randomly from the population. The sampling-error adjustments take both within-family and within-neighborhood clustering into account.

Table 9.5 shows regression results for the PSID-based completed-schooling model presented in chapter 6, and it includes standard errors calculated on the assumption of simple random sampling (this reproduces the results presented in chapter 6), as well as sampling errors calculated from the OSIRIS REPERR sampling-error program. A separate column shows the ratio of these two sets of standard errors.

There are striking differences in the effects of this adjustment by race, in part reflecting the fact that whites tend to live in more heterogeneous neighborhoods. For whites, the properly computed standard errors are only about 10 percent to 20 percent higher, on average, than standard errors computed under the assumption of simple random sampling. None of the coefficients—at either the neighborhood or the family level—that is statistically significant under the assumption of simple random sampling loses its statistical significance when the clustering is taken into account.

In contrast, the adjustments more than double the standard errors for blacks for most variables, and the conclusions regarding the statistical significance of measures at both the neighborhood and family level change as well. For black men and women, the apparently significant effects of neighborhood-level ethnic diversity and family-level income lose their statistical significance with the increase in standard errors. The effect of maternal education retains its statistical significance for both of these groups. For black women, the significance level of the high-SES neighbor coefficient drops from $p < .01$ to $p < .10$. The lesson appears to be that it is very important to account for clustering in black samples, but not as important for white samples.

The sampling designs in the upstate New York, Atlanta, and Adolescent Pathways samples were developed with an eye toward a set of research questions aligned more closely to the within-neighborhood estimation of pathways to child and adolescent outcomes than to the estimation of between-neighborhood differences in child outcomes based on census-tract data. Specifically, they oversampled subjects from poor families and neighborhoods in urban areas, and they contain many more observations per tract than the national samples—in some cases, up to one hundred observations per tract. Both of these elements increase the precision of their estimate of within-neighborhood effects of family and individual characteristics on developmental outcomes for this population, but because of reduced dispersion of neighborhoods relative to an unclustered population sample, the efficiency of estimates of neighborhood effects is reduced. An important topic for future research is to gauge the extent of inefficiency.

TABLE 9.5 Standard Error Estimates with and Without Correction for Serial Correlation

| | White Males | | | White Females | | | Black Males | | | Black Females | | |
|---|---|---|---|---|---|---|---|---|---|---|---|---|
| | SRS | Complex | Ratio: Complex/SRS | SRS | Complex | Ratio: Complex/SRS | SRS | Complex | Ratio: Complex/SRS | SRS | Complex | Ratio: Complex/SRS |
| Neighborhood factors | | | | | | | | | | | | |
| Low SES | -.02 (.20) | -.02 (.21) | 1.1 | -.06 (.19) | -.06 (.19) | 1.0 | -.14 (.11) | -.14 (.20) | 1.8 | .10 (.11) | .10 (.23) | 2.1 |
| High SES | .43* (.11) | .43* (.12) | 1.1 | .38* (.10) | .38* (.11) | 1.1 | .06 (.13) | .06 (.30) | 2.3 | .51* (.13) | .51 (.29) | 2.2 |
| Male joblessness | .19 (.15) | .19 (.16) | 1.1 | -.04 (.13) | -.04 (.12) | 0.9 | .06 (.10) | .06 (.23) | 2.3 | .03 (.10) | .03 (.25) | 2.5 |
| Family concentration | -.14 (.09) | -.14 (.14) | 1.6 | .04 (.09) | .04 (.09) | 1.0 | -.08 (.06) | -.08 (.14) | 2.3 | .12 (.07) | .12 (.15) | 2.1 |
| Ethnic diversity | .06 (.11) | .06 (.09) | 0.8 | .18 (.11) | .18 (.14) | 1.3 | .24* (.09) | .24 (.14) | 1.6 | .18* (.08) | .18 (.13) | 1.6 |
| Family characteristics | | | | | | | | | | | | |
| Family income/ needs | .27* (.05) | .27* (.05) | 1.0 | .26* (.04) | .26* (.07) | 1.8 | .22* (.06) | .22* (.19) | 3.2 | .15* (.07) | .15 (.13) | 1.9 |
| Female head | -.42 (.27) | -.42 (.33) | 1.2 | -.12 (.25) | -.12 (.27) | 1.1 | -.29* (.14) | -.29 (.30) | 2.1 | -.00 (.14) | -.00 (.23) | 1.6 |
| Mother's education | .23* (.04) | .23* (.04) | 1.0 | .24* (.03) | .24* (.04) | 1.2 | .09* (.03) | .09* (.04) | 1.3 | .16* (.03) | .16* (.04) | 1.3 |
| Constant | 16.22 | 16.22 | | 11.04 | 11.04 | | 14.05 | 14.05 | | 14.46 | 14.46 | |
| N | 785 | 785 | | 821 | 821 | | 858 | 858 | | 931 | 931 | |
| R² | .24 | .24 | | .26 | .26 | | .08 | .08 | | .11 | .11 | |

*Indicates coefficient is more than twice its standard error. SRS refers to sampling errors calculated under the assumption of simple random sampling. Complex refers to standard errors calculated to account for serial correlation. Ratio: Complex/SRS is the ratio of the Complex and SRS standard errors. Adjustments for serial correlation were made with the OSIRIS REPERR sampling error program.

*Source:* Panel Study of Income Dynamics.

## SUMMARY

The rather simplistic models used in earlier chapters to gauge causal effects of neighborhoods are susceptible to many sources of possible bias. Some concerns are based on measurement issues dealt with in other chapters of the volume; other concerns center on how we specify our causal models of these effects. We have tried to provide a taxonomy of five potential problems regarding model specification and then to provide empirical illustrations, where possible, of strategies for dealing with these issues. Still others stem from data-analytic and sampling strategies used to obtain estimates of neighborhood effects.

The most commonly cited model-specification problem for developmentalists arises when one ignores perspectives that emphasize the interactive relations among contextual processes, social location, and individual development (for example, Bronfenbrenner 1989). In the empirical work represented in this volume we have examined at least some of these relations by conducting within-group analyses of pathways from neighborhood and family conditions to individual outcomes.

The specification problem of greatest concern to economists and sociologists stems from the fact that families choose the neighborhoods in which they live, rather than being randomly assigned to them. If unmeasured factors affect these choices and how their children develop, then our regression approach may produce biased estimates of the causal role neighborhood factors play. Fortunately, one of our data sources contained unusually rich measures of typically unmeasured characteristics, so we were able to conduct a direct test for possible bias. We found virtually no evidence that adjustments for typically unmeasured family factors changed the estimated effects of neighborhood, once adjustments for typically measured factors had been incorporated.

We also have approached the selection-bias problem using instrumental-variables procedures, taking advantage of the fact that the PSID provided measures of the characteristics of the neighborhoods in which mothers lived after all of their children had left home. These characteristics are certainly correlated with neighborhood characteristics of children during adolescence but arguably have only a weak correlation to the unmeasured parental characteristics whose spurious effects we are trying to avoid. Somewhat surprisingly, neighborhood characteristics became more uniformly important after this procedure was applied. We may indeed have solved the selection-bias problem using this approach, although the data are also consistent with the interpretation that neighborhood characteristics are a proxy for unmeasured family-level SES or mother's ability and that the instrumental-variables procedure is adjustment for measurement error but not selection bias.

The theoretically appealing transaction model suggests that our practice of controlling for family-level characteristics when looking for neighborhood effects may well overcontrol and induce a downward bias in the estimated neighborhood effects. Although our cross-sectional data sets were not designed to test the transaction model, we went ahead and specified its key hypothesis and found strong support for the utility of this model and its place in the future modeling of neighborhood and family influences on child and adolescent development.

Also revealing were our analyses in which we relaxed some of our assumptions about the functional form of our basic regression models and examined the possibility that suppression effects and threshold effects may be at work in the relations between neighborhood and outcome variables. These additional analyses allowed us to understand better why, within black samples, the simple bivariate relations between educational performance from childhood through adulthood and the presence of high-SES neighbors in the individual's community is so weak. Our additional analyses revealed that, in black samples, when sufficient numbers of high-SES neighbors are present and, for males, when these potential role models are themselves black, the positive effects on educational attainment hold.

Our final point of concern involved the implications of using OLS regression techniques on data drawn from three levels of observation—individual, family, and neighborhood. Here we argue that, given the well-measured census-based neighborhood data available to us, the optimal sampling scheme for estimating neighborhood effect would be one observation per neighborhood. The fact that all of our data sets collect multiple observations per neighborhood reduces the efficiency of estimation by introducing serial correlation. Our PSID-based estimates showed that OLS standard errors are understated by 10 percent to 20 percent for most measures for whites, but by much more than that for blacks. Since the multisite and local samples have considerably more clustering, we would expect even greater OLS-based understatement of standard errors from them. This topic is an important one for future research.

Taken together, our empirical illustrations suggest that "true" neighborhood effects may be larger than what our oversimplified models suggest, although the levels of statistical significance we report from our OLS regressions are somewhat overstated.

## NOTES

1. In the empirical chapters of this volume we include demographic variables as moderators in our regression equations, and in chapters 8, 10, and 12, we conduct within-group analyses, to examine gender- and ethnic-specific pathways from neighborhood conditions to development outcomes. However, as stated earlier, an important next step for the field is to develop and include more refined measures of the dynamics of race, class, and gender to assess how they shape the effects of neighborhood conditions on development. Also to be examined are interactions among neighborhood and broader contextual conditions as they affect developmental outcomes.

2. We are grateful to John Bound, Charles Brown, Anne Case, Christopher Jencks, David Lam, and Susan Mayer for helping us think through the issues involved in the instrumental-variables approach. They should not, however, be held responsible for our choice of instrument.

3. Although mothers may not give weight to the likely effects of future neighborhoods on children, there may still be a positive correlation between the characteristics of the new neighborhoods and PARENTING. The extent to which the instrumental-variables approach purges NEIGHBOR of its offending correlation with PARENTING is an inverse function of this correlation.

4. We also experimented with a change version of the transaction model in which *changes* in four important characteristics of family context (HOME learning, warmth, social support, and depression) were related to the initial levels of neighborhood and other family, and individual-level variables. The results were qualitatively similar to what was found in the cross-sectional model. The low-SES, male-joblessness, and family-concentration factors were never significant predictors of changes in parental characteristics. High-SES was a negative and borderline significant predictor of changes in social support, while the ethnic-diversity factor was a negative and significant predictor of both HOME learning and warmth.

5. Sociologists and developmentalists differ somewhat in how they define suppression effects. Sociologists define them as instances where omitted exogenous variables have opposite-signed correlations with dependent and included exogenous measures. Developmentalists tend to be more inclusive in their definition and also use the term to cover other situations in which a simple correlation between included exogeneous and dependent variables is lower in the absence of an omitted variable.

6. Race-specific, neighborhood-based income-distribution data are not available in the census data files, so we could not compute exact percentages of high-SES African American and white individuals within neighborhoods, nor could we identify for subgroup analyses the high- versus low-SES African American families within neighborhoods.

7. Gary Solon and Tom Cook provided many helpful comments on this section.

8. The Bryk and Raudenbush model uses a single independent variable that may be measured at the level of either the child or the neighborhood, with the neighborhood-level measure constructed by aggregating the individual-level observations within each neighborhood. Since our child- and neighborhood-level measures come from different sources, we use distinct variables. Our discussion ignores the fact that the family constitutes a third hierarchical level and that some of the data sets contain observations on siblings.

9. A third type of research question can also be posed—how neighborhood conditions moderate or change relationships within neighborhoods or how individual and family characteristics moderate or change the effects of neighborhoods on outcomes. These questions call for the estimation of additional parameters in equation 9.2. While these questions are important and of relevance to the empirical and theoretical work represented in this volume, they do not raise additional issues for the methodological discussion in this section.

10. It can be shown that the OLS and generalized least squares estimators of $\beta_1$ and $\beta_2$ are weighted averages of the "within" and "between" estimators and that, in general, GLS is more efficient, since OLS places too much weight on the between-neighborhood variation (Greene 1990, 489–90).

11. This is not to say that our census-based neighborhood measures are error-free measures of the crucial conceptual dimensions of neighborhood influences, such as role models or resources. We mean that our measures of neighborhood demographic composition contain relatively little error in describing the neighborhood's demographic composition.

12. Here we ignore the fact that it is usually more costly to conduct interviews in different neighborhoods than in the same neighborhood. The trade-off between interviewer travel costs and inefficiency introduced by clustering observations within neighborhoods has long been the concern of sampling statisticians.

13. It is possible, but somewhat more difficult, to come to the same conclusion by thinking in terms of optimal experimental designs rather than optimal sampling schemes. Suppose one faced the problem of selecting observations optimal for distinguishing among our five neighborhood factors. If we define neighborhoods according to whether they have low or high scores on each of the five factors, then there are $2^5 = 32$ different kinds of neighborhoods from which observations should be selected. Since neighborhood type is defined on the basis of information that is independent of the cases chosen for the analysis, there is no advantage to selecting additional observations within a given cell of this thirty-two-cell design before ensuring that all cells are represented. As with the sampling schemes, maximum dispersion of the selected cases across neighborhood type is the key to maximum statistical leverage in estimating neighborhood effects.

14. Even more dispersion could be obtained by sampling exclusively from the extremes of the neighborhood distribution rather than taking a more equal selection-probability population sample.

# 10

# Neighborhood Effects and Federal Policy

*Jeffrey S. Lehman and Timothy M. Smeeding*

In this chapter, we reflect on what the social science research included in this volume implies for federal policy. How should Congress react to this new learning about neighborhood effects on children? What direction should policy makers take from this new scholarship? We approach these questions slowly and carefully, because they subsume some very difficult general questions about the relationship between academic scholarship and the domain of public policy, and about the relationship of federal policy to children in prospering, as well as failing, neighborhoods. By making these general questions explicit in the first portion of this chapter, we hope to make it easier to grapple with the specific questions later on.

## GOAL OF FEDERAL POLICY

We presume that the overarching goal of federal policy is to deploy public resources toward the efficient and equitable promotion of public goals, particularly providing a fair opportunity for upward social and economic mobility for all Americans. Stating our premise so baldly helps to signal some of the deeply contested normative issues that shape and reshape debates over federal policy, particularly as it affects local neighborhoods and their residents. What are appropriate public goals? What role do political leaders play in shaping those goals? How large a pool of public resources is available to promote those goals? Faced with scarce resources, how should priorities be established among worthy goals? Which level of government should be responsible for reaching worthy goals? And, if the federal government is to take the lead, how should state and local governments be involved in shaping and implementing these policies?

One strand of academic policy analysis holds that social science scholarship has little to contribute to the discussion of such normative issues. The issues seem too big, too philosophical, too personal, or too political to be susceptible to scientific evaluation. By this line of thinking, all social scientists can do is study and describe the world they see and the way that different forms of governmental activity influence that world. Yet, the world cannot be subdivided so neatly. In almost any public debate, the positions of "principle" or "philosophy" are mixed together with empirical assumptions about how people behave or about how the world at large works. Some of those assumptions can be tested. Thus, individuals who oppose a guaranteed minimum income may say that they believe able-bodied people should not be allowed to depend on state support if work is available. But when pressed for reasons, they may say that, otherwise, so many people would quit their jobs that we would face an intolerable labor shortage and a large tax burden to support nonworkers. While all individuals can weigh in on the first statement, social scientists in particular may well have something useful to say about the second proposition.

But the linkages between normative debates and empirical analysis go in the opposite direction as well. A social scientist's choice of what problem to study is influenced by a sense of what seems important. That may reflect a personal judgment about what normative goals the public agenda ought to be directed toward and about what social facts might help one to sensibly develop such an agenda. Or it may reflect an assessment of what normative goals seem to be dominating the public debate at a particular moment and of what social facts might be most salient in shaping that debate.

Even more importantly, the social scientist's methodology may reflect certain conventional normative assumptions about how people behave. The economist may be methodologically committed to an assumption that people are wealth maximizers. The anthropologist may be methodologically committed to an assumption that cultural norms are adaptive and functional, given a particular set of environmental constraints. The developmental psychologist may be committed to the notion that parents can be trusted to do whatever is good for their children. An average citizen's acceptance of the social scientist's findings might therefore properly depend on her or his willingness to accept those methodological and normative commitments as well.

To ask what the research findings presented in this volume imply for the policy arena is therefore to ask how those findings, and their normative and methodological underpinnings, relate to the political environment in which they are being received. We therefore begin by offering our own assessment of that environment.

The reader should be forewarned that modesty is a virtue not to be ignored in this chapter. When research results are mixed, when existing policy has only small or uncertain effects on outcomes, when large-scale efforts ("social engineering") have a very high absolute dollar cost and a high opportunity cost, and when the ultimate determinants of child well-being (much less the effects of neighborhoods on well-being) remain elusive, modest responses may be called for. But this is not to say that zero federal policy response is the appropriate policy direction either—going slow is not the same as doing nothing.

# THE CURRENT POLITICAL ENVIRONMENT

American social welfare policy has long been characterized by conflicts, constraints, and uncertainty. The dominant commitment to a government of limited scope made ours a late arrival on the scene of welfare states and has left it relatively small in comparison with those of other industrialized nations. Fears for the work-disincentive effects of public assistance have made the programs categorical, have seriously limited the generosity of cash programs, and have thus created some set of their own disincentives for people to escape welfare. We seem to prefer social programs and benefits tied to work or to noncash benefits that reduce recipients' choices. And our federal structure of governmental authority has made implementation a central concern in the design of any national program.

## POLITICAL CONSENSUS ON GOALS

It would seem, however, that in today's political environment, some rough consensus has emerged concerning some of the appropriate goals of federal action. In particular, we mention three sets of goals: (1) the goal of making investments in children; (2) the goal of reducing poverty, promoting individual dignity, and enhancing opportunity for social mobility; and (3) the goal of minimizing crime and social disorder.

MAKING INVESTMENTS IN CHILDREN    Central to America's self-understanding is the ideology that offers every child a "reasonably fair opportunity" (albeit not an "equal" opportunity) to prosper economically. Children are deemed to be morally blameless, and society is thought to have an obligation to mitigate the most extreme inequalities that follow from the accident of birth. A parallel ideology would hold that "children belong to everyone" (or, more parochially, investments in children redound to the whole society). At least since 1935, those ideologies have justified federal support for various forms of assistance to deprived children (although the federal entitlement to many forms of support ended in 1996). And the easier it has been for the federal government to ensure that a given program helps children without "leaking" over and helping their parents, the easier it has been to garner support for the program. (The 1996 federal legislation requiring time limits for a mother's receipt of welfare is a case in point.) However, U.S. programs and policy thinking have still not progressed to the level of those in other modern nations where all children receive universal benefits (child allowances) due only to their citizenship or where governments provide insurance for child support payments to the custodial parents of children living with only one natural parent.

REDUCING POVERTY AND PROMOTING DIGNITY AND OPPORTUNITY    The goal of reducing poverty, promoting individual dignity, and enhancing opportunity for social mobility is more deeply contested, more heavily qualified, and more weakly respected than the goal identified in the prior paragraph. Nonetheless, it appears to us that, at least since the time of President Lyndon Johnson's Great Society, Americans have been disturbed by the presence of poverty amid affluence. Moreover, they believe that the federal government has a role to play in fighting poverty, at least as long as other public commitments are not sacrificed for the cause. The sentiment for federal intervention appears especially strong when individuals, particularly families with children, who are willing and able to work find themselves unable to earn enough to live above the poverty line. However, appropriate policy action to meet these sentiments has been only slowly forthcoming, even for the working poor. And while most Americans agree that "welfare dependency" is a major social problem, there appears to be little or no consensus about how best to attack the problem. In fact, current policy thinking and the 1996 legislation have resulted in marked state-by-state variation in welfare policy.

MINIMIZING CRIME AND SOCIAL DISORDER    The maintenance of civil order is a defining characteristic of civil society. For the most part, America has left that critical task to the jurisdiction of state and local governments. If and when those governments prove inadequate to the task, however, local crime is easily transformed into a national issue. During the mid-1990s, concern over urban violence was voiced frequently at the highest levels of government. That concern was highest when it intersected with the goal of investment in children: when crime seemed to touch the schools children attend or the neighborhoods where they live (Hechinger 1994). And, with the 1994 crime bill, federal policy produced "three strikes (convictions) and you're out (lifetime imprisonment)" legislation, a hundred thousand new police, hundreds of new jails, and more gun-control laws. Neighborhood safety and protection from violent crime are two overriding issues that policy makers of all political stripes support.

Historically, the federal government has pursued the goal of minimized crime and social disorder primarily by designing programs defined by reference to the traits of individuals and families, as opposed to the traits of neighborhoods or communities. Eligibility for Medicaid, Aid to Families with Dependent Children (AFDC), food stamps, the Women, Infants, and Children (WIC) program, Head Start, and school lunches depends on the characteristics of the child and the family, not on the characteristics of the place where the child lives. Such an approach to program definition is politically attractive. It does not require Congress to specify in advance which districts get more resources and which get fewer; inequalities in the distribution of resources flow, after the fact, from the application of seemingly neutral principles. And as long as a child's "need" depends more heavily on individual and family-level traits than on neighborhood-level traits, such programs are a logical and efficient response (Diamond 1994). While the aggregation of large majorities of poor people in specific locations (underclass areas) may produce situations where economies of scale in service delivery and in program implementation argue for a strategy of community- or neighborhood-based service centers, these are still individual and family programs, not neighborhood programs per se.

Nonetheless, over the years the federal government has at times sought to pursue its social welfare goals through programs that use the neighborhood or the community as their unit of analysis. The first such program to be pursued on a grand scale was Urban Renewal, a program that targeted "blighted" communities because of a belief that visible structural decay was an important contributing factor to the decline of community structures. Thereafter such diverse efforts as Community Action, Model Cities, and (most recently) Empowerment Zones and Enterprise Communities have attempted to bring federal resources to bear on social needs and problems that are defined by reference to specific geographic areas. At still other times, the federal government has sponsored programs that are designed to help specific geographic spaces in a different way. It has taken resources that were collected through national-level taxes and transmitted them to state and local units of government. The programs have varied in the amount of discretion they have left to the decentralized governmental entities concerning how the funds are to be spent: Community Development Block Grants have afforded great discretion to local political leaders, while Head Start funds have come with many more strings attached.

In all these programs, the same design issues have presented themselves. Should the details of program administration be dictated uniformly "from above," or should they vary from jurisdiction to jurisdiction as they are developed in cooperation with state and local governmental and private-sector representatives? Should the workers who implement the programs be employees of the federal government, of local government, or of private nonprofit or for-profit organizations? How should the initiatives be interrelated to assume a coherent set of programs for youth and families with multiple problems?

## DOMESTIC POLICIES OF THE MID-1990s

During its first year, the Clinton administration frequently signaled its interest in pursuing the connection between federal policy and the goals of social welfare. President Clinton and prominent members of his government spoke frequently on such matters as ending welfare as we know it, putting America to work, investing in all Americans, assisting the underclass, and empowering distressed communities to join the economic mainstream. The first year's legislative and administrative agenda included the following items: a substantial expansion of the Earned Income Tax Credit (to $25 billion per year in 1996); increased funding for Head Start; the enactment of limited direct federal assistance to businesses that invest in "empowerment zones" and "enterprise communities" that are locally nominated but federally chosen; the passage of an anticrime package that included the so-called Brady bill; and the grant of waivers to states interested in experimenting with radical modifications in federal-state welfare programs, particularly the AFDC program. The second year's domestic agenda promised an emphasis on health-care reform, crime, and perhaps welfare reform, but the only major success was the crime bill.

The third and fourth years of the Clinton administration resulted in the Personal Responsibility and Work Opportunity Reconciliation Act of 1996. The new welfare bill eliminates entitlements. Under the new bill, states receive block grants to run AFDC and Job Opportunity and Base Skills (JOBS) programs, and each state determines its own eligibility criteria for receipt of benefits. Welfare recipients are required to work for their benefits after two years, and the legislation has set ambitious deadlines for states to enforce these work requirements. Five-year limits for welfare receipt have been implemented; however, states will be permitted to exempt up to 20 percent of the caseload from this limit. Unmarried teen parents are required to live with an adult (or under adult supervision) in order to receive benefits, and no family cap was set (but states have flexibility to establish them). In addition, states have the option to receive waivers to operate their own welfare-to-work programs without adhering to all of the federal guidelines.

From his first days in office, President Clinton has made a point of publicly including William Julius Wilson in his inner circle of advisors about the federal role in social welfare policy. That last development, as much as anything else, captures the political significance of research by social scientists about how neighborhoods and neighborhood policies affect child development and the importance of these findings to policy formation and implementation. A brief review of Wilson's thesis is therefore useful to understanding some of the impetus behind federal policy.

## THE WILSON THESIS AND FEDERAL POLICY

The publication in 1987 of Wilson's *The Truly Disadvantaged* was a significant event on many levels. It had a substantial impact on public debate about race and urban poverty; it had a clear impact on the thinking of then Arkansas governor Bill Clinton; and it triggered a resurgence of foundation support for social science research in those domains. Not the least significant of the book's effects was to stimulate renewed and heightened interest in the sociological and ethnographic investigation of neighborhoods. A critical link in Wilson's complex thesis about the emergence of an urban underclass during the 1970s was the proposition that declining neighborhoods and the disintegration of community social buffers led directly to a decline in what might generally be termed youth outcomes—the likelihood that a child will finish high school, become regularly employed, and avoid producing children outside marriage.

Because of its importance, Wilson's thesis needs to be summarized in some detail. Wilson claims that the emergence of an urban underclass resulted, in the first instance, from the development of socially isolated neighborhoods (Wilson 1987). Those neighborhoods, he claims, were produced through the interaction of several important macrostructural changes in American society after World War II—most notably, (1) the great migration of southern blacks to segregated northern cities; (2) the shift in the black community's age profile (tilted toward youth); (3) the restructuring of the American economy away from manufacturing and the relocation of remaining American manufacturing out of central cities, with the consequent drop in demand for unskilled urban labor; and (4) the opening up of the suburbs to middle-class blacks and their consequent out-migration from inner cities. The neighborhoods were socially isolated in the sense that their residents lacked contact with individuals and institutions representing mainstream society. According to Wilson, that lack of contact left ghetto residents cut off from job networks and engendered a set of ghetto-specific norms and behaviors that made steady work even less likely.

What followed from this social isolation was a downward spiral of neighborhood dislocation. Employment plummeted, marriage and education lost their attractiveness, and crime rose. The cycle became self-perpetuating as families living in those neighborhoods had to cope with the set of experiences that Wilson called concentration effects. In his more recent work (Wilson 1996), Wilson has argued that during the 1980s those concentration effects interacted with the arrival of crack cocaine, AIDS, and rising homelessness, on the one hand, and the drop in countercyclical governmental interventions, on the other. The cycle became even more vicious as flight from the cities accelerated and urban racial tensions heightened in an atmosphere of mutual recrimination. At the same time, Wilson stresses that the vicious circle is only partly self-perpetuating: the concentration effects are produced by dynamic processes, and those processes have situational bases that are susceptible to change through public and private action (Wilson 1991a).

Wilson's emphasis on social isolation and concentration effects has renewed interest in the neighborhood as a unit of analysis, an interest that had flagged during the 1970s and 1980s. Wilson's argument resonated with the intuitions of a great many people in both the scholarly and political communities, not to mention the average person thinking about buying a house. It suggested that some children were growing up to experience substantially less satisfying lives than they would have experienced if their families had lived in a different neighborhood, even if all other elements in their lives, such as family structure, were the same. Wilson's theory was not about small marginal differences in well-being; it was about the difference between a life of productivity in the economic mainstream and a life of marginalized despair.

And yet, Wilson's thesis also has an optimistic side. It suggests to us that these neighborhood effects could be mitigated through the right policy interventions. To be sure, it is not at all obvious what the "right" kinds of policy intervention might be. Even if one knows that neighborhood effects both exist and are significant, it is not at all obvious how one should go about designing and implementing effective policy responses. For instance, it is not clear whether policies should be aimed at improving neighborhoods, helping people move out of poor neighborhoods, or enhancing the job markets in cities (Wilson 1996). Not all of the neighborhoods dealt with in this book are as bad as the Chicago neighborhoods where Wilson based his studies. Nonetheless, knowledge about neighborhood effects can help to shape and direct the development of government programs at all levels.

## OUR MODEL OF CHILD WELL-BEING AND ISSUES IT RAISES FOR URBAN POLICY

Optimists and believers in neighborhood-based theories should also be exposed to a dose of modesty. The effects and channels by which public policy directed toward neighborhoods or toward families affect children's well-being are complex and not always obvious (Smeeding 1995). Chapter 2 of this volume lays out a skeletal micromodel of child well-being that helps organize our thinking about how neighborhoods affect and are affected by changes in child well-being and other factors. A brief review of the multidisciplinary nature of this model will help us understand the complicated nature of child well-being and the forces—neighborhood and otherwise—that might bring about positive child outcomes.

Until recently, many social scientists (economists and sociologists, especially) and most public policy analysts have measured children's well-being by their parents' well-being. They have used measurable socioeconomic variables that are really inputs into children's well-being: variables such as household consumption, income, wealth, household capital goods, and neighborhood characteristics. Social standing or the lack thereof has also been measured largely by parent's characteristics until children reach the age of majority, labor force participation, or criminal institutionalization, whichever comes first. Beyond birth-weight and Apgar scores, which qualify a newborn's vitality, children have not traditionally been individual social, economic, and statistical entities as far as state record keeping and social scientists' household survey practices have been concerned. Most large-scale (macro-oriented) household surveys have included little more than their age and sex. Most of the databases that are exceptions to this rule were used earlier in this volume to help ferret out neighborhood effects on families and children.

Developmental psychologists, educators, anthropologists, and pediatricians approach children's well-being from the other, or micro, end of the spectrum. That is, they employ direct measures of some aspect of children's well-being: cognitive, social, intellectual, educational, or other developmental outcome measures are used by psychologists, educators, and anthropologists; and physical and mental health status is used by pediatricians. The measures are usually for a small subset of children drawn from a local sample or institution. Even when the children studied vary widely by background or health status (as do many of the children studied here), the economic, social, environmental, and other contextual measures on which the macrodisciplines focus are often poorly measured or ignored.

It is to their great credit that the scholars represented in this volume are wedded to the idea of marrying these two perspectives to produce a more holistic approach to measuring the impact of various forces, and ultimately to analyzing the impact of public policy, on children. If we are truly to measure the impact of adult-focused programs like welfare reform on children's well-being, or if we ultimately want to find out why some children in poor neighborhoods succeed while others do not, these two perspectives must be brought together, if not wedded (Chase-Lansdale and Brooks-Gunn 1995). Important public policy questions regarding such things as the relative effects on children of family-based subsidies and neighborhood-based initiatives can only be addressed in this manner.

The model developed in chapter 2 is intended to suggest the types of conditions, processes, and life events that shape children's lives and well-being. It is an attempt to represent the "big picture," and it highlights the role of neighborhoods and communities in affecting child outcomes. Various exogenous (to the neighborhood) forces such as economic restructuring, migration, and existing public policies create an environment that presents the constraints and opportunities facing children and their families at a point in time. Public policy may affect children's well-being by affecting any of the variables that directly or indirectly influence the child: family, peers, other adults, or such neighborhood features as stability, ethnic and racial heterogeneity, social organizations, and cultural values (Chase-Lansdale and Brooks-Gunn 1995).

These clusters of static variables set the stage for the dynamic processes involving the family and the community that also contribute to child development. Together, they shape various measurable child outcomes, including health status and educational attainment.

How should neighborhood effects and policy responses be viewed through the lens of this model? Immediately, we realize that it is not enough to know, as a general proposition, that neighborhoods matter. *It matters how neighborhoods matter.* That is, one needs to know the mediators: social organizations and networks; cultural processes; and parental, peer, and other processes that link to neighborhoods and to children's developmental courses. Consider one example. The Omnibus Budget Reconciliation Act of 1993 and the Crime Bill of 1994 call for the identification of "empowerment zones" demonstrating various characteristics (such as community plans) to be designated by the secretary of Housing and Urban Development after having been nominated by the relevant state and local governments. Under the 1993 Act, to be contenders, zones and communities must satisfy specific criteria with regard to size and must have a condition of pervasive poverty, unemployment, and general economic distress. In addition, the relevant "state and local governments must have committed themselves to a strategic plan" that would include direct public investments in the nominated area and provide indirect support for private for-profit and nonprofit institutions to do likewise. Once chosen, the communities receive various awards (from $20 million to $100 million) to implement their plans.

But what, precisely, are the kinds of investments that institutions should be making in the empowerment zones? What kinds of activities should be subsidized? It depends on why we are concerned about these neighborhoods. Our concern here is the effect of bad neighborhoods on children. To be sure, there are a host of reasons why a government might be concerned about depressed neighborhoods that have nothing to do with concentration effects on child development. But let us assume (accurately, in this case) that at least part of the motivation for the creation of empowerment zones is a desire to respond to the implications of Wilson's thesis. Then, we would contend, it matters *how* children are affected by growing up in neighborhoods that suffer from concentrated high unemployment, crime, and social decay.

Suppose, for example, that high levels of neighborhood unemployment are detrimental to children because those children are deprived of a particular kind of socializing experience: that of interacting socially with adult neighbors whose lives are structured around the experience of steady employment (and who are likely to reflect the primacy of employment in their lives through their conversations). If that is the major mediating mechanism, then the logical aim of policy intervention should be to subsidize the employment of adults who reside in the neighborhood, regardless of where the job is located. But now suppose, conversely, that high levels of neighborhood unemployment are detrimental to children because those children are deprived of a different kind of socializing experience: that of observing a critical mass of adult neighbors at work in steady jobs during the day. In that case, the logical aim of policy intervention would be to subsidize the employment of adult neighbors in neighborhood jobs that are visible to children. One policy stresses job creation regardless of place; the other stresses job creation *within* a specific neighborhood. Both polices affect family well-being and, presumably then, parental and family processes. But only the second directly affects neighborhoods as well. Moreover, the exact ways by which each of these policies filters down to children—directly or indirectly (via the mediators of social organizations, cultural processes, or family efforts)—is not well known.

In fact, Congress chose subsidies that were closer to the latter description than to the former. To oversimplify somewhat, in the 1993 Employment Zone law, employers were given wage subsidies for wages paid to zone residents if they work in the zone (although admittedly even if they work in places not accessible to children), and additional tax incentives were granted to businesses that carry out substantially all their operations within the zone, as long as at least 35 percent of their employees are zone residents. In the 1994 Crime Bill, considerably greater flexibility in the use of federal funds was allowed, but the funds were still targeted on specific areas and on the plan of action for their use. Whether these were the right choices is not important for the current purposes. Similarly, we are not concerned here with whether Congress was right to emphasize employment policy; we would make the same point if the centerpiece had been anticrime policy or school assistance policy. The point is that, in deciding which type of policy to pursue, it matters *how* children are affected by their environments.

## WHAT THE RESEARCH MIGHT HAVE FOUND AND WHAT THESE FINDINGS MIGHT HAVE IMPLIED

Since the publication of *The Truly Disadvantaged* (1987), social scientists have been systematically testing various elements of Wilson's thesis. Variations have been proposed, stressing factors other than those Wilson emphasized or emphasizing differently the overall story's various aspects. And one particularly significant piece of Wilson's analysis that has received special attention is his suggestion that some neighborhoods have significant, independent, detrimental effects on the life courses of the children who grow up in them. That particular aspect is one that gave rise to this book and that produced neighborhoods and communities as key elements in our structural model. To give an appropriate sense of the policy significance of the research that is reported in this book, it is useful to consider what is sometimes referred to as Sherlock Holmes's "dog that didn't bark." It is useful to think more generally about what the researchers might have found and what that might have implied for public policy. We consider three "silent dogs," three possibilities that did *not* come about from the findings in this book: (1) a finding of *no* neighborhood effects, (2) a finding that children who grow up in "bad" neighborhoods end up doing "better" than children who grow up in "average" neighborhoods (a "survivor's effect"), and (3) a finding that children who grow up in "bad" neighborhoods end up doing "worse" than children who grow up in "average" neighborhoods (the anticipated findings).

### POSSIBILITY: NO DISCERNIBLE NEIGHBORHOOD EFFECTS

The research in this volume could have discerned no distinct neighborhood effects whatsoever. The so-called common analyses in chapters 4, 5, 6, 7, and 8 could have concluded that measurable characteristics of the neighborhood added nothing to our ability to explain variation in child outcomes, once we included a full range of individual- and family-level variables. What would that have implied?

First, we should note that such a finding would have been surprising. Casual empiricism would suggest that most people strongly believe that neighborhoods matter, and in recent years, researchers have tended to find such effects, although the policy significance of their magnitude has been a subject of much debate. And among the many methodological hurdles that confront researchers in this field, at least one has been noted to generate a potential bias in favor of finding such effects: the fact that most, if not all, individuals have *some* control over which neighborhood they live in means it is easy to attribute certain effects to neighborhoods that in fact reflect unmeasured family characteristics (see chapter 9; Tienda 1989). Of course, studies that overcome any such bias and find no neighborhood effects could themselves have been methodologically contaminated. The research methodology might have been unable to reveal neighborhood influences that were really there. The research might have been trapped with census data that required *neighborhoods* to be defined differently from the sociological neighborhoods that have real-world effects (as discussed in volume 2). The thirty-five census-tract variables available to the researchers might not have captured some characteristics of neighborhoods (such as school characteristics or levels of gang activity) that are highly relevant to child development. Traits that were deemed family traits might have been shaped by neighborhood characteristics before they could be measured. The samples might have been too small. Nonlinear effects might have been invisible to linear models. Interneighborhood social linkages might be ignored. And the researchers might have failed to test for an interaction that was in fact present (see chapter 5).

But if no neighborhood effects had been discerned, and if a policy maker had been comfortable enough with the methodology to place weight on that finding, there would have been clear policy implications. In a world of limited resources, one would be more inclined to move slowly on neighborhood-level interventions wherever one could as easily (as efficiently, and with no greater collateral costs) implement macroeconomic, family-level, or individual-level interventions. Thus:

1. One would be inclined to continue to emphasize programs that respond to *individual* children's needs for education, health care, nutrition, and general income support, where needs are measured without regard to the child's place of residence.

2. One would be inclined to continue to emphasize programs that direct adult education, training, and wage subsidies to individual adults in need, without regard to their neighbors' employment situations.

3. And one would be inclined to continue to emphasize the importance of macroeconomic policies that influence the resources available to children's family environments and shape the longer-term opportunities those children will enjoy when they are older.

## POSSIBILITY: "BAD" NEIGHBORHOODS LEAD CONSISTENTLY TO "BETTER" OUTCOMES THAN "AVERAGE" NEIGHBORHOODS

Jencks and Mayer (1990) have identified several neighborhood-effects models. Two of those varieties are competition models (in which children compete with their peers for access to scarce developmentally significant resources) and relative deprivation models (in which a child's developmentally significant self-concept is shaped by comparison with peers). Both types of neighborhood-effects models predict that, even after one accounts for a full range of individual- and family-level characteristics, the presence of certain "bad" neighborhood attributes will be associated with positive child outcomes, as children thrive from being the "biggest fish" in their local ponds. Consistent with such models, the common analyses could have found that children who live in low-SES neighborhoods do better than comparable children who live in middle-SES or high-SES neighborhoods. What would that have implied? Once again, such findings would have been noteworthy. They would have been inconsistent with the spirit of evaluations of the Gautreaux housing voucher program (Rosenbaum 1991), and they would accordingly have complicated straightforward arguments for "deconcentrating the inner city poor" (Schill 1992).

## POSSIBILITY: "BAD" NEIGHBORHOODS LEAD CONSISTENTLY TO "WORSE" CHILD OUTCOMES THAN "AVERAGE" NEIGHBORHOODS

Two other neighborhood-effects models identified by Jencks and Mayer (1990) are contagion theories (in which child development is shaped by peer behavior) and collective socialization theories (in which child development is shaped by adult role modeling and monitoring). These labels connote subsets of more general categories: theories that stress peer influence (whether or not one would want to brand it with the pejorative *contagion*) and theories that stress community resources (including, but not limited to, role modeling and mentoring). Both peer-influence and community-resource theories predict that, even after one accounts for a full range of individual- and family-level characteristics, the presence of certain "bad" neighborhood attributes will be associated with negative child outcomes.[1] Consistent with such theories, the common analyses in chapters 4 through 8 could have shown that children who live in low-SES neighborhoods do worse than comparable children who live in middle-SES or high-SES neighborhoods. What would that have implied?

In thinking about government policy more generally, such findings would have implied only that one would have needed to read the mediator analyses with great care. Peer-influence theories have very different policy implications from community-resource theories. Or, to return to the more general theme stressed in this chapter, the mediators would matter.

Consider, for example, the possibility that the mediator analyses had found that children in low-SES neighborhoods did worse because, as Wilson theorized, the individuals living in that neighborhood lacked the wherewithal to produce an adequate stock of critical community resources (such as social buffers, quality schools, job networks, or physical security). Responsive policies might then involve systematic efforts (1) to identify which such resources were critical to child development and then (2) to make the production of such resources less dependent on the individuals who live in a particular neighborhood. Such efforts might involve simple funds transfers from one governing body to another, in the form of revenue sharing or block grants. Or, more grandly, they might involve more aggressive transformation of metropolitan governance structures along the lines advocated by Rusk (1993).

Or, consider the possibility that the mediator analyses had shown that children in low-SES neighborhoods did worse because their peers spoke a different language from the Standard American English that is most efficacious in the job market. That is the "language of segregation" theory advanced by Massey and Denton (1993). Responsive policies might take any of several directions. They might attempt to restructure the likely peer environments that children would find themselves in, through heightened attacks on residential segregation, or, as a fall-back strategy, through heightened efforts to promote school integration even in a society where residential segregation persists. Or, more speculatively, they might explore ways to generalize the strategies that have allowed immigrant nonspeakers of Standard American English to penetrate the American job market.

Or, consider a more complex mediation possibility. Suppose that the mediator analyses had shown that children in low-SES neighborhoods did worse because of the interaction of three forces:

1. High degree of perceived rewards for investing time in socially unproductive or even antisocial activities. The perception of such rewards could be acquired from heeding peer influences or from weighing the costs and benefits of criminal activity as opposed to legal costs (Anderson 1994; Freeman 1991b).

2. Low degree of perceived rewards for investing time in skills acquisition. This absence could be because the rewards are in fact not there, given constrained job opportunities. Or, it could be because informational resources (in the form of either peer influence or community resources such as role models or counselors) are not present to show children that the rewards are in fact there.

3. Low degree of effective assistance with skills acquisition, for example, due to poor-quality schools.

Once again, responsive policies might take any of several different courses. Community-level efforts to raise the perceived cost of antisocial activities might involve counseling, the criminal justice system, or public support for private authoritarian institutions. Strategies for giving children more heterogeneous opportunities for peer interaction were discussed earlier. Strategies for increasing the availability of returns to investment in skills acquisition might depend on why such investment had been found to be currently ineffective; Lehman (1994) provides a general review of such strategies. Strategies for increasing the availability of effective assistance with skills acquisition might involve school finance reform or support for extracurricular education-and-training programs. They might also involve programs to produce safer schools.

To be sure, even if the research in this volume had provided powerful support for one or another peer-influence or community-resource theory of neighborhood effects, and even if one were to conclude on the basis of such research that a policy intervention along one of the foregoing lines was appropriate, it would still not be clear what role the federal government should be playing and how states and localities might implement these interventions. That is an important overarching question to which we will return.

In summary, the silent dog analogies and the model review in the previous section point to the sequential nature of our enterprise: (1) What is the nature and type of neighborhood effect? (2) How large, consistent, and linear are these effects? (3) Even if we know that these effects are worth the attention of policy makers (that is, as an identified problem), do we know enough about the mediators through which they operate to be able to design effective policies to offset or neutralize the effects? Knowledge of the problem does not always point to knowledge of an effective solution.

## THE RESEARCH FINDINGS AND FEDERAL POLICY: WHAT WAS FOUND

Having carefully and deliberately set the context for interpreting the findings of this body of research, we turn from silent dogs to those that at least made some noise. We begin by noting that it is somewhat risky to distill the nuanced and still-warm findings of many different researchers into a thematic synopsis. But that must be done if those findings are to be accessible and useful to policy makers. And several themes do appear to have emerged clearly within the research findings of this volume. The following eight themes strike us as being of the greatest potential policy interest.

### THE RESEARCHERS FOUND MEASURABLE NEIGHBORHOOD EFFECTS

Consistently, across data sets and across ages, the researchers found that models with neighborhood variables were able to explain more of the variance in child outcomes than models without neighborhood variables. This fits with our (and others) general reactions to the Wilson hypothesis, with investigations of its veracity in other locations, and with common sense: different neighborhoods have different problems and hence different types of effects on the children who live in them.

The neighborhood effects that were found were in some respects more consistent with community-resource theories and in some respects more consistent with adult-level contagion theories (peer contagion effects for children per se could only be inferred from these data). The presence of high-SES neighbors seemed to be associated with good child outcomes, for at least some children, in three of the five age groups (chapters 4, 5, and 8). The presence of low-SES neighbors did not seem to be associated with bad child outcomes for any of the age groups and may have been associated with better behavior by early adolescent African American girls in the Atlanta sample (chapter 6). The presence of high rates of neighborhood male joblessness did seem to be associated with bad child outcomes, for at least some children (chapter 6), but not consistently across samples.

The variety of neighborhood effects suggests that it would be a mistake to focus exclusively on male joblessness as the key element in the causal process of neighborhood decline. While male joblessness, particularly as it manifests itself in the lives of African American youth, is a key problem to be solved, it is far from the only problem, and it may not even be the primary problem in primarily African American neighborhoods.

SOME NEIGHBORHOOD EFFECTS WERE FOUND AT ALL AGES    Even after controlling for family-level variables, the researchers found that the presence of high-SES neighbors contributed to better outcomes in the cognitive domain for the three- and four-year-olds they studied (chapter 4).

THE NEIGHBORHOOD EFFECTS THAT WERE FOUND VARIED BY RACE AND GENDER    As indicated in chapters 4, 5, and 8, the association of high-SES neighbors with positive outcomes was stronger for whites than for blacks. In all the chapters, race and gender differences were common. For now, we only note that this finding may significantly complicate policy design.

THE MEDIATOR ANALYSES WERE OFTEN INDETERMINATE, BUT YIELDED INTERESTING ALTERNATIVE HYPOTHESES TO ACCOUNT FOR COMPLEX INTERACTIONS AMONG VARIABLES, SUCH AS RACE AND GENDER    Several different chapters suggested interactions among a child's race, the child's neighborhood quality, and the child's perceptions of home and school support, although these interactions were not always consistent. For example, high-SES neighborhoods were not associated with the same kinds of positive outcomes for black males as for white males. Mediator analysis suggested that black males from high-SES neighborhoods were less likely to find schools supportive than black males from low-SES neighborhoods. Thus, other benefits from living in a high-SES neighborhood may have been offset (or "suppressed" in the vernacular) by harms in the school context. The precise reason for the school-context effect remains unclear.

THE NEIGHBORHOOD EFFECTS WERE GENERALLY MUCH WEAKER THAN THE EFFECTS OF FAMILY-LEVEL AND INDIVIDUAL-LEVEL FACTORS    While some of the neighborhood variables were significant predictors, they were always secondary predictors. In no case did they explain as much of the variance in child outcomes as the family-level and individual-level variables did.

THE DATA DID NOT ALWAYS PERMIT THE RESEARCHERS TO DISTINGUISH LINEAR, ADDITIVE NEIGHBORHOOD EFFECTS FROM NONLINEAR, "EPIDEMIC-STYLE" NEIGHBORHOOD EFFECTS    A finding that the fraction of high-SES neighbors in a neighborhood is positively associated (in a way identifiable through linear regression analysis) with good child outcomes is consistent with either of two possibilities. The relationship might be linear, so that moving a high-SES neighbor out of one neighborhood into another would harm the outcomes in the original neighborhood in a way that roughly corresponds to the benefits it would provide for the outcomes in the new neighborhood. But it might also be nonlinear, so that moving a high-SES neighbor from a well-off neighborhood to a neighborhood with very few high-SES residents would provide benefits to the new neighborhood without harming the outcomes in the original neighborhood (see Brooks-Gunn et al. 1993a).

THE RESEARCHERS' OWN METHODOLOGICAL RESERVATIONS COUNSEL POLICY MAKERS TO EXERCISE CAUTION IN RELYING TOO HEAVILY ON THEIR FINDINGS    Volume 2 includes discussions of potential sources of bias, as well as alternative methodologies for tapping the many meanings and nuances of *neighborhood.* Among the many ways that social science research differs from a Sherlock Holmes mystery—a particularly important difference—concerns the inferences one should draw from "silent dogs." Some of those methodological limitations imply that, even if the "dogs did not bark" for these researchers, a different research methodology or measure of neighborhood might have coaxed them into action. The research here has thus *not* shown that any of the policy responses discussed in this section are necessarily wrongheaded. The arguments in favor of those approaches were not refuted; rather, they were only held in abeyance.

## THE RESEARCH FINDINGS AND FEDERAL POLICY: WHAT THE FINDINGS IMPLY

The research in this volume has taken advantage of the most sophisticated interdisciplinary theories available, has embraced multidisciplinary teams of well-qualified researchers, and has exploited some rich and well-constructed data sets. However, it may have little to say to federal policy makers concerning neighborhood effects on children. For a first attempt at such a multiphased and difficult collaboration, this result should have been expected. The most extreme potential findings—ones that could have, in theory, supported a simpler vision of the world—did not materialize. Instead, we have received additional support for the proposition that the world is complex. And so, the most significant debates about the future course of policy on behalf of children growing up in distressed urban neighborhoods should continue unabated.

To us, that implies at least three things:

First, if the federal government is already undertaking macroeconomic, family-level, and individual-level programs that help low-income children who live in distressed urban neighborhoods, this research does not suggest any reasons for those efforts to cease.

This research joins the existing literature suggesting that family income matters most to child development. If the federal government can use macroeconomic policy to promote employment opportunities for low-income parents and to supplement earned income, such a policy should continue to be understood as promoting child development. If the federal government can use redistributive transfers to boost family incomes, such transfers should continue to be understood as promoting child development as well. If anything, this research supports continued efforts to develop new forms of family-level and individual-level intervention that are likely to help low-income children who live in distressed urban neighborhoods. Some form of universal health insurance guaranteeing access to basic preventive and acute health care for all children—a federal policy initiative not yet enacted—is surely an obvious place to begin. But it is certainly not the place to stop. Moreover, the belief that nothing can be done, or worse, that federal policy hurts poor families more than it helps them is clearly *not* supported by the research described in this volume.

Second, if the federal government is already undertaking neighborhood-oriented (or community-oriented) programs that help low-income children who live in distressed urban neighborhoods, this research does not suggest any reasons for those efforts to cease.

The evaluation literature suggests that Head Start and the WIC program are effective federal initiatives (NAS 1993; National Commission on Children 1991). To encourage expanded support for Head Start, one might point to chapter 4's finding that neighborhood effects show up even before school begins, but that seems unnecessary, since Head Start attempts to influence individual-level characteristics through an intervention that is at once neighborhood-based and family-directed. Sampson (1993) has aptly observed that it is a common fallacy to believe that, when one uses a community as one's unit of analysis, all of one's observations result from "community processes" rather than from the cumulative effects of the actions of the individuals who happen to compose the community at that moment (see also Sampson and Morenoff vol. 2). As is often the case, such an observation about the empirical analysis of social phenomena can be translated into an analogous admonition about the analysis of the effects of social programs. Here, we would note that it is also a fallacy to assume that a "community-based program" makes sense only if community processes are significant and the program influences those processes. A community-based program may simply be the most effective way to reach the individuals who live there. Anticrime programs and neighborhood-safety programs might be couched in the same terms.

> Third, we still have breathtakingly little knowledge about the effects of public interventions on child development, and about the way neighborhood effects on children are mediated. Accordingly, it would seem premature (or at least a significant leap of faith) to press for some bold, new, nationally mandated, universal effort to address neighborhood effects. Conversely, there would seem to be great potential value in federal support for carefully structured programmatic experimentation, coupled with rigorous evaluation, in order to augment that knowledge.

## IMPLICATIONS OF THE RESEARCH FINDINGS FOR STATE AND LOCAL POLICY

In volume 2, Brown and Richman discuss some of the existing state and local initiatives that are already a potential source of programmatic experimentation. How should federal efforts dovetail with those initiatives? We would offer the following tentative suggestions, both substantive and procedural.

### SUBSTANTIVE SUGGESTIONS: THE LOCI OF ADDITIONAL INQUIRY

The research findings in this volume do not dictate a determinate list of fields for policy experimentation and evaluation. Nonetheless, we would be surprised if any reader of volumes 1 and 2 did not come away with an appetite whetted for a better understanding of the dynamics of neighborhood effects. The following list reflects our own personal sense of domains for fruitful experimentation in public interventions:

JOBS AND THEIR CORRELATES    In the research in this volume, *high socioeconomic status* was defined in terms of an annual income of thirty thousand dollars—a level that almost invariably requires one and perhaps even two family members to have a good job, one with good benefits, including health insurance. Jobs and male joblessness were the variables that most frequently generated independent effects on the development of children in the neighborhood. What kinds of policy interventions might increase employment levels? A number of concrete proposals have been on the table for several years, and many have been implemented in different ways. Various forms of government-run welfare-to-work transitional programs and education-and-training programs have received substantial trial and evaluation over the years (Aber, Brooks-Gunn, and Maynard 1995; Gueron and Pauly 1991; Heckman 1994; Maynard 1995; S. Smith 1995; T. Smith 1993). We would expect the marginal returns from further trial and evaluation in those domains to be diminishing rapidly. Other proposals, some directly and others indirectly linked to work promotion, have received less experimental testing. The following strike us as the most promising candidates.

*Guaranteed Public-Sector Employment*   The literature on past efforts is dated and inconclusive (Lehman 1994). Moreover, there are strong theoretical arguments for the proposition that the current dynamics of racial distrust require more radical interventions than ever before. The New Hope demonstration project in Milwaukee is evaluating such an experiment (Aikman 1993; Hollister 1993). More such experiments, if targeted to areas of high joblessness and few job openings, would provide opportunities for careful, up-to-date evaluation.

*Transportation*   The literature on the so-called spatial mismatch is conflicting and inconclusive (see Burtless and Mishel 1993). Nonetheless, there is almost irresistible intuitive appeal to the proposition that job opportunities expand greatly if one has ready access to an effective means of transportation. Senator Bill Bradley introduced legislation in the mid-1990s called the Mobility for Work Act that would expand support for public transit systems in twenty metropolitan areas. But as attractive a service as public transportation is likely to be on many levels, its impact on the lives of low-income children living in distressed urban neighborhoods is likely to be slow and unmeasurable. A better-targeted, less-expensive, and more easily evaluated alternative experiment would be to provide target groups with private transportation vouchers or "car stamps"—in-kind subsidies for welfare-to-work program enrollees to rent or purchase transportation services, including cars (Smeeding 1994).

*Child Care*   As was true for transportation, there is almost irresistible intuitive appeal to the proposition that job opportunities expand greatly for parents who have ready access to a reliable source of quality day care (Chase-Lansdale and Brooks-Gunn 1995; Hofferth and Chaplin 1994). An example is the Expanded Child Care Options Project, a demonstration project which was intended to provide a comprehensive and systematic long-range test of the impact of different forms of child-care assurance on adults and children in low-income families (Hollister 1993). Regrettably, this project was not funded.

*Nonpublic Employment and Training Initiatives and Placement*  In recent years, private for-profit entrepreneurs such as America Works and Maximus (two for-profit human resource firms providing job placement services) have attracted attention for their efforts to help welfare recipients obtain and keep positions in the formal economy (Aikman 1993). It is at least theoretically conceivable that the interpersonal dynamics of dealing with a for-profit service, coupled with a well-structured profit motive, *could* make such services more effective than their public-sector counterparts. But absent rigorous evaluation, it remains just as conceivable that such services are merely skimming the most motivated participants and claiming substantial credit for outcomes in which their own contributions were slight. Additional experimentation, coupled with rigorous evaluation, seems both feasible and desirable.

Note that in conducting evaluations of interventions such as these, the primary concern must be long-term differential impact. Neither car stamps nor public-service employment should be required to catapult beneficiaries into high-income positions. The question is whether, over the long term, they can be said to have helped beneficiaries move onto a path that might lead to such a position where no such path existed before.

SOCIAL CAPITAL  The quantitative research described in this volume did not attempt to capture in its independent variables the kinds of private, community-based institutions that Wilson referred to in his discussion of "social buffers." Yet much of the theoretical and qualitative discussion suggests that such institutions can make an important difference in children's lives. A literature on community-based organizations documents (usually, although not invariably, through case study) the systematic efforts by planners, social workers, and organizers to nurture such organizations (Mayer 1981; Naparstek 1993; Sullivan 1993). Substantial attention has been given to the efforts of community-based financial institutions and housing-oriented community development corporations to redevelop neighborhoods that are the locus of concentrated urban poverty (Aikman 1993; Sullivan 1993).

Yet that same literature is explicit about how difficult it is to carefully evaluate research concerning such institutions (Aikman 1993). Our knowledge about what kinds of public interventions are most likely to enable such programs to survive remains impressionistic, more a reflection of a priori theory than post hoc evaluation (Connell, Aber, and Walker 1996; Lehman and Lento 1992). And if they do survive, we know very little about how to measure their effects on neighborhood processes (as opposed to their effects on the individuals who live there). Ultimately, social scientists may have little to offer in the way of evaluative rigor to supplement local policy makers' hunches about which of these programs are effective and which are not. But at this point it would seem worthwhile to support efforts to develop evaluation protocols that would identify the most rigorous evaluations of such potentially critical programs (see Brown and Richman vol. 2; Aber and Connell vol. 2; Sampson 1993).

PUBLIC SAFETY   The quantitative research described in this volume was unable to include measures of neighborhood safety in the research designs. Yet a significant qualitative literature and growing epidemiological and psychiatric literatures suggest that some of the most destructive effects of ghetto neighborhoods are associated with the extremely high levels of violence found there (Earls 1992; Fagan 1993; Marans and Cohen 1994; Sampson 1993). The need to develop interventions that bolster mechanisms of social control, especially of teenage boys, is an old one, but it seems to have taken on pressing significance and policy importance in recent years. While we remain unconvinced that more prisons and longer jail sentences offer a long-term, cost-effective solution for reducing crime and increasing public safety, other public safety innovations warrant ongoing study.

DRUGS   Too often in the urban landscape the buying, selling, and consuming of illicit drugs are highly correlated with violence, imprisonment, and neglected children. Regulation and criminalization continue to enjoy only mixed success. But the case for decriminalization remains speculative (Nadelman 1989). Any local experiments that do take place should certainly be evaluated rigorously.

SCHOOLS   Some of the most interesting mediator analysis in this volume concerned the interaction among race, gender, neighborhood, and the child's perception of the degree of support available in school. We still do not know nearly enough about the role schools play in exaggerating or mitigating the effects of variable neighborhood quality. Also, we do not know nearly enough about the differential effects schools may have on children of different races and genders or about how the school environment interacts with and may influence the home learning environment. But, the Atlanta and upstate New York data sets seem to promise exceptionally rich sources of further research on these topics. Moreover, schools may be much better equipped than the larger neighborhood to provide effective loci for delivery of social and health services, and to provide safe havens from violence, guns, and drugs. While the growing segregation by race, income, and poverty status in American schools is becoming all too apparent (Orfield 1993), schools still provide a focal point of intensive, synergistic interventions that can be effectively targeted on children in bad neighborhoods.

## POLICY ANALOGUES OF INTERACTION EFFECTS
## AND NONLINEARITIES

We mentioned earlier that observations about the empirical analysis of social phenomena can be translated into an analogous admonition about the analysis of social programs' effects. The empirical research reported in this volume made at least two methodological observations whose analogues in the policy domain warrant discussion.

The first such observation concerns so-called interaction effects—the fact that when one finds two characteristics (such as race and poverty) in the same observational unit (neighborhood or individual), the effects may be different from the linear sum of the effects of finding the two characteristics in isolation. In the policy domain, the analogous concept is "synergy." At least as a theoretical matter, it is possible that Program A (for example, child care) might have no effects on its own, and Program B (for example, transportation assistance) might have no effects on its own, but that the *simultaneous* implementation of Program A and Program B might have significant effects. In recent years, several commentators have pressed the theoretical case for interactions among policy interventions on behalf of low-income children who live in distressed urban neighborhoods. These arguments have sometimes been expressed as calls for "integrated services" or "one-stop shopping."

The abstract possibility of programmatic synergy does not strike us as sufficient to justify experiments that randomly mix and match different combinations of interventions. But where there are strong theoretical reasons to expect synergistic benefits, experimental interventions can be designed to test for them directly. This volume itself offers two fruitful approaches to developing theoretical criteria for ascertaining when synergistic benefits are likely to be obtained: (1) the theoretical discussion of individual development processes and (2) the theoretical discussion of neighborhood process (chapters 1 and 2). And the chapter by Brown and Richman in volume 2 on state and local policy implications indicates that such synergism might be integrated with various types of "social capital" at the neighborhood level to produce positive outcomes.

The second such observation concerns so-called nonlinearities: the fact that when a significant level of a phenomenon is present, the effects on behavior may be more than double the effects that exist at half that level. (The best-known application in the social science context is probably Schelling's [1971] analysis of "tipping" in racially segregated neighborhoods.) In the policy domain, this phenomenon has a direct analogue: at least as a theoretical matter, it is possible that Program A (for example, counseling) might have no effects at one level (for instance, one hour per week) but might have significant effects at a much higher level (for instance, one hour per day). And that possibility is frequently invoked in political debates, sometimes defensively to distinguish past experimental failures (for example, "the fact that lightly funded state enterprise zones have failed to produce significant results tells us little about whether heavily funded federal enterprise zones would") and sometimes offensively as an argument for "saturation" ("if we spend a huge amount in a massive intervention, we are bound to make a difference").

Our own intuition is that nonlinearities pervade the policy domain. At the low end, virtually any successful program is likely to produce no detectable benefits if it is attempted on a small enough scale. At the high end, our sense is not that one is likely to see accelerating benefits from a single program, but the opposite—that one is more likely to see diminishing marginal returns. (This is different from the possibility of beneficial interactions among multiple programs, discussed previously; but as we noted, our intuition is to believe that one should have a priori theoretical reasons to suspect the presence of such interactions before investing in the testing of them.) The net result is that experimental interventions are likely to provide the most valuable information for those who want to assess the cost of benefits of a prospective policy if the effects of several, significantly different levels of intervention are tested simultaneously. That is what would have been attempted in the Expanded Child Care Options Project (Hollister 1993). And the positive impact of the MDRC evaluation of the GAIN program in Riverside County, California (as compared to other counties in California), points to the importance of organizational culture in achieving good results for welfare-to-work programs (Gueron 1994).

## PROCEDURAL SUGGESTIONS: THE LEVERS OF FEDERALISM

One of the most problematic questions under our federal system concerns the design of federally supported programs. Indeed, the devolution from federal to state control of a number of social programs is now occurring. How much specificity in design should be handled at the federal level and how much left to more decentralized units of activity? How much administration should be carried out by federal employees and how much by others? How much funding should come from the federal purse and how much from others?

These questions arise most strongly in the context of full-scale national programs, but they arise in the context of federally supported experiments as well. In the past, the federal government has sometimes launched and monitored localized experiments and evaluations on its own. Sometimes it has been able to do so through new appropriations of funds (for example, the Experimental Housing Allowance Program [EHAP], and the Seattle and Denver Income Maintenance Experiments [SIME/DIME] programs). Sometimes it has been able to do so in conjunction with programs of cooperative federalism (as with MDRC evaluations of JOBS in California). And sometimes it has been able to do so by placing conditions on program grants to state and local units of government (as with JTPA programs).

We do not have strong a priori commitments about how such questions of allocation should be dealt with in the context of experimentation. We do believe, however, that close attention to the problems associated with the policy analysis of neighborhood-level interventions might provide some useful insights. In particular, we would stress the specific domains of implementation and evaluation.

Two of the most vexing problems in funding and evaluating new experiments may not involve high-level design. Rather, those problems may be at the level of implementation and evaluation (see Brooks-Gunn et al. vol. 2). At the level of implementation, we would emphasize that whether a program has beneficial effects or not may depend as much on who runs it as on how it is structured (Manski 1990). That fact creates something of a theoretical conundrum in the formation of federal policy. Are we interested in experiments that involve the best imaginable quality of implementation? Or are we interested in experiments that involve only a representative quality of implementation? The former approach may leave us overly optimistic about what benefits may flow from generalizing an experimental intervention. (That is what some have argued about the early evaluations of the Head Start demonstration program conducted at the Perry Preschool in Ypsilanti, Michigan.) But the latter approach may leave us overly pessimistic about what is feasible.

We would argue that, at least at the stage of experiment and evaluation, it makes more sense to design experiments involving the best available mode of implementation. That approach allows one to treat any benefits found as a plausible upper bound on the benefits to be obtained from a generalized, replicated program. Moreover, careful evaluation should permit systematic discussion of how expensive or difficult it might be to generalize and replicate successes.

What forms of implementation are most likely to maximize success? Once again, one should be wary of overgeneralizations. But some of the best impressionistic accounts of neighborhood-level interventions share two common themes: charismatic leadership and participatory development. Energetic, creative, and charismatic leaders can sustain programs that would otherwise fail (Aikman 1993; T. Smith 1993). Participation of residents in program development can have two benefits: it can leave them more committed to making sure the program succeeds (Aikman 1993; Halpern 1993), and, perhaps even more significantly, it can generate an important "product"— higher levels of human capital in community residents (Brown and Richman vol. 2; Kahn and Kamerman 1996).

At the level of evaluation, we would emphasize two related observations. First, new evaluation research should be shaped by basic theory and research (see Aber and Connell vol. 2). To the extent that variations in neighborhood context can shape individual child development outcomes, one should also expect that variations in neighborhood context will shape the results of programmatic intervention. Comprehensive evaluations should explore between-neighborhood variations in program effects, as well as within-neighborhood variations between control and intervention subjects, in order to provide the most useful information to policy makers. Second, evaluators must be sensitive to the point about implementation made in the preceding paragraphs. Several observers have suggested that idiosyncratic features of program implementation, such as leaders' charisma and community participation in development, may be critical to program success or failure. To the extent that evaluators can track and measure such characteristics, evaluations are likely to be much more meaningful.

And we would conclude with two observations about the problem of funding. First, federal administrators are unlikely to have access to the sorts of information that might allow them to discern which leaders will be perceived as charismatic by the community and which leaders will be able to galvanize community participation. Over the past few decades, however, private foundations have been actively involved in making precisely those kinds of distinctions. It might therefore make sense for federal funds to be disbursed as matching grants directed toward programs that are willing to submit to rigorous evaluation and that have also been able to obtain equivalent levels of funding from major foundation sources.

Second, one of the most important unanswered research questions is also an important unanswered funding question. As we have noted, confirmation of the existence of neighborhood effects does not answer the question of whether those effects are linear or nonlinear. If the effects are nonlinear, a case can be made that when major programs are implemented on a universal level, such as the assistance to schools that educate poor students pursuant to Title I, funds should be distributed in a nonlinear manner as well. However, if the effects are related (for example) in a linear manner to the rate of child poverty in the neighborhood, then any disproportionate distribution of those funds might be less effective than a proportionate distribution would be. More basic research is thus likely to continue to pay policy dividends well into the future.

## CONCLUSION

Perhaps we should conclude by pointing out one traditional type of urban policy we did *not* mention in our experimentation recommendations. Specially targeted federal assistance for urban economic development is *not* on our list of priorities. To the extent that such activities promote political patronage and other objectives unrelated to antipoverty or child development goals, we believe that federal efforts should be designed to do the least harm

(Bartik 1994). The case for massive "neighborhood" economic development policy remains unmade.

On the other hand, we would be remiss if we did not observe that research outside this volume already makes a compelling case to support policy reform. It is now apparent that full-year, full-time work will not by itself ensure that parents with little education or experience will be able to lift their children out of poverty (Jencks and Edin 1993) or that such initiatives will result in enhanced child development (Aber, Brooks-Gunn, and Maynard 1995; Wilson, Ellwood, and Brooks-Gunn 1995; Zaslow et al. 1995). The expected earnings trajectories for undereducated single parents are so low that longer-term income support is necessary if many families with children are to escape poverty (Burtless 1994; Danziger and Lehman 1996). The expansion and extension of the Earned Income Tax Credit (EITC) is helpful; it may be sufficient for two-parent families when both can work and parent as a team. But for single parents the EITC is not enough. Substitutes for the absent parent in the form of child care and child support are also needed. Child care may come from family members or via government subsidy to formal providers. Child support may come from absent fathers (formally or informally), government child-support assurances, or even refundable income tax credits. The point is that something *beyond* work and the EITC—a comprehensive income-support package (Cherlin 1995; Garfinkel and McLanahan 1995; Rainwater 1993)—is necessary if we are going to turn work into a vehicle by which single parents have better choices for their children.

It is unfortunate that much of today's welfare reform rhetoric is more concerned with state governments' choices and opportunities than with poor children's choices and opportunities. We remain hopeful that in the end a compassionate concern for the vulnerable will lead to constructive income-support reform. Beyond the domain of income support, the research in this volume has not led us to abandon the sense of priorities we held before we were exposed to it. We would support carefully designed experimental efforts to give both adults and their children a better set of true life choices: residential mobility, an education, a job, and a sense of hope. And we would make "neighborhood" policy a secondary priority, except where required to promote a safe environment in which "people" policy and income-support policy reforms can operate.

It is perhaps predictable that a chapter discussing the federal policy implications of social science research concerned with the effects of poor neighborhoods on children should be cautious. Calls for experimentation, further evaluation, and still more research are de rigueur. But our conformity to that norm should not be read as in any way critical of the careful research discussed in this volume. If the dogs are standing mute, good researchers have to leave policy makers to make their own chorus of sounds. We can only hope the sounds will be ones we would like to hear.

---

This paper was originally prepared for the SSRC Committee for Research on the Urban Underclass, Working Group on Communities and Neighborhoods, Family Processes and Individual Development Conference, May 19–20, 1994, Baltimore, Maryland, and has been revised based on conference discussion and on comments received subsequently. The support of the Russell Sage Foundation and the Center for Advanced Study in the Behavioral Sciences is gratefully acknowledged. The authors would like to thank Esther Gray, Karin D'Agostino, and Leslie Lindzey for secretarial assistance and Michael McLeod, Susan Mayer, and Greg Duncan for helpful comments. We, however, assume all responsibility for errors of commission and omission.

## NOTES

1. Jencks and Mayer (1990) note that if peer-influence effects are linear, so that "good eggs" are equally beneficial for their neighbors wherever they are, and "bad apples" equally harmful, the argument for the social benefits of "deconcentrating" the bad apples is much more complicated than the argument is if the effects are nonlinear. Crane (1991a, 1991b) found such nonlinear "epidemic" effects in his analysis of dropping out and teenage childbearing using 1970 census data. His findings are consistent with the enthnographic account of teenage pregnancy in E. Anderson (1991). But Clark (1992) was unable to find such effects in her analysis of dropping out, using 1980 census data.

# 11

## Lessons Learned and Future Directions for Research on the Neighborhoods in Which Children Live

*Jeanne Brooks-Gunn, Greg J. Duncan, Tama Leventhal,*
*and J. Lawrence Aber*

I n this first volume of *Neighborhood Poverty*, our working group has attempted to provide a state-of-the-art quantitative assessment of whether, and in what ways, the neighborhood conditions in which children are raised influence their achievement, behavior, and mental health. Strengths of our approach in *Policy Implications in Studying Neighborhoods* include the use of longitudinal data and a consistent set of well-conceived census-based measures of the demographic composition of neighborhoods, as well as the recognition reflected in our analyses that the influence of context depends on a child's level of development. (Our second volume contains commentaries on conceptual, methodological, and theoretical approaches to assessing neighborhood effects using a variety of approaches. In essence, the second volume offers insights into the limitations of our approach and ideas on how the next generation of neighborhood studies might be conducted). In this summary chapter, we provide a brief overview of what we found, as well as thoughts about future directions for neighborhood-based research.

## THEORETICAL FRAMEWORK

In chapters 1 and 2, we outlined the theoretical framework employed in the two volumes of *Neighborhood Poverty*. The major theoretical ground broken in these volumes was the integration of urban sociological models of neighborhood and community influences and models of development in context. The former drew heavily from the social disorganization and sociostructural perspectives (Coleman 1988; Jencks and Mayer 1990; Sampson 1992; Sampson and Morenoff vol. 2; Shaw and McKay 1942), and the latter from ecological models of human development in context (Bronfenbrenner 1979b). Taken together, the integrated model provides a more holistic understanding of the process through which neighborhoods could influence development.

To review our framework, three types of processes—neighborhood and community, social and interpersonal, and individual—which affect individual outcomes, were considered (see figure 2.1). Our model of child development ordered these processes from the most distal (neighborhood) to the more proximal (individual). As suggested by several prominent sociologists, most notably Wilson (1991), these processes are all influenced by exogenous forces (for example, globalization, economic restructuring, migration, public policies). Noteworthy here is the inclusion of community processes in models of human development, as developmentalists typically focus on interpersonal and individual processes. In general, when community influences are investigated by developmentalists, schools rather than institutions such as social services and parental workplace or neighborhood conditions (for example, ethnic heterogeneity, male joblessness) are explored. The six studies analyses tried to move beyond the current paradigm to include community influences other than just school into a developmentally oriented framework. The dimensions of community context included were structure and composition, social organization, and cultural and symbolic processes, all of which have been identified in the sociological, economic, and anthropological literature as central to individual outcomes (see figure 2.2). Cultural and symbolic processes, however, were not examined in the census-based analyses but are explored in volume 2.

Also of importance is the inclusion of both direct and indirect effects of neighborhoods, as well as the other processes, on individual outcomes. Neighborhoods may directly affect child development vis-à-vis the presence of resources such as libraries and parks. Indirectly, neighborhoods may influence parenting behavior or may affect the self-system and motivational processes, all of which in turn have implications for children's development. The particular mechanisms through which neighborhoods exert their influence on children may vary as a function of the age of the individual. For example, neighborhoods may have more indirect effects on young children (see for example, chapter 5) and more direct effects on adolescents (see for example, chapter 8). Accordingly, the six studies analyses examined four developmental epochs—preschool (three to seven years old), school age (eight to ten years old), young adolescence (eleven to sixteen years old), and late adolescence (seventeen to twenty years old). Certainly, the analyses presented in this volume support our hypothesis regarding differential effects of neighborhoods over the life course. To fully examine this issue also required investigating multiple domains of development (cognitive/academic, social/ emotional), which differ with age as well. Again, we found that the neighborhood factors in the analyses that mattered most differed across the developmental outcomes (discussed in detail in the following section).

Finally, it is worthwhile to acknowledge that community effects may be bi-directional in that individuals may shape the character of the neighborhood. While we did not examine such effects, we considered four dimensions of development—person, process, context, and time—to broaden our understanding of how neighborhoods influence development (Bronfenbrenner 1979, 1989). Our neighborhood analyses by definition highlighted context, and also incorporated person characteristics (age/epoch, gender, race/ethnicity), and to some extent process (chapters 5 and 7).

## WHAT WE FOUND

Bearing caution in mind, we arrived at the following general conclusions. First, while neighborhood conditions were often significant predictors of children's development, the *size* of the estimated effects of neighborhood conditions was usually much smaller than the estimated effects of family-level conditions. For example, when available in the data, family-level measures such as family income and maternal schooling were almost always fairly powerful predictors of children's cognitive development; these measures and family structure were usually significant predictors of behavioral development as well. In contrast, both the size and statistical significance of coefficients on the neighborhood measures were usually smaller than those of family-level measures. Thus, it appears that families still should be viewed as the key agents in promoting positive development in children.

A second result surprised us: Neighborhood conditions were often significant predictors of developmental outcomes around the time of transition to school. It is commonly assumed that the scope for neighborhood effects grows as children pass from early to middle childhood, and from middle childhood to adolescence. Implicit in this view is the assumption that neighborhood influences are direct and that they depend on the amount of time children spend away from their parents and homes. Our theoretical discussion pointed to potentially important *indirect* effects of neighborhood contexts on young children—through daycare; the safety and stimulation of parks, playgrounds, and other neighborhood resources; the parenting practices of others observed outside the home; and the parenting practices within children's homes.

Parallel analyses of two data sets containing observations on children aged three to six showed that the concentration of affluent families in a child's neighborhood was a significant predictor of cognitive development, perhaps because of the greater resources and opportunities for enrichment associated with affluent neighbors. There was also some evidence that the extent of male joblessness in the neighborhood exacerbated problem behavior of African American children.

Our data sets across childhood development showed the most powerful neighborhood effects in the early childhood years and in the late adolescence years. Less powerful effects were found in between. Since we had expected that neighborhood effects would grow with age, this result puzzles us. We see two possible explanations, one methodological and one substantive. The methodological explanation would be that the data sets covering the middle-childhood and early adolescent years were the ones with restricted geographical ranges and for which the detection of neighborhood effects would be more difficult. In other words, our data sets may not have been up to the task of detecting the neighborhood effects in the middle-childhood ranges. The substantive explanation would be that the effect of the neighborhood environments really is less important than that of other environments—family and, in this case, schools. Only new research with better designs to evaluate neighborhood effects across different developmental epochs can resolve this uncertainty.

Living in areas with greater concentrations of middle-class neighbors was associated with greater achievement for adolescents, as it was with enhanced cognitive development and early achievement among young children. Our theories point to a number of possible causes, ranging from the resources and neighborhood services that affluent neighbors bring with them, to the kinds of role models and direct labor-market connections they might provide. For African American males, but none of the other groups, we found interesting threshold effects and interactions. The benefits of middle-class neighbors for African American males came only when there were substantial numbers of such neighbors and, it appears, when the middle-class neighbors were themselves African American.

## LIMITATIONS

The volume's empirical approach to assessing neighborhood effects is a simple one that relates, by using multiple regression techniques, child outcomes to neighborhood and family conditions. Our methodological chapter sheds light on how such an approach could either overstate or understate the "true" causal role played by neighborhood conditions.

Our primary worries are three. First, our neighborhood-based measures of demographic composition are only tenuously linked to the theoretical processes by which neighborhood conditions affect children. This may lead us to understate true neighborhood effects. Second, the geographic range from which some of our samples are drawn is quite restricted. This, too, will probably lead us to understate true neighborhood effects and prevent us from identifying the neighborhood dimensions that matter the most. And third, our estimates fail to adjust fully for the process by which parents choose (or are constrained to live in) the neighborhoods in which they live. If important but unmeasured factors such as maternal depression or parental concern for children's development affect both choice of neighborhood and children's development, then their omission from our analyses will probably lead us to overstate neighborhood effects.

Given these concerns, we must be cautious about drawing firm conclusions regarding the size and nature of neighborhood effects. In the instance where our analyses are based on geographically dispersed samples, our approach can perhaps be regarded as providing a set of upper-bound estimates on the importance of the *demographic composition* of the neighborhoods in which children are raised. Restricted as it is to census-based measures, our approach can say little about the influence of neighborhood conditions that are not highly correlated with our demographic measures. On the positive side, our approach appears to be particularly useful in suggesting what compositional measures do *not* seem to matter. For example, much has been written on the detrimental effects of large numbers of jobless men in a neighborhood. The extent of male joblessness is measured well by the census, but it often fails to be a significant predictor of children's achievement-related outcomes. This suggests that any theory should concentrate on other dimensions of neighborhood conditions when child achievement is the focus. At the same time, male joblessness seems to be associated with behavioral outcomes, at least at some particular ages. If replicated, such findings should lead to more hypothesis generating and empirical testing of the possible mechanisms that might account for such specific associations between neighborhood composition and developmental outcomes.

## PROMISING AVENUES FOR FUTURE RESEARCH

As is generally true for empirical work like ours, our efforts were bounded by limitations in theory and data. In what directions, both theoretical and empirical, should future research on neighborhood effects move?

Our first recommendation is to go beyond the measures gathered in the decennial census. Although they provide an exceedingly rich and well-measured characterization of the sociodemographic characteristics of children's neighborhoods, the census-based measures bore weak relations to the theoretical concepts of interest. For example, nowhere in the decennial census are there questions about (1) the "social capital" that binds neighbors together and helps parents keep track of their children, (2) public services such as police protection, (3) key characteristics of the peer groups available to children in the neighborhood, or (4) other key neighborhood compositional factors such as the level of violence and substance abuse in the neighborhood. In our second volume, three of these possible pathways and neighborhood characteristics are discussed in detail. In chapter 1 Sampson and Morenoff argue persuasively for the conceptual importance of a neighborhood's social capital. And the analysis presented by Darling and Steinberg in chapter 6, which is based on a sample-generated, rather than census-generated, set of contextual measures, illustrates the empirical importance of direct measures of the characteristics of peer networks. Leventhal, Brooks-Gunn, and Kamerman in chapter 11 address issues of public resource variation by neighborhood. New research investigates the effects of neighborhood violence and drugs (Aber, Brown, Chaudry, Jones, and Samples 1996) and the effects of collective efficacy in communities (Sampson et al. forthcoming).

Our second recommendation is to focus future studies on the dimensions of family and developmental processes that might explain why neighborhood conditions affect children as they do. Our two data sets on young children offered the best such data and showed that the home learning environment played a mediating role. Other theoretically driven measures of process—for example, parental supervision or monitoring, family organization, consistency in routines, parental self-efficacy—were not available in our data sets, preventing us from estimating the mediated models needed to provide a convincing explanation of how neighborhood effects work. And other mediating developmental processes are just beginning to be explored (Aber, Brown and Jones 1995; Aber, Brown et al. 1996; Connell, Spencer, and Aber 1994).

A third recommendation is to use housing demonstrations as a control for the assignment of families to neighborhoods. Unmeasured characteristics of families associated with the process by which families are sorted into neighborhoods may impart a bias, probably downward, to our estimates of neighborhood effects. Using demonstrations circumvents this problem.

Although the ethical problems of randomly assigning families to neighborhoods may appear insurmountable, there are in fact experiments or quasi experiments that provide something close to random assignment. For example, in the Gautreaux housing relocation project, nearly four thousand families were involved in a court-ordered subsidized program that arranged for private housing, much of it in Chicago suburbs, but some of it in the city of Chicago itself (see chapter 1). Research based on these data show an impressive series of differences, both in the employment outcomes for adults and in developmental outcomes for their children, for the families assigned to the suburban locations (Rosenbaum and Popkin 1991). Specifically, among families who moved to the suburbs, mothers were more likely to be employed than mothers in families who stayed in the central city. Further, of those who had never been employed, mothers who moved to the suburbs were more likely than those who stayed to be employed. However, there were no differences between those who moved to the suburbs and those who stayed in the city in wages earned or families living in poverty (Rosenbaum and Popkin 1991). When looking at child outcomes, youth who moved to the suburbs were more likely to graduate from high school, take college-preparatory courses, attend college, and enter the workforce than youth from comparable families who stayed in the central city (Rosenbaum, Rubinowitz, and Kulieke 1986).

A study of moving to cluster-based low-income housing in middle-class neighborhoods in Yonkers from public housing in poor Yonkers communities is under way as well. Early analyses suggest that adolescents' social networks are changed dramatically by the move to middle-class neighborhoods, even though the youth, by and large, are still attending the same schools that they did before the move (Briggs 1996).

Even more ambitious is Moving to Opportunity, a five-city relocation project recently launched by the Department of Housing and Urban Development, based on true randomized assignment. At least two thousand families are being assigned to one of three groups—those staying in public housing, those receiving Section 8 vouchers for relocation to private housing within the city, and those receiving vouchers (and help in finding housing) for moving to communities where 10 percent or fewer of the residents are poor. A primary question is whether or not children and youth will exhibit greater school engagement, higher achievement scores, and decreased school dropout in the affluent neighborhoods (movers to middle-class neighborhoods) than in the poor neighborhoods (stayers). Likewise, it is possible to look at potential mechanisms through which such effects, if found, will operate. For example, do mothers in the mover families exhibit different parenting practices and behaviors than mothers in the stayer families? If our findings from the non-experimental studies reported in this volume reflect causal processes, then we might expect differences to emerge in provision of stimulating experiences in the home and possibly organization of daily activities and planning for future activities. Such differences, in part, may account for the (expected) differences in school achievement. At the same time, if the behavior-problem findings from the work reported in the volume hold true, then the children moving to the affluent communities may not exhibit lower rates of behavior problems, since, in general, the receiving communities have primarily white residents (and our findings indicate that decreased behavior problems were seen only in black children moving to affluent neighborhoods with black residents). Since the vast majority of the Moving to Opportunity families are black and Latino, then moves to affluent neighborhoods with few blacks or Latinos may not be beneficial for certain domains of child well-being.

## QUASI-EXPERIMENTAL STUDIES OF FAMILIES' RESIDENTIAL MOBILITY

Our fourth recommendation is to investigate neighborhoods' effects on child and family well-being is by examining residential mobility. In a recent study of African American, multigenerational families, we have looked at neighborhoods using the following tract distinctions: concentration of people, adult presence, racial similarity, employment, and neighborhood SES. Even though the sample did not have great variability in neighborhood conditions, we found a neighborhood effect for the economic and social capital resources (that is, high SES, employment [more employed and educated males], and adult presence) for young adult mothers, but not for teenage mothers vis-à-vis residential mobility patterns (Gordon et al. in press). The young adult mothers resided apart from the homes of their female kin when the kin lived in extremely impoverished neighborhoods. This analysis also highlights another point, which has to do with understanding the process through which neighborhoods influence children and families. In this case, neighborhood influences appear to be operating through moving. To date, most studies of neighborhood effects have not addressed how moving affects children's lives. Although not necessarily an experimental variable, residential mobility is a powerful means of investigating the effects of neighborhoods on children's development (and selection in terms of what factors are associated with families moving—choice of neighborhood residence) and remains a promising avenue for future research on neighborhoods.

## DIRECT MEASUREMENT OF NEIGHBORHOOD CONDITIONS

Our fifth recommendation is that multilevel designs be developed that provide direct measures of the important conceptual dimensions of neighborhood conditions and processes, as well as family-level mediators. This goal requires moving beyond the census-based measurement of the demographic conditions to a design in which questions about neighborhood context are included in the questionnaires administered to a clustered sample of children and their parents. The neighborhood-level measures would then be obtained by aggregating the responses of all of the individuals living in a given neighborhood cluster or aggregating a community survey (see Cook et al. vol. 2).

The benefit of such a strategy is that it provides precise measurement of many important neighborhood dimensions. The drawback, however, is that a given sample size provides far less variability across different kinds of neighborhood contexts than the alternative strategy, using unclustered samples and census-based measurement of neighborhood conditions. In future research designs, investigators need to pay careful attention to the trade-offs between the precision of measurement of neighborhood effects and the amount of variability across neighborhood contexts.

The ideal research design must also cope with the problem of bias resulting from the nonrandom assignment of families to neighborhood types. As is clear from the methodological discussion in chapter 9, the bias problem is caused by the omission of measures of parental characteristics that influence both choice of neighborhood and children's cognitive and behavioral development. Short of capitalizing on an experimental design, what is needed in future research designs is the explicit measurement of these typically unmeasured characteristics.

Our emphasis on measurement of neighborhood conditions from sources other than the decennial census should not be taken to indicate that developmental data matched through addresses to census-based data are without value. To the contrary, the availability, precision, and scope of census-based measures speak to their utility for neighborhood research, especially if they can be linked to developmental data with measures of family process and other conditions that either help to explain neighborhood effects or help to correct for the problem of nonrandom selection of families across neighborhood. There is much to be learned about neighborhood effects from studies that use census-based sources of data. At the same time, alternative procedures for measuring neighborhoods need to be nurtured. Some of the most promising alternative methodologies, discussed extensively in volume 2, are briefly mentioned here.

One approach is systematic social observation (Barnes-McGuire and Reiss 1993; Taylor, Gottfredson, and Brower 1984) or a windshield survey (Burton 1996; Spencer et al. vol. 2). This approach is not widely used and is still in its formative stages. Using a structured format, trained observers characterize neighborhoods. Usually, the block or street on which the residence is located is the target of the observation, although an adjacent street often is observed as well (see Spencer et al. vol. 2). Unlike the information ascertained from census-tract data, this method provides information on neighborhoods' physical features (such as lighting, traffic flow, housing disrepair, and commercial establishments) and social organizational features (such as types of people on the streets, and the presence of public behaviors such as drug use, prostitution, or drinking) (Earls and Barnes-McGuire 1994; Sampson et al. forthcoming).

Somewhat a variant of systematic social observation, another approach to measuring neighborhoods entails videotaping of neighborhoods. Neighborhood dimensions are then coded after the data collection. This technique is also amenable to studying organizational features of neighborhoods. Videotaping and coding are being employed in the Chicago Project on Human Development (Earls and Barnes-McGuire 1994), an ongoing study, based on an accelerated longitudinal design that is following seven age cohorts. The sample is stratified by neighborhood type, based on SES and ethnic density. Given the sophistication of the research design employed, psychometric and validity data for this technique should be informative.

Individuals' ratings are another strategy. Neighborhood residents are asked to provide information on their neighborhoods, yielding their perceptions of the neighborhoods. Particularly useful data ascertained from this approach include perceptions of safety (Furstenberg and Hughes vol. 2), neighborhood cohesion and hassles (Aber and Jones 1995; Seidman et al. 1995), and availability of community resources (Simcha-Fagan and Schwartz 1986), as information on crime and social services is not readily available from the census-tract data. Information on community attachment and social capital can also be ascertained (see Korbin and Coulton vol. 2; Simcha-Fagan and Schwartz 1986).

These ratings may come from three different sources. First, key informants who are not participating in the study may be asked to provide information. For example, in the Chicago Project on Human Development, approximately nine thousand residents have been randomly sampled from over eighty neighborhood clusters (approximately twenty to fifty per cluster) to ascertain ratings on neighborhood dimensions (Earls and Buka 1997). Second, leaders in the community may be interviewed for rating of community characteristics. This approach was used in the Chicago and Yonkers Projects (Crain personal communication). Finally, the last approach is participants' ratings of communities. Although, the most widely used approach, participants' ratings are the least desirable because the community ratings are confounded with outcome ratings.

In terms of future research designs, we advocate a multimethod approach to assessing neighborhoods. Of particular interest is how the different levels of information (individual perception, direct observation, census aggregation) are interrelated, as well as how the three levels are associated with family behavior and child development. Since neighborhood methodology is still in its infancy, methodological cross-validation is essential for progress. It is also possible that different types of assessment may differentially predict child development and family behavior, depending on the domain under investigation.

## IMPLICATIONS FOR USE OF CENSUS DATA

Chapter 10 is filled with thoughtful commentary on how our research results might translate into policies at the federal level. Here we offer supplementary comments, some of which are inspired by the revolutionary policy changes at the federal level passed in 1995 and 1996.

A first observation is based on the purely descriptive information presented in chapter 3. Building on the annual Census Bureau reports of the poverty status of black and white families, they provide a cross-tabulation of long-run poverty at the family level *and* at the neighborhood level. Stunning in their results are the much greater ethnic differences in socioeconomic status when neighborhood conditions are combined with family conditions. White children who are poor are dispersed across neighborhood types, with some living in very poor neighborhoods but many living in neighborhoods with moderate or even low levels of poverty (Brooks-Gunn and Duncan 1997).

The picture is very different for black children, both poor and nonpoor, for whom high-poverty neighborhoods are much more prevalent. A substantial majority of white children escape poverty at both the family and neighborhood levels, while very few black children do (chapter 3; Brooks-Gunn, Klebanov, and Duncan 1996). As large as the ethnic differences in economic well-being appear to be in Census Bureau data, the true gap, based on more comprehensive measurement of children's environments, is much larger.

Another observation concerns impending changes in federal statistical policy. Essential components of most of our studies of neighborhood effects were measures of neighborhood conditions gathered as part of the decennial census. Simple demographic information on the number and ages of a neighborhood's population come from the "short form" administered to all households on April 1 of every census year. Approximately one in six households fill out a more detailed "long form," which contains much more valuable economic information such as family income and poverty status and the employment and education status of household members. Despite the great value and relatively low marginal cost of obtaining the long-form information, it appears that some or even all of the long-form data may not be gathered in future censuses. It behooves us to educate legislators about the research value of these data. (On the other hand, the Census Bureau plans to develop a new annual community survey that would make it possible to examine yearly changes in community characteristics in large jurisdictions and fix running averages in smaller jurisdictions.)

## NEIGHBORHOOD CHARACTERISTICS AND CHILD OUTCOMES

We conclude by raising, once again, the issue of what neighborhood characteristics might be most relevant for child and adolescent outcomes. These characteristics might operate directly or indirectly, in the latter case through the family, peer, or school systems (or some combination of all three). Six characteristics are included in our somewhat abbreviated list: income, human capital, ethnic integration, social capital, social disorganization, and safety (Brooks-Gunn, Rauh, and Leventhal forthcoming). Some of these characteristics are better defined by census geocoding than are others.

### INCOME

Among developmentalists, neighborhood poverty is perhaps one of the most widely investigated dimensions of neighborhoods because residence in an impoverished neighborhood has implications for child-care settings, schools, and peer groups (Mayer and Jencks 1989; NICHD Child Care Study 1997; Phillips 1991). The research presented in this volume suggests that neighborhood SES is one of the most important neighborhood characteristics associated with child development (particularly IQ) and maternal behavior, such as parenting. Further, Wilson's (1987, 1991a, 1991b, 1996) seminal analysis of postindustrial structural changes suggests that increases in the number of poor and jobless people in inner-city neighborhoods is associated with behavioral manifestations (such as teen childbearing and crime) among these neighborhoods' residents.

Neighborhood income is typically assessed in terms of neighborhood poverty and neighborhood affluence using census-tract data. Neighborhoods with poverty rates of 40 percent or more (of the nonelderly population) are often termed ghetto neighborhoods (Jargowsky and Bane 1990; Wilson 1991a, 1991b). However, in this volume, this relatively extreme rate of poverty is not always used to define poor neighborhoods (see Brooks-Gunn, Duncan, et al. 1993). Research suggests that the concentrations of poor and affluent neighbors have differential effects on child and adolescent development. Research based on 1980 census data, the most recent data until the 1990 census data, has employed two indicators that incorporate the income distribution. Accordingly, "low income" has been designated as the fraction of families in the census tract with incomes under $10,000, and "affluence" has been designated as the fraction of families with incomes over $30,000 (chapter 3; Brooks-Gunn, Klebanov, and Duncan, 1996). These measures of neighborhood income were correlated with five neighborhood factors identified in this volume: Low SES, High SES, Male Joblessness, Ethnic Diversity, and Family Concentration. These neighborhood factors correspond with some of the constructs discussed here, indicating that neighborhood income is highly associated with other neighborhood characteristics. If limited variability in neighborhood conditions exists, a neighborhood risk composite, which consists of summing the first three factors identified, can be used (see chapter 3).

## HUMAN CAPITAL

*Human capital* is defined as skills, knowledge, and capabilities acquired by individuals. Through application of these abilities, human capital facilitates productive activity (Coleman 1987). Human capital can in turn build an economic base in neighborhoods, and the presence of individuals with human capital (that is, those who are educated or employed) in a community, may provide role models for children and youth.

At the neighborhood level, human capital is evaluated in terms of employment and education. Measures of human capital rely on census-tract data and include the percentage of high school graduates in a tract, the percentage of unemployed individuals in a tract, and the percentage of professionals in a tract. Neighborhood unemployment is typically broken down by age (that is, twenty-five years and younger) and gender, such that the percentage of young males unemployed and the percentage of females unemployed are considered independently; however, the percentage of unemployed young males is the most frequently used variable, as was seen in chapter 3's analyses.

## ETHNIC INTEGRATION

Ethnic integration involves the ethnic heterogeneity or homogeneity of a neighborhood. Various researchers (for example, Sampson 1992; Sampson and Morenoff vol. 2) have suggested that a high degree of ethnic heterogeneity has led in part to an erosion of neighborhood social networks. Others (for example, Wilson 1991a, 1991b) have argued that social isolation of blacks and Latinos in inner cities has contributed to urban poverty.

Accordingly, ethnic integration is usually assessed with census-tract measures of the percentage of different ethnic groups in the tract. Ethnic diversity did not emerge as a significant predictor in most of the analyses reported here. Using other outcomes and other procedures to define ethnic diversity within neighborhoods, some scholars, particularly ethnographers, have suggested that ethnic diversity within poor neighborhoods may not be beneficial for some outcomes (see Garcia Coll et al. 1997; Jarrett vol. 2; Korbin and Coulton vol. 2). One suggestive finding in chapter 4 is that African American children from ethnically diverse neighborhoods had lower verbal abilities than their peers in less ethnically diverse neighborhoods. Further, chapter 5 showed that families residing in ethnically integrated neighborhoods had home environments marked by lower cognitive stimulation, less maternal warmth, and lower levels of social support than children residing in more ethnically homogeneous neighborhoods.

A recent study funded by the MacArthur Foundation seeks to study ethnic integration more closely (MacArthur Foundation's Network on Successful Midlife). A two-site study (Chicago and New York) was undertaken as part of a national study on midlife development (Midlife Development Inventory; MIDI) to focus on ethnic and racial minorities, who would be underrepresented in the national investigation. In Chicago the ethnic groups examined were Mexican Americans and Puerto Ricans, and in New York the groups were African Americans, Dominican Americans, and Puerto Ricans. The sampling frame identified families in neighborhoods that varied in SES and ethnic density. SES was based on a median split for the ethnic group. Figures such as 10 percent to 20 percent designated low concentration of a particular ethnic group, and figures ranging from 50 percent to 70 percent designated high concentration. Preliminary analyses with respect to ethnic density suggest that among middle-aged adults, living in a high-density neighborhood is associated with poor physical health and is marginally associated with decreased psychological well-being (Hughes in preparation). This study promises to provide insight on how neighborhood ethnic integration is related to development (without being confounded with neighborhood SES).

In an ancillary study funded by the Foundation for Child Development, we are more intensively investigating the Chicago MIDMAC families with children. In this study, we are attempting to better understand the process by which urban poverty transmits its adverse effects to the developing child, especially among immigrant populations for whom traditional research instruments may not be appropriate. We are particularly interested in how families are connected to the communities in which they reside, how this "embeddedness" can be measured, and whether the degree of embeddedness moderates the impact of community conditions, such as ethnic integration, on family functioning.

Initial analyses examining parenting in the larger MIDMAC sample indicate that the percentage of whites in the tract is associated with ratings of parent-child relations and child outcomes more than either ethnic density or SES (Hughes, Chen-Cross, Leventhal, and Brooks-Gunn in preparation).

## SOCIAL CAPITAL

Coleman (1987) used the construct of social capital to describe the phenomenon that comes about through changes in the relationships among persons that facilitate action. Social capital exists in relations among persons (in communities) and can be conceptualized as the intersection of families and neighborhoods. Social capital includes several components: interpersonal ties and reciprocity, norms and sanctions, information, stability, opportunity, and quality of life.

Since social capital is not economic or tangible, it is assessed primarily through interviews and systematic social observation rather than census-tract characteristics. Interview questions consist of having members rate their participation in various community activities (involving blocks, churches, schools, clubs, and so on) in order to assess social cohesion and social networks (Furstenberg and Hughes vol. 2; Korbin and Coulton vol. 2; Seidman et al. 1995; Simcha-Fagan and Schwartz 1986). Residents are also asked about informal networks with neighbors, as with sharing information about schools, asking for advice, having parties, or monitoring neighbors' homes (Simcha-Fagan and Schwartz 1986). Clearly, these networks are the crux of social capital and tap the different dimensions just listed (Coleman 1988; Granovetter 1985). In order to assess norms and sanctions, participants are sometimes asked to rate (on a Likert-type scale) how likely it is that they would intervene in various circumstances, as when a child is holding a gun, a child is left home alone during the evening, or someone is selling drugs in plain sight (see Korbin and Coulton vol. 2). Norms and sanctions can also be evaluated via systematic social observation. For example, the observer records whether or not children are supervised, whether people are selling drugs, and so on. Observation of information channels involves noting visible signs, notices, postings about local programs, and announcements of community meetings or events (Barnes-McGuire and Reiss 1993). Participants can also rate the quality and cohesion of their neighborhood. For example, "My neighborhood is a good place to live/raise children" (Seidman et al. 1995; Simcha-Fagan and Schwartz 1986). Alternatively, observers can evaluate the physical environment in order to assess quality of life (Barnes-McGuire and Reiss 1993; Burton 1996; Spencer et al. vol. 2). Stability can be measured by assessing census-tract data on residential mobility (as in the research reported in this volume) and by asking participants whether or not they consider their current neighborhood their "true home" (Simcha-Fagan and Schwartz 1986) or how they perceive the number of renters in the neighborhood and the number of people moving in and out of the neighborhood (see Korbin and Coulton vol. 2). Opportunity might be measured in terms of human capital as previously discussed.

## SOCIAL DISORGANIZATION

Social disorganization entails the disruption of local community social organization, usually characterized by rates of crime, delinquency, and deviant behaviors (Kornhauser 1978; Sampson and Groves 1989; Shaw and McKay 1942, 1969). According to this view, the degree of social organization in a community reflects the establishment of social relationships in the community and the content and consensus of values (see Sampson and Morenoff vol. 2).

Social disorganization has been assessed through multiple methods. Census-tract data on a number of community structural factors are used to evaluate social disorganization, including residential instability, family concentration (crowded housing), and ethnic heterogeneity (Sampson and Morenoff vol. 2; Shaw and McKay 1942). Interview data and systematic social observation provide information on community processes associated with social disorganization. Specifically, systematic observation entails having observers rate housing density, the condition of available housing, the amount of trash accumulation, the number of vacant lots and buildings, the number of businesses present, as well as the amount of prostitution, public drinking and drug use, and public arguing and shouting that occurs (Barnes-McGuire and Reiss 1993; Burton 1996; Spencer et al. vol. 2). Participants may also be asked to rate the presence of activities and attributes such as fights, murders, burglary, gang activity, loitering, trash throwing, drug use, and residential mobility (Korbin and Coulton vol. 2; Simcha-Fagan and Schwartz 1986).

## SAFETY

Safety entails the degree to which individuals feel physically threatened in their community. Researchers have argued that residing in a dangerous neighborhood has implications for parenting and family management (Furstenberg and Hughes vol. 2; Garbarino and Sherman 1980).

The most common means of assessing safety is via participant ratings. Residents are asked to indicate how worried they are about events such as being mugged, being robbed (see Korbin and Coulton vol. 2). Participants can also rate the magnitude of these problems (see Furstenberg and Hughes vol. 2). These types of measures yield participants' perceptions of safety. Systematic social observation entails evaluating the lighting, police presence, neighborhood-watch signs, buildings with bars and barbed wire, traffic, and so on (Barnes-McGuire and Reiss 1993; Burton 1996; Spencer et al. vol. 2).

Table 11.1 presents a summary of the major methodological and conceptual approaches to assessing neighborhoods discussed in this section. As our review indicates, many of the neighborhood constructs are overlapping, tapping similar yet distinct neighborhood constructs (Furstenberg and Hughes vol. 2). We return to these issues in volume 2 of *Neighborhood Poverty: Policy Implications in Studying Neighborhoods*.

## CONCLUSION

In conclusion, we are encouraged by the results of *Context and Consequences for Children,* because they provide a first look at possible effects of neighborhood residence on children, as well as potential pathways through

*(Text continues on page 296.)*

TABLE 11.1  Summary of Conceptual and Methodological Approaches to Assessing Neighborhoods

| Neighborhood Constructs | Methodological Approach | Sample Measures | Source |
|---|---|---|---|
| Income | Census-tract data | Percent of families in tract w/income <$10,000; percent of families w/income >$30,000 (1979 dollars) | Duncan et al. 1994 |
| Human capital | Census-tract data | Percent of high school graduates; percent unemployed young males; percent professionals | Crane 1991; Duncan and Aber chapter 3; Wilson 1991a, 1991b |
| Ethnic integration | Census-tract data | Percent of minorities; percent of specific racial/ethnic group | Sampson 1992; Sampson and Morenoff vol. 2 |
| Social capital | Census-tract data | Concentration of poverty (40 percent or more); residential mobility | Jargowsky and Bane 1990; Sampson 1992; Sampson and Morenoff vol. 2; Wilson 1991a, 1991b |
| | Individual ratings | Participation in community activities and informal networks among neighbors; likelihood intervene in various situations; ratings of quality of neighborhood; ratings of stability of neighborhood; ratings of neighborhood cohesion | Furstenberg 1993; Korbin and Coulton vol. 2; Seidman et al. 1995; Simcha-Fagan and Schwartz 1986 |
| | Systematic social observation | Observation of behavior of children, youth, and adults; observation of information channels (for example, signs); observations of physical environment | Barnes-McGuire and Reiss 1993; Burton 1996; Spencer et al. vol. 2; Taylor et al. 1984 |

TABLE 11.1  *Continued*

| Neighborhood Constructs | Methodological Approach | Sample Measures | Source |
|---|---|---|---|
| Social disorganization | Census-tract data | Residential mobility; family concentration (crowded housing); ethnic heterogeneity | Sampson and Morenoff vol. 2; Shaw and McKay 1942 |
| | Individual ratings | Ratings of problems concerning condition of housing, trash accumulation, prostitution, public drinking and drug use, vacant lots and buildings, public arguing and fighting, presence of businesses, residential mobility | Korbin and Coulton vol. 2; Simcha-Fagan and Schwartz 1986 |
| | Systematic social observation | Observations of housing density, condition of housing, trash accumulation, prostitution, public drinking and drug use, vacant lots and buildings, public arguing and fighting, presence of businesses | Barnes-McGuire and Reiss 1993; Burton 1996; Spencer et al. vol. 2; Taylor et al. 1984 |
| Safety | Individual ratings | Ratings of how worried they are about events (for example, walking alone at night, being mugged); ratings of magnitude of problems (for example, murder, rape, robbery) | Furstenberg 1993; Furstenberg and Hughes vol. 2; Korbin and Coulton vol. 2 |
| | Systematic social observation | Observation of lighting, police presence, neighborhood-watch signs, buildings with bars and wire, traffic | Barnes-McGuire and Reiss 1993; Burton 1996; Spencer et al. vol. 2; Taylor et al. 1984 |

which neighborhood residence might have an impact. At the same time, we do not believe that these results in any way present definitive knowledge of neighborhood effects. In part, this is due to limitations of the measures of neighborhood used (that is, census-based tract-level characteristics). Also, because many of the data sets do not have particularly rich measures of family and peer processes, convincing demonstration of the ways in which neighborhood effects are mediated by families and peers could not be made. Perhaps it would be more accurate to say, however, that the process measures were not chosen because of their value for looking at neighborhood effects, rather than that the measures were not rich. Of particular interest, though, are the findings in chapters 4 and 5, which investigated neighborhood effects on child outcomes and potential mediating family process variables of neighborhood effects. These findings suggest that the quality of the home learning environment mediated some of the neighborhood effects on children's verbal ability and behavior problems (see chapters 4 and 5).

Perhaps the most striking finding is that the dimension of census-tract residence that matters the most, across these studies, is economic condition. As previously noted, neighborhood income is highly correlated with other neighborhood conditions, including single parenthood, receipt of public assistance, and high school completion. These issues are difficult to tease apart in the real world (as compared to the statistical world). Within the broad rubric of neighborhood SES, what matters is high SES, rather than low SES. Clearly, children growing up in affluent neighborhoods appear to do better than children in low-income neighborhoods. Consistent with theories of collective socialization as identified by Jencks and Mayer (1990), results of the six studies suggest that affluent neighbors impart benefits to children and their absence, rather than the presence of low-income neighbors, is associated with adverse effects for children. Hypothesized mechanisms of influence according to these theories include availability of resources, adult role models, and monitoring. Wilson (1991a, 1991b) has argued that the middle-class flight from inner-city neighborhoods has led to social isolation of African Americans and Latinos in concentrated areas of poverty and resultant negative outcomes for children and families. Thus, our findings on the importance of high-SES neighbors are consistent with this perspective.

It is also possible that the low-income effect could not be explored adequately in these data sets. We may see low-income neighborhood effects only for extremely poor neighborhoods—in keeping with Wilson's thesis. Perhaps we did not find a low-income effect because our low-SES neighborhood category includes more than the extremely poor neighborhoods where 40 percent or more of the residents are poor. Perhaps more fine-grained analyses that separate out near-poor, poor, and extremely poor neighborhoods would reveal an effect of extremely poor neighborhood residence. In addition, investigations of families' residential mobility (quasi-experimental and experimental studies) are another way to explore neighborhood-SES effects on child and family well-being.

Alternatively, with the exception of very poor neighborhoods, it may be that neighborhood affluence matters more than neighborhood low and middle SES, as was found in the two national data sets and the Infant Health and Development Program. There also is increasing evidence from several recent studies that neighborhood affluence has a positive effect on children's achievement throughout the school years (Ensminger et al. 1995; Entwisle et al. 1994; Kupersmidt et al. 1995). That is, middle-income neighborhoods and low-income neighborhoods (leaving aside the very low-income neighborhoods) may have similar effects on children—which is another way of interpreting our findings. It may be that affluent neighbors really do have more resources and characteristics conducive to child well-being than do middle-income or low-income neighborhoods.

In sum, the six studies' analyses presented in this volume are among the first systematic examinations of neighborhood effects on child and adolescent development. Our review of the findings clearly points to the importance of neighborhood affluence on child and adolescent outcomes. In this chapter, we reviewed some of the shortcomings of the six studies, as well as of the census-based measures employed, and suggested some alternative approaches to assessing neighborhood effects in terms of process, design, and methodological tools. Finally, we highlighted what neighborhood characteristics might be most relevant to children and youth and how best to assess these dimensions.

We hope this volume has heightened the interest in better understanding the processes through which neighborhoods affect children and families, and we hope it will influence the next generation of neighborhood studies.

---

We would like to thank the Foundation for Child Development for their support. We also would like to acknowledge the National Institute of Child Health and Human Development Research Network on Child and Family Well-Being and the National Institute of Health and Human Development Research Network on Middle Childhood.

# References

Aber, J. L. 1994. "Poverty, Violence and Child Development: Untangling Family and Community-Level Effects." In *Threats to Optimal Development: Integrating Biological, Psychological and Social Risk Factors*, vol. 27, edited by C. Nelson. Hillsdale, N.J.: Lawrence Erlbaum Associates.

Aber, J. L., L. Allen, E. Seidman, and S. M. Jones. 1996. "Pathways to Depression and Aggression in High-Risk, Urban Youth: The Role of Proximal Developmental Processes." *Development and Psychopathology.*

Aber, J. L., J. Brooks-Gunn, and R. Maynard. 1995. "Effects of Welfare Reform on Teenage Parents and Their Children." *The Future of Children: Critical Issues for Children and Youth* 5(2): 53–71.

Aber, J. L., J. Brown, N. Caudry, S. M. Jones, and F. Samples. 1996. "The Evaluation of the Resolving Conflict Creativity Program: An Overview." *American Journal of Preventative Medicine* S12(5): 82–90.

Aber, J. L., and S. M. Jones. 1995. "Neighborhood Influences on Adolescent Antisocial Behavior and Psychological Symptoms." Paper presented at the Biennial Meeting of the Society for Research in Child Development, Indianapolis, Ind. (March 30–April 2, 1995).

Aber, J. L., E. Seidman., L. Allen, C.. Mitchell, R. Garfinkel. 1995. "Poverty Related Risks and the Psychsocial Adaptation of Urban Youth: Testing Mediational Models." Unpublished manuscript.

Achenbach, T. M., and C. S. Edelbrock. 1981. *Behavioral Problems and Competencies Reported by Parents of Normal and Disturbed Children Aged Four to Sixteen*. Monographs of the Society for Research in Child Development, series 188, vol. 46, no. 1. Chicago: University of Chicago Press.

———. 1984. "Psychopathology of Childhood." *Annual Review of Psychology* 35: 227–56.

———. 1987. *Manual for the Youth Self-Report and Profile*. Burlington, Vt.: University of Vermont Department of Psychiatry.

Achenbach, T. M., C. S. Edelbrock, and C. T. Howell. 1987. "Empirically-Based Assessment of the Behavioral/Emotional Problems of Two- and Three-Year-Old Children." *Journal of Abnormal Psychology* 15(4): 629–50.

Achenbach, T. M., C. T. Howell, H. C. Quay, and C. K. Conners. 1991. *National Survey of Problems and Competencies among Four- to Sixteen-Year-Olds*. Monographs of the Society for Research in Child Development, series 225, vol. 56, no. 13. Chicago: University of Chicago Press.

Aikman, L. 1993. "Fighting Urban Poverty: Lessons from Local Intervention Programs." Memorandum prepared for SSRC Policy Conference on Persistent Urban Poverty, Washington, D.C. (November 9–10).

Ainsworth, M., M. C. Blehar, E. Waters, and S. Wall. 1978. *Patterns of Attachment: A Psychological Study of the Strange Situation*. Hillsdale, N.J.: Lawrence Erlbaum Associates.

Alexander, L. L., and D. R. Entwisle. 1989. *Achievement in the First Two Years of School: Patterns and Processes.* Monographs of the Society for Research in Child Development series 218, vol. 53, no. 2.

Allen, J., J. L. Aber, and B. Leadbeater. 1990. "Adolescent Behavior Problems: The Influence of Attachment and Autonomy." *Psychiatric Clinics of North America* 13(3): 455–67.

Allen, L., J. L. Aber, E. Seidman, J. Denner, and C. Mitchell. 1996. "Midlife Parenting in a Black and Latina Urban Sample: Effects of Adolescent Change across a School Transition." In *When Children Grow Up: Development and Diversity in Midlife Parenting,* edited by C. Ryff and M. Seltzer. Chicago: Chicago University Press.

Allen, L., Y. Bat-Chava, and E. Seidman. 1995. "Ethnic Identity in Neighborhood and School Context: Effects on Depression among African-American, Latino and European American Urban Adolescents." Unpublished manuscript.

Allen, L., J. Denner, H. Yoshifawa, E. Seidman, and J. L. Aber. 1996. "Acculturation and Depression among Black and Latina Urban Girls." In *Urban Girls,* edited by B. Leadbeater and N. Way. New Haven, Conn.: Yale University Press.

Allen J., B. Leadbeater, and J. L. Aber. 1994. "The Development of Problem Behavior Syndromes in At-Risk Adolescents." *Development and Psychopathology* 6(2): 323–42.

Anastasi, A. 1988. *Psychological Testing.* 6th ed. New York: Macmillan.

Anderson, D. 1994. "The Crime Funeral." *New York Times Magazine,* July 4.

Anderson, E. 1985. "The Social Context of Youth Employment Programs." In *Youth Employment and Training Programs: The Yedpa Years,* edited by C. Betsey, R. G. Hollister, and M. G. Papageorgiou. Washington, D.C.: National Academy Press.

———. 1990. *Street Wise: Race, Class, and Change in an Urban Community.* Chicago: University of Chicago Press.

———. 1991. "Neighborhood Effects on Teenage Pregnancy." In *The Urban Underclass,* edited by C. Jencks and P. Peterson. Washington, D.C.: Brookings Institution.

Astone, N. M., and S. S. McLanahan. 1991. "Family Structure, Parental Practices, and High School Completion." *American Sociological Review* 56: 309–20.

Auletta, K. 1982. *The Underclass.* New York: Vintage Press.

Baker, P. C., C. K. Keck, F. L. Mott, and S. V. Quinlan. 1993. *NLSY Child Handbook—Revised Edition: A Guide to the 1986–1990 National Longitudinal Survey of Youth Child Data.* Columbus, Ohio: Center for Human Resource Research, Ohio State University.

Baker, P. C., and F. L. Mott. 1989. *NLSY Child Handbook 1989: A Guide and Resource Document for the National Longitudinal Survey of Youth 1986 Child Data.* Columbus, Ohio: Center for Human Resources Research, Ohio State University.

Baltes, P. B., D. L. Featherman, and R. M. Lerner. 1990. *Life-Span Development and Behavior.* Hillsdale, N.J.: Lawrence Erlbaum Associates.

Bandura, A. 1971. "Vicarious and Self-Reinforcement Processes." In *The Nature of Reinforcement,* edited by R. Glaser. New York: Academic Press.

———. 1977. *Social Learning Theory.* New Jersey: Prentice-Hall.

Bane, M. J., and P. A. Jargowsky. 1988. "Urban Poverty Areas: Basic Questions Concerning Prevalence, Growth, and Dynamics." In *Concentrated Urban Poverty in America,* edited by M. G. H. McGeary and L. E. Lynn Jr. Washington, D.C.: National Academy Press.

Barnes-McGuire, J., and A. Reiss. 1993. *Systematic Social Observation Manual: Project on Human Behavior in Chicago Neighborhoods.* Report prepared for Foundation for Child Development. Mass.: Author.

Baron, R. M., and D. A. Kenny. 1986. "The Moderator-Mediator Variable Distinction in Social Psychological Research: Conceptual, Strategic, and Statistical Considerations." *Journal of Personality and Social Psychology* 51(6): 1173–82.

Baroody, A. J., K. E. Gannon, R. Berent, and H. P. Ginsburg. 1984. "The Development of Basic Formal Mathematics Abilities." *Acta Paedologica* 1(2): 133–150.

Bartik, T. 1994. *"What Should the Federal Government Be Doing about Urban Economic Development?"* Upjohn Institute Working Paper 94-25. Kalamazoo, Mich.: Upjohn Institute.

Baydar, N., and J. Brooks-Gunn. 1991. "Effects of Maternal Employment and Child-Care Arrangements in Infancy on Preschoolers' Cognitive and Behavioral Outcomes: Evidence from the Children of the NLSY." *Developmental Psychology* 27(6): 932–45.

Baydar, N., J. Brooks-Gunn, F. F. Furstenberg, Jr. 1993. "Early Warning Signs of Functional Illiteracy: Predictors in Childhood and Adolescence." *Child Development* 64(3): 815–29.

Benasich, A. A., J. Brooks-Gunn, D. Spiker, and G. Black. 1997. "Maternal Attitudes and Knowledge about Child Development." In *Helping Low Birth Weight, Premature Babies*, edited by R. T. Gross, D. Spiker, and W. C. Haynes. Palo Alto, Calif.: Stanford University Press

Berlin, L. J., J. Brooks-Gunn, D. Spiker, and M. J. Zaslow. 1995. "Examining Observational Measures of Emotional Support and Cognitive Stimulation in Black and White Mothers of Preschoolers." *Journal of Family Issues* 16(5): 664–86.

Blalock, H. 1984. "Contextual-Effects Models: Theoretical and Methodological Issues." *Annual Review of Sociology* 10: 353–72.

Bott, E. 1957. *Family and Social Network*. London: Havistock.

Bound, J., C. Brown, G. Duncan, and W. Rodgers. 1994. "Evidence on the Validity of Cross-sectional and Longitudinal Labor Market Data." *Journal of Labor Economics* 12(3): 345–68.

Bowman, H., and A. Viveros-Long. 1981. *Balancing Jobs and Family Life*. Philadelphia, Pa.: Temple University Press.

Boyce, T. 1983a. "The Family Routines Inventory: Development and Validation." *Social Science Medicine* 17(4): 201–11.

———. 1983b. "The Family Routines Inventory: Theoretical Origins." *Social Science Medicine* 17(4): 193–200.

Bradbury, K. L., K. E. Case, and C. R. Dunham. 1989. "Geographic Patterns of Mortgage Lending in Boston, 1982–1987." Unpublished manuscript.

Bradley, R. H., and B. M. Caldwell. 1980. "The Relation of the Home Environment, Cognitive Competence, and IQ among Males and Females." *Child Development* 51: 1140–48.

Bradley, R. H., B. M. Caldwell, S. L. Rock, C. T. Ramey, K. E. Barnard, C. Gray, M. A. Hammond, S. Mitchell, A. W. Gottfried, L. Sigel, and D. L. Johnson. 1989. "Home Environment and Cognitive Development in the First Three Years of Life: A Collaborative Study including Six Sites and Three Ethnic Groups in North America." *Developmental Psychology* 25: 217–35.

Bradley, R. H., D. J. Mundfrom, L. Whiteside, P. H. Casey, and K. Barrett. 1994. "A Factor Analytic Study of the Infant-Toddler and Early Childhood Versions of the HOME Inventory Administered to White, Black, and Hispanic American Parents of Children Born Preterm." *Child Development* 65: 880–88.

Bradley, R. H., L. Whiteside, D. J. Mundfrom, P. H. Casey, K. J. Kelleher, and S. K. Pope. 1994. "Early Indications of Resilience and Their Relation to Experiences in the Home Environments of Low Birthweight, Premature Children Living in Poverty." *Child Development* 65: 346–60.

Briggs, X. N. 1996. "Brown Kids in White Suburbs: Housing Mobility, Neighborhood Effects and the Social Capital of Poor Youth." Ph.D. diss. Teachers College, New York.

Brim, O. G., Jr., and J. Kagan. 1980. *Constancy and Change in Human Development.* Cambridge, Mass.: Harvard University Press.

Bronfenbrenner, U. 1979a. "Contexts of Child Rearing: Problems and Prospects." *American Psychologist* 34: 844–850.

———. 1979b. *The Ecology of Human Development: Experiments by Nature and Design.* Cambridge, Mass.: Harvard University Press.

———. 1986. "Ecology of the Family as a Context for Human Development." *Developmental Psychology* 22(6): 723–42.

———. 1988. "Interacting Systems in Human Development: Research Paradigms: Present and Future." In *Persons in Context: Developmental Processes,* edited by N. Bolger, A. Caspi, G. Downey, and M. Moorehouse. New York: Cambridge University Press.

———. 1989. "Ecological Systems Theory." In *Annals of Child Development—Six Theories of Child Development: Revised Formulations and Current Issues,* edited by R. Vasta. Greenwich, Conn.: JAI Press.

Bronfenbrenner, U., P. Moen, and J. Garbarino. 1984. "Child, Family and Community." In *Review of Child Development Research,* vol. 7, edited by R. Parke. Chicago: University of Chicago Press.

Brooks-Gunn, J. 1990. "Promoting Healthy Development in Young Children: What Educational Interventions Work?" In *Improving the Life Chances of Children at Risk,* edited by D. E. Rogers and E. Ginzberg. Boulder, Colo.: Westview Press.

———, 1995. "Children and Families in Communities: Risk and Intervention in the Bronfenbrenner Tradition". In *Examining Lives in Context: Perspective on the Ecology of Human Development,* edited by P. Moen, G. H. Elder, and K. Lusher. Washington D.C.: American Psychological Association Press.

———, 1996. "Big City Kids and Their Families: Intergeneration of Research and Practice." In *Children and Their Families in Big Cities,* edited by A. J. Kahn and S. B. Kammerman. New York: Cross-National Studies Program.

Brooks-Gunn, J., B. Brown, G. R. Duncan, and K. A. Moore. 1995. "Child Development in the Context of Family and Community Resources: An Agenda for National Data Collection." In *Integrating Federal Statistics on Children: Report of a Workshop,* National Research Council Institute of Medicine. Washington, D.C.: National Academy Press.

Brooks-Gunn, J., and P. L. Chase-Lansdale. 1991. "Children Having Children: Effects on the Family System." *Pediatric Annals* 20(9): 467–81.

———, 1995. "Adolescent Parenthood." In *Handbook of Parenting,* vol. 3, edited by M. Bornstein. Hillsdale, N.J.: Lawrence J. Erlbaum and Associates.

Brooks-Gunn, J., J. Denner, and P. K. Klebanov. 1995. "Families and Neighborhoods as Contexts for the Education." *Changing Populations, Changing Schools: Ninety-fourth Yearbook of the National Society for the Study of Education, Part II,* edited by E. Flaxman and A. H. Passow. Chicago Ill.: National Society for the Study of Education.

Brooks-Gunn, J., and G. R. Duncan. 1997. "Growing Up Poor: Consequences for Children and Youth." *Futures of Children.*

Brooks-Gunn, J., G. J. Duncan, P. K. Klebanov, and N. Sealand. 1993. "Do Neighborhoods Influence Child and Adolescent Development?" *American Journal of Sociology* 99(2): 353–95.

Brooks-Gunn, J., and F. F. Furstenberg, Jr. 1987. "Continuity and Change in the Context of Poverty: Adolescent Mothers and Their Children." *The Malleability of Children*, edited by J. J. Gallagher and C. T. Ramey. Baltimore: Brookes Publishing.

Brooks-Gunn, J., R. T. Gross, H. C. Kraemer, D. Spiker, and S. Shapiro. 1992. "Enhancing the Cognitive Outcomes of Low-Birth-Weight, Premature Infants: For Whom Is the Intervention Most Effective?" *Pediatrics* 89: 1209–15.

Brooks-Gunn, J., G. Guo, and F. F. Furstenberg Jr. 1993. "Who Drops Out of and Who Continues beyond High School? A Twenty-year Follow-up of Black Urban Youth." *Journal of Research on Adolescence* 3(3): 271–94.

Brooks-Gunn, J., P. K. Klebanov, and G. J. Duncan. 1996. "Ethnic Differences in Children's Intelligence Test Scores: Role of Economic Deprivation, Home Environment and Maternal Characteristics." *Child Development* 67: 396–408.

Brooks-Gunn, J., P. K. Klebanov, and F. Liaw. 1995a. "The Learning, Physical, and Emotional Environment of the Home in the Context of Poverty: The Infant Health and Development Program." *Children and Youth Services Review* 17(1-2): 251–76.

———. 1995b. "The Provision of Learning Experiences in the Context of Poverty: The Infant Health and Development Program." *Children and Youth Services Review* 17(2): 231–50.

Brooks-Gunn, J., P. K. Klebanov, F. Liaw, and G. J. Duncan. 1995. "Toward an Understanding of the Effects of Poverty upon Children." In *Children of Poverty: Research, Health Care, and Policy Issues,* edited by H. E. Fitzgerald, B. M. Lester, and B. Zuckerman. New York: Garland Press.

Brooks-Gunn, J., P. K. Klebanov, F. R. Liaw, and D. Spiker. 1993. "Enhancing the Development of Low-Birth-Weight, Premature Infants: Changes in Cognition and Behavior over the First Three Years." *Child Development* 64(3): 736–53.

Brooks-Gunn, J., C. McCarton, P. H. Casey, M. C. McCormick, C. R. Bauer, J. C. Bernbaum, J., Tyson, M. Swanson, F. C. Bennett, D. T. Scott, J. Tonascia, and C. L. Meinert. 1994. "Early Intervention in Low Birth Weight, Premature Infants: Results Through Age 5 Years from the Infant Health and Development Program." *Journal of the American Medical Association* 272(16): 1257–62.

Brooks-Gunn, J., and R. L. Paikoff. 1992. "Changes in Self Feelings during the Transition towards Adolescence." In *Childhood Social Development: Contemporary Perspectives,* edited by H. McGurk. East Sussex, England: Lawrence Erlbaum Associates.

———. 1993. " 'Sex Is a Gamble, Kissing Is a Game': Adolescent Sexuality, Contraception, and Pregnancy." *Promoting the Health of Adolescents: New Directions for the Twenty-first Century,* edited by S. G. Millstein, A. C. Petersen, and E. O. Nightingale. New York: Oxford University Press.

Brooks-Gunn, J., V. Rauh, and T. Leventhal. Forthcoming. "Equivalence and Conceptually-Anchored Research with Children of Color." In *Children of Color,* edited by H. E. Fitzgerald, B. M. Lester, and B. Zuckerman. New York: Garland Press.

Brooks-Gunn, J., and E. O. Reiter. 1990. "The Role of Pubertal Processes in the Early Adolescent Transition." *At the Threshold: The Developing Adolescent,* edited by S. Feldman and G. Elliott. Cambridge, Mass.: Harvard University Press.

Brown, B. B. 1990. "Peer Groups and Peer Cultures." *At the Threshold: The Developing Adolescent*, edited by S. Feldman and G. Elliott. Cambridge, Mass.: Harvard University Press.

Bryant, B. 1985. "The Neighborhood Walk: Sources of Support in Middle Childhood." *Monographs of the Society for Research on Child Development*, 50(3).

Bryk, A., and S. Raudenbush. 1989. "Methodology for Cross-Level Organizational Research." *Research in Organizational Behavior* 7: 233–73.

Bryk, A. S., and W. Raudenbush. 1992. *Hierarchical Linear Models: Applications and Data Analysis Methods*. Newbury Park, Calif.: Sage Publications.

Buckner, J. C. 1986. "The Development of an Instrument and Procedure to Assess the Cohesiveness of Neighborhoods." Ph.D. diss., University of Maryland, College Park.

———. 1988. "The Development of an Instrument to Measure Neighborhood Cohesion." *American Journal of Community Psychology* 16: 771–91.

Bursik, R. J., Jr. 1988. "Social Disorganization and Theories of Crime and Delinquency: Problems and Propects." *Criminology* 26: 519–52.

Burtless, G. 1994. *"The Employment Prospects of Welfare Recipients."* Paper prepared for Urban Institute Conference on Self-Sufficiency and the Low Wage Labor Market, Arlington, Va. (April 20, 1994).

Burtless, G., and L. Mishel. 1993. *"Recent Wage Trends: The implications for Low-Wage Workers."* Memorandum prepared for SSRC Policy Conference on Persistent Urban Poverty, Washington, D.C. (November 9–10, 1993).

Burton, L. 1991. "Caring for Children: Everyday Life in Two High-Risk Neighborhoods." *American Enterprise* (May/June): 34–37.

———. 1996. *Neighborhood Assessment of Community Characteristics*. Rev. ed. Harrisburg, Pa.: Author.

Burton, L. M., K. Allison, and D. A. Obeidallah. 1995. "Social Context and Adolescents: Perspectives on Development among Inner-City African-American Teens." In *Pathways through Adolescence: Individual Development in Relation to Context*, edited by L. Crockett and A. C. Crouter. Hillsdale, N.J.: Lawrence Erlbaum Associates.

Burton, L. M., D. A. Obeidallah, and K. Allison. Forthcoming. "Ethnographic Perspectives on Social Context and Adolescent Development among Inner-City African-American Teens." In *Ethnography and Human Development: Context and Meaning in Social Inquiry*, edited by D. Jessor, A. Colby, and R. Shweder. Chicago: University of Chicago Press.

Caldwell, B. M., and R. H. Bradley. 1984. *Home Observation for Measurement of the Environment*. Little Rock, Ark.: University of Arkansas Press.

Case, A. C., and L. F. Katz. 1991. "The Company You Keep: The Effects of Family and Neighborhood on Disadvantaged Youths." Working Paper 3705. Cambridge, Mass.: National Bureau of Economic Research.

Casper, L. M. 1996. "Who's Minding Our Preschoolers?" *Current Population Reports*, series p70, no. 53. Washington: U.S. Government Printing Office.

Cauce, A. M., R. D. Felner, and J. Primavera. 1982. "Social Support in High-Risk Adolescents: Structural Components and Adaptive Impact." *American Journal of Community Psychology* 10: 417–28.

Chase-Lansdale, P. L., and J. Brooks-Gunn, eds. 1995. *Escape from Poverty: What Makes a Difference for Children?* New York: Cambridge University Press.

Chase-Lansdale, P. L., J. Brooks-Gunn, and E. S. Zamsky. 1994. "Young African-American Multigenerational Families in Poverty: Quality of Mothering and Grandmothering." *Child Development* 65: 373–93.

Chase-Lansdale, P. L., and R. A. Gordon. 1996. "Economic Hardship and the Development of Five- and Six-Year-Olds: Neighborhood and Regional Perspectives." *Child Development* 67: 3338-67.

Chase-Lansdale, P. L., F. L. Mott, J. Brooks-Gunn, and D. Phillips. 1991. "Children of the NLSY: A Unique Research Opportunity." *Developmental Psychology* 27(6): 918–31.

Cherlin, A. J. 1995. "Child Care for Poor Children: Policy Issues." In *Escape from Poverty: What Makes a Difference for Poor Children?* edited by P. L. Chase-Lansdale and J. Brooks-Gunn. New York: Cambridge University Press.

Choldin, H. 1984. "Subcommunities: Neighborhoods and Suburbs in Ecological Perspective." In *Sociological Human Ecology*, edited by M. Micklin and H. Choldin. Boulder, Colo.: Westview.

Chow, J., and C. Coulton 1992. "Was There a Social Transformation of Urban Neighborhoods in the Eighties? A Decade of Changing Structure in Cleveland, Ohio." Center for Urban Poverty and Social Change, Case Western Reserve University, Cleveland, Ohio. Unpublished manuscript.

Cicchetti, D. 1989. "How Research on Child Maltreatment Has Informed the Study of Child Development: Perspectives from Developmental Psychopathology." *Child Maltreatment: Theory and Research on the Causes and Consequences of Child Abuse and Neglect*, edited by D. Cicchetti and V. Carlson. Cambridge: Cambridge University Press.

Cicchetti, D., and R. Rizley. 1981. "Developmental Perspectives on the Etiology, Intergenerational Transmission and Sequelae of Child Maltreatment." In *Developmental Perspectives on Child Maltreatment*, edited by R. Rizley and D. Cicchetti. San Francisco, Calif.: Jossey-Bass.

Clark, R. L. 1992. "Neighborhood Effects on Dropping Out of School Among Teenage Boys." Washington, D.C.: Urban Institute. Mimeographed.

Clark, R. M. 1983. *Family Life and School Improvement: Why Poor Black Children Succeed or Fail.* Chicago: University of Chicago Press.

Clasen, D. R., and B. B. Brown. 1985. "The Multidimensionality of Peer Pressure in Adolescence." *Journal of Youth and Adolescence* 14: 451–68.

Cohen, J. B., and R. S. Lazarus. 1977. *Social Support Questionnaire.* Berkeley: University of California.

Coleman, J. S. 1988. "Social Capital in the Creation of Human Capital." *American Journal of Sociology* 94: S95–S120.

———. 1990. *Foundations of Social Theory.* Cambridge, Mass.: Harvard University Press.

Coleman, J. S., and T. Hoffer. 1987. *Public and Private High Schools: The Impact of Communities.* New York: Basic Books.

Collins, W. A., ed. 1984. *Development during Middle Childhood: The Years from Six to Twelve.* Washington, D.C.: National Academy Press.

Collins, W. A., and M. Gunnar. 1990. "Social and Personality Development." *Annual Review of Psychology* 41: 387–416.

Collins, W. A., and G. Russell. 1991. "Mother–Child and Father–Child Relationships in Middle Childhood and Adolescence: A Developmental Analysis." *Developmental Review* 11: 99–136.

Conger, R. D., K. J. Conger, and G. Elder. 1997. "Family Economic Hardship and Adolescent Academic Performance: Mediating and Moderating Processes." In *Consequences of Growing Up Poor*, edited by G. J. Duncan and J. Brooks-Gunn. New York: Russell Sage Foundation.

Connell, J. P. 1990. "Context, Self, and Action: A Motivational Analysis of Self-system Processes across the Life Span." In *The Self in Transition: Infancy to Childhood*, edited by D. Cicchetti and M. Beeghly. Chicago: University of Chicago Press.

Connell, J. P., J. L. Aber, and G. Walker. 1995. "How Do Urban Communities Affect Youth? Using Social Services to Inform the Design and Evaluation of Comprehensive Community Initiatives." In *New Approaches to Evaluating Community Interventions*, edited by J. P. Connell, A. C. Kubish, L. Schorr, and C. Weiss. Washington, D.C.: The Aspen Institute.

———. 1996. "Using Social Sciences Research to Inform the Design and Evaluation of Comprehensive Community Initiatives for Children and Families: A Case Study from the Youth Field." In *Children and Their Families in Big Cities: Strategies for Service Reform*, edited by A. J. Kahn and S. B. Kamerman. New York: Cross-National Studies Program.

Connell, J. P., and W. Furman. 1984. "The Study of Transitions: Conceptual and Methodological Considerations. In *Continuity and Discontinuity in Development*, edited by R. Emde and R. Harmon. New York: Plenum Press.

Connell, J. P., B. L. Halpern-Felsher, E. Clifford, W. Crichlow, and P. Usinger. 1995. "Hanging in There: Contextual and Psychological Factors Contributing to Urban African-American Students' Engagement, Performance and Decision to Stay in School." *Journal of Research on Adolescence* 10: 41–63.

Connell, J. P., L. Pierson, and J. Wellborn. 1992. "Research/Assessment Package for Schools (Student, Teacher, and Parent Version 2)." Technical Report 100. Institute for Research and Reform in Education.

Connell, J. P., and R. Ryan. 1987. "Motivation and Development in the Social Context of School." *International Society for the Study of Behavioral Development Newsletter* 1–2.

Connell, J. P., M. B. Spencer, and J. L. Aber. 1994. "Educational Risk and Resilience in African American Youth: Context, Self, Action, and Outcomes in School." *Child Development* 65: 493–506.

Connell, J. P., and J. Wellborn. 1991. "Competence, Autonomy, and Relatedness: A Motivational Analysis of Self-system Processes." In *Minnesota Symposium on Child Development*, vol. 22, edited by M. Gunnar and A. Sroufe. Hillsdale, N.J.: Lawrence Erlbaum Associates.

Conte, V. A., and M. J. Salamon. 1982. "An Objective Approach to the Measurement and Use of Life Satisfaction." *Measurement and Evaluation in Guidance* 15: 194–200.

Corcoran, M., R. Gordon, D. Laren, and G. Solon. 1992. "The Association between Men's Economic Status and Their Family and Community Origins." *Journal of Human Resources* 27(4): 575–601.

Coulton, C. J. 1996. "Effects of Neighborhoods on Families and Children: Implications for Services." In *Children and Their Families in Big Cities: Strategies for Service Reform*, edited by A. J. Kahn and S. B. Kamerman. New York: Cross-National Studies Program, Columbia University School of Social Work.

Coulton, C. J., J. Korbin, M. Su, and J. Chow. 1995. "Community Level Factors and Child Maltreatment Rates." *Child Development* 66: 1262–76.

Coulton C. J., and S. Pandey. 1992. "Geographic Concentration of Poverty and Risk to Children in Urban Neighborhoods." *American Behavioral Scientist* 35(3): 238–57.

Coulton, C., S. Pandey, and J. Chow. 1990. "Concentration of Poverty and the Changing Ecology of Low-Income, Urban Neighborhoods: An Analysis of the Cleveland Area." *Social Work Research and Abstracts* 26: 5–16.

Crandall, V. C., W. Katkovsky, and V. J. Crandall. 1965. "Children's Beliefs in Their Own Control of Reinforcements in Intellectual-Academic Achievement Situations." *Child Development* 36: 91–109.

Crane, J. 1991a. "Effects of Neighborhoods on Dropping Out of School and Teenage Childbearing." In *The Urban Underclass*, edited by C. Jencks and P. Peterson. Washington, D.C.: Brookings Institution.

———. 1991b. "The Epidemic Theory of Ghettos and Neighborhood Effects on Dropping Out and Teenage Chilbearing." *American Journal of Sociology* 96(5): 1226–59.

Crichlow, W., and R. Vito. 1989. "Evaluation of Intervention Projects for At-Risk Students: Comparative Results of the Rochester Assessment Package for Schools Administered at Five At-Risk Project Schools." University of Rochester, Rochester, New York. Unpublished manuscript.

Crockett, L. J., and A. C. Petersen. 1993. "Adolescent Development: Health Risks and Opportunities for Health Promotion." In *Promoting the Health of Adolescents*, edited by S. G. Millstein, A. C. Petersen, and E. O. Nightingale. New York: Oxford University Press.

Csikszentmihalyi, M., R. Larson, and S. Prescott. 1977. "The Ecology of Adolescent Activity and Experience." *Journal of Youth and Adolescence* 6: 281–94.

Danziger, S. K., and S. Danziger, eds. 1995. [Special issue on child poverty and social policies] *Children and Youth Service Review* 17(1).

Danziger, S., and J. Lehman. 1996. "How Will Welfare Recipients Fare in the Labor Market?" *Challenge* (March–April): 30–35.

Darling, N., L. Steinberg, and M. Gringlas. 1993. "Community Integration and Value Consensus as Forces for Socialization: A Test of the Functional Community Hypothesis." Paper presented at the Society for Research on Child Development Biennial Meeting. New Orleans (March 1993).

Datcher, L. 1982. "Effects of Community and Family Background on Achievement." *Review of Economics and Statistics* 64(1): 32–41.

Diamond, P. 1994. *"The Emerging Realities for Addressing Urban Poverty and Decline in the United States."* Washington, D.C.: White House (July 26, 1994). Mimeographed.

Dodge, K. 1986. "A Social-Information Processing Model of Social Competence in Children." In *Minnesota Symposium on Child Psychology*, vol. 18, edited by M. Perlmutter. Hillsdale, N.J.: Lawrence Erlbaum Associates.

Dodge, K. S., and J. D. Coie. 1987. "Social-Information-Processing Factors in Reactive and Proactive Aggression in Children's Peer Groups." *Journal of Personality and Social Psychology* 53: 1146–58.

Dornbusch, S. M., L. P. Ritter, and L. Steinberg. 1991. "Community Influences on the Relation of Family Statuses to Adolescent School Performance: Differences between African Americans and Non-Hispanic Whites. *American Journal of Education* 38(4): 543–67.

Doucette-Gates, A., J. Brooks-Gunn, and P. L. Chase-Lansdale. Forthcoming. "Adolescent Research: The Role of Bias and Equivalence." In *Studying Minority Adolescence*, edited by V. McLoyd and L. Steinberg. Hillsdale, N.J.: Lawrence Erlbaum Associates.

Drillien, C. M. 1964. *The Growth and Development of the Prematurely Born Infant*. Edinburgh: Livingstone.

Duncan, G. J. 1994. "Families and Neighbors as Sources of Disadvantage in the Schooling Decisions of Black and White Adolescents." *American Journal of Education*, 103(1): 20–53.

Duncan, G. J., and J. Brooks-Gunn, eds. 1997. *Consequences of Growing Up Poor*. New York: Russell Sage Foundation.

Duncan, G. J., J. Brooks-Gunn, and P. Klebanov. 1994. "Economic Deprivation and Early Childhood Development." *Child Development* 65(2): 296–318.

Duncan, G. J., and S. D. Hoffman. 1991. "Teenage Underclass Behavior and Subsequent Poverty: Have the Rules Changed?" In *The Urban Underclass*, edited by C. Jencks and P. Peterson. Washington, D.C.: Brookings Institution.

Duncan, G., and W. Rodgers. 1991. "Has Children's Poverty Become More Persistent?" *American Sociological Review* 56: 538–50.

Dunn, H. G. 1986. "Sequelae of Low Birthweight: The Vancouver Study." *Clinics in Developmental Medicine* 95/96.

Dunn, J. 1983. "Sibling Relationships in Early Childhood." *Child Development* 54: 787–811.

Dunn, L. M., and L. M. Dunn. 1981. *Peabody Picture Vocabulary Test—Revised*. Circle Pines, Minn.: American Guidance Service.

Dunn, L. M., and F. C. Markwardt. 1970. *Peabody Individual Achievement Test Manual*. Circle Pines, Minn.: American Guidance Service.

Dunst, C. J., V. Jenkins, and C. M. Trivette. 1984. "The Family Support Scale: Reliability and Validity." *Journal of Individual Family and Community Wellness* 1(4): 45–52.

Earls, F. 1992. "A Commentary on Papers of the Working Group on the Social Ecology of Crime and Drugs." Paper presented at the Research Conference on the Urban Underclass, Ann Arbor, Mich. (June 1992).

Earls, F. S., and J. Barnes-McGuire. 1994. *Fourth Annual Progress Report: Developmental Epidemiology Research Unit, Judge Baker Children's Center*. Boston, Mass.: Harvard School of Public Health.

Earls, F. S., and S. L. Buka. 1997. "Project on Human Development in Chicago Neighborhoods." Report presented to the National Institute of Justice, no. 163495. Washington, D.C.: National Institute of Justice.

Eccles, J., and C. Midgley. 1990. "Changes in Academic Motivation and Self-perception during Early Adolescence." In *From Childhood to Adolescence: A Transition Period? Advances in Adolescent Development: An Annual Book Series*, vol. 2, edited by R. Montemayor, G. Adams, and T. Gullotta. Thousand Oaks, Calif.: Sage Publications.

Eccles, J. S., C. Midgley, A. Wigfield, C. M. Buchanan, D. Reuman, C. Flanagan, and D. MacIver. 1993. "The Impact of Stage–Environment Fit in Young Adolescents' Experiences in School and in Families." *American Psychologist* 48: 90–101.

Edin, K., and L. Lein. 1997. *Making Ends Meet*. New York: Russell Sage Foundation.

Elder, G. 1974. *Children of the Great Depression*. Chicago: University of Chicago Press.

Elliott, D. S., S. Menard, B. Rankin, A. Elliott, W. J. Wilson, and D. Huizinga. Forthcoming. *Overcoming Disadvantage: Successful Youth Development in High Risk Neighborhoods*. Chicago: University of Chicago Press.

Emde, R. N. 1980. "Emotional Availability: A Reciprocal Award System for Infants and Parents with Implications for the Prevention of Psychosocial Disorders." In *Parent–Infant Relationship*, edited by P. M. Taylor. New York: Grune and Stratton.

Ensminger, M. E., R. P. Lamkin, and N. Jacobson. 1996. "School Leaving: A Longitudinal Perspective Including Neighborhood Effects." *Child Development* 67: 2400–2416.

Entwisle, D. R., and K. L. Alexander. 1992. "Summer Setback: Race, Poverty, School Composition, and Mathematics Achievement in the First Two Years of School." *American Sociological Review* 57: 72–84.

———. 1993. "Entry into School: The Beginning School Transition and Educational Stratification in the U.S." *Annual Review of Sociology* 19: 401–23.

Entwisle, D. R., K. L. Alexander, and L. S. Olson. 1994. "The Gender Gap in Math: Possible Origins in Neighborhood Effects." *American Sociological Review* 59: 822–38.

Entwisle, D. R., and N. M. Astone. 1994. "Some Practical Guidelines for Measuring Youth's Race/Ethnicity and Socioeconomic Status." *Child Development* 65(6): 1521–40.

Entwisle, D. R., and L. A. Hayduk. 1982. *Early School: Cognitive and Affective Outcomes.* Baltimore, Md.: Johns Hopkins University Press.

Erikson, E. 1950. *Childhood and Society.* New York: Norton.

Esbensen, F., and D. Huizinga. 1990. "Community Structure and Drug Use: From a Social Disorganization Perspective." *Justice Quarterly* 7(4): 691–709.

Evans, W. N., W. E. Oates, and R. M. Schwab. 1992. "Measuring Peer Group Effects: A Study of Teenage Behavior." *Journal of Political Economy* 100: 966–91.

Fagan, J. 1993. "Crime, Drugs and Neighborhood Change: The Effects of Deindustrialization on Social Control in Inner Cities." Memorandum prepared for SSRC Policy Conference on Persistent Urban Poverty, Washington, D.C. (November 9–10, 1993).

Farley, R. 1997. *The New American Reality: Who We Are, How We Got Here, Where We Are Going.* New York: Russell Sage Foundation.

Feldman, S., and G. R. Elliott, eds. 1990. *At the Threshold: The Developing Adolescent.* Cambridge, Mass.: Harvard University Press.

Fine, M., and N. Zane. 1989. "Bein' Wrapped Too Tight: When Low-Income Women Drop Out of High School." In *Dropouts from School: Issues, Dilemmas, and Solutions,* edited by L. Weis, E. Farrar, and H. G. Petrie. Albany: State University of New York Press.

Fischer, C. S. 1977. *Networks and Places: Social Relations in the Urban Setting.* New York: Free Press.

———. 1982. *To Dwell among Friends: Personal Networks in Town and City.* Chicago: University of Chicago Press.

Fitzgerald, H. E., B. M. Lester, and B. Zuckerman, eds. 1995. *Children of Poverty: Research, Health, and Policy Issues.* New York: Garland Press.

Freeman, R. B. 1991a. "Employment and Earning of Disadvantaged Young Men in a Labor Shortage Economy." In *The Urban Underclass,* edited by C. Jencks and P. E. Peterson. Washington, D.C.: Brookings Institution.

———. 1991b. *"Crime and the Economic Position of Disadvantaged Youth."* Working Paper 4027. Cambridge, Mass.: National Bureau of Economic Research.

Freudenburg, W. 1986. "The Density of Acquaintanceship: An Overlooked Variable in Community Research?" *American Journal of Sociology* 92: 27–63.

Furstenberg, F. F. 1993. "How Families Manage Risk and Opportunity in Dangerous Neighborhoods." In *Sociology and the Public Agenda,* edited by W. J. Wilson. Newbury Park, Calif.: Sage Publications.

Furstenberg, F. F., Jr., J. Brooks-Gunn, and P. Morgan. 1987. *Adolescent Mothers in Later Life.* New York: Cambridge University Press.

Galster, G. C. 1986. "More than Skin Deep: The Effect of Housing Discrimination on the Extent and Pattern of Racial Residential Segregation in the United States." In *Housing*

*Discrimination and Federal Policy*, edited by J. M. Goering. Chapel Hill: University of North Carolina Press.

———. 1990a. "Racial Discrimination in Housing Markets during the 1980's: A Review of the Audit Evidence." *Journal of Planning Education and Research* 9: 165–75.

———. 1990b. "Racial Steering by Real Estate Agents: Mechanisms and Motives." *Review of Black Political Economy* 19: 39–63.

———. 1990c. "Racial Steering in Urban Housing Markets: A Review of the Audit Evidence." *Review of Black Political Economy* 18: 105–29.

Gans, H. J. 1961. "The Balanced Community: Homogeneity and Heterogeneity in Residential Areas." *Journal of the American Institute of Planners* 27: 176–84.

Garbarino, J. 1977. "The Human Ecology of Child Maltreatment: A Conceptual Model for Research." *Journal of Marriage and the Family* (November): 721–35.

Garbarino, J., and A. Crouter, 1978. "Defining the Community Context for Parent–Child Relations: The Correlates of Child Maltreatment." *Child Development* 49: 604–16.

Garbarino, J., and D. Sherman. 1980. "High-Risk Neighborhoods and High-Risk Families: The Human Ecology of Child Maltreatment." *Child Development* 51: 188–98.

Garcia Coll, C. G. Lamberty, R. Jenkins, H. P. MacAdoo, K. Crnic, B. H. Wasik, H. Garcia Vazquez. 1996. "An Integrative Model for the Study of Developmental Competencies in Minority Children." *Child Development* 67(5): 1891-1914.

Garfinkel, I., and S. McLanahan. 1995. "The Effects of Child Support on Child Well-being and Proposals for the Future." In *Escape from Poverty: What Makes a Difference for Poor Children?* edited by P. L. Chase-Lansdale and J. Brooks-Gunn. New York: Cambridge University Press.

Garmezy, N., and M. Rutter. 1983. *Stress, Coping and Development in Children*. Baltimore, Md.: Johns Hopkins University Press.

Garner, C. L., and S. W. Raudenbush. 1991. "Neighborhood Effects on Educational Attainment: A Multilevel Analysis." *Sociology of Education* 64: 251–62.

Gephart, M. A. 1989. "Neighborhoods and Communities in Concentrated Poverty." *Items* 43(4): 84–92.

Gilligan, C. 1993. *In a Different Voice: Psychological Theory of Women's Development*. Cambridge, Mass.: Harvard University Press.

Goldberg, D. P. 1972. *The Detection of Psychiatric Illness by Questionnaire*. London: Oxford University Press.

———. 1978. *Manual of the General Health Questionnaire*. Great Britain: NFER Publishing.

Gordon, R. A., P. L. Chase-Lansdale, J. L. Matjasko, and J. Brooks-Gunn. Forthcoming. "Young Mothers Living with Grandmothers and Living Apart: How Neighborhood and Household Contexts Relate to Multigenerational Coresidence in African-American Families." *Applied Developmental Science*.

Gottfried, A. W. 1984. *Home Environment and Early Cognitive Development*. New York: Academic Press.

Gottschalk, Peter. 1995. "Is the Correlation in Welfare Participation Across Generations Spurious?" Mimeo. Boston College, Chestnut Hill, Mass.

Graber, J. A., J. Brooks-Gunn, and A. C. Peterson, eds. 1996. *Transitions through Adolescence: Interpersonal Domains and Context*. Hillsdale, N.J.: Lawrence Erlbaum Associates.

Graber, J. A., and J. S. Dubas, eds. 1997. *New Directions for Child Development: Leaving Home*, vol. 71. San Francisco: Jossey-Bass.

Gramlich, E., D. Laren, and N. Sealand. 1992. "Moving into and out of Poor Urban Areas." *Journal of Policy Analysis and Management* 11: 273–87.

Granovetter, M. 1985. "Economic Action and Social Structure: The Problem of Embeddedness." *American Journal of Sociology* 91(3): 481–510.

Green, R. K., and M. J. White. 1994. "Measuring the Benefits of Homeowning: Effects on Children." Working Paper 93. Center for the Study of the Economy and the State, University of Chicago.

Greene, W. H. 1993. *Econometric Analysis*, 2d ed. New York: Macmillan.

Grunau, R. V. E. 1986. "Educational Achievement." In *Sequelae of Low Birthweight: The Vancouver Study*, edited by H. G. Dunn. Philadelphia, Pa.: Lippincott.

Gueron, J. 1994. "Employment and Training for Low Skill Workers: A Summary of The Evidence." Seminar presented at the Russell Sage Foundation, New York (May 6, 1994).

Gueron, J., and E. Pauly. 1991. *From Welfare to Work*. New York: Russell Sage Foundation.

Halpern, R. 1993. "Neighborhood-Based Services and Best Practice in the Inner City: A Memo in Two Parts." Memorandum prepared for SSRC Policy Conference on Persistent Urban Poverty, Washington, D.C. (November 9–10, 1993).

Halpern-Felsher, B. L. 1994. "Ethnic Differences in the Influence of Neighborhood and Family Poverty on Adolescents' School Support and Risk." Poster presented at the Fifth Biennial Meeting of the Society for Research on Adolescence, San Diego, Calif.

Halpern-Felsher, B. L., and J. P. Connell. 1995. "Sources of Diversity in African-American Children's Performance and Adjustment in Elementary School: The Roles of Context, Self, and Action." University of California, San Francisco. Unpublished manuscript.

Hare, B. R. 1977. "Racial and Socioeconomic Variations in Preadolescence Area Specific and General Self-esteem." *International Journal of Intercultural Relations* 1(3): 31–51.

Harris, D. 1995. "Exploring the Determinants of Adult Black Identity: Context and Process." *Social Forces* 74: 227–41.

Harter, S. 1983. "Competence as a Dimension of Self-evaluation: Toward a Comprehensive Model of Self-worth." In *The Development of the Self*, edited by R. Leahy. New York: Academic Press.

Harter, S., N. R. Whitesell, and P. S. Kowalski. 1992. "Individual Differences in the Effects of Educational Transitions on Young Adolescents' Perceptions of Competence and Motivational Orientation." *American Educational Research Journal* 29: 777–807.

Hartup, W. 1989. "Social Relationships and Their Developmental Significance." *American Psychologist* 44(2):120–26.

———. 1992. "Peer Relations in Early and Middle Childhood." *Handbook of Social Development: A Lifespan Perspective, Perspectives in Developmental Psychology*, edited by V. B. VanHasselt and M. Hersen. New York: Plenum Press.

Hauser, R. 1970. "Context and Consex: A Cautionary Tale." *American Journal of Sociology* 75: 645–64.

Hauser, R. H., B. Brown, and W. Prosser, eds. Forthcoming. *Indicators of Children's Well-Being*. New York: Russell Sage Foundation.

Haveman, R., and B. Wolfe. 1994. *Succeeding Generations: On the Effects of Investments in Children*. New York: Russell Sage Foundation.

Haveman, R., B. Wolfe, and J. Spaulding. 1991. "Childhood Events and Circumstances Influencing High School Completion." *Demography* 28(1): 133–57.

Havighurst, R. J. 1953. *Human Development and Education*. New York: McKay.

Hawley, A. 1950. *Human Ecology: A Theory of Community Structure*. New York: Ronald Press.

Hayes, C. D., J. L. Palmer, M. Zaslow, eds. 1990. *Who Cares for America's Children: Child Care Policy for the 1990's*. Washington, D.C.: National Academy Press.

Heath, S. B., and M. W. McLaughlin. 1991. "Community Organizations as Family: Endeavors that Engage and Support Adolescent Youth." *Phi Delta Kappan* 72(8): 623–27.

———. 1993. *Identity and Inner-City Youth: Beyond Ethnicity and Gender*. New York: Teachers College Press.

Hechinger, F. M. 1994. "Saving Youth from Violence." *Carnegie Quarterly* 39(1): 1–11.

Heckman, J. 1994. "Is Job Training Oversold?" *Public Interest* (Spring): 91–115.

Herman, J. F., J. A. Heins, and D. S. Cohen. 1987. "Children's Spatial Knowledge of Their Neighborhood Environment." *Journal of Applied Developmental Psychology* 8: 1–15.

Hill, M. S. 1992. *The Panel Study of Income Dynamics: A User's Guide*. Beverly Hills, Calif: Sage Publications.

Hirsch, P. M. 1975. "Organizational Effectiveness and the Institutional Environment." *Administrative Science Quarterly* 20: 327–44.

Hofferth, S. L., and D. Chaplin. 1994. *Child Care Quality versus Availability: Do We Have to Trade One for the Other?* Washington, D.C.: Urban Institute.

Hofferth, S. L., and D. A. Phillips. 1991. "Child Care Policy Research." *Journal of Social Issues* 47: 1–13.

Hogan, D., N. M. Astone, and E. M. Kitagawa. 1985. "Social and Environmental Factors Influencing Contraceptive Use among Black Adolescents." *Family Planning Perspectives* 17: 165–69.

Hogan, D. P., and E. M. Kitagawa. 1985. "The Impact of Social Status, Family Structure and Neighborhood on the Fertility of Black Adolescents." *American Journal of Sociology* 90(4): 825–55.

Hollister, R. G. 1993. "Social Policy Research through Major Data Gathering Projects: Four Contemporaneous Examples." Memorandum prepared for SSRC Policy Conference on Persistent Urban Poverty, Washington, D.C. (November 9–10).

Hoy, E. A., J. M. Bill, and D. H. Sykes. 1988. "Very Low Birthweight: A Long-Term Developmental Impairment?" *International Journal of Behavioral Development* 11: 37–67.

Hughes, D., L. Chen-Cross, T. Leventhal, and J. Brooks-Gunn. In Preparation. *MacArthur Foundation's Network on Successful Midlife (MIDMAC): Parenting Outcomes*. New York: McArthur Foundation.

Hunter, A. 1974. *Symbolic Communities: The Persistence and Change of Chicago's Local Communities*. Chicago: University of Chicago Press.

Huston, A. C., ed. 1991. *Children in Poverty: Child Development and Public Policy*. Cambridge, Mass.: Cambridge University Press.

Huston, A. C., C. Garcia-Coll, and V. C. McLoyd, eds. 1994. *Child Development* [Special issue on children and poverty] 65(2).

Hyman, D. 1985. *Community Systems and Human Services: An Ecological Approach to Policy, Planning, and Management.* Dubuque, Iowa: Kendall/Hunt.

Ianni, F. A. 1989. *The Search for Structure: A Report on American Youth Today.* New York: Free Press.

Infant Health and Development Program (IHDP) 1990. "Enhancing the Outcomes of Low Birthweight, Premature Infants: A Multisite Randomized Trial." *Journal of the American Medical Association* 263(22): 3035–42.

Institute of Medicine. 1985. *Preventing Low Birthweight.* Washington, D.C.: National Academy Press.

Jargowsky, P. A. 1994. "Ghetto Poverty among Blacks in the 1980's." *Journal of Policy Analysis and Management* 13(2): 288–310.

———. 1997. *Poverty and Place: Ghettos, Barrios, and the American City.* New York: Russell Sage Foundation.

Jargowsky, P. A., and M. J. Bane. 1990. "Ghetto Poverty: Basic Questions." In *Inner City Poverty in the United States*, edited by L. E. Lynn Jr. and M. G. H. McGeary. Washington, D.C.: National Academy Press.

———. 1991. "Ghetto Poverty in the United States, 1970–1980." In *The Urban Underclass*, edited by C. Jencks and P. Peterson. Washington, D.C.: Brookings Institution.

Jarrett, R. L. 1990. "A Comparative Examination of Socialization Patterns among Low-Income African-Americans, Chicano, Puerto Ricans, and Whites: A Review of the Ethnographic Literature." Loyola University of Chicago. Unpublished manuscript.

———. 1994. "Community Context, Intrafamilial Processes, and Social Mobility Outcomes: Ethnographic Contributions to the Study of African-American Families and Children in Poverty. In *Ethnicity and Diversity*, edited by G. E. Brookings and M. B. Spencer. Hillsdale, N.J.: Lawrence Erlbaum Associates.

———. 1995. "Growing Up Poor: The Family Experiences of Socially Mobile Youth in Low Income African-American Neighborhoods." *Journal of Adolescent Research* 10(1): 111–35.

Jencks, C. 1988. "Deadly Neighborhoods." *New Republic* 13: 23–32.

Jencks, C., and K. Edin. 1993. "Welfare." In *Rethinking Social Policy*, edited by C. Jencks. New York: Harper Collins.

Jencks, C., and S. E. Mayer. 1990. "The Social Consequences of Growing Up in a Poor Neighborhood." In *Inner-City Poverty in the United States*, edited by L. E. Lynn Jr. and M. G. H. McGeary. Washington, D.C.: National Academy Press.

Jencks, C. and P. E. Peterson, eds. 1991. *The Urban Underclass.* Washington, D.C.: The Brookings Institution.

Johnson, J. J. 1986. *Life Events as Stressors in Childhood and Adolescence.* Newbury Park, Calif.: Sage Publications.

Johnson, J. H., and S. M. McCutcheon. 1980. "Assessing Life Stress in Older Children and Adolescents: Preliminary Findings with the Life Events Checklist." In *Stress and Anxiety*, edited by I. G. Sarason and C. D. Spielberger. Washington, D.C.: Hemisphere.

Jones, S. M., J. L. Aber, L. Allen, and E. Seidman. 1996. "Pathways to Aggression and Depression in High-Risk Urban Youth: The Role of Proximal Developmental Processes." Paper presented at the sixth biennial meeting of the Society for Research in Adolescence. Boston, Mass. (March 7–10, 1996).

Kahn, A. J., and S. B. Kamerman, 1996. *Children and Their Families in Big Cities: Strategies for Service Reform.* New York: Cross-National Studies Program, Columbia University School of Social Work.

Kardiner, A., and L. Ovesey. 1951. *Mark of Oppression: Explorations in the Personality of the American Negro*. New York: Norton.

Kasarda, J. D. 1988. "Jobs, Migration, and Emerging Urban Mismatches." In *Urban Change and Poverty*, edited by M. G. McCeary and L. E. Lynn Jr. Washington D.C.: National Academy Press.

————. 1990a. "City Jobs and Residents on a Collision Course: The Urban Underclass Dilemma." *Economic Development Quarterly* 4: 313–19.

————. 1990b. "Urban Industrial Transition and the Underclass." *Annals of the American Academy of Political and Social Science* 501: 26–47.

Kaufman, J. E., and J. E. Rosenbaum. 1992. "The Education and Employment of Low-Income Black Youth in White Suburbs." *Educational Evaluation and Policy Analysis* 14(3): 229–40.

Keating, D. P. 1990. "Adolescent Thinking." In *At the Threshold*, edited by S. Feldman and G. Elliott. Cambridge, Mass.: Harvard University Press.

Kellam, S. G., M. E. Ensminger, J. Branch, C. H. Brown, and J. P. Fleming. 1980. "The Woodlawn Mental Health Longitudinal Community Epidemiological Project." In *Longitudinal Research in the United States*, edited by S. A. Mednick and M. Harway. Hingham, Mass.: Martinus Nijhoff Publishing.

Kirschenman, J., and K. M. Neckerman. 1991. "We'd Love to Hire Them, But . . .": The Meaning of Race for Employers." In *The Urban Underclass*, edited by C. Jencks and P. E. Peterson. Washington, D.C.: The Brookings Institution.

Klebanov, P. K., J. Brooks-Gunn, and G. J. Duncan. 1994. "Does Neighborhood and Family Poverty Affect Mothers' Parenting, Mental Health, and Social Support?" *Journal of Marriage and the Family* 56(2): 441–55.

Klebanov, P. K., J. Brooks-Gunn, and M. C. McCormick. 1994a. "Classroom Behavior of Very Low Birth Weight Elementary School Children." *Pediatrics* 94(5): 700–708.

————. 1994b. "School Achievement and Failure in Very Low Birth Weight Children." *Journal of Developmental and Behavioral Pediatrics* 15(4): 248–56.

Klein, N. 1988. "Children Who Were Very Low Birthweight: Cognitive Abilities and Classroom Behavior at Five Years of Age." *Journal of Special Education* 22(1): 41–54.

Klein, N., M. Hack, J. Gallagher, and A. A. Fanaroff. 1985. "Preschool Performance of Children with Normal Intelligence Who Were Very Low-Birth-Weight Infants." *Pediatrics* 75: 531–37.

Kopp, C. B. 1982. "Antecedents of Self-regulation: A Developmental Perspective." *Developmental Psychology* 18(2): 199–214.

Korenman, S., J. E. Miller, and J. E. Sjaastad. 1995. "Longterm Poverty and Child Development in the United States: Results from the NLSY." *Children and Youth Services Review* 17(1): 127–56.

Kornhauser, R. 1978. *Social Sources of Delinquency*. Chicago: University of Chicago Press.

Kupersmidt, J. B., P. C. Griesler, M. E. de Rosier, C. J. Patterson, and P. W. Davis. 1995. "Childhood Aggression and Peer Relations in the Context of Family and Neighborhood Factors." *Child Development* 66(2): 360–75.

Ladner, J. A. 1971. *Tomorrow's Tomorrow: The Black Woman*. New York: Doubleday.

Land, K., P. McCall, and Cohen, L. 1990. "Structural Covariates of Homicide Rates: Are There Any Invariances across Time and Space?" *American Journal of Sociology* 95: 922–63.

Laumann, E. O., J. Galaskiewicz, and P. V. Marsden. 1978. "Community Structure as Interorganizational Linkages." *Annual Review of Sociology* 4: 455–84.

Lavrakas, P. J. 1982. "Fear of Crime and Behavioral Restrictions in Urban and Suburban Neighborhoods." *Population and Environment* 5: 242–64.

Lehman, J. 1994. "Updating Urban Policy." *Confronting Poverty*, edited by S. Danziger, G. Sandefur, and D. Weinberg. Cambridge, Mass.: Harvard University Press.

Lehman, J., and S. Danziger. Forthcoming. "Turning Our Backs on the New Deal: The End of Welfare in 1996." In *Race, Poverty, and Domestic Policy*, edited by C. M. Henry. New Haven: Yale University Press.

Lehman, J., and R. Lento. 1992. "Law School Support for Community-Based Economic Development in Low-Income Urban Neighborhoods." *Journal of Urban and Contemporary Law* 42: 65–84.

Lerner, J. A., T. S. Inui, E. W. Trupin, and E. Douglas. 1985. "Preschool Behavior Can Predict Future Psychiatric Disorders." *Journal of the American Academy of Child Psychiatry* 24(1): 42–48.

Lerner, R. M. 1982. "Children and Adolescents as Producers of Their Own Development." *Developmental Review* 2: 342–70.

Leventhal, T., J. Brooks-Gunn, and S. Kammerman. 1997. "Communities as Place, Face, and Space: Provision of Services to the Poor, Urban Children and Their Families." In *Neighborhood Poverty*, vol. 2, edited by J. Brooks-Gunn, G. J. Duncan, and J. L. Aber. New York: Russell Sage Foundation.

Leventhal, T., J. A. Graber, and J. Brooks-Gunn. 1996. "The Adolescent Transition into Young Adulthood: When a Job Is Not Just a Job." Paper presented as part of the symposium "Youth and Employment: An Interdisciplinary Perspective" at the Biennial Meeting of the Society for Research on Adolescence, Boston, Mass., (March 6, 1996).

Liaw, F., and J. Brooks-Gunn. 1994. "Cumulative Familial Risks and Low-Birthweight Children's Cognitive and Behavioral Development." *Journal of Clinical Child Psychology* 23(4): 360–72.

Lillard, D. R. 1993. "Neighborhood Effects on Educational Attainment." Research Paper 93-5. Ithaca: New York State College of Human Ecology, Cornell University.

———. 1994. "Differences in Neighborhood Effects on the Educational Attainment of Men and Women." Research Paper 93-7, Ithaca: New York State College of Human Ecology, Cornell University.

Links, Paul S. 1983. "Community Surveys of the Prevalence of Childhood Psychiatric Disorders: A Review." *Child Development* 54: 531–48.

Logan, J., and H. Molotch. 1987. *Urban Fortunes: The Political Economy of Place*. Berkeley: University of California Press.

Lord, F. M., and M. R. Novick. 1968. *Statistical Theories of Mental Test Scores*. Reading, Mass.: Addison-Wesley.

Maccoby, E., and J. Martin. 1983. "Socialization in the Context of the Family: Parent–Child Interaction." *Handbook of Child Psychology, Vol. 4: Socialization, Personality, and Social Development*, edited by E. M. Hetherington. New York: Wiley.

MacLeod, J. 1987. *Ain't No Makin' It: Leveled Aspirations in a Low-Income Neighborhood*. Boulder, Colo.: Westview Press.

Magnusson, D., H. Stattin, and V. L. Allen. 1985. "Biological Maturation and Social Development: A Longitudinal Study of Some Adjustment Processes for Mid-adolescence to Adulthood." *Journal of Youth and Adolescence* 14: 267–283.

Manski, C. F. 1990. "Where We Are in the Evaluation of Federal Social Welfare Programs." *Focus* 12(4): 1–5.

Marans, S. R., and D. J. Cohen. 1994. "Children and Inner-City Violence: Strategies for Intervention." *Psychological Effects of War and Violence on Children*, edited by L. Leavitt and N. Fox. Mahwah, N. J.: Lawrence Erlbaum Associates.

Massey, D. S. 1990. "American Apartheid: Segregation and the Making of the Underclass." *American Journal of Sociology* 96: 329–58.

———. 1993. *American Apartheid: Segregation and the Making of the Underclass* Cambridge, Mass.: Harvard University Press.

Massey, D. S., and N. A. Denton. 1989. "Hypersegregation in U.S. Metropolitan Areas: Black and Hispanic Segregation along Five Dimensions." *Demography* 26: 373–391.

———. 1993. *American Apartheid.* Cambridge, Mass.: Harvard University Press.

Massey, D. S., and M. L. Eggers. 1990. "The Ecology of Inequality: Minorities and the Concentration of Poverty, 1970–1980." *American Journal of Sociology* 95(5): 1153–88.

Massey, D. S., A. B. Gross, and M. L. Eggers. 1991. "Segregation, the Concentration of Poverty, and the Life Chances of Individuals." *Social Science Research* 20(4): 397–420.

Massey, D., and S. Kahaiaupuni. 1993. "Public Housing and the Concentration of Poverty." *Social Science Quarterly* 74: 109–22.

Masten, A., J. Neeman, and S. Andenas. 1994. "Life Events and Adjustment in Adolescents: The Significance of Event Independence, Desirability, and Chronicity." *Journal of Research on Adolescence* 4(1):71–97.

Mayer, N. 1981. *Keys to the Growth of Neighborhood Development Organizations.* Washington, D.C.: Urban Institute.

Mayer, S. E., and C. Jencks. 1989. "Growing Up in Poor Neighborhoods: How Much Does It Matter?" *Science* 243: 1441–45.

Maynard, R. 1995. "Teenage Childbearing and Welfare Reform: Lessons from a Decade of Demonstration and Evaluation Research." *Children and Youth Services Review* 17(1/2): 309–32.

McCarton, C., J. Brooks-Gunn, and J. Tonascia. 1994. "The Cognitive, Behavioral and Health Status of Mainland Puerto Rican Children in the Infant Health and Development Program." In *Health and Development of Puerto Rican Mothers and Children in the Mainland,* edited by C. Garcia Coll and G. Lamberty. New York: Plenum.

McCarton, C., J. Brooks-Gunn, I. Wallace, C. Bauer, F. Bennett, J. Bernbaum, I. R. Broyles, P. Casey, J. McCormick, P. Scott, J. Tyson, J. Tonascia, and C. Meinert. 1997. "Results at Eight Years of Intervention for Low Birthweight Premature Infants: The Infant Health and Development Program." *Journal of the American Medical Association* 227(2): 126–32.

McCormick, M. C. 1985. "The Contribution of Low Birthweight to Infant Mortality and Childhood Morbidity." *New England Journal of Medicine* 312: 82–90.

———. 1989. "Long-term Follow-up of NICU Graduates." *Journal of the American Medical Association* 261: 1767–72.

McCormick, M. C., and J. Brooks-Gunn. 1989. "Health Care for Children and Adolescents." In *Handbook of Medical Sociology,* edited by H. Freeman and S. Levine. Englewood Cliffs, N.J.: Prentice Hall.

McCormick, M. C., J. Brooks-Gunn, T. Shorter, J. H. Holmes, and M. C. Heagarty. 1989. "Factors Associated with Maternal Rating of Infant Health in Central Harlem." *Developmental and Behavioral Pediatrics* 10(3): 139–44.

McCormick, M. C., J. Brooks-Gunn, T. Shorter, C. Y. Wallace, J. H. Holmes, and M. C. Heagarty. 1987. "The Planning of Pregnancy among Long-Income Women in Central Harlem." *American Journal of Obstetrics and Gynecology* 156(1): 145–49.

McCormick, M. C., J. Brooks-Gunn, K. Workman-Daniels, J. Turner, and G. Peckham. 1992. "The Health and Developmental Status of Very Low Birth Weight Children at School Age." *Journal of the American Medical Association* 267(16): 2204–8.

McCormick, M. C., S. L. Gortmacker, and A. M. Sobol. 1990. "Very Low Birth Weight Children: Behavior Problems and School Difficulty in a National Sample." *Journal of Pediatrics* 117(5): 687–93.

McLanahan, S. S., N. M. Astone, and N. F. Marks. 1991. "The Role of Mother-Only Families in Reproducing Poverty." In *Children in Poverty: Child Development and Public Policy*, edited by A. Huston. Cambridge: Cambridge University Press.

McLanahan, S. S., and K. Booth. 1989. "Single Mothers and Their Children: Problems, Reproduction, and Politics." *Journal of Marriage and the Family* 51(August): 557–80.

McLanahan, S., and G. D. Sandefur. 1994. *Growing Up with a Single Parent: What Hurts, What Helps*. Cambridge, Mass.: Harvard University Press.

McLoyd, V. C. 1990a. "The Impact of Economic Hardship on Black Families and Development." *Child Development* 61: 311–46.

———. 1990b. "Minority Children: Introduction to the Special Issue [on minority children]." *Child Development* 61: 263–66.

McLoyd, V., and L. Steinberg. Forthcoming. *Research on Minority Adolescents: Conceptual Methodological, and Theoretical Issues*. Hillsdale, N.J.: Lawrence Erlbaum Associates.

Merriwether–de Vries, C., L. M. Burton, and L. Eggeletion. 1996. "Early Parenting and Intergenerational Family Relationships within African-American Families." In *Transitions through Adolescence: Interpersonal Domains and Context*, edited by J. A. Graber, J. Brooks-Gunn, and A. C. Petersen. Mahwah, N.J.: Lawrence Erlbaum Associates.

Merry, S. 1981. *Urban Danger: Life in a Neighborhood of Strangers*. Philadelphia: Temple University Press.

Mischel, W., Y. Shoda, and P. Peake. 1988. "The Nature of Adolescent Competencies Predicted by Preschool Delay of Gratification." *Journal of Personality and Social Psychology* 54(4): 687–96.

Mischel, W., Y. Shoda, and M. Rodriguez. 1989. "Delay of Gratification in Children." *Science* 244: 933–38.

Moen, P., G. H. Elder, and K. Lusher, eds. 1995. *Examining Lives in Context: Perspective on the Ecology of Human Development*. Washington, D.C.: American Psychological Association Press.

Moos, R. H., R. C. Cronkite, A. G. Billings, and J. W. Finney, 1986. *Health and Daily Living Form Manual*. Palo Alto, Calif.: Veterans Administration and Stanford University Medical Centers.

Mosher, D. L., and M. Sirkin. 1984. "Measuring in a Macho Personality Constellation." *Journal of Research in Personality* 8: 150–64.

Moss, P., and C. Tilly. 1991. *Why Black Men Are Doing Worse in the Labor Market: A Review of Supply-Side and Demand-Side Explanations*. New York: Social Science Research Council.

———. 1995. "Skills and Race in Hiring: Quantitative Findings from Face to Face Interviews." *Eastern Economic Journal* 21: 357–74.

Nadelman, E. 1989. "Drug Prohibition in the U.S.: Costs, Consequences and Alternatives." *Science* 249(Sept. 1): 939–46.

Naparstek, A. 1993. "Rethinking Poverty through a Community-Building Approach: Policy Memorandum on Community Reinvestment." Memorandum prepared for SSRC Policy Conference on Persistent Urban Poverty, Washington, D.C. (November 9–10).

National Academy of Sciences (NAS). 1993. "Head Start: Final Report." Mimeographed.

National Commission on Children. 1991. *Beyond Rhetoric*. Washington, D.C.: National Commission on Children.

Neisser, U. 1986. *The School Achievement of Minority Children: New Perspectives*. Hillsdale, N.J.: Lawrence Erlbaum Associates.

Nettles, S., and J. Pleck. 1994. "Risk, Resilience and Development: The Multiple Ecologies of Black Adolescents in the United States." In *Stress, Risk, and Resilience in Children and Adolescents: Processes, Mechanisms, and Interventions*, edited by R. J. Haggerty, L. R. Sherrod, N. Garmezy, and M. Rutter. New York: Cambridge University Press.

Newman, K. 1996. "Working Poor: Low Wage Employment in the Lives of Harlem Youth." In *Transitions through Adolescence: Interpersonal Domains and Context*, edited by J. A. Graber, J. Brooks-Gunn, and A. Petersen. Hillsdale, N. J.: Lawrence Erlbaum Associates.

NICHD Child Care Research Network. 1997. Poverty and Patterns of Child Care. In *Consequences of Growing Up Poor*, edited by G. J. Duncan and J. Brooks-Gunn. New York: Russell Sage Foundation.

Nickel, R. E., C. B. Forrest, and F. N. Lamson. 1982. "School Performance of Children with Birth Weights of 1000 g or Less." *American Journal of Disease of Children* 136: 105–10.

O'Brien, R. M. 1990. "Estimating the Reliability of Aggregate-Level Variables Based on Individual-Level Characteristics." *Sociological Methods and Research* 18: 473–504.

O'Brien, R., K. Pittman, and M. Cahill. 1992. "Building Supportive Communities: Local Approaches to Enhancing Community Youth Services and Support." Baltimore, Md.: Center for Youth Development, International Youth Foundation.

Ogbu, J. U. 1985. "A Cultural Ecology of Competence among Inner-City Blacks." In *Beginnings: Social and Affective Development of Black Children*, edited by M. B. Spencer, G. K. Brookins, and W. R. Allen. Hillsdale, N.J.: Lawrence Erlbaum Associates.

———. 1991. "Minority Coping Responses and School Experience." *Journal of Psychohistory* 18(4): 433–56.

Orfield, G. 1993. "The Growth of Segregation in American Schools: Changing Patterns of Separation and Poverty since 1968." Harvard University. Mimeographed.

Osterman, P. 1991. "Welfare Participation in a Full Employment Economy: The Impact of Neighborhood." *Social Problems* 38(4): 475–91.

Parham, T. A., and J. E. Helms. 1981. "The Influence of Black Student's Racial Identity Attitudes on Preferences for Counselor's Race." *Journal of Counseling Psychology* 28: 250–57.

Patterson, C. J., J. B. Kupersmidt, and N. A. Vaden. 1990. "Income Level, Gender, Ethnicity, and Household Composition as Predictors of Children's School-Based Competence." *Child Development* 61: 485–94.

Peeples, F. and R. Loeber. 1994. "Do Individual Factors and Neighborhood Context Explain Ethnic Differences in Juvenile Delinquency?" *Journal of Quantitative Criminology* 10(2): 141–57.

Petersen, A. C., B. Compas, J. Brooks-Gunn, M. Stemmler, S. Ely, and K. Grant. 1993. "Depression in Adolescence." *American Psychologist* 48(2):155–68.

Peterson, J. L., and Zill N. 1986. "Marital Disruption, Parent-Child Relationships, and Behavior Problems in Children." *Journal of Marriage and the Family* 48: 295–307.

Phillips, D. 1991. "With a Little Help: Children in Poverty and Child Care." In *Children in Poverty: Child Development and Public Policy*, edited by A. Huston. New York: Cambridge University Press.

Phillips, D., and S. Hofferth. 1991. "Child Care Policy and Research." *Journal of Social Issues* 47(2):1–13.

Piaget, J. 1973. *The Child and Reality: Problems of Genetic Psychology.* New York: Grossman.

Popkin, S. J., J. E. Rosenbaum, and P. M. Meaden. 1993. "Labor Market Experiences of Low-Income Black Women in Middle-Class Suburbs: Evidence from a Survey of Gautreaux Program Participants." *Journal of Policy Analysis and Management* 12(3): 556–73.

Public/Private Ventures. 1995. *Community Ecology and Youth Resilience.* Philadelphia: Annie E. Casey Foundation.

Rainwater, L. 1995. "Sex, Families, Race, Poverty, and Welfare," *American Enterprise* 66: 33–34.

———. 1993. "The Social Wage in the Income Package of Working Parents." Luxembourg Income Study. Working Paper 89. Luxembourg: LIS.

Ramey, C. T., D. Bryant, J. J. Sparling, and B. H. Wasik. 1985. "Educational Interventions to Enhance Development." In *The At-Risk Infant: Psycho/Social/Medical Aspects*, edited by S. Harel and N. J. Anastasiow. Baltimore, Md.: Brooks Publishing.

Ramey, C. T., D. M. Bryant, B. H. Wasik, J. J. Sparling, K. H. Fendt, and L. M. LaVange. Forthcoming. "The Infant Health and Development Program for Low Birthweight, Premature Infants: Program Elements, Family Participation, and Child Intelligence." *Pediatrics.*

Reiss, A. J., Jr. 1986. "Why Are Communities Important in Understanding Crime?" In *Communities and Crime*, edited by A. J. Reiss Jr. and M. Tonry. Chicago: University of Chicago Press.

Ricketts, E. R., and R. Mincy. 1989. "The Growth of the Underclass: 1970–1980." Changing Domestic Priorities Discussion Paper, April 1989. Washington, D.C.: Urban Institute.

Ricketts, E. R., and I. V. Sawhill. 1988. "Defining and Measuring the Underclass." *Journal of Policy Analysis and Management* 7: 316–25.

Rosenbaum, J. E. 1991. "Black Pioneers—Do Their Moves to the Suburbs Increase Economic Opportunity for Mothers and Children?" *Housing Policy Debate* 2(4): 1179–1213.

Rosenbaum, J., N. Fishman, A. Brett, and P. Meaden. 1993. "Can the Kerner Commission's Housing Strategy Improve Employment, Education and Social Integration for Low-Income Blacks?" *North Carolina Law Review* 71(5):1519–56.

Rosenbaum, J. E., M. J., Kulieke, and L. S. Rubinowitz. 1988. "White Suburban Schools' Responses to Low-Income Black Children: Sources of Successes and Problems." *Urban Review* 20(1): 28–41.

Rosenbaum, J. E., and P. Meaden. 1992. "Harassment and acceptance of Low-Income Black Youth in White Suburban Schools." Working Paper 92-6. Evanston, Ill.: Center for Urban Affairs and Policy Research, Northwestern University.

Rosenbaum, J. E., and S. J. Popkin. 1991. "Employment and Earnings of Low-Income Blacks Who Move to Middle-Class Suburbs." In *The Urban Underclass*, edited by C. Jencks and P. Peterson. Washington D.C.: Brookings Institution.

———. 1992. "The Gautreaux Program: An Experiment in Racial and Economic Integration." *The Center Report: Current Policy Issues* 2(1).

Rosenbaum, J. E., S. J. Popkin, J. E. Kaufman, and J. Rusin. 1991. "Social Integration of Low-Income Black Adults in Middle-Class White Suburbs." *Social Problems* 38(4): 448–61.

Rosenbaum, J. E., L. S. Rubinowitz, and M. J. Kulieke. 1986. *Low-Income Black Children in White Suburban Schools.* Evanston, Ill.: Center for Urban Affair and Policy Research, Northwestern University.

Rowlison, R., and R. D. Felner. 1988. "Major Life Events, Hassles and Adaptation in Adolescence: Confounding in the Conceptualization and Measurement of Life Stress and Adjustment Revisited." *Journal of Personality and Social Psychology* 55: 432–44.

Rusk, D. 1993. *Cities without Suburbs*. Baltimore: Johns Hopkins University Press.

Rutter, M. 1987. "Psychosocial Resilience and Protective Mechanisms." *American Journal of Orthopsychiatry* 57: 316–31.

Ryan, R., and J. P. Connell. 1989. "Locus of Causality in the Academic and Social Domains: A Motivational Analysis of Children's Rationales for Action." *Journal of Personality and Social Psychology* 5: 749–61.

Saigal, S., P. Szatmari, P. Rosenbaum, D. Campbell, and S. King. 1990. "Intellectual and Functional Status at School Entry of Children Who Weighed 1000 Grams or Less at Birth: A Regional Perspective of Births in the 1980s." *Journal of Pediatrics* 116: 409–16.

Sameroff, A. J., and M. J. Chandler. 1975. "Reproductive Risk and the Continuum of Caretaking Casualty." In *Review of Child Development Research*, vol. 4, edited by F. D. Horowitz. Chicago: University of Chicago Press.

Sameroff, A. J., and R. Seifer. 1983. "Familial Risk and Child Competence." *Child Development* 54(5): 1254–68.

Sameroff, A. J., R. Seifer, A. Baldwin, and C. Baldwin. 1993. "Stability of Intelligence from Preschool to Adolescence: The Influence of Social and Family Risk Factors." *Child Development* 64: 80–97.

Sameroff, A. J., R. Seifer, R. Barocas, M. Zax, and S. Greenspan. 1987. "Intelligence Quotient Scores of 4-Year-Old Children: Social-Environmental Risk Factors." *Pediatrics* 79(3): 343–50.

Sampson, R. J. 1988. "Local Friendship Ties and Community Attachment in Mass Society: A Multilevel Systemic Model." *American Sociological Review* 53: 766–79.

———. 1991. "Linking the Micro- and Macro-level Dimensions of Community Social Organization." *Social Forces* 70(1): 43–64.

———. 1992. "Family Management and Child Development: Insights from Social Disorganization Theory." In *Advances in Criminological Theory*, vol. 3, edited by J. McCord. New Brunswick, N.J.: Transaction Books.

———. 1993. "Concentrated Urban Poverty and Crime: A Synopsis of Prior Community-level Research." Background Memorandum for the Social Science Research Council Policy Conference on Persistent Urban Poverty. Washington, D.C. (November 9–10, 1993).

Sampson, R. J., and W. B. Groves. 1989. "Community Structure and Crime: Testing Social-Disorganization Theory." *American Journal of Sociology* 94(4): 774–802.

Sampson, R. J., and J. H. Laub. 1994. "Urban Poverty and the Family Context of Delinquency: A New Look at Structure and Process in a Classic Study." *Child Development* 65(2): 523–40.

Sampson, R. J., S. W. Raudenbush, and F. Earls. Forthcoming. "Neighborhoods and Violent Crime: A Multilevel Study of Collective Efficacy." *Science*.

Sattler, J. M. 1988. *Assessment of Children*. 3rd ed. San Diego, Calif.: Jerome M. Sattler.

Savin-Williams, R. C., and T. J. Berndt. 1990. "Friendship and Peer Relations." In *At the Threshold: The Developing Adolescent*, edited by S. S. Feldman and G. R. Elliott. Cambridge, Mass.: Harvard University Press.

Scarr, S., and K. McCartney. 1983. "How People Make Their Own Environments: A Theory of Genotype-Environment Effects." *Child Development* 54: 424–35.

Schelling, T. 1971. "Dynamic Models of Segregation." *Journal of Mathematical Sociology* 1:143–86.

Schill, M. 1992. "Deconcentrating the Inner City Poor." *Chicago-Kent Law Review* 67: 795–853.

Schwirian, K. 1983. "Models of Neighborhood Change." *Annual Review of Sociology* 9: 83–102.

Scott, D. T., C. R. Bauer, H. C. Kraemer, and J. Tyson. 1989. "Neonatal Health Index for Preterm Infants." *Pediatric Research* 25(4): 263a.

Seidman, E. 1991. "Growing Up the Hard Way: Pathways of Urban Adolescents." *American Journal of Community Psychology* 19: 173–201.

Seidman, E., L. Allen, J. L. Aber, C. Mitchell, and J. Fienman. 1994. "The Impact of School Transitions on the Self-system and Social Context of Poor Urban Youth." *Child Development* 65: 507–22.

Seidman, E., L. Allen, J. L. Aber, C. Mitchell, J. Fienman, H. Yoshikawa, K. A. Comtois, J. Golz, R. L. Miller, B. Ortiz-Torres, and G. C. Roper. 1995. "Development and Validation of Adolescent Perceived Microsystem Scales: Social Support, Daily Hassles and Involvement." *American Journal of Community Psychology* 23(3): 355–88.

Shaw, C., and H. McKay. 1942. *Juvenile Delinquency and Urban Areas.* Chicago: University of Chicago Press.

Sherrod, L. R., R. J. Haggerty, and D. L. Featherman. 1993. "Introduction: Late Adolescence and the Transition to Adulthood." *Journal of Research on Adolescence* 3(3):217–26.

Simcha-Fagan, O., and J. E., Schwartz. 1986. "Neighborhood and Delinquency: An Assessment of Contextual Effects." *Criminology* 24(4): 667–704.

Simmons, R. G., R. Burgeson, S. Carlton-Ford, and D. A. Blyth. 1987. The Impact of Cumulative Change in Early Adolescence." *Child Development* 58: 1220–34.

Simmons, R. G., S. L. Carlton-Ford, D. A. Blyth. 1987. "Predicting How a Child Will Cope with the Transition to Junior High School." In *Biological-Psychosocial Interactions in Early Adolescence. Child Psychology*, edited by R. M. Lerner and T. T. Foch. Hillsdale, N.J.: Lawrence Erlbaum Associates.

Skinner, E. A., J. Wellborn, and J. P. Connell. 1990. "What It Takes to Do Well in School and Whether I've Got It: The Role of Perceived Control in Children's Engagement and School Achievement." *Journal of Educational Psychology* 82: 22–32.

Skogan, W. 1986. "Fear of Crime and Neighborhood Change." In *Communities and Crime*, edited by A. J. Reiss Jr. and M. Tonry. Chicago: University of Chicago Press.

Smeeding, T. M. 1994. "Car Stamps: Economic Mobility for the Geographically Challenged." Syracuse University, Syracuse, N.Y. Mimeographed.

———. 1995. "An Interdisciplinary Model for Studying Poor Children." In *Escape from Poverty: What Makes a Difference for Poor Children?* edited by P. L. Chase-Lansdale and J. Brooks-Gunn. New York: Cambridge University Press.

Smeeding, T. M., and B. B. Torrey. 1988. "Poor Children in Rich Countries." *Science* 247 (Nov. 11): 1135–40.

Smetana, J. G. 1988. "Adolescents' and Parents' Conceptions of Parental Authority." *Child Development* 59:321–35.

Smith, S. 1995. "Two-Generation Programs: A New Intervention Strategy and Directions for Future Research." In *Escape from Poverty: What Makes a Difference for Poor Children?* edited by P. L. Chase-Lansdale and J. Brooks-Gunn. New York: Cambridge University Press.

Smith, T. J. 1993. "Improving Practice in the Youth Employment Field." Memorandum prepared for SSRC Policy Conference on Persistent Urban Poverty, Washington, D.C. (November 9–10).

Smith, J. R., J. Brooks-Gunn, and P. K. Klebanov. 1997. "Consequences of Growing Up Poor for Young Children." In *Consequences of Growing Up Poor*, edited by G. J. Duncan and J. Brooks-Gunn. New York: Russell Sage Foundation.

Snow, 1983. "Literacy and Language: Relationships during the Preschool Years." *Harvard Educational Review* 53(2): 165–89.

Snyder, T. D. 1996. *Digest of Education Statistics* (NCES 96-133). Washington, DC: U.S. Department of Education, National Center for Education Statistics.

Sparling, J., I. Lewis, C. T. Ramey, B. H. Wasik, D. M. Bryant, and L. M. La Vange. 1991. "Partners, a Curriculum to Help Premature, Low-Birth-Weight Infants Get Off to a Good Start." *Topics in Early Childhood Special Education* 11: 36–55.

Spencer, M. B. 1985. "Cultural Cognition and Social Cognition as Identity Factors in Black Children's Personal-Social Growth." In *Beginnings: Social and Affective Development of Black Children*, edited by M. B. Spencer, G. K. Brookins, and W. R. Allen. New York: Lawrence Erlbaum Associates.

———. 1986. "Risk and Resilience: How Black Children Cope with Stress." *Journal of Social Science* 71(1): 22–26.

———. 1987. "Black Children's Ethnic Identity Formation: Risk and Resilience of Castelike Minorities." In *Children's Ethnic Socialization*, edited by J. S. Phinney and M. J. Rotheram. Thousand Oaks, Calif.: Sage Publications.

———. 1988. "Persistent Poverty of African American Youth: A Normative Study of Developmental Transitions in High-Risk Environments." Unpublished proposal submitted to and funded by the Spencer and Ford Foundations. Atlanta, Ga.: Emory University.

———. 1990. "Development of Minority Children: An Introduction." *Child Development* 61(2): 267–69.

———. 1995. "Old Issues and New Theorizing about African American Youth: A Phenomenological Variant of Ecological Systems Theory." In *Black Youth: Perspectives on Their Status in the United States*, edited by R. L. Taylor. Westport, Conn.: Praeger.

Spencer, M. L., J. Blumenthal, and E. Richards. 1995. "Caring for Poor Children: Child Care and Children of color." *Escape from Poverty: What Makes a Difference for Poor Children?* edited by P. L. Chase-Lansdale and J. Brooks-Gunn. New York: Cambridge University Press.

Spencer, M. B., and S. Dornbusch. 1990. "Challenges in Studying Minority Youth." In *At the Threshold: The Developing Adolescent*, edited by S. Feldman and G. R. Elliott. Cambridge, Mass.: Harvard University Press.

Spencer, M. B., and C. Markstrom-Adams. 1990. "Identity Processes among Racial and Ethnic Minority Children in America." *Child Development* 61: 290–310.

Spencer, M. B., D. P. Swanson, and M. Cunningham. 1991. "Ethnicity, Ethnic Identity, and Competence Formation: Adolescent Transition and Cultural Transformation." *Journal of Negro Education* 60: 366–87.

Spiker, D., H. Kraemer, N. A. Constantine, and D. Bryant. Forthcoming. "Reliability and Validity of Behavior Problem Checklists as Measures of Stable Traits in Low Birth Weight, Premature Preschoolers." *Child Development*.

Sroufe, A. 1979. "The Coherence of Individual Development: Early Care, Attachment and Subsequent Developmental Issues." *American Psychologist* 34: 194–210.

———. 1983. "Infant–Caregiver Attachment and Patterns of Adaptation to Preschool: The Roots of Maladaptation and Competence." In *Minnesota Symposium on Child Psychology*, vol. 16, edited by M. Perlmutter. Hillsdale, N. J.: Lawrence Erlbaum Associates.

Sroufe, A., R. Cooper, G. DeHart, M. Marshall, and U. Bronfenbrenner. 1992. *Child Development: Its Nature and Course*. New York: McGraw-Hill.

Steinberg, L. 1987. "Single Parents, Stepparents, and Susceptibility of Adolescents to Antisocial Peer Pressure." *Child Development* 58: 269–75.

———. 1989. "Communities of Families and Education." In *Education and the American Family: A Research Synthesis*, edited by W. Weston. New York: New York University Press.

Steinberg, L., and N. Darling. 1993. "The Broader Context of Social Influence in Adolescence." In *Adolescence in Context*, edited by R. Silbereisen and E. Todt. New York: Springer.

Steinberg, L., S. Dornbusch, and B. Brown. 1992. "Ethnic Differences in Adolescent Achievement in Ecological Perspective." *American Psychologist* 47(6): 723–29.

Steinberg, L., S. D. Lamborn, S. M. Dornbusch, and N. Darling. 1992. "Impact of Parenting Practices on Adolescent Achievement: Authoritative Parenting, School Involvement, and Encouragement to Succeed." *Child Development* 63: 1266–81.

Steinberg, L., N. S. Mounts, S. D. Lamborn, and S. M. Dornbusch. 1991. "Authoritative Parenting and Adolescent Adjustment Across Varied Ecological Niches." *Journal of Research on Adolescence* 1(1): 19–36.

Stevenson, J., N. Richman, and P. Graham. 1983. "Behavior Problems and Language Abilities at Three Years and Behavior Deviance at Eight Years." *Child Psychology and Psychiatry* 16(2): 215–30.

Stewart, R. 1983. "Sibling Attachment Relationships: Child–Infant Interactions in the Strange Situation." *Developmental Psychology* 19: 192–99.

Stipek, D., R. Feiler, D. Daniels, and S. Milburn. 1995. "Effects of Different Instructional Approaches on Young Achievement." *Child Development* 66(1): 209–23.

Sugland, B. W., M. Zaslow, J. R. Smith, J. Brooks-Gunn, D. Coates, C. Blumental, K. A. Moore, T. Griffin, and R. Bradley 1995. "The Early Childhood HOME Inventory and HOME–Short Form in Differing Racial/Ethnic Groups: Are There Differences in Underlying Structure, Internal Consistency of Subscales, and Patterns of Prediction?" *Journal of Family Issues* 16: 632–63.

Sullivan, M. L. 1989. *Getting Paid: Youth, Crime and Work in the Inner City*. Ithaca, N.Y.: Cornell University Press.

———. 1993a. "Community Development as an Anti-poverty Strategy." Memorandum prepared for SSRC Policy Conference on Persistent Urban Poverty, Washington, D.C. (November 9–10).

———. 1993b. *More than Housing: How Community Development Corporations Go about Changing Lives and Neighborhoods*. New York: New School for Social Research.

Tatum, B. D. 1987. *Assimilation Blues: Black Families in a White Community*. New York: Greenwood Press.

Taub, R. 1988. *Community Capitalism*. Boston, Mass.: Harvard Business School Press.

Taub, R., G. Taylor, and J. Dunham. 1984. *Paths of Neighborhood Change*. Chicago: University of Chicago Press.

Taylor, R., and J. Covington. 1988. "Neighborhood Changes in Ecology and Violence." *Criminology* 26: 553–90.

Taylor, R. B., S. Gottfredson, and S. Brower. 1994. "Local Crime as a Natural Hazard: Implications for Understanding the Relationship between Disorder and Fear of Crime." *American Journal of Community Psychology* 18(5): 619–41.

Terman, L. M., and M. A. Merrill. 1973. *Stanford-Binet Intelligence Scale: Manual for the Third Revision. Form L-M*. Boston, Mass.: Houghton Mifflin.

Tienda, M. 1989. "Poor People and Places: Deciphering Neighborhood Effects on Policy Outcomes." In *Macro-Micro Linkages in Sociology*, edited by J. Huber. Newbury Park, Calif.: Sage Publications.

————. 1991. "Poor People and Poor Places: Deciphering Neighborhood Effects on Poverty Outcomes." In *Macro–Micro Linkages in Sociology*, edited by J. Haber. Newberry, Calif.: Sage.

Tweed, D. L., H. F. Goldsmith, D. S. Jackson, D. Stiles, D. S. Rae, and M. Kramer. 1990. "Racial Congruity as a Contextual Correlate of Mental Disorder." *American Journal of Orthopsychiatry* 60: 392–403.

Unger, D. G., and A. Wandersman. 1985. "The Importance of Neighbors: The Social, Cognitive, and Affective Components of Neighboring." *American Journal of Community Psychology* 13: 139–69.

U. S. House of Representatives. 1994. *Background Material and Data on Programs Within the Jurisdiction of the Committee on Ways and Means (1994 Green Book)*. Washington: U. S. Government Printing Office.

Velez, C. N., J. Johnson, and P. Cohen. 1989. "A Longitudinal Analysis of Selected Risk Factors for Child Psychopathology." *Journal of the American Academy of Child and Adolescent Psychiatry* 28: 861–64.

Vito, R. C. 1993. "Why Students Become 'At-Risk.'" Ph.D. diss., University of Rochester, Rochester, N.Y.

Vohr, B. R., and C. T. G. Coll. 1985. "Neurodevelopmental and School Performance of Very Low-Birth-Weight Year Infants: A Seven-Year Longitudinal Study." *Pediatrics* 76: 345–50.

Wachs, T. D., and G. E. Gruen. 1982. *Early Experience and Human Development*. New York: Plenum Press.

Wacquant, L. J. D., and W. J. Wilson. 1989. "Poverty, Joblessness and the Social Transformation of the Inner City." In *Welfare Policy for the 1990's*, edited by P. Cottingham and D. Ellwood. Cambridge, Mass.: Harvard University Press.

Wallace, R., and D. Wallace. 1990. "Origins of Public Health Collapse in New York City: The Dynamics of Planned Shrinkage, Contagious Urban Decay and Social Disintegration." *Bulletin of the New York Academy of Medicine* 66: 391–434.

Wechsler, D. 1967. *Wechsler Preschool and Primary Scale of Intelligence*. San Antonio, Tex.: Psychological Corporation.

Wellborn, J., and J. P. Connell. 1987. "RAPS-S: Rochester Assessment Package for Schools, Student Report." University of Rochester, Rochester, N.Y. Unpublished manuscript.

Werner, E. E. 1994. "Overcoming the Odds." *Journal of Developmental and Behavioral Pediatrics* 15(2): 131–36.

Werner, E. E., and R. S. Smith. 1992. *Overcoming the Odds*. Ithaca, N.Y.: Cornell University Press.

White, M. J. 1987. *American Neighborhoods and Residential Differentiation*. New York: Russell Sage Foundation.

White, R. 1959. "Motivation Reconsidered: The Concept of Competence." *Psychological Review* 66: 297–333.

————. 1960. "Competence and Psychosexual Development." In *Nebraska Symposium on Motivation*, edited by M. R. Jones. Lincoln: University of Nebraska Press.

Williams, T., and W. Kornblum. 1985. *Growing Up Poor*. Lexington. Mass.: Lexington Books.

Willis, P. 1977. *Learning to Labor: How Working-Class Kids Get Working-Class Jobs*. New York: Columbia University Press.

Wilson, W. J. 1987. *The Truly Disadvantaged: The Inner City, the Underclass and Public Policy*. Chicago: University of Chicago Press.

———. 1991a. "Public Policy Research and *The Truly Disadavantaged*." In *The Urban Underclass*, edited by C. Jencks and P. E. Peterson. Washington, D.C.: Brookings Institution.

———. 1991b. Studying Inner City Social Dislocations: The Challenge of Public Agenda Research. *American Sociological Review* 56(1): 1–14.

———. 1993. "The Underclass: Issues, Perspectives, and Public Policy." In *The Ghetto Underclass: Social Science Perspectives*, edited by W. J. Wilson. Newbury Park, Calif.: Sage Publications.

———. 1994. "Crisis and Challenge: Race and the New Urban Poverty." The 1994 Reyerson Lecture, University of Chicago.

———. 1996. *When Work Disappears: The World of the New Urban Poor*. New York: Alfred A. Knopf.

Wilson, J. B., D. T. Ellwood, and J. Brooks-Gunn. 1995. "Welfare to Work through the Eyes of Children: The Impact on Parenting of Movement from AFDC to Employment." In *Escape from Poverty: What Makes a Difference for Children?* edited by P. L. Chase-Lansdale and J. Brooks-Gunn. New York: Cambridge University Press.

Youniss, J. and J. Smollar. 1985. *Adolescent Relations with Mothers, Fathers, and Friends*. Chicago: University of Chicago Press.

Zaslow, M. J., K. A. Moore, D. R. Morrison and M. J. Coiro. 1995. "The Family Support Act and Children: Potential Pathways of Influence." *Children and Youth Service Review* 17(1/2): 231–50.

Zill, N. 1988. "Behavior, Achievement, and Health Problems among Children in Stepfamilies: Findings from a National Survey of Child Health." In *Impact of Divorce, Single Parenting, and Stepparenting on Children*, edited by E. M. Hetherington and J. D. Arasteh. Hillsdale, N.J.: Lawrence Erlbaum Associates.

Zill, N., and C. A. Schoenborn. 1990. "Developmental, Learning, and Emotional Problems: Health of Our Nation's Children, United States, 1988. In *Advance Data: From Vital and Health Statistics of the National Center for Health Statistics*, no. 190. Washington, D.C.: U.S. Government Printing Office.

# Index

Boldface numbers refer to figures and tables.